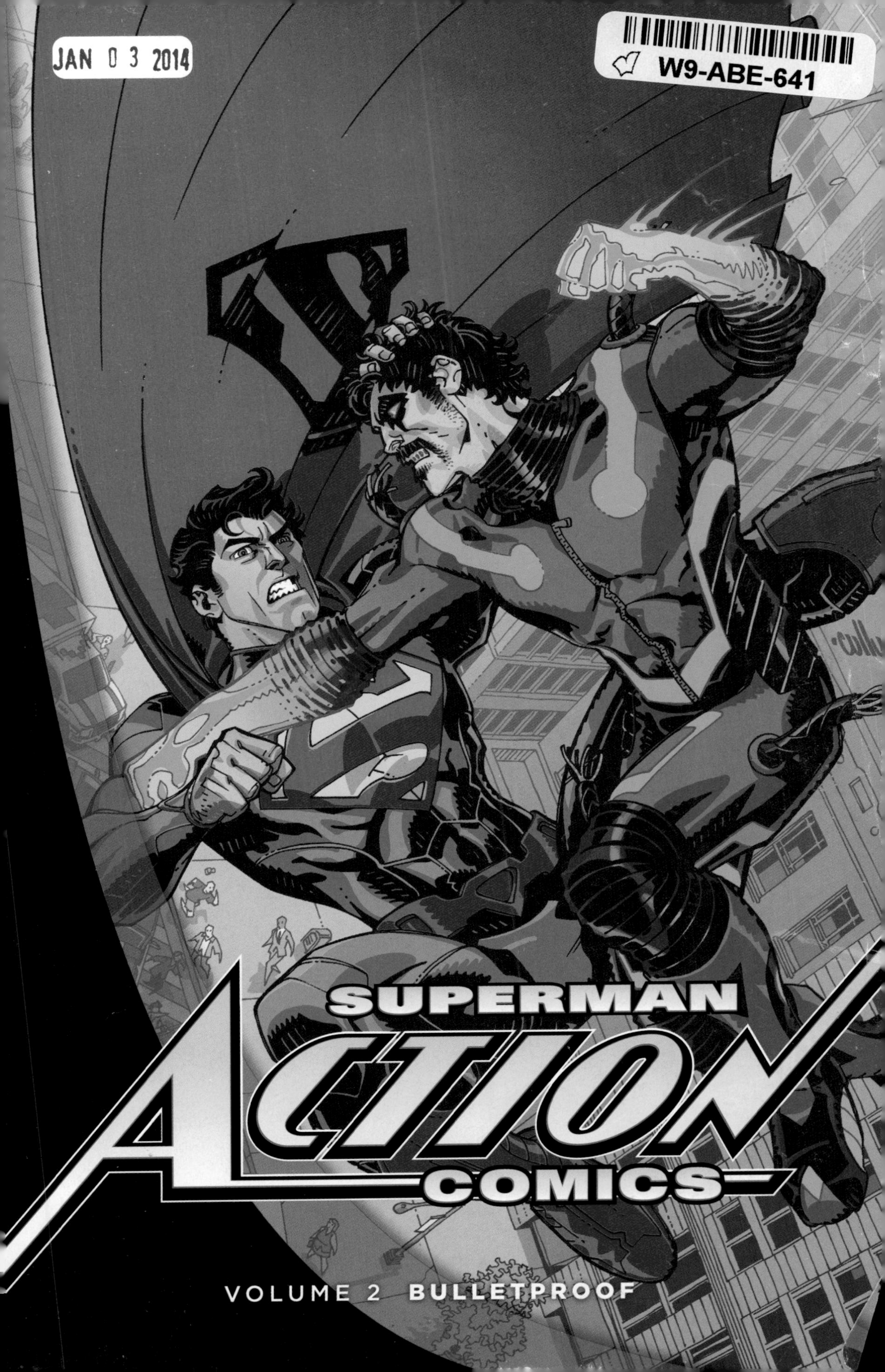
SUPERMAN
ACTION
COMICS
VOLUME 2 BULLETPROOF

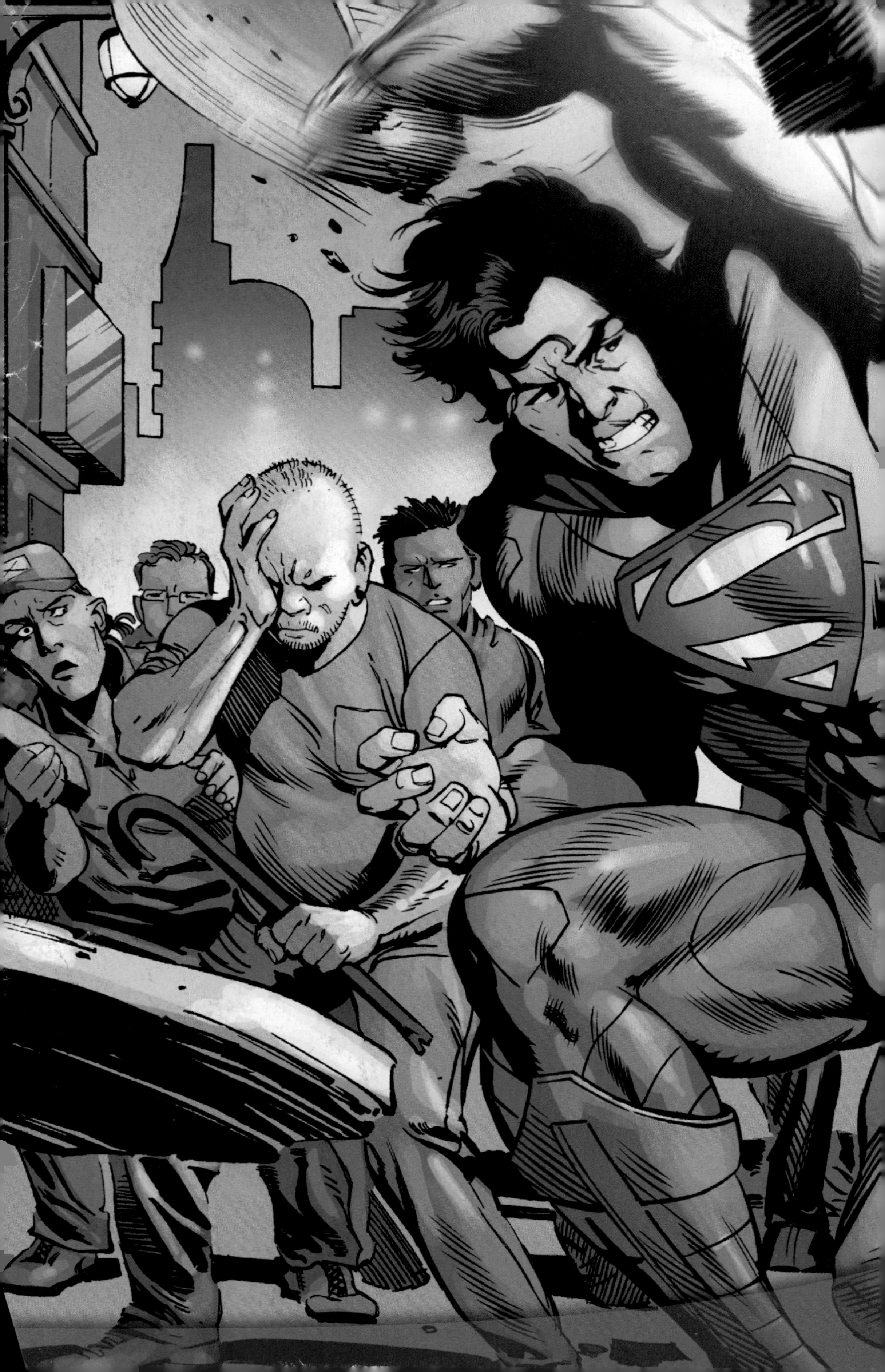

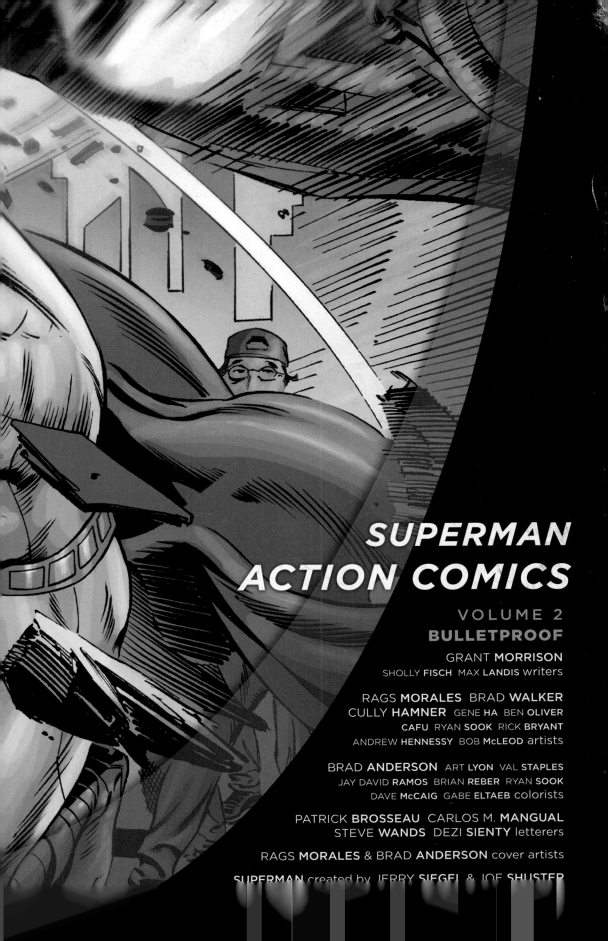

SUPERMAN
ACTION COMICS

VOLUME 2
BULLETPROOF

GRANT **MORRISON**
SHOLLY **FISCH**   MAX **LANDIS** writers

RAGS **MORALES**   BRAD **WALKER**
CULLY **HAMNER**   GENE **HA**   BEN **OLIVER**
CAFU   RYAN **SOOK**   RICK **BRYANT**
ANDREW **HENNESSY**   BOB **McLEOD** artists

BRAD **ANDERSON**   ART **LYON**   VAL **STAPLES**
JAY DAVID **RAMOS**   BRIAN **REBER**   RYAN **SOOK**
DAVE **McCAIG**   GABE **ELTAEB** colorists

PATRICK **BROSSEAU**   CARLOS M. **MANGUAL**
STEVE **WANDS**   DEZI **SIENTY** letterers

RAGS **MORALES** & BRAD **ANDERSON** cover artists

SUPERMAN created by JERRY **SIEGEL** & JOE **SHUSTER**

MATT IDELSON Editor – Original Series WIL MOSS Associate Editor – Original Series PETER HAMBOUSSI Editor
ROBBIN BROSTERMAN Design Director – Books ROBBIE BIEDERMAN Publication Design

BOB HARRAS Senior VP – Editor-in-Chief, DC Comics

DIANE NELSON President DAN DIDIO and JIM LEE Co-Publishers GEOFF JOHNS Chief Creative Officer
JOHN ROOD Executive VP – Sales, Marketing and Business Development
AMY GENKINS Senior VP – Business and Legal Affairs NAIRI GARDINER Senior VP – Finance
JEFF BOISON VP – Publishing Planning MARK CHIARELLO VP – Art Direction and Design
JOHN CUNNINGHAM VP – Marketing TERRI CUNNINGHAM VP – Editorial Administration
ALISON GILL Senior VP – Manufacturing and Operations HANK KANALZ Senior VP – Vertigo and Integrated Publishing
JAY KOGAN VP – Business and Legal Affairs, Publishing JACK MAHAN VP – Business Affairs, Talent
NICK NAPOLITANO VP – Manufacturing Administration SUE POHJA VP – Book Sales
COURTNEY SIMMONS Senior VP – Publicity BOB WAYNE Senior VP – Sales

SUPERMAN – ACTION COMICS VOLUME 2: BULLETPROOF

DC Comics, 1700 Broadway, New York, NY 10019
A Warner Bros. Entertainment Company.
Printed by RR Donnelley, Salem, VA, USA. 11/08/13 First Printing.
HC ISBN: 978-1-4012-4101-8
SC ISBN: 978-1-4012-4254-1

SUSTAINABLE
FORESTRY
INITIATIVE

Certified Chain of Custody
At Least 20% Certified Forest Content
www.sfiprogram.org
SFI-01042
APPLIES TO TEXT STOCK ONLY

Library of Congress Cataloging-in-Publication Data

Morrison, Grant, author.
Superman — Action Comics. Volume 2, Bulletproof / Grant Morrison, Rags Morales.
pages cm
"Originally published in single magazine form in Action Comics 9-12, 0; Action Comics Annual 1."
ISBN 978-1-4012-4101-8
1. Graphic novels. I. Morales, Rags, illustrator. II. Title. III. Title: Bulletproof.
PN6728.S9M733 2013
741.5'973—dc23
                                    2013000117

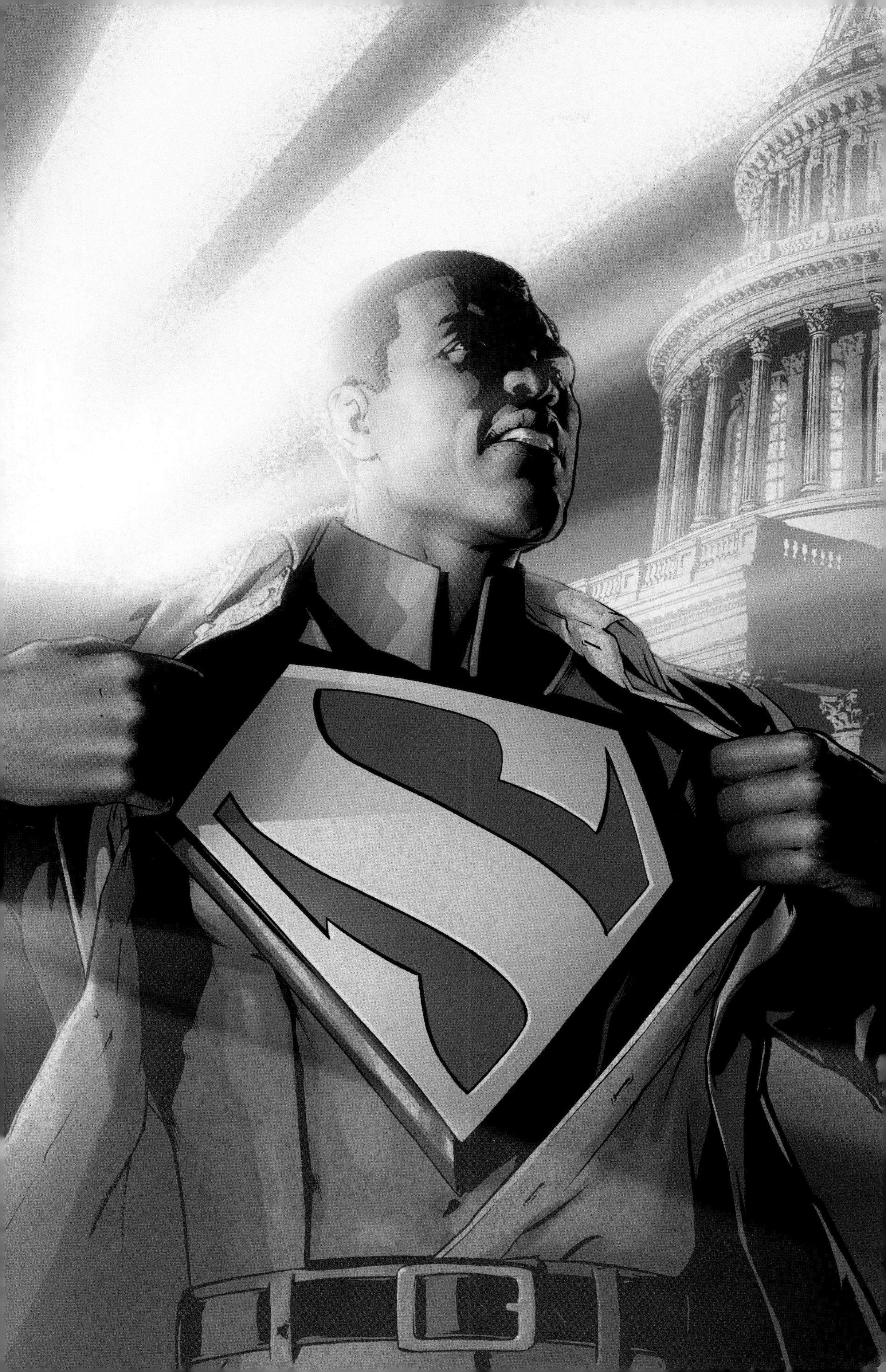

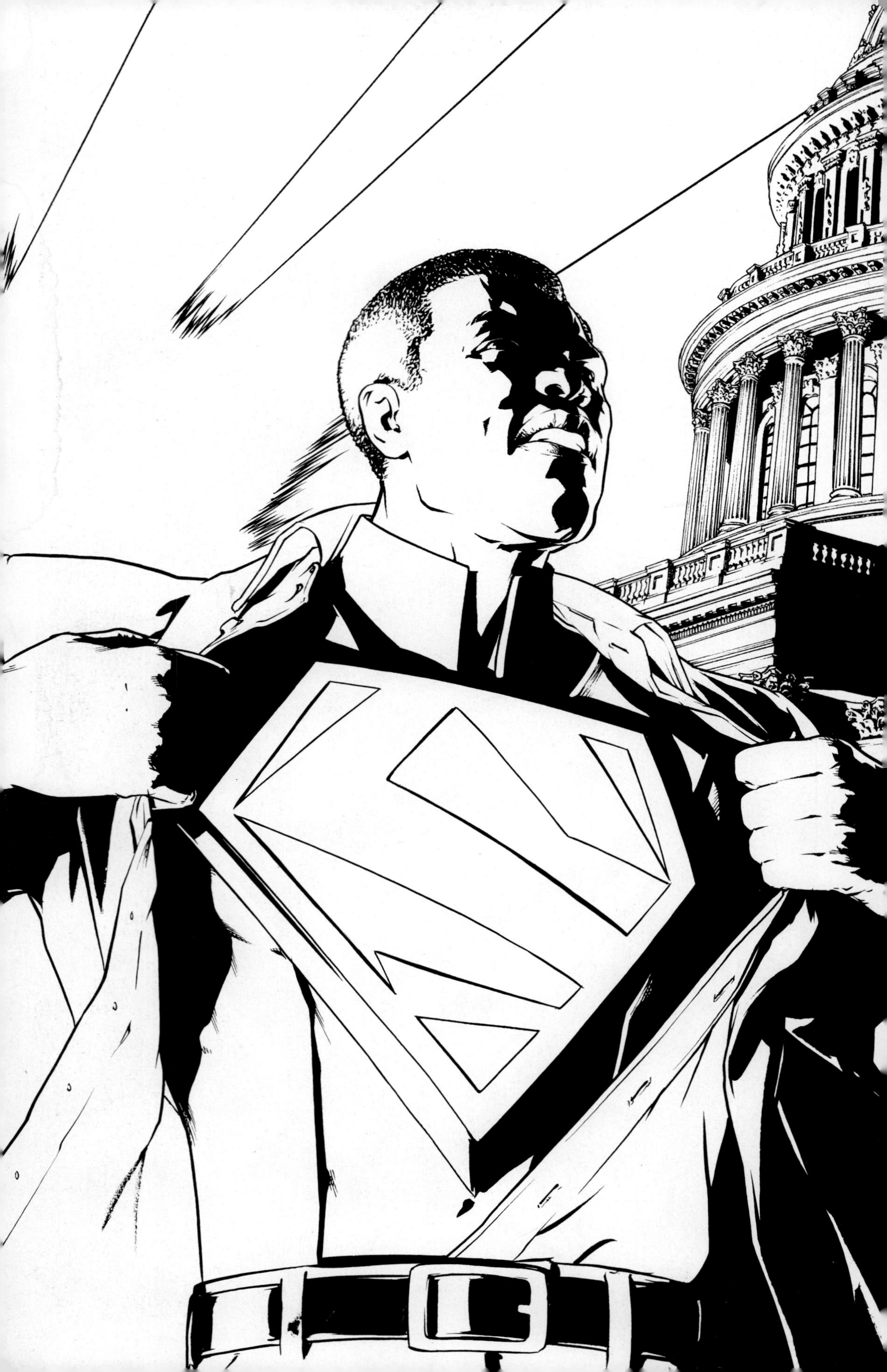

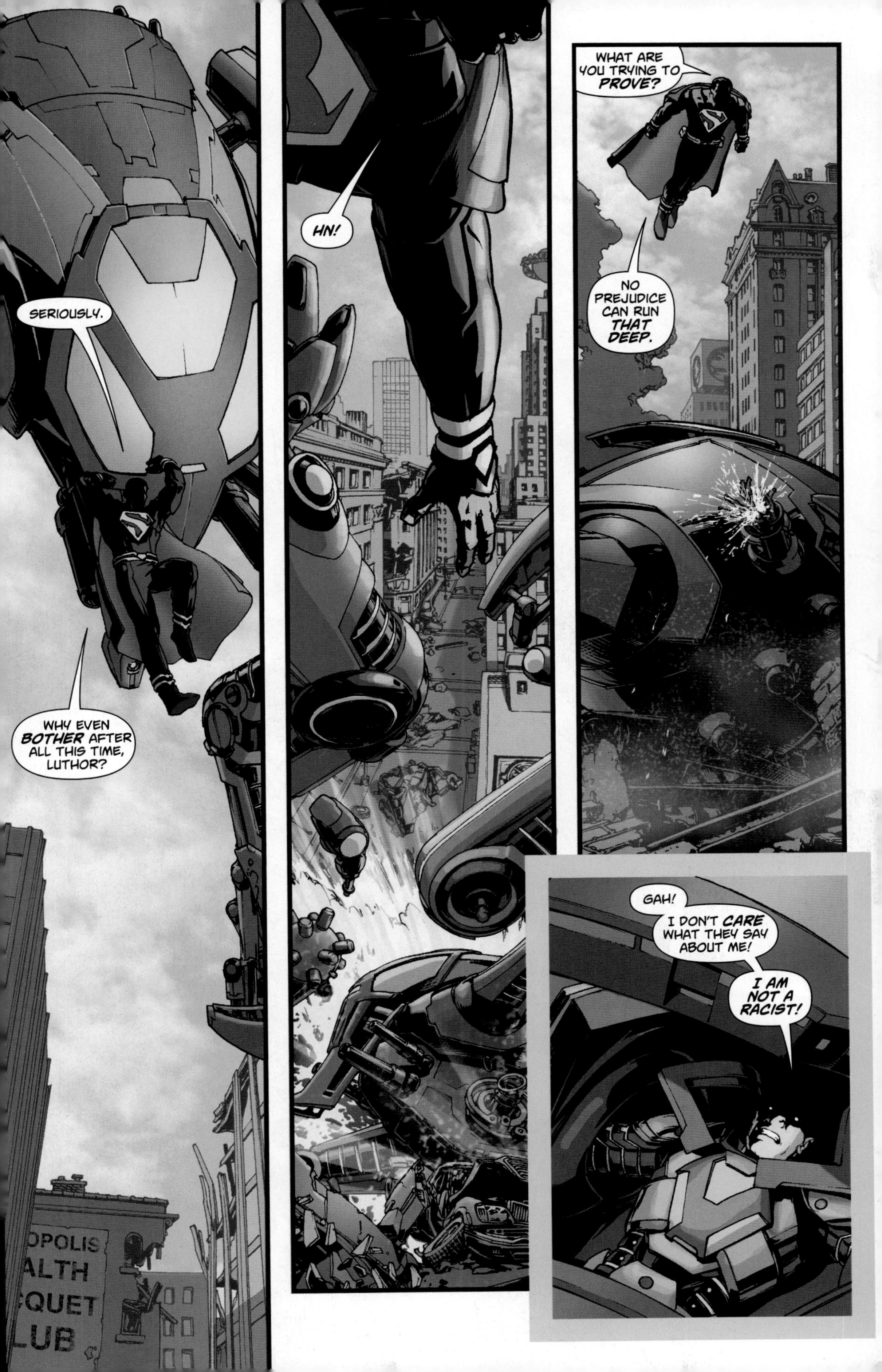
SERIOUSLY.
WHY EVEN BOTHER AFTER ALL THIS TIME, LUTHOR?
HN!
WHAT ARE YOU TRYING TO PROVE?
NO PREJUDICE CAN RUN THAT DEEP.
GAH!
I DON'T CARE WHAT THEY SAY ABOUT ME!
I AM NOT A RACIST!
OPOLIS
ALTH
CQUET
LUB

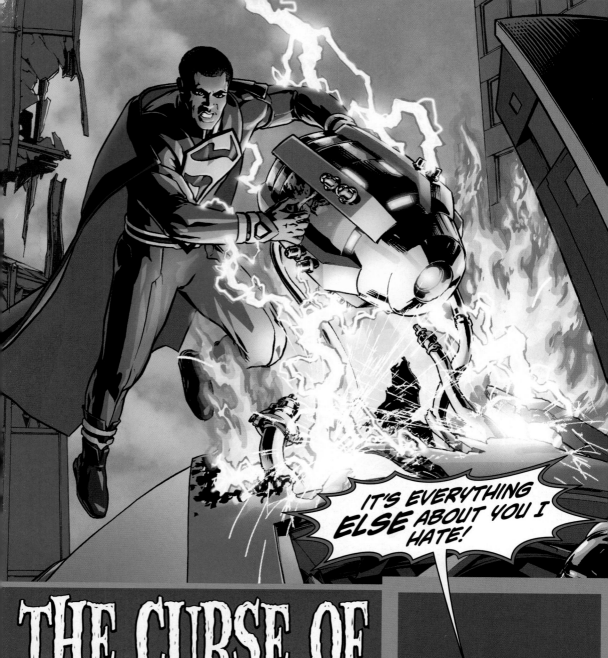

IT'S EVERYTHING *ELSE* ABOUT YOU I HATE!

THE CURSE OF SUPERMAN

GRANT MORRISION WRITER

GENE HA ARTIST **ART LYON** COLORIST

PATRICK BROSSEAU LETTERER GENE HA & ART LYON COVER

RAGS MORALES & BRAD ANDERSON VARIANT COVER

WIL MOSS ASSOCIATE EDITOR MATT IDELSON EDITOR

SUPERMAN CREATED BY JERRY SIEGEL & JOE SHUSTER

DON'T *EVER* FORGET THAT!

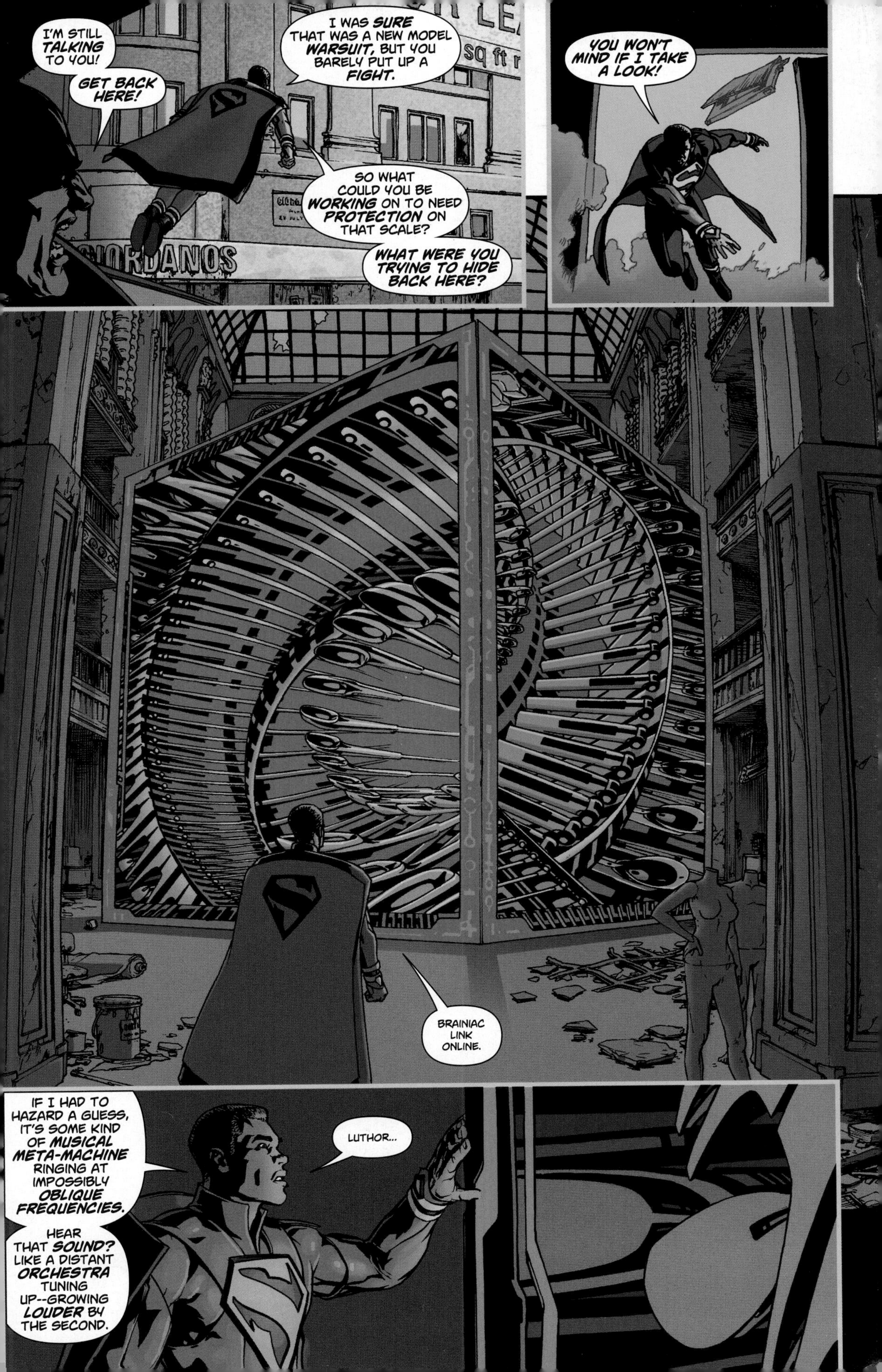
I'M STILL TALKING TO YOU!
GET BACK HERE!
I WAS SURE THAT WAS A NEW MODEL WARSUIT, BUT YOU BARELY PUT UP A FIGHT.
SO WHAT COULD YOU BE WORKING ON TO NEED PROTECTION ON THAT SCALE?
WHAT WERE YOU TRYING TO HIDE BACK HERE?
GIORDANOS
YOU WON'T MIND IF I TAKE A LOOK!
BRAINIAC LINK ONLINE.
IF I HAD TO HAZARD A GUESS, IT'S SOME KIND OF MUSICAL META-MACHINE RINGING AT IMPOSSIBLY OBLIQUE FREQUENCIES.
HEAR THAT SOUND? LIKE A DISTANT ORCHESTRA TUNING UP--GROWING LOUDER BY THE SECOND.
LUTHOR...

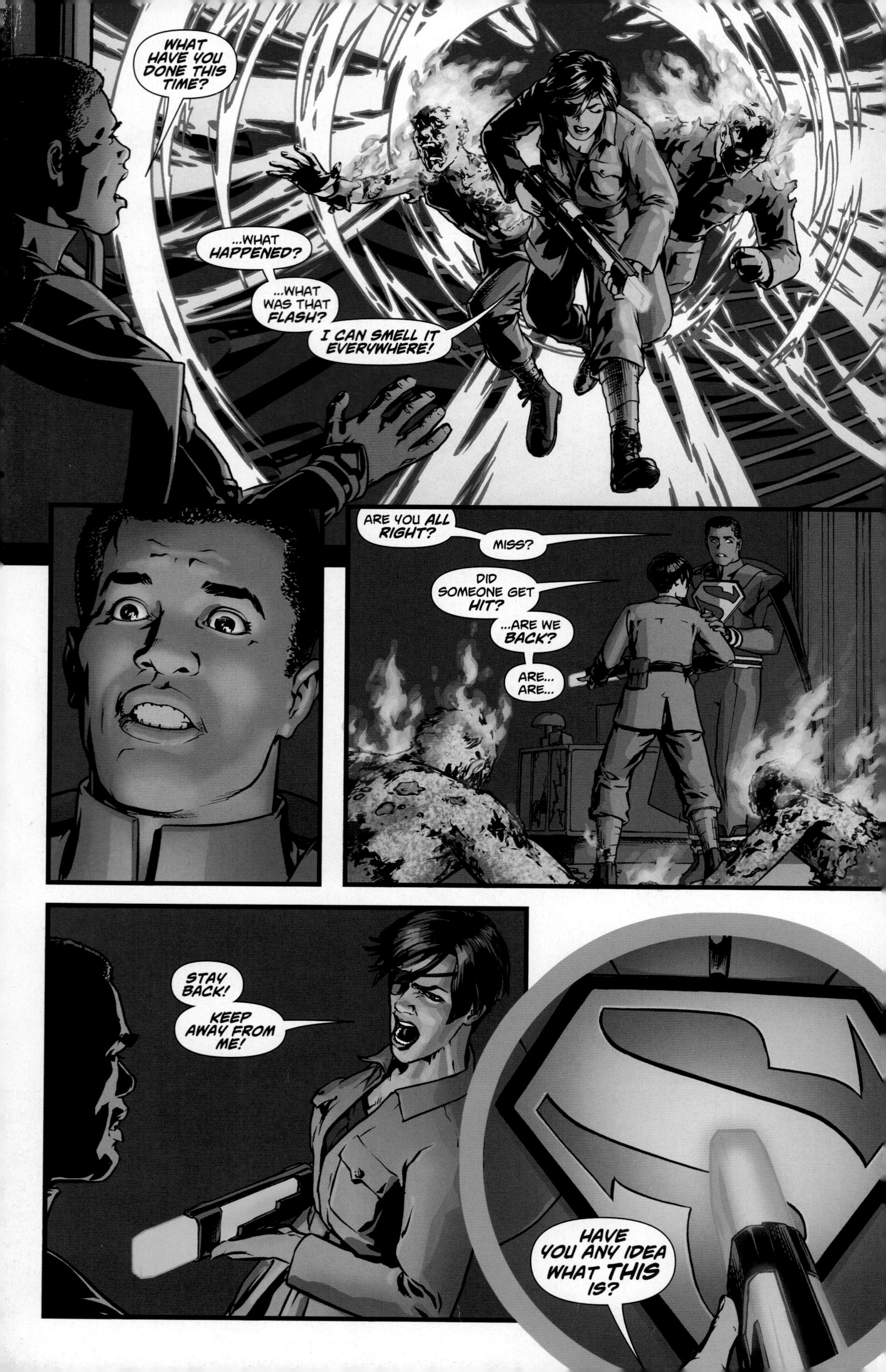
WHAT HAVE YOU DONE THIS TIME?
...WHAT HAPPENED?
...WHAT WAS THAT FLASH?
I CAN SMELL IT EVERYWHERE!
ARE YOU ALL RIGHT?
MISS?
DID SOMEONE GET HIT?
...ARE WE BACK?
ARE... ARE...
STAY BACK!
KEEP AWAY FROM ME!
HAVE YOU ANY IDEA WHAT THIS IS?

BACK!

...I...

YOU'RE IMMUNE TO *K-LASER.*

K-LASER?

IT'S--IT'S A *HATE-POWERED* WEAPON FROM THAT--THAT *OTHER* PLACE, WITH *OPTIMAN*--

CLARK WAS *RIGHT*-- CLARK...?

NNNN

LLLLUHH-LUH

CLARK!

OH, JIMMY!

OH NO, NO, NO!

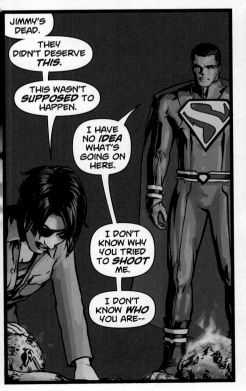

JIMMY'S DEAD.

THEY DIDN'T DESERVE *THIS.*

THIS WASN'T *SUPPOSED* TO HAPPEN.

I HAVE NO *IDEA* WHAT'S GOING ON HERE.

I DON'T KNOW WHY YOU TRIED TO *SHOOT* ME.

I DON'T KNOW *WHO* YOU ARE--

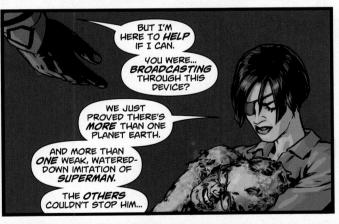

BUT I'M HERE TO *HELP* IF I CAN.

YOU WERE... *BROADCASTING* THROUGH THIS DEVICE?

WE JUST PROVED THERE'S *MORE* THAN ONE PLANET EARTH.

AND MORE THAN *ONE* WEAK, WATERED-DOWN IMITATION OF *SUPERMAN.*

THE *OTHERS* COULDN'T STOP HIM...

WHAT MAKES *YOU* SO DIFFERENT?

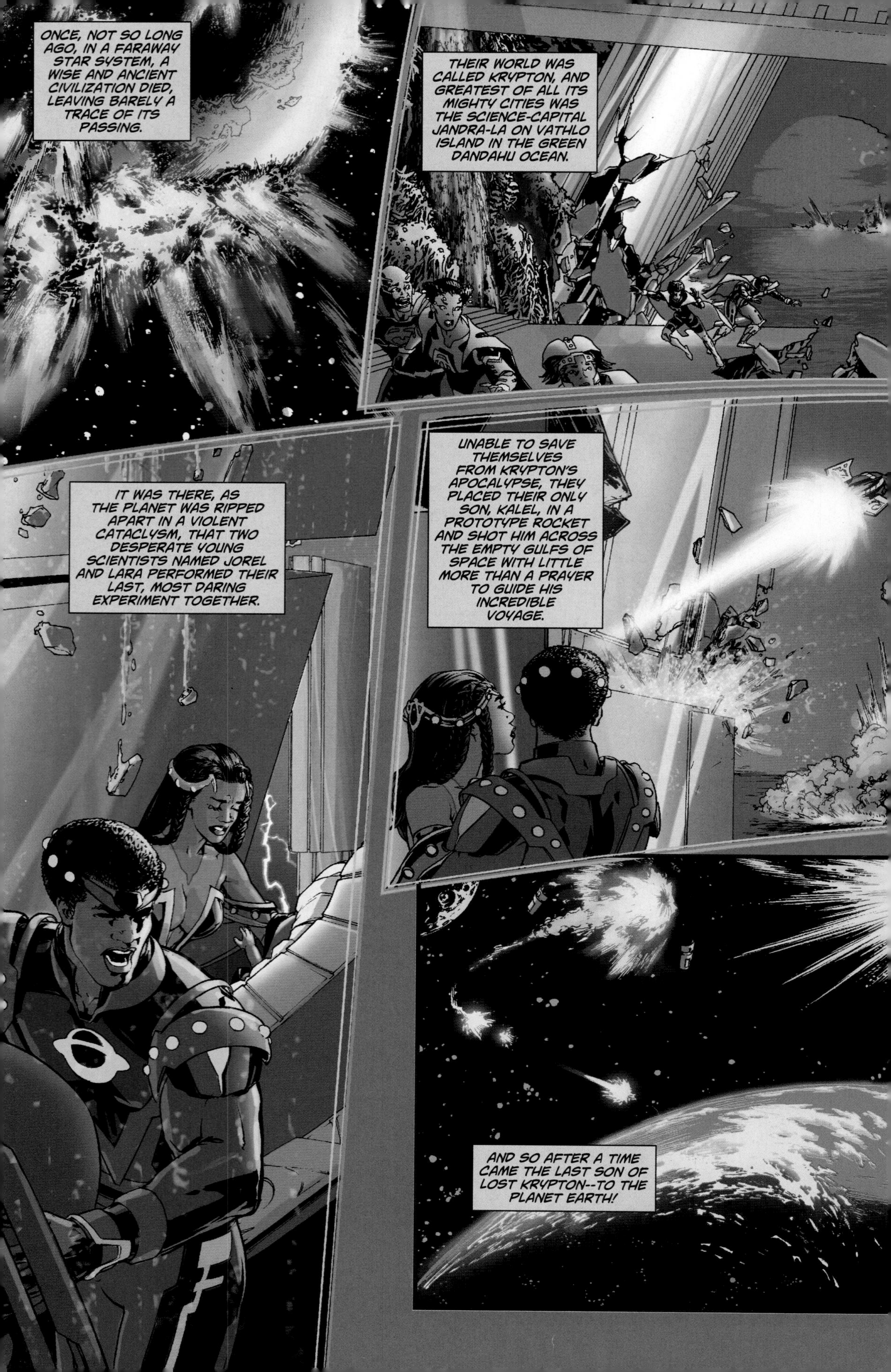
ONCE, NOT SO LONG AGO, IN A FARAWAY STAR SYSTEM, A WISE AND ANCIENT CIVILIZATION DIED, LEAVING BARELY A TRACE OF ITS PASSING.
THEIR WORLD WAS CALLED KRYPTON, AND GREATEST OF ALL ITS MIGHTY CITIES WAS THE SCIENCE-CAPITAL JANDRA-LA ON VATHLO ISLAND IN THE GREEN DANDAHU OCEAN.
IT WAS THERE, AS THE PLANET WAS RIPPED APART IN A VIOLENT CATACLYSM, THAT TWO DESPERATE YOUNG SCIENTISTS NAMED JOREL AND LARA PERFORMED THEIR LAST, MOST DARING EXPERIMENT TOGETHER.
UNABLE TO SAVE THEMSELVES FROM KRYPTON'S APOCALYPSE, THEY PLACED THEIR ONLY SON, KALEL, IN A PROTOTYPE ROCKET AND SHOT HIM ACROSS THE EMPTY GULFS OF SPACE WITH LITTLE MORE THAN A PRAYER TO GUIDE HIS INCREDIBLE VOYAGE.
AND SO AFTER A TIME CAME THE LAST SON OF LOST KRYPTON--TO THE PLANET EARTH!

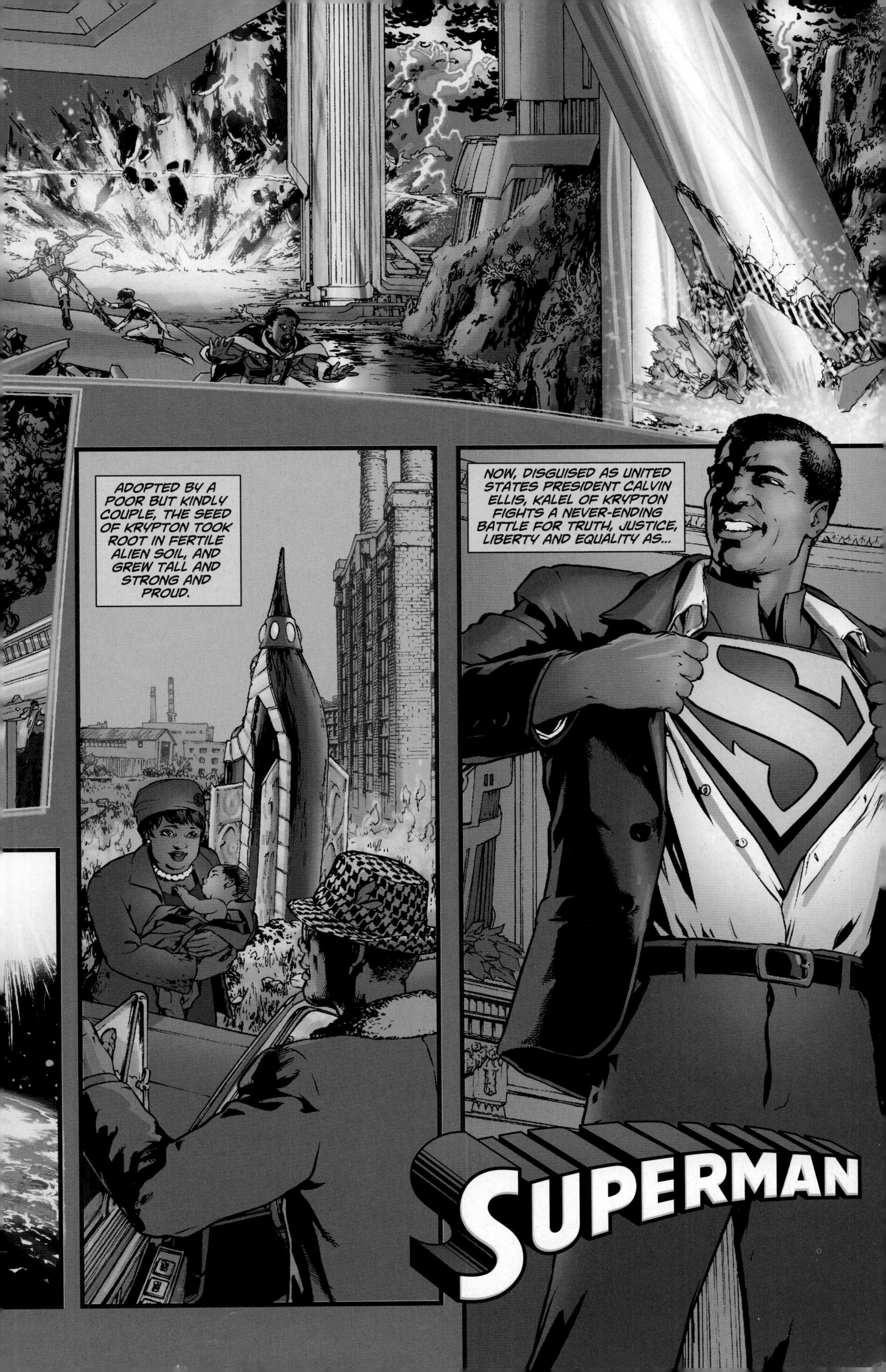
ADOPTED BY A POOR BUT KINDLY COUPLE, THE SEED OF KRYPTON TOOK ROOT IN FERTILE ALIEN SOIL, AND GREW TALL AND STRONG AND PROUD.
NOW, DISGUISED AS UNITED STATES PRESIDENT CALVIN ELLIS, KALEL OF KRYPTON FIGHTS A NEVER-ENDING BATTLE FOR TRUTH, JUSTICE, LIBERTY AND EQUALITY AS...
SUPERMAN

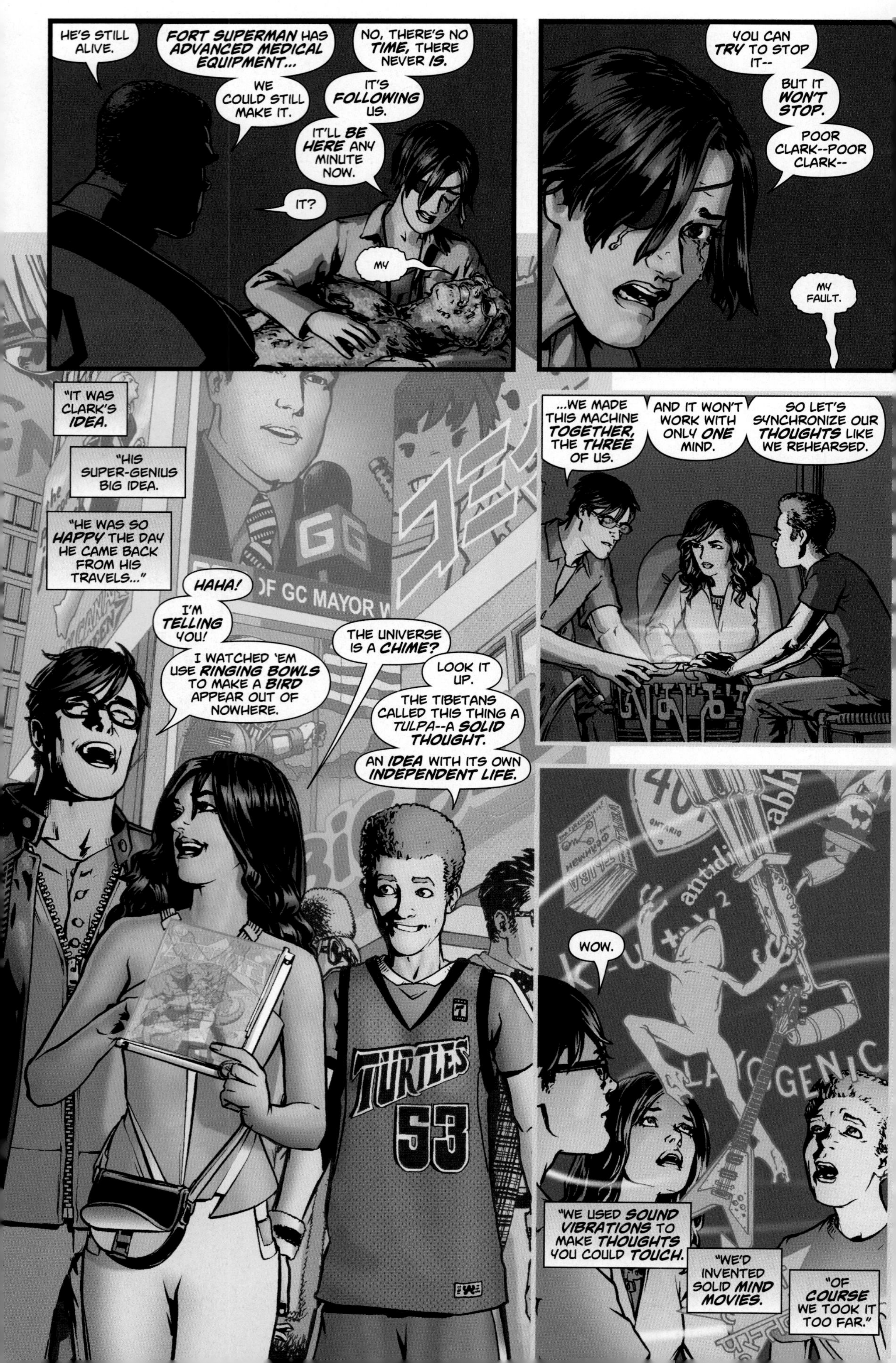
HE'S STILL ALIVE.
FORT SUPERMAN HAS ADVANCED MEDICAL EQUIPMENT...
WE COULD STILL MAKE IT.
NO, THERE'S NO TIME, THERE NEVER IS.
IT'S FOLLOWING US.
IT'LL BE HERE ANY MINUTE NOW.
IT?
MY
YOU CAN TRY TO STOP IT--
BUT IT WON'T STOP.
POOR CLARK--POOR CLARK--
MY FAULT.
"IT WAS CLARK'S IDEA.
"HIS SUPER-GENIUS BIG IDEA.
"HE WAS SO HAPPY THE DAY HE CAME BACK FROM HIS TRAVELS..."
OF GC MAYOR W
HAHA!
I'M TELLING YOU!
I WATCHED 'EM USE RINGING BOWLS TO MAKE A BIRD APPEAR OUT OF NOWHERE.
THE UNIVERSE IS A CHIME?
LOOK IT UP.
THE TIBETANS CALLED THIS THING A TULPA--A SOLID THOUGHT.
AN IDEA WITH ITS OWN INDEPENDENT LIFE.
TURTLES
53
...WE MADE THIS MACHINE TOGETHER, THE THREE OF US.
AND IT WON'T WORK WITH ONLY ONE MIND.
SO LET'S SYNCHRONIZE OUR THOUGHTS LIKE WE REHEARSED.
ONTARIO
antidi
WOW.
"WE USED SOUND VIBRATIONS TO MAKE THOUGHTS YOU COULD TOUCH.
"WE'D INVENTED SOLID MIND MOVIES.
"OF COURSE WE TOOK IT TOO FAR."

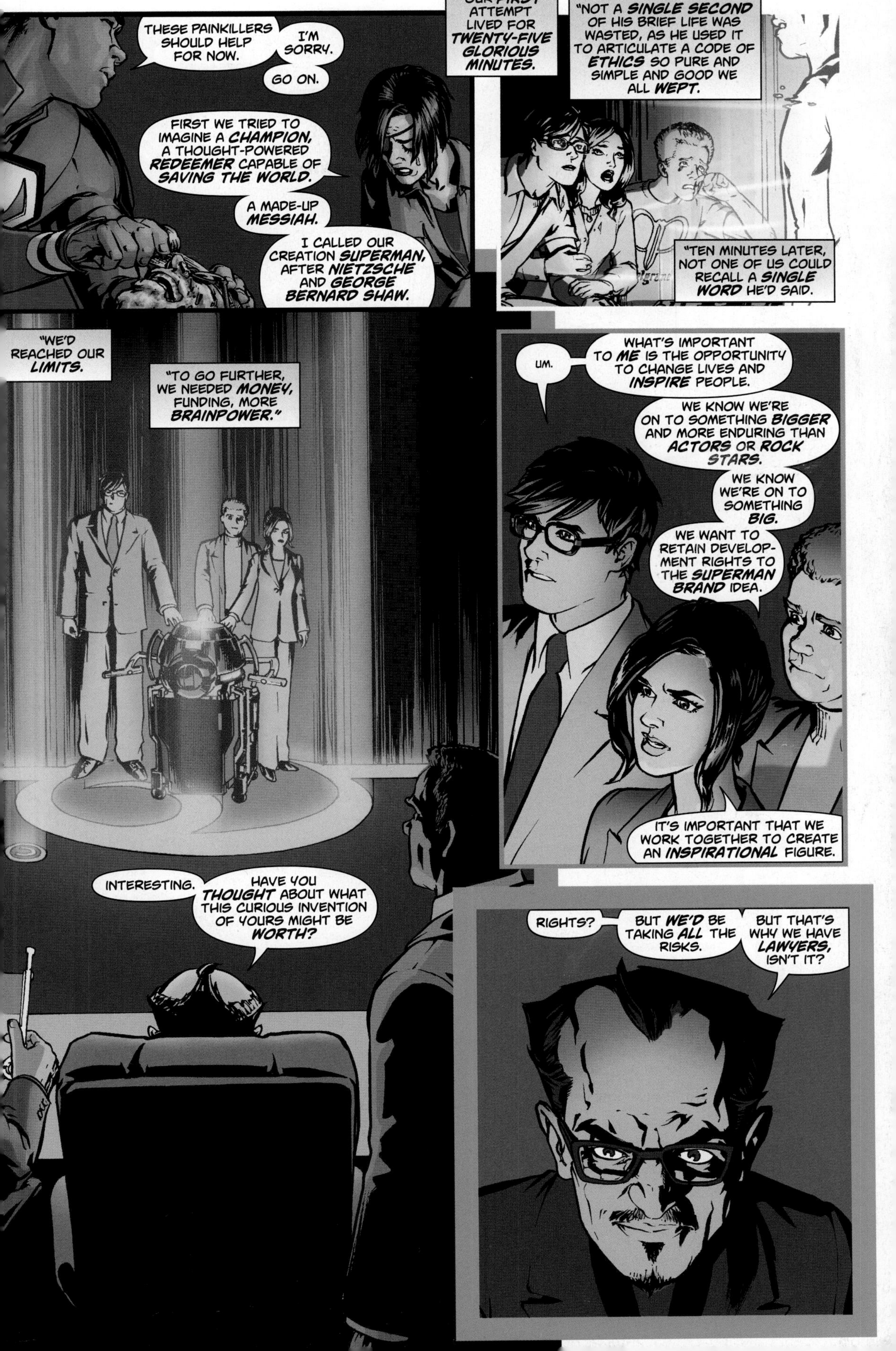
THESE PAINKILLERS SHOULD HELP FOR NOW.
I'M SORRY.
GO ON.
FIRST WE TRIED TO IMAGINE A CHAMPION, A THOUGHT-POWERED REDEEMER CAPABLE OF SAVING THE WORLD.
A MADE-UP MESSIAH.
I CALLED OUR CREATION SUPERMAN, AFTER NIETZSCHE AND GEORGE BERNARD SHAW.
"OUR FIRST ATTEMPT LIVED FOR TWENTY-FIVE GLORIOUS MINUTES.
"NOT A SINGLE SECOND OF HIS BRIEF LIFE WAS WASTED, AS HE USED IT TO ARTICULATE A CODE OF ETHICS SO PURE AND SIMPLE AND GOOD WE ALL WEPT.
"TEN MINUTES LATER, NOT ONE OF US COULD RECALL A SINGLE WORD HE'D SAID.
"WE'D REACHED OUR LIMITS.
"TO GO FURTHER, WE NEEDED MONEY, FUNDING, MORE BRAINPOWER."
INTERESTING.
HAVE YOU THOUGHT ABOUT WHAT THIS CURIOUS INVENTION OF YOURS MIGHT BE WORTH?
UM.
WHAT'S IMPORTANT TO ME IS THE OPPORTUNITY TO CHANGE LIVES AND INSPIRE PEOPLE.
WE KNOW WE'RE ON TO SOMETHING BIGGER AND MORE ENDURING THAN ACTORS OR ROCK STARS.
WE KNOW WE'RE ON TO SOMETHING BIG.
WE WANT TO RETAIN DEVELOPMENT RIGHTS TO THE SUPERMAN BRAND IDEA.
IT'S IMPORTANT THAT WE WORK TOGETHER TO CREATE AN INSPIRATIONAL FIGURE.
RIGHTS?
BUT WE'D BE TAKING ALL THE RISKS.
BUT THAT'S WHY WE HAVE LAWYERS, ISN'T IT?

YOU **DO** HAVE LAWYERS?

YES?

OVERCORP

LAWYERS?

FORGET IT.

THE WHOLE **SUPERMAN** THING WAS WAY TOO **MACHO** AND AGGRESSIVE ANYWAY--WE SHOULD THINK UP A **CARTOON CHARACTER** KIDS CAN **ACTUALLY** PLAY WITH!

THE GUY'S A **REPTILE.**

ON THE **OTHER HAND,** EVERYONE WILL KNOW OUR **NAMES** AFTER THIS.

WE CAN'T TAKE IT ANY FURTHER ON OUR **OWN.**

GUYS, THEY'LL **STEAL** THE IDEA IF WE **DON'T** SELL IT.

THAT'S IT.

THE **DOTTED LINE.**

YOU WON'T **REGRET** THIS.

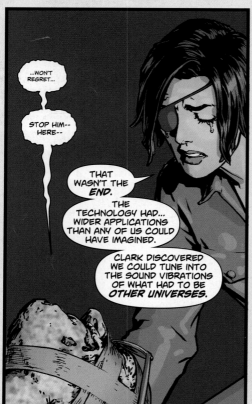

...WON'T REGRET...

STOP HIM-- HERE--

THAT WASN'T THE **END.**

THE TECHNOLOGY HAD... WIDER APPLICATIONS THAN ANY OF US COULD HAVE IMAGINED.

CLARK DISCOVERED WE COULD TUNE INTO THE SOUND VIBRATIONS OF WHAT HAD TO BE **OTHER UNIVERSES.**

...I DON'T UNDERSTAND WHAT YOU DID **WRONG.**

WE **SOLD OUT!**

THEY HAD **500 EXPERTS** LINED UP, THINKING IN **HARMONY** TO STREAMLINE THE **SUPERMAN BRAND** FOR MAXIMUM CROSS-SPECTRUM, WIDE PLATFORM APPEAL.

THEY BUILT A VIOLENT, TROUBLED, FACELESS **ANTI-HERO,** CONCEALING A TRAGIC **SECRET LIFE,** A GLOBAL MARKETING **ICON.**

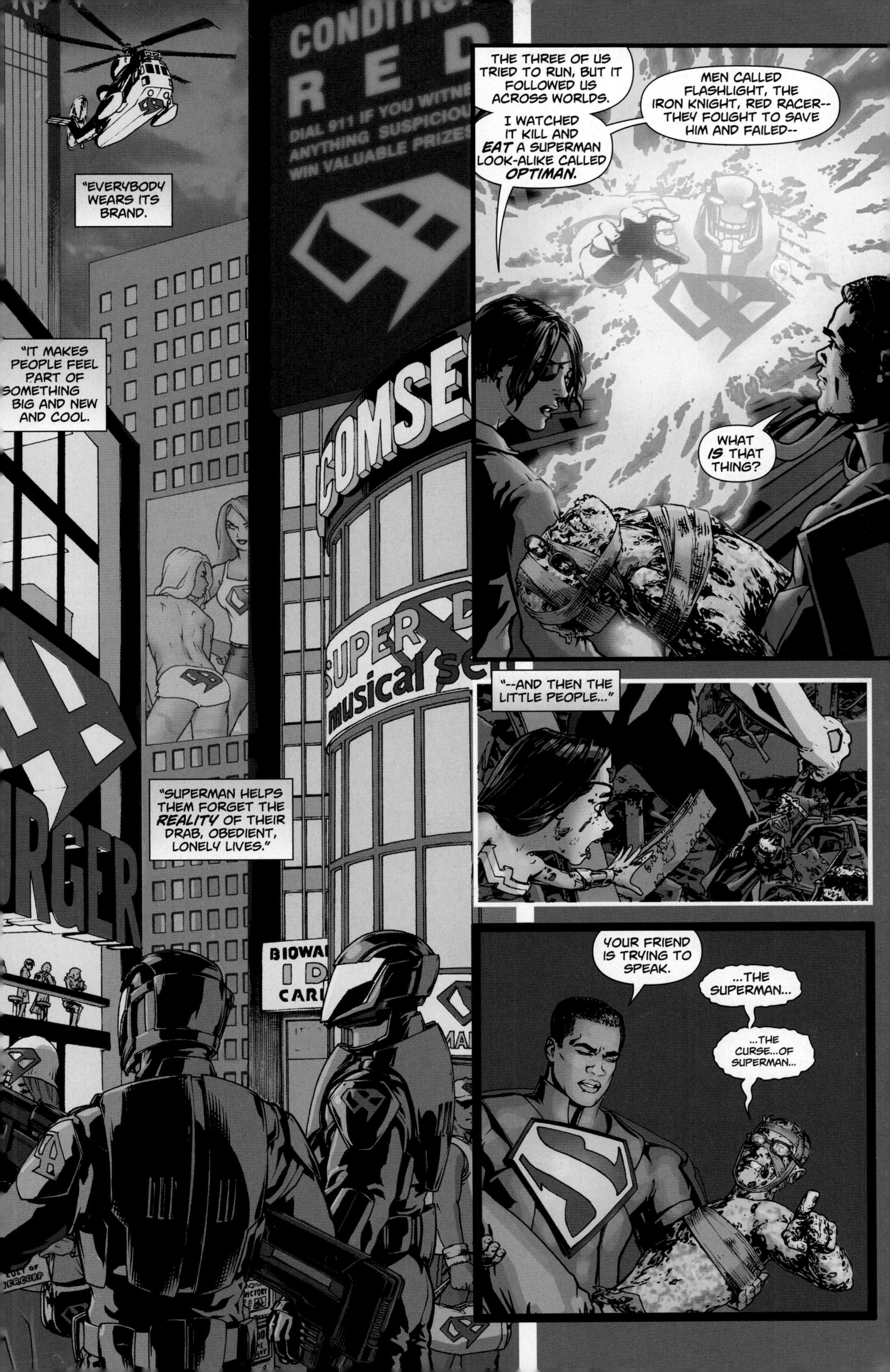
CONDITION
R E D
DIAL 911 IF YOU WITNE
ANYTHING SUSPICIOU
WIN VALUABLE PRIZES
"EVERYBODY WEARS ITS BRAND.
"IT MAKES PEOPLE FEEL PART OF SOMETHING BIG AND NEW AND COOL.
"SUPERMAN HELPS THEM FORGET THE REALITY OF THEIR DRAB, OBEDIENT, LONELY LIVES."
COMSE
SUPER
musical se
URGER
BIOWA
I D
CAR
THE THREE OF US TRIED TO RUN, BUT IT FOLLOWED US ACROSS WORLDS.
I WATCHED IT KILL AND EAT A SUPERMAN LOOK-ALIKE CALLED OPTIMAN.
MEN CALLED FLASHLIGHT, THE IRON KNIGHT, RED RACER-- THEY FOUGHT TO SAVE HIM AND FAILED--
WHAT IS THAT THING?
"--AND THEN THE LITTLE PEOPLE..."
YOUR FRIEND IS TRYING TO SPEAK.
...THE SUPERMAN...
...THE CURSE...OF SUPERMAN...

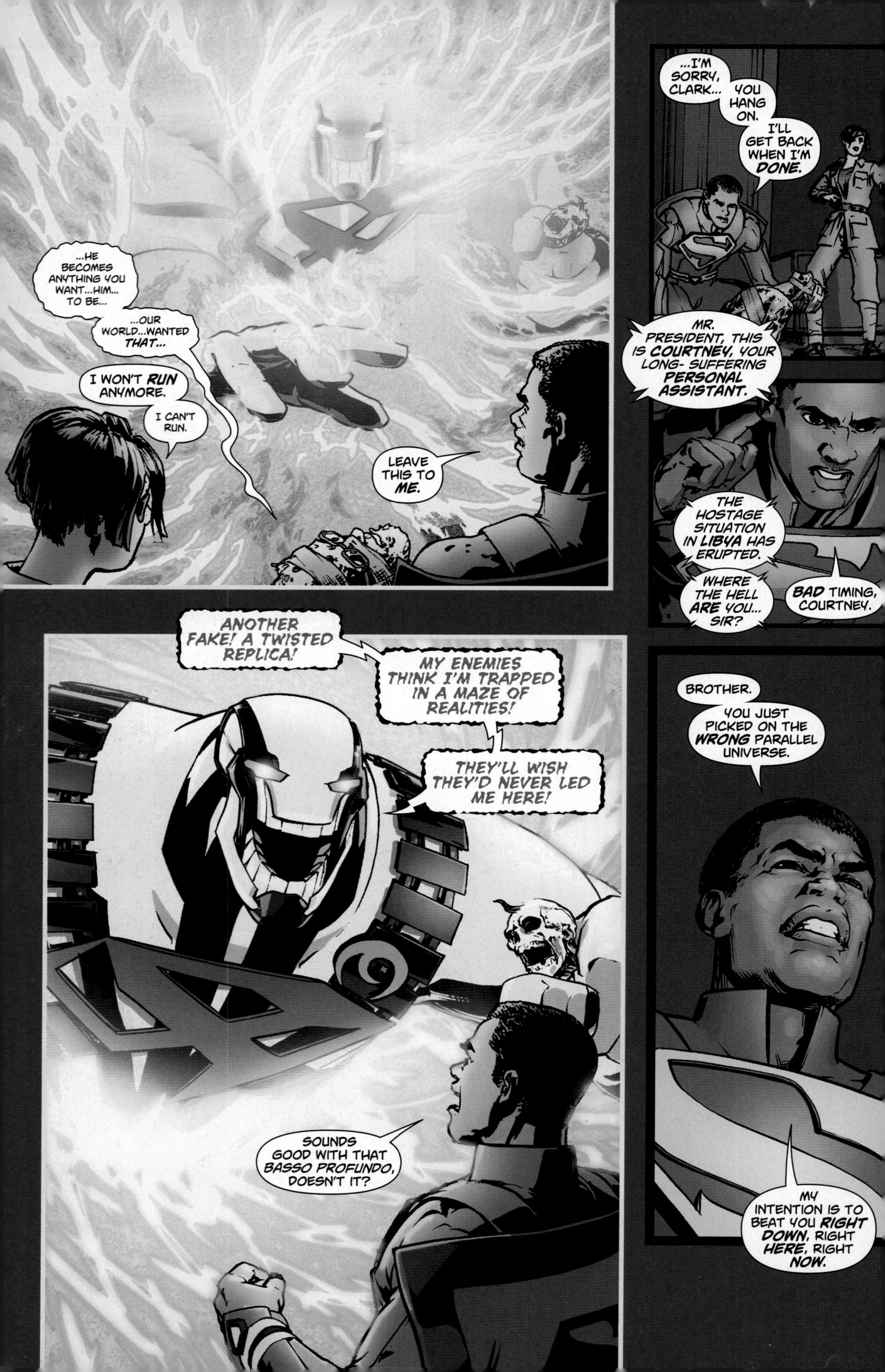

...HE BECOMES ANYTHING YOU WANT...HIM... TO BE...
...OUR WORLD...WANTED THAT...
I WON'T RUN ANYMORE.
I CAN'T RUN.
LEAVE THIS TO ME.
...I'M SORRY, CLARK...
YOU HANG ON.
I'LL GET BACK WHEN I'M DONE.
MR. PRESIDENT, THIS IS COURTNEY, YOUR LONG- SUFFERING PERSONAL ASSISTANT.
THE HOSTAGE SITUATION IN LIBYA HAS ERUPTED.
WHERE THE HELL ARE YOU... SIR?
BAD TIMING, COURTNEY.
ANOTHER FAKE! A TWISTED REPLICA!
MY ENEMIES THINK I'M TRAPPED IN A MAZE OF REALITIES!
THEY'LL WISH THEY'D NEVER LED ME HERE!
SOUNDS GOOD WITH THAT BASSO PROFUNDO, DOESN'T IT?
BROTHER.
YOU JUST PICKED ON THE WRONG PARALLEL UNIVERSE.
MY INTENTION IS TO BEAT YOU RIGHT DOWN, RIGHT HERE, RIGHT NOW.

BRAINIAC! WHILE I'M BUSY, YOU'RE IN CHARGE.

LIBYA.

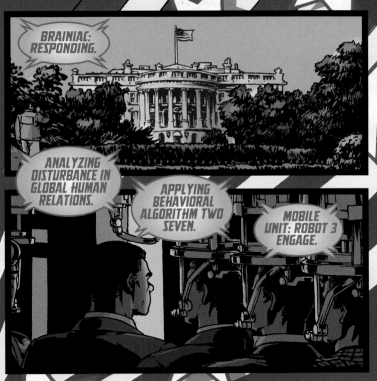

BRAINIAC: RESPONDING.

ANALYZING DISTURBANCE IN GLOBAL HUMAN RELATIONS.

APPLYING BEHAVIORAL ALGORITHM TWO SEVEN.

MOBILE UNIT: ROBOT 3 ENGAGE.

RESPONDING.

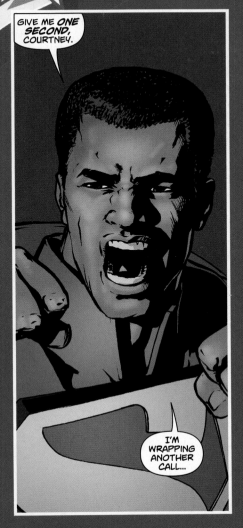

GIVE ME ONE SECOND, COURTNEY.

I'M WRAPPING ANOTHER CALL...

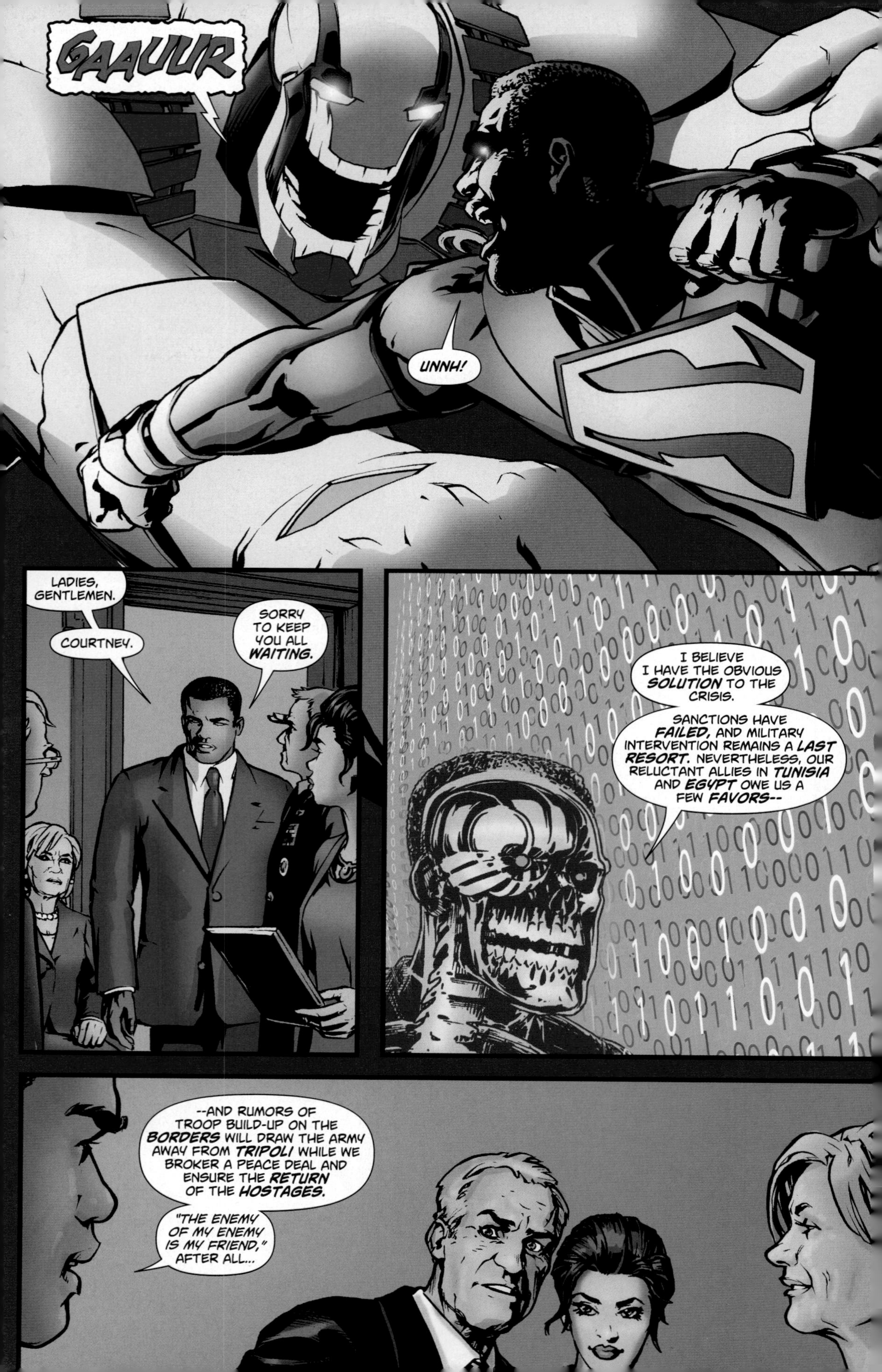
GAAUUR
UNNH!
LADIES, GENTLEMEN.
COURTNEY.
SORRY TO KEEP YOU ALL WAITING.
I BELIEVE I HAVE THE OBVIOUS SOLUTION TO THE CRISIS.
SANCTIONS HAVE FAILED, AND MILITARY INTERVENTION REMAINS A LAST RESORT. NEVERTHELESS, OUR RELUCTANT ALLIES IN TUNISIA AND EGYPT OWE US A FEW FAVORS--
--AND RUMORS OF TROOP BUILD-UP ON THE BORDERS WILL DRAW THE ARMY AWAY FROM TRIPOLI WHILE WE BROKER A PEACE DEAL AND ENSURE THE RETURN OF THE HOSTAGES.
"THE ENEMY OF MY ENEMY IS MY FRIEND," AFTER ALL...

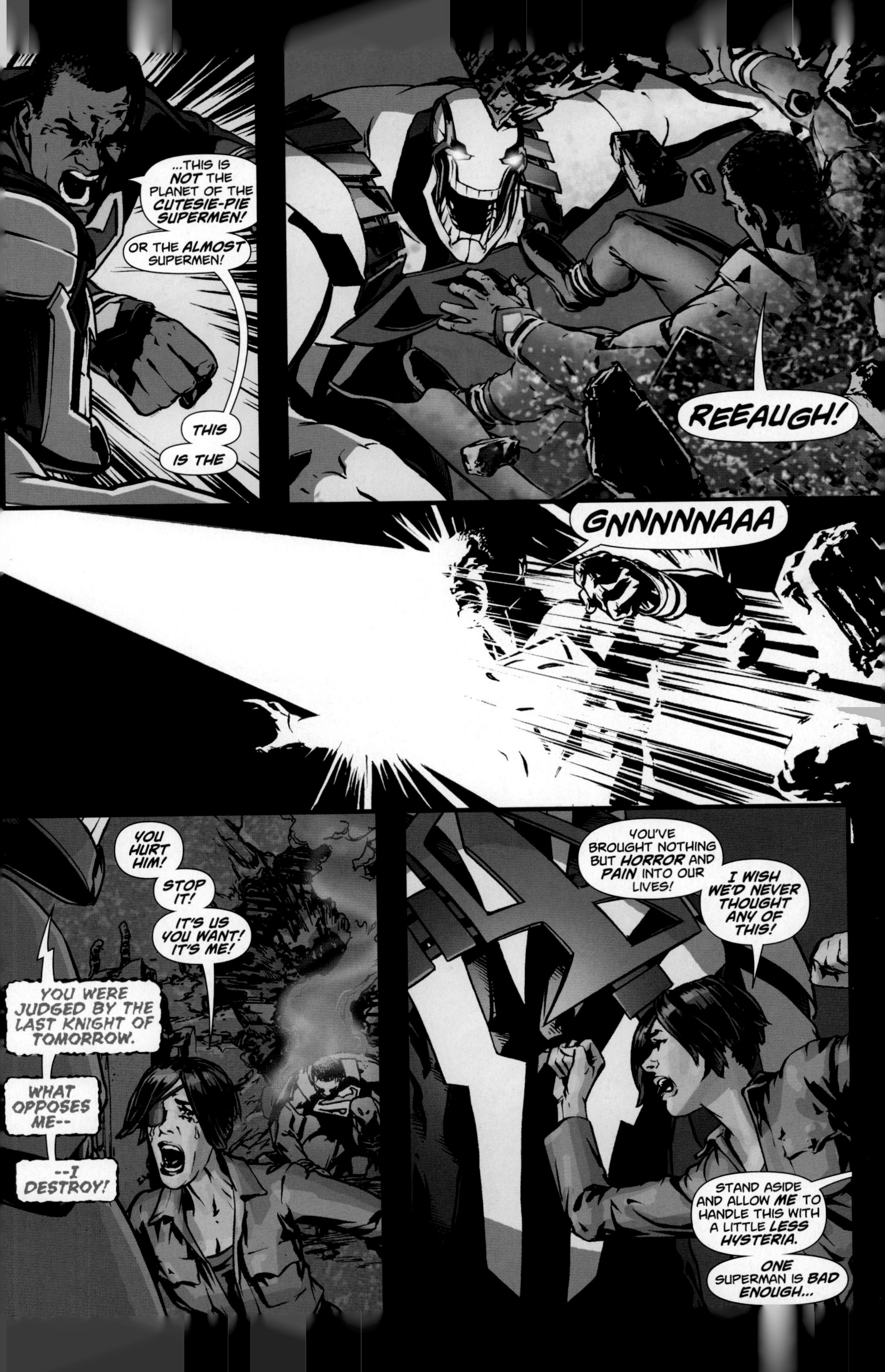
...THIS IS NOT THE PLANET OF THE CUTESIE-PIE SUPERMEN!
OR THE ALMOST SUPERMEN!
THIS
IS THE
REEAUGH!
GNNNNNAAA
YOU HURT HIM!
STOP IT!
IT'S US YOU WANT! IT'S ME!
YOU WERE JUDGED BY THE LAST KNIGHT OF TOMORROW.
WHAT OPPOSES ME--
--I DESTROY!
YOU'VE BROUGHT NOTHING BUT HORROR AND PAIN INTO OUR LIVES!
I WISH WE'D NEVER THOUGHT ANY OF THIS!
STAND ASIDE AND ALLOW ME TO HANDLE THIS WITH A LITTLE LESS HYSTERIA.
ONE SUPERMAN IS BAD ENOUGH...

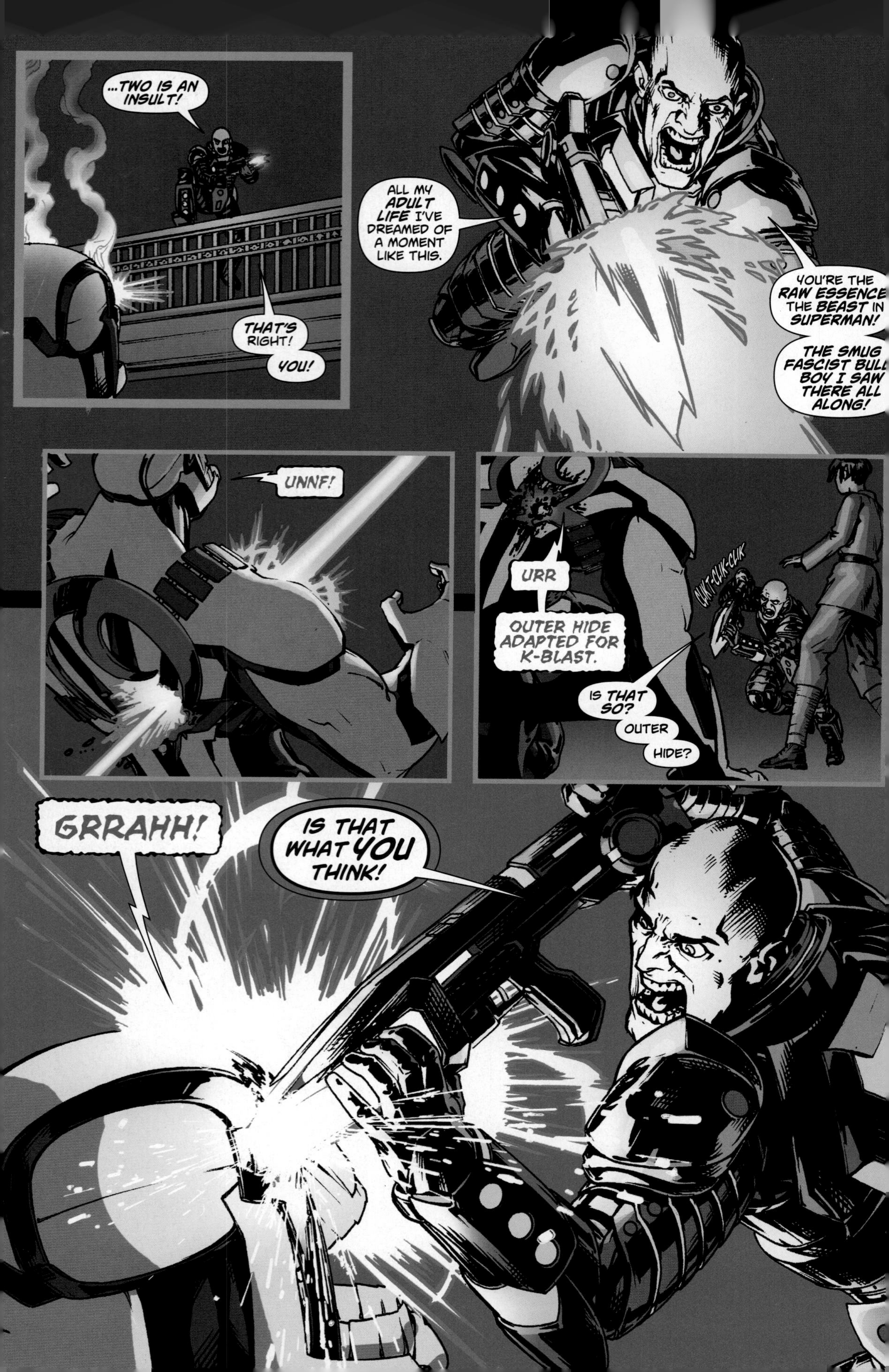
...TWO IS AN INSULT!
THAT'S RIGHT!
YOU!
ALL MY ADULT LIFE I'VE DREAMED OF A MOMENT LIKE THIS.
YOU'RE THE RAW ESSENCE THE BEAST IN SUPERMAN!
THE SMUG FASCIST BULL BOY I SAW THERE ALL ALONG!
UNNF!
URR
OUTER HIDE ADAPTED FOR K-BLAST.
CLIK-CLIK-CLIK
IS THAT SO?
OUTER
HIDE?
GRRAHH!
IS THAT WHAT YOU THINK!

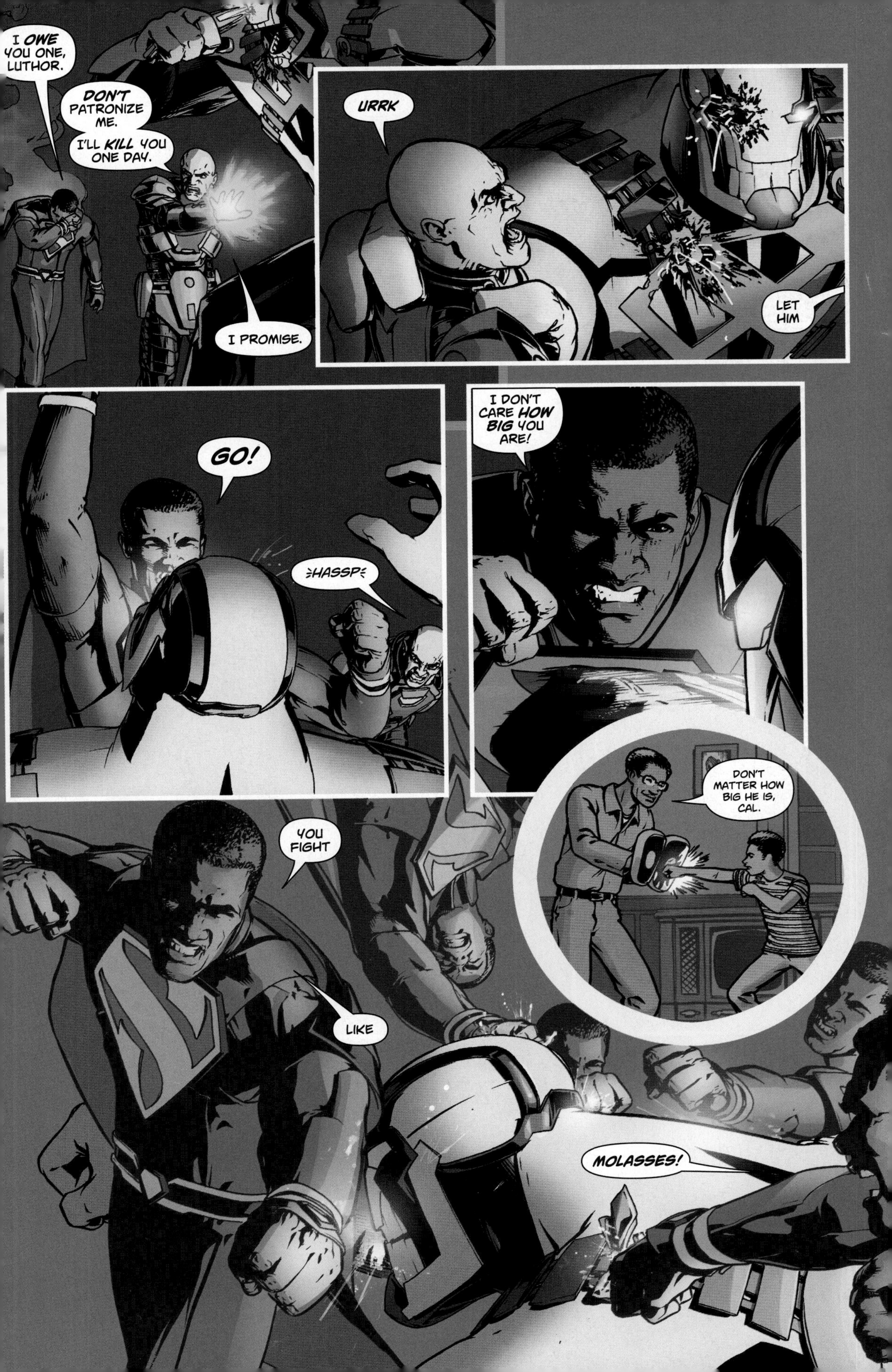
I OWE YOU ONE, LUTHOR.
DON'T PATRONIZE ME.
I'LL KILL YOU ONE DAY.
I PROMISE.
URRK
LET HIM
GO!
HASSP
I DON'T CARE HOW BIG YOU ARE!
DON'T MATTER HOW BIG HE IS, CAL.
YOU FIGHT
LIKE
MOLASSES!

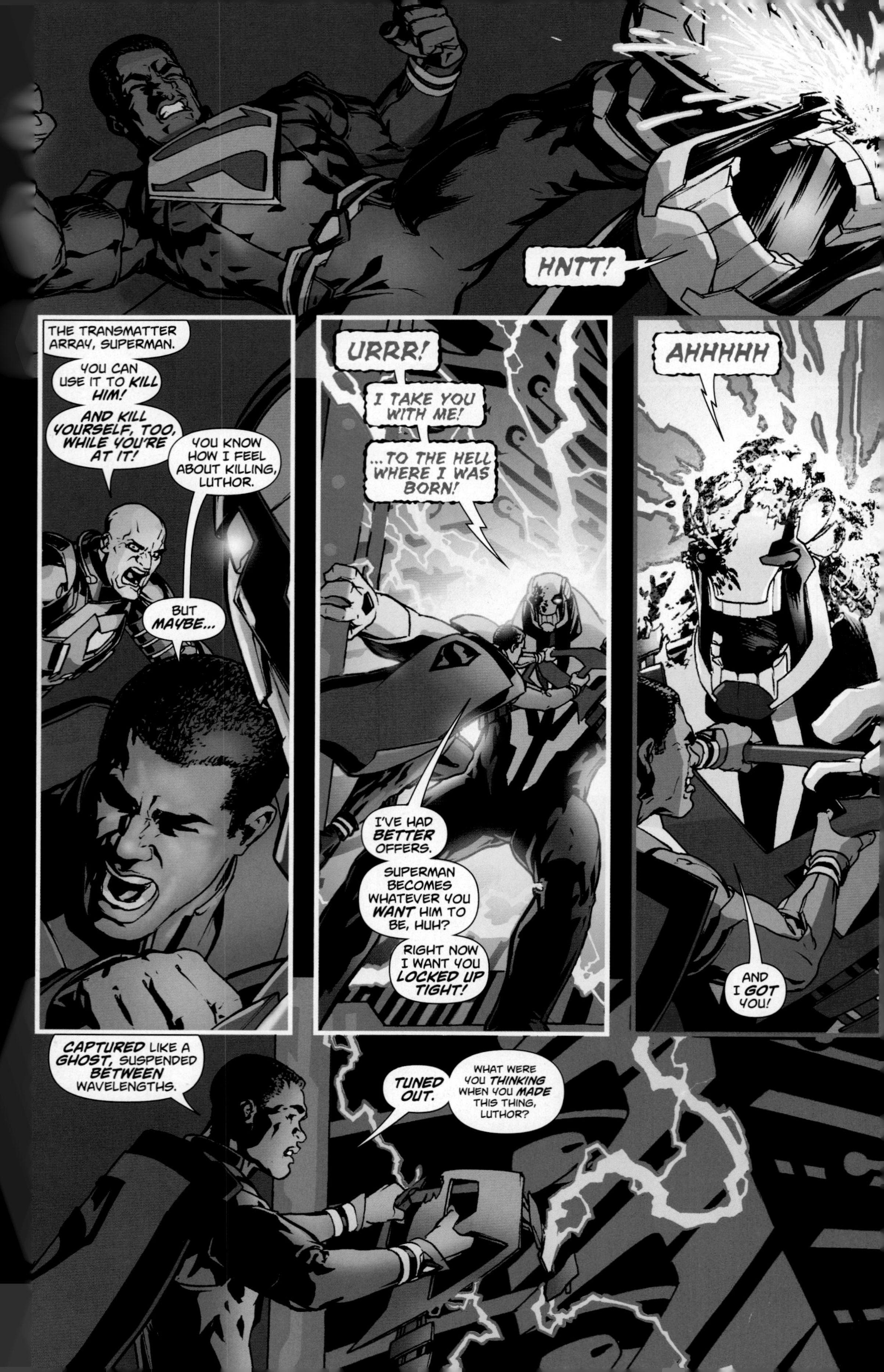
HNTT!
THE TRANSMATTER ARRAY, SUPERMAN.
YOU CAN USE IT TO KILL HIM!
AND KILL YOURSELF, TOO, WHILE YOU'RE AT IT!
YOU KNOW HOW I FEEL ABOUT KILLING, LUTHOR.
BUT MAYBE...
URRR!
I TAKE YOU WITH ME!
...TO THE HELL WHERE I WAS BORN!
I'VE HAD BETTER OFFERS.
SUPERMAN BECOMES WHATEVER YOU WANT HIM TO BE, HUH?
RIGHT NOW I WANT YOU LOCKED UP TIGHT!
AHHHHH
AND I GOT YOU!
CAPTURED LIKE A GHOST, SUSPENDED BETWEEN WAVELENGTHS.
TUNED OUT.
WHAT WERE YOU THINKING WHEN YOU MADE THIS THING, LUTHOR?

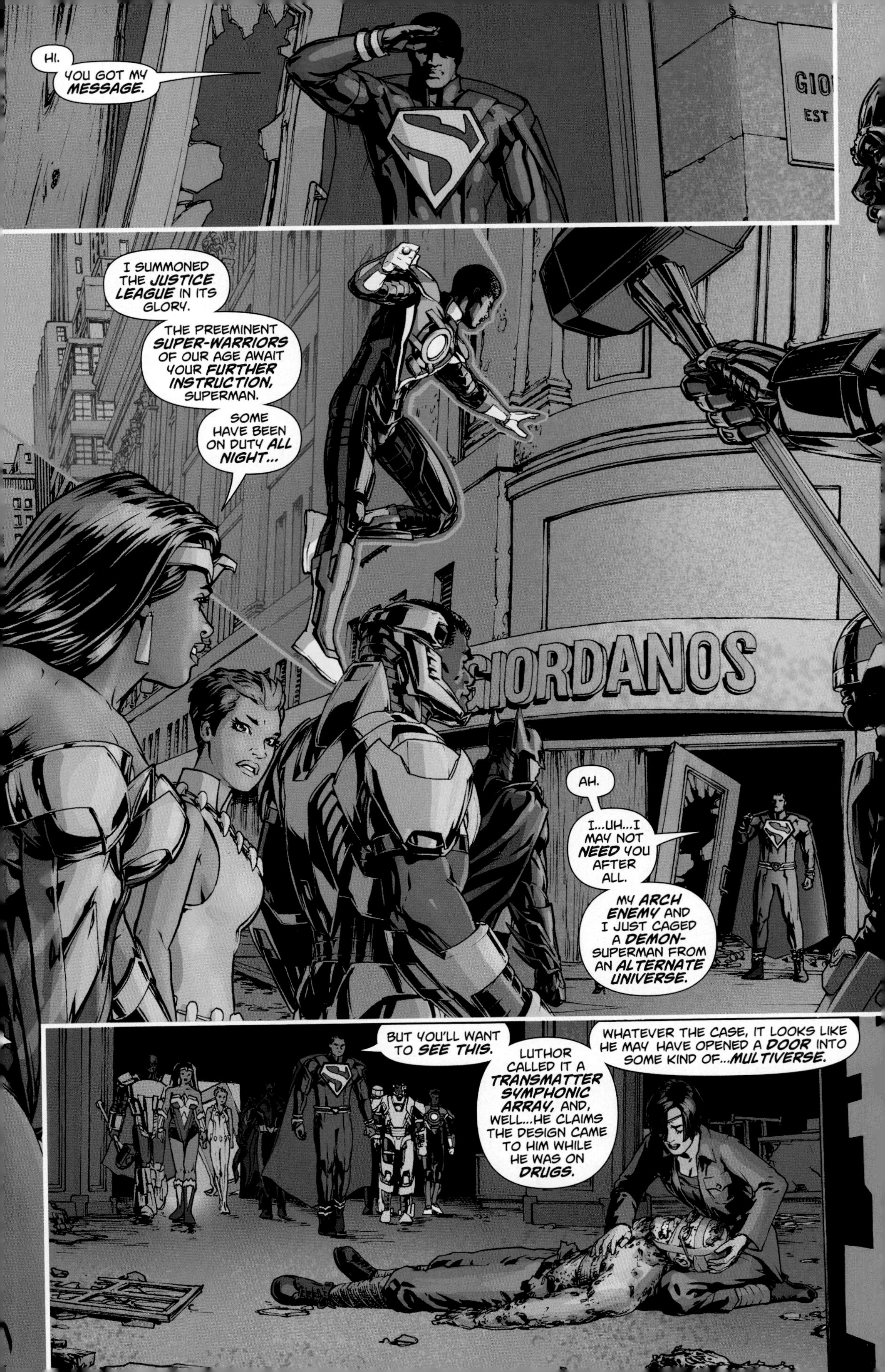
HI.
YOU GOT MY MESSAGE.
GIO
EST
I SUMMONED THE JUSTICE LEAGUE IN ITS GLORY.
THE PREEMINENT SUPER-WARRIORS OF OUR AGE AWAIT YOUR FURTHER INSTRUCTION, SUPERMAN.
SOME HAVE BEEN ON DUTY ALL NIGHT...
GIORDANOS
AH.
I...UH...I MAY NOT NEED YOU AFTER ALL.
MY ARCH ENEMY AND I JUST CAGED A DEMON-SUPERMAN FROM AN ALTERNATE UNIVERSE.
BUT YOU'LL WANT TO SEE THIS.
LUTHOR CALLED IT A TRANSMATTER SYMPHONIC ARRAY, AND, WELL...HE CLAIMS THE DESIGN CAME TO HIM WHILE HE WAS ON DRUGS.
WHATEVER THE CASE, IT LOOKS LIKE HE MAY HAVE OPENED A DOOR INTO SOME KIND OF...MULTIVERSE.

...I COULDN'T *SAVE* HIM.

BUT THERE'S A STILL THE CHANCE OF A SUCCESSFUL *LAZARUS REVIVAL* IN MY LAB.

IN THE MEANTIME--

YOU'RE WELCOME TO *STAY HERE* AS LONG AS YOU LIKE.

WHAT *CHOICE* DO I HAVE?

WHAT'S LEFT?

I'M IN *SHOCK.*

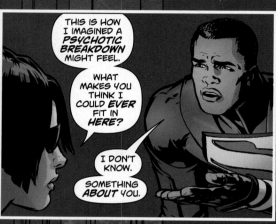

THIS IS HOW I IMAGINED A *PSYCHOTIC BREAKDOWN* MIGHT FEEL.

WHAT MAKES YOU THINK I COULD *EVER* FIT IN *HERE?*

I DON'T *KNOW.*

SOMETHING *ABOUT* YOU.

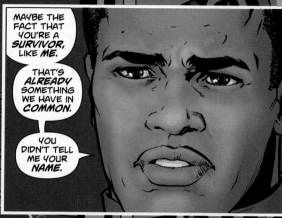

MAYBE THE FACT THAT YOU'RE A *SURVIVOR,* LIKE *ME.*

THAT'S *ALREADY* SOMETHING WE HAVE IN *COMMON.*

YOU DIDN'T TELL ME YOUR *NAME.*

ME?

I'M *LOIS.*

MY NAME'S *LOIS LANE.*

I GUESS YOU MUST BE *SUPERMAN* DONE RIGHT.

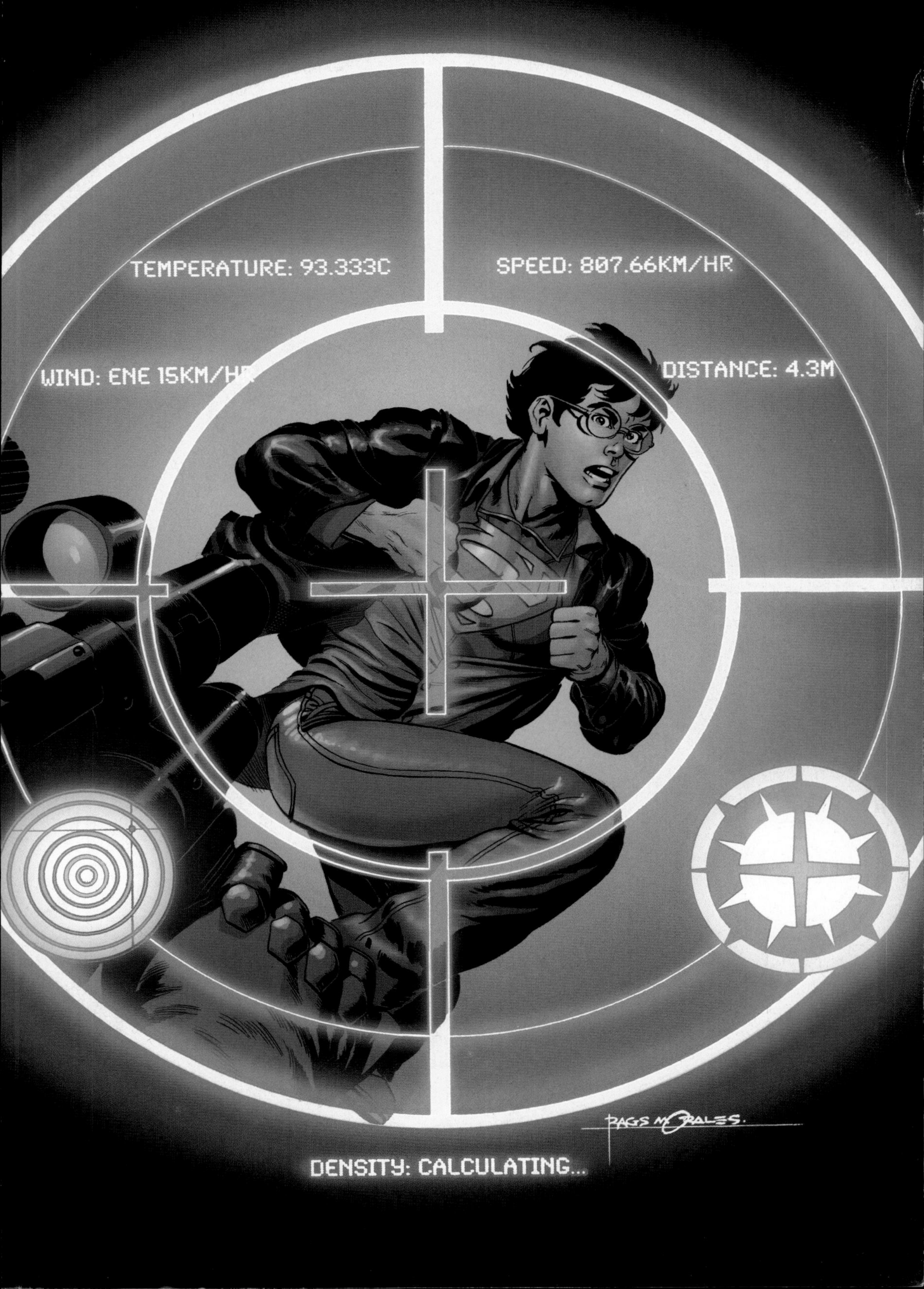
TEMPERATURE: 93.333C
SPEED: 807.66KM/HR
WIND: ENE 15KM/HR
DISTANCE: 4.3M
RAGS MORALES.
DENSITY: CALCULATING...

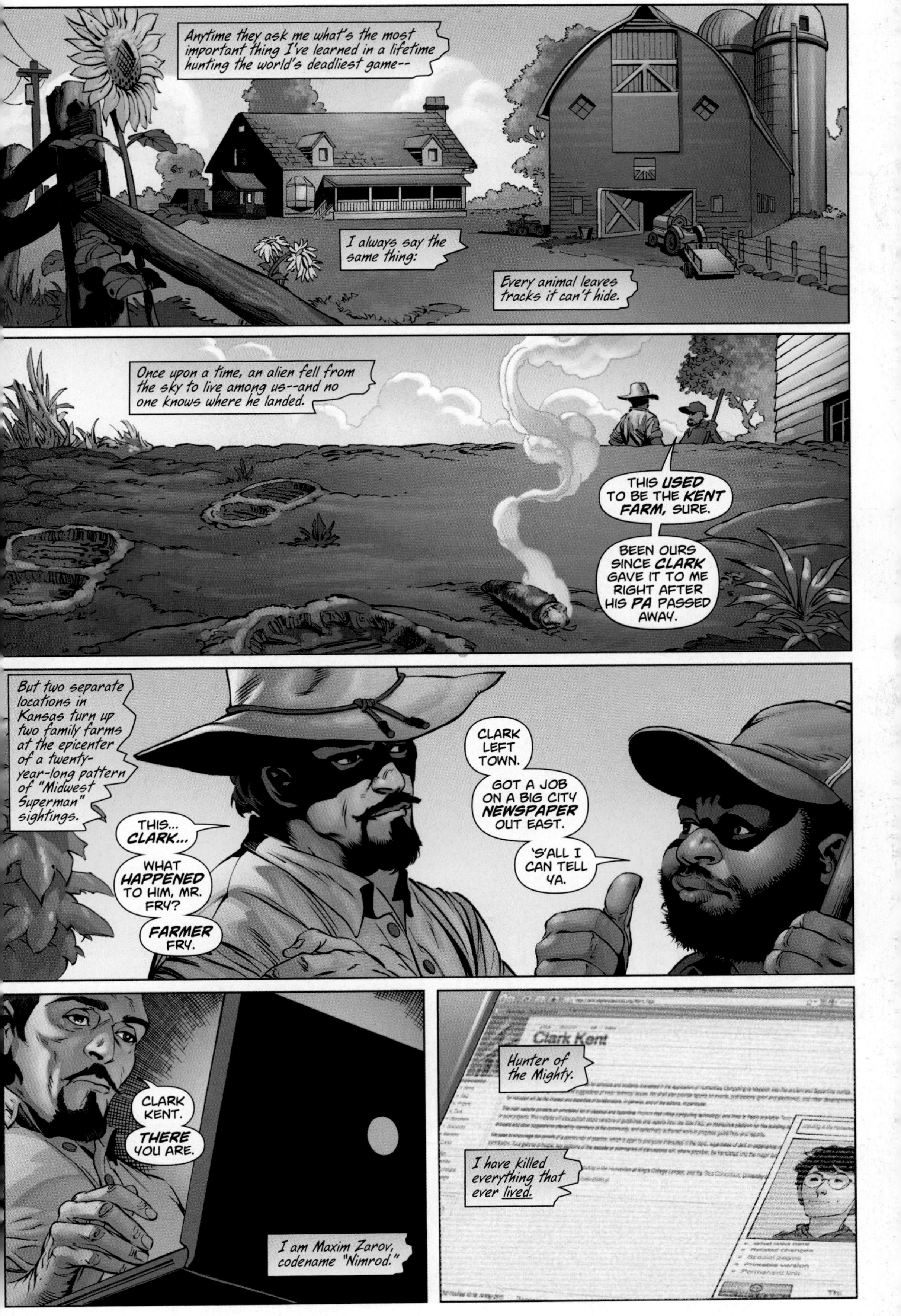

Anytime they ask me what's the most important thing I've learned in a lifetime hunting the world's deadliest game--
I always say the same thing:
Every animal leaves tracks it can't hide.
Once upon a time, an alien fell from the sky to live among us--and no one knows where he landed.
THIS USED TO BE THE KENT FARM, SURE.
BEEN OURS SINCE CLARK GAVE IT TO ME RIGHT AFTER HIS PA PASSED AWAY.
But two separate locations in Kansas turn up two family farms at the epicenter of a twenty-year-long pattern of "Midwest Superman" sightings.
THIS... CLARK...
WHAT HAPPENED TO HIM, MR. FRY?
FARMER FRY.
CLARK LEFT TOWN.
GOT A JOB ON A BIG CITY NEWSPAPER OUT EAST.
'S'ALL I CAN TELL YA.
CLARK KENT. THERE YOU ARE.
I am Maxim Zarov, codename "Nimrod."
Clark Kent
Hunter of the Mighty.
I have killed everything that ever lived.

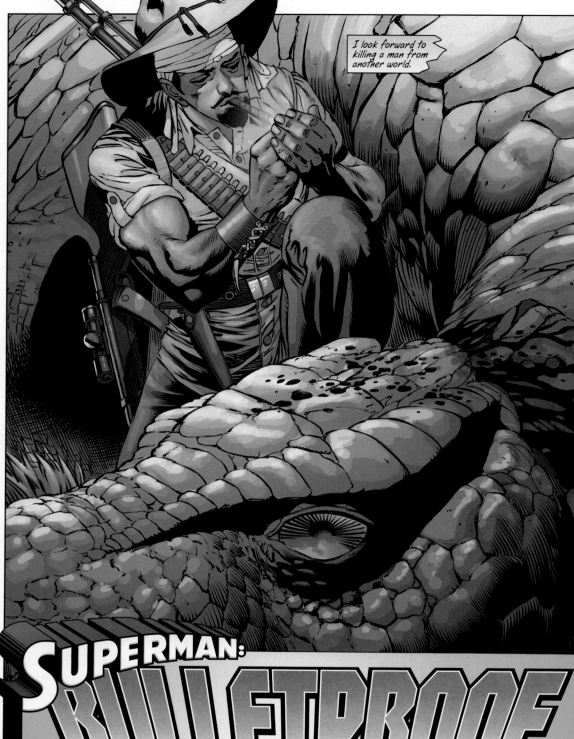

I look forward to killing a man from another world.

SUPERMAN: BULLETPROOF

GRANT MORRISION WRITER RAGS MORALES PENCILLER RICK BRYANT INKER
BRAD ANDERSON COLORIST PATRICK BROSSEAU LETTERER RAGS MORALES & BRAD ANDERSON COVER
BRYAN HITCH & PAUL MOUNTS VARIANT COVER WIL MOSS ASSOCIATE EDITOR MATT IDELSON EDITOR
SUPERMAN CREATED BY JERRY SIEGEL & JOE SHUSTER

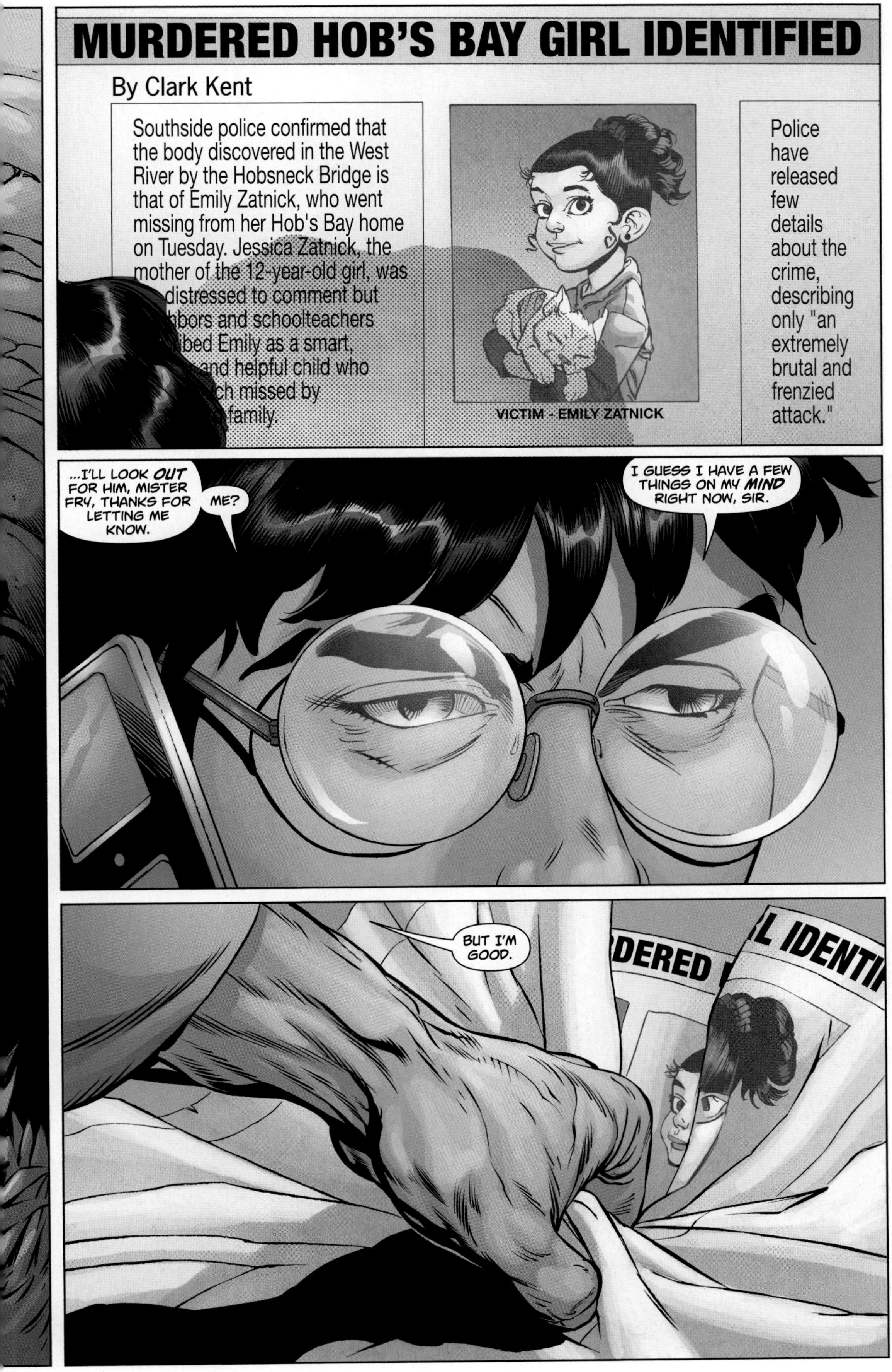

MURDERED HOB'S BAY GIRL IDENTIFIED
By Clark Kent
Southside police confirmed that the body discovered in the West River by the Hobsneck Bridge is that of Emily Zatnick, who went missing from her Hob's Bay home on Tuesday. Jessica Zatnick, the mother of the 12-year-old girl, was
distressed to comment but
hbors and schoolteachers
ibed Emily as a smart,
and helpful child who
ch missed by
family.
VICTIM - EMILY ZATNICK
Police have released few details about the crime, describing only "an extremely brutal and frenzied attack."
...I'LL LOOK OUT FOR HIM, MISTER FRY, THANKS FOR LETTING ME KNOW.
ME?
I GUESS I HAVE A FEW THINGS ON MY MIND RIGHT NOW, SIR.
BUT I'M GOOD.
DERED
L IDENTI

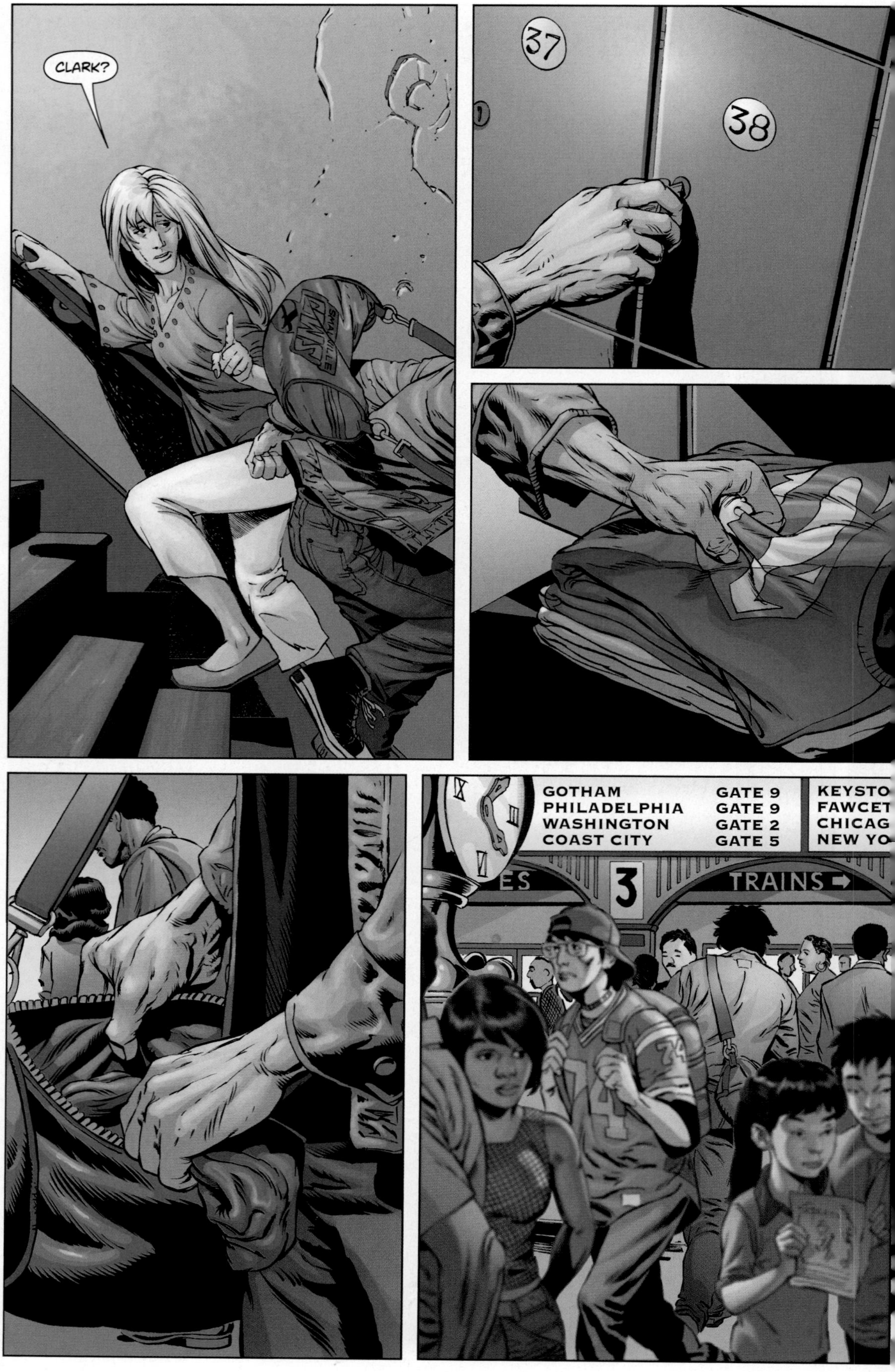
CLARK?
37
38
GOTHAM GATE 9
PHILADELPHIA GATE 9
WASHINGTON GATE 2
COAST CITY GATE 5
3
TRAINS

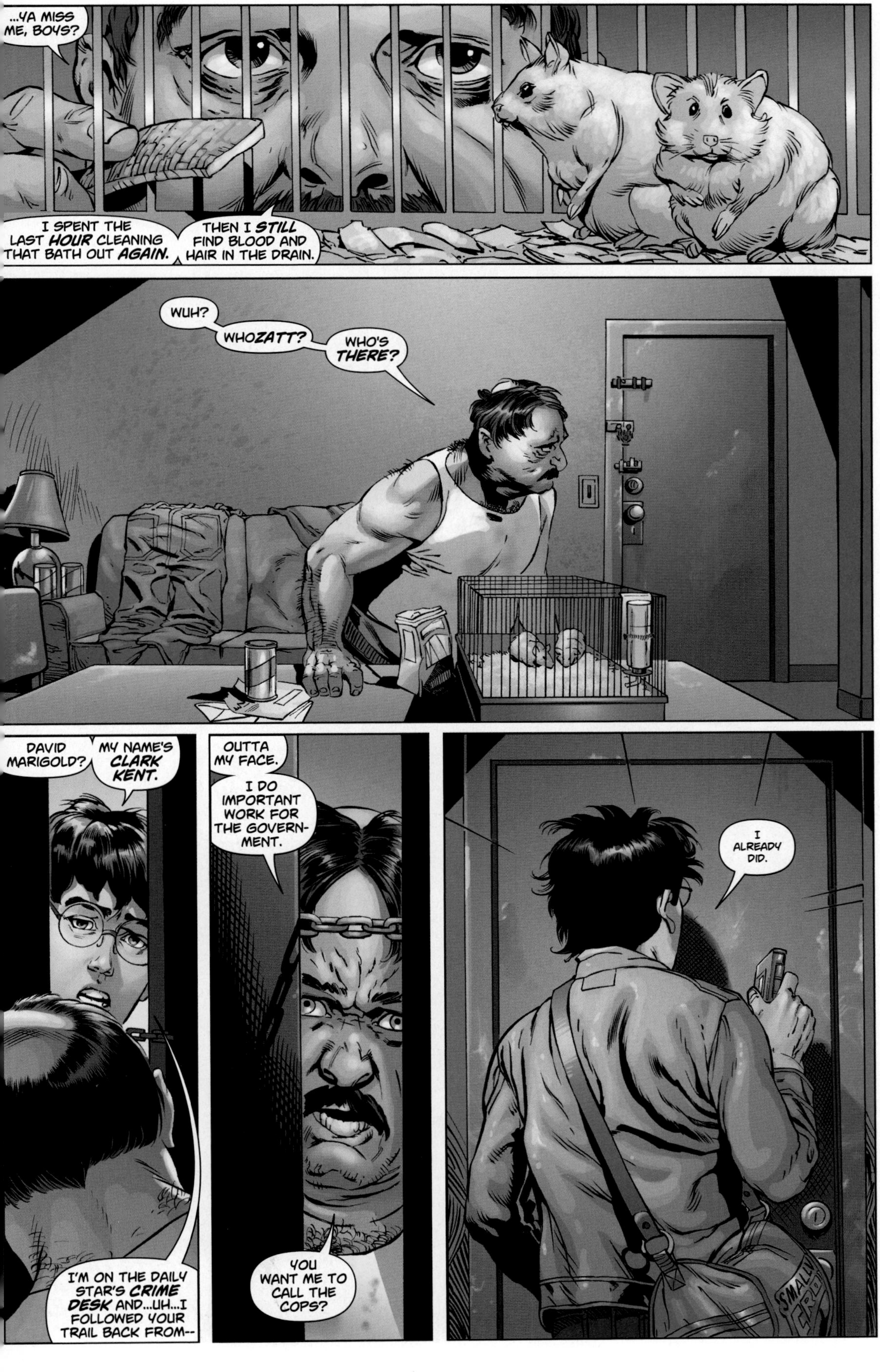
...YA MISS ME, BOYS?
I SPENT THE LAST HOUR CLEANING THAT BATH OUT AGAIN.
THEN I STILL FIND BLOOD AND HAIR IN THE DRAIN.
WUH?
WHOZATT?
WHO'S THERE?
DAVID MARIGOLD?
MY NAME'S CLARK KENT.
I'M ON THE DAILY STAR'S CRIME DESK AND...UH...I FOLLOWED YOUR TRAIL BACK FROM--
OUTTA MY FACE.
I DO IMPORTANT WORK FOR THE GOVERNMENT.
YOU WANT ME TO CALL THE COPS?
I ALREADY DID.

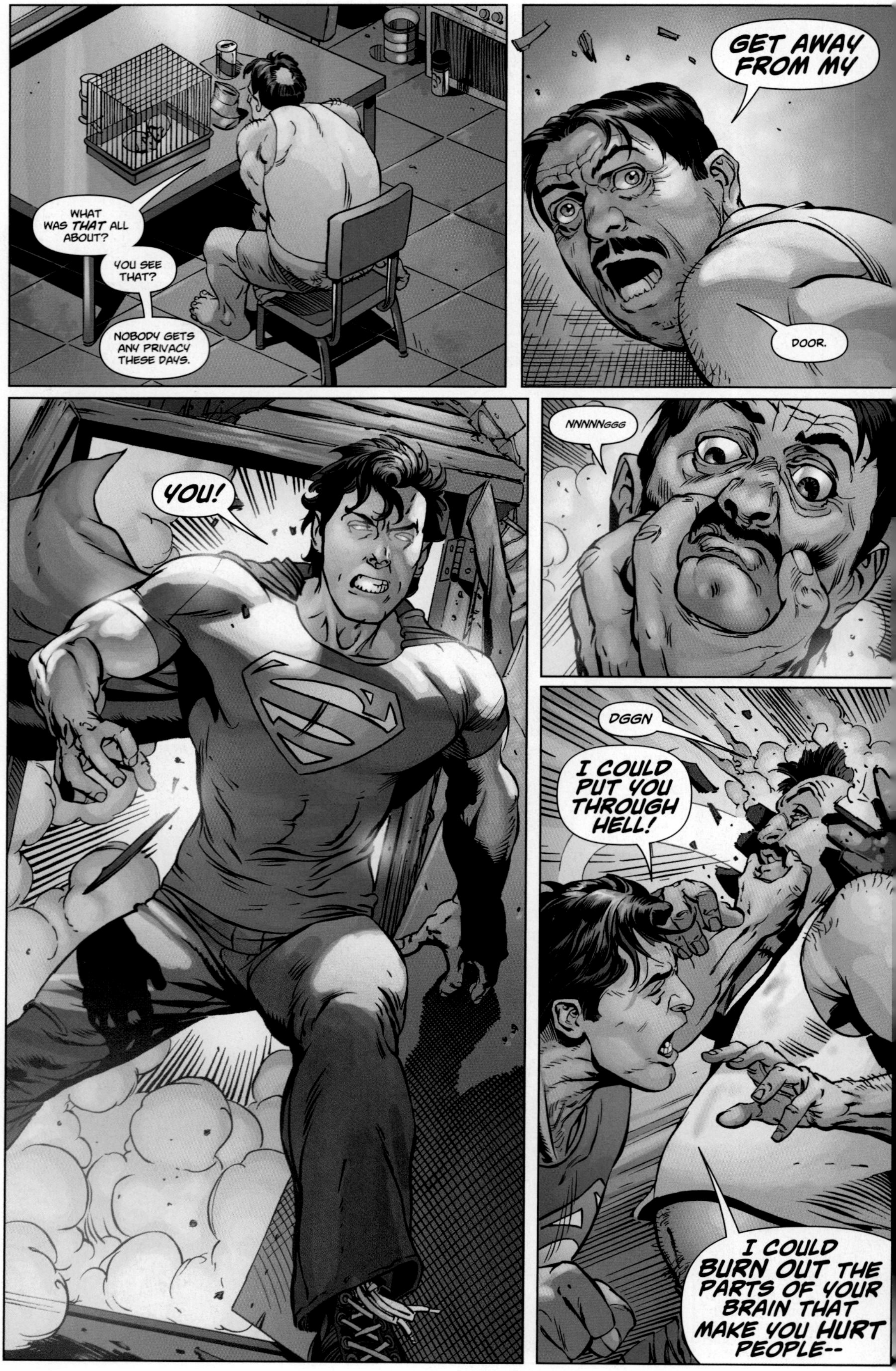
WHAT WAS THAT ALL ABOUT?
YOU SEE THAT?
NOBODY GETS ANY PRIVACY THESE DAYS.
GET AWAY FROM MY
DOOR.
YOU!
NNNNNGGG
DGGN
I COULD PUT YOU THROUGH HELL!
I COULD BURN OUT THE PARTS OF YOUR BRAIN THAT MAKE YOU HURT PEOPLE--

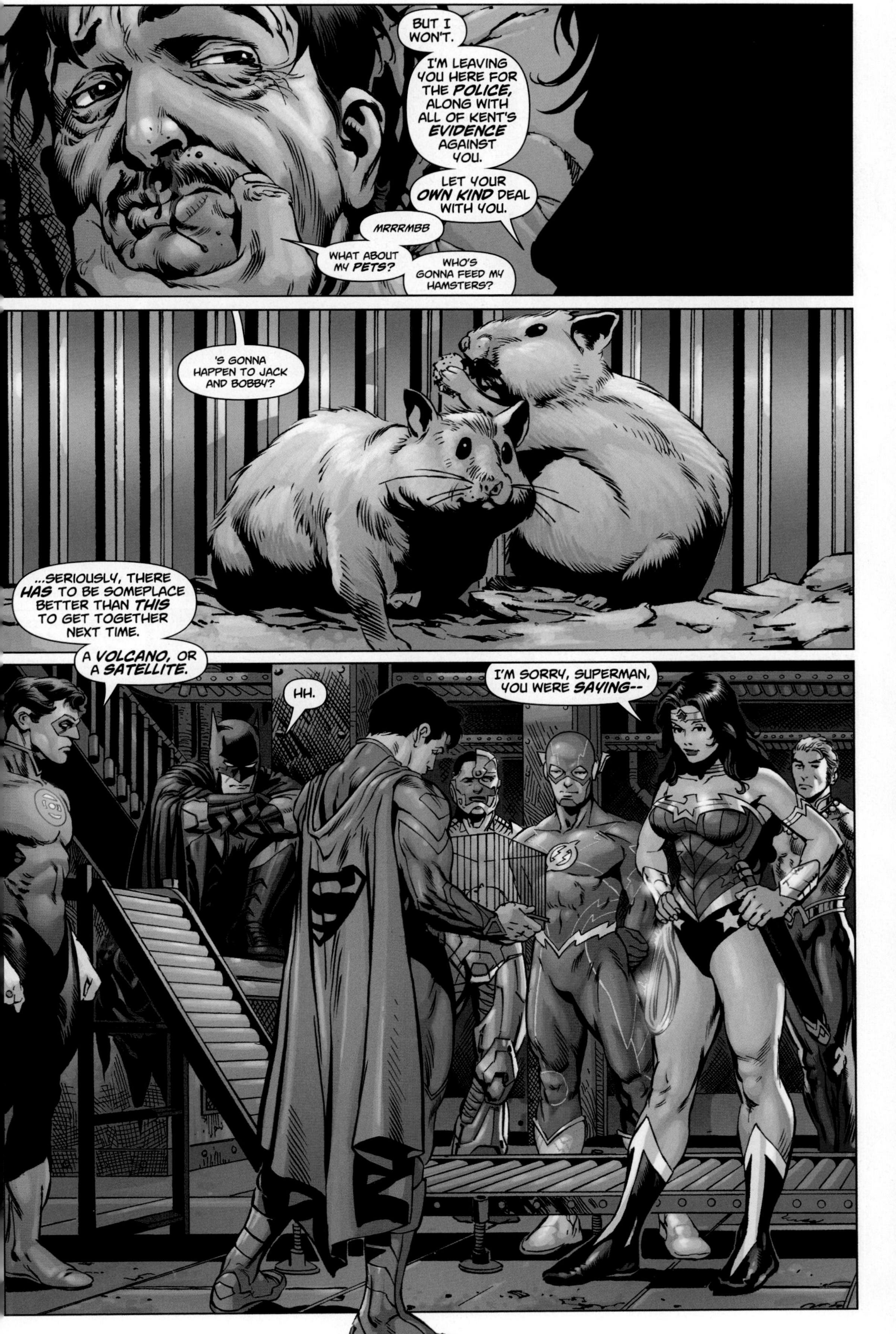

BUT I WON'T.
I'M LEAVING YOU HERE FOR THE POLICE, ALONG WITH ALL OF KENT'S EVIDENCE AGAINST YOU.
LET YOUR OWN KIND DEAL WITH YOU.
MRRRMBB
WHAT ABOUT MY PETS?
WHO'S GONNA FEED MY HAMSTERS?
'S GONNA HAPPEN TO JACK AND BOBBY?
...SERIOUSLY, THERE HAS TO BE SOMEPLACE BETTER THAN THIS TO GET TOGETHER NEXT TIME.
A VOLCANO, OR A SATELLITE.
HH.
I'M SORRY, SUPERMAN, YOU WERE SAYING--

NOBODY WANTS TWO ADORABLE *HAMSTERS* AND NOBODY WANTS TO START TACKLING POVERTY IN *SOMALIA?*

SO WHAT DO WE DO *NOW?* SIT IN A BARN UNTIL SOME MORE EVIL *ALIENS* TURN UP?

WHAT'S YOUR *POINT,* SUPERMAN?

I THOUGHT I'D MADE IT *CLEAR.*

THIS WORLD IS *CRYING OUT* FOR *CHANGE,* FOR *FAIRNESS,* AND *JUSTICE* AND...

I'M IN A ROOM WITH THE KING OF AN UNDERSEA *EMPIRE,* AN AMAZON *PRINCESS* AND A *BILLIONAIRE* PLAYBOY.

PLAYBOY? WHAT GAVE YOU *THAT* IDEA?

OH, I *FORGOT.* YOU'RE A *JOURNALIST.* A SNOOP.

HOW DID YOU--?

BATMAN, I DIDN'T MEAN--

PLEASE.

DOES IT MATTER *HOW* YOU DISGUISE YOURSELVES TO WALK IN THIS WORLD?

WE ALL WANT TO MAKE IT BETTER.

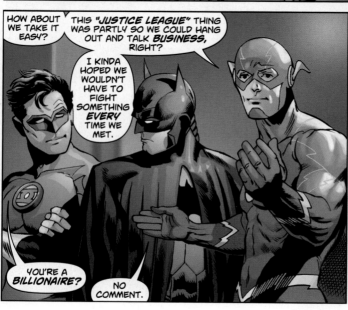

HOW ABOUT WE TAKE IT EASY?

THIS *"JUSTICE LEAGUE"* THING WAS PARTLY SO WE COULD HANG OUT AND TALK *BUSINESS,* RIGHT?

I KINDA HOPED WE WOULDN'T HAVE TO FIGHT SOMETHING *EVERY* TIME WE MET.

YOU'RE A *BILLIONAIRE?*

NO COMMENT.

LOOK, I THINK WE CAN ALL *SYMPATHIZE* WITH OUR *SUPERMAN* HERE.

BUT I DON'T WANT TO BE PART OF A GANG OF AUTHORITARIAN *LIVING WEAPONS* FROM *AMERICA.*

I WON'T MARCH INTO COUNTRIES *UNINVITED* TO "FIX" PROBLEMS WE BARELY UNDER-STAND.

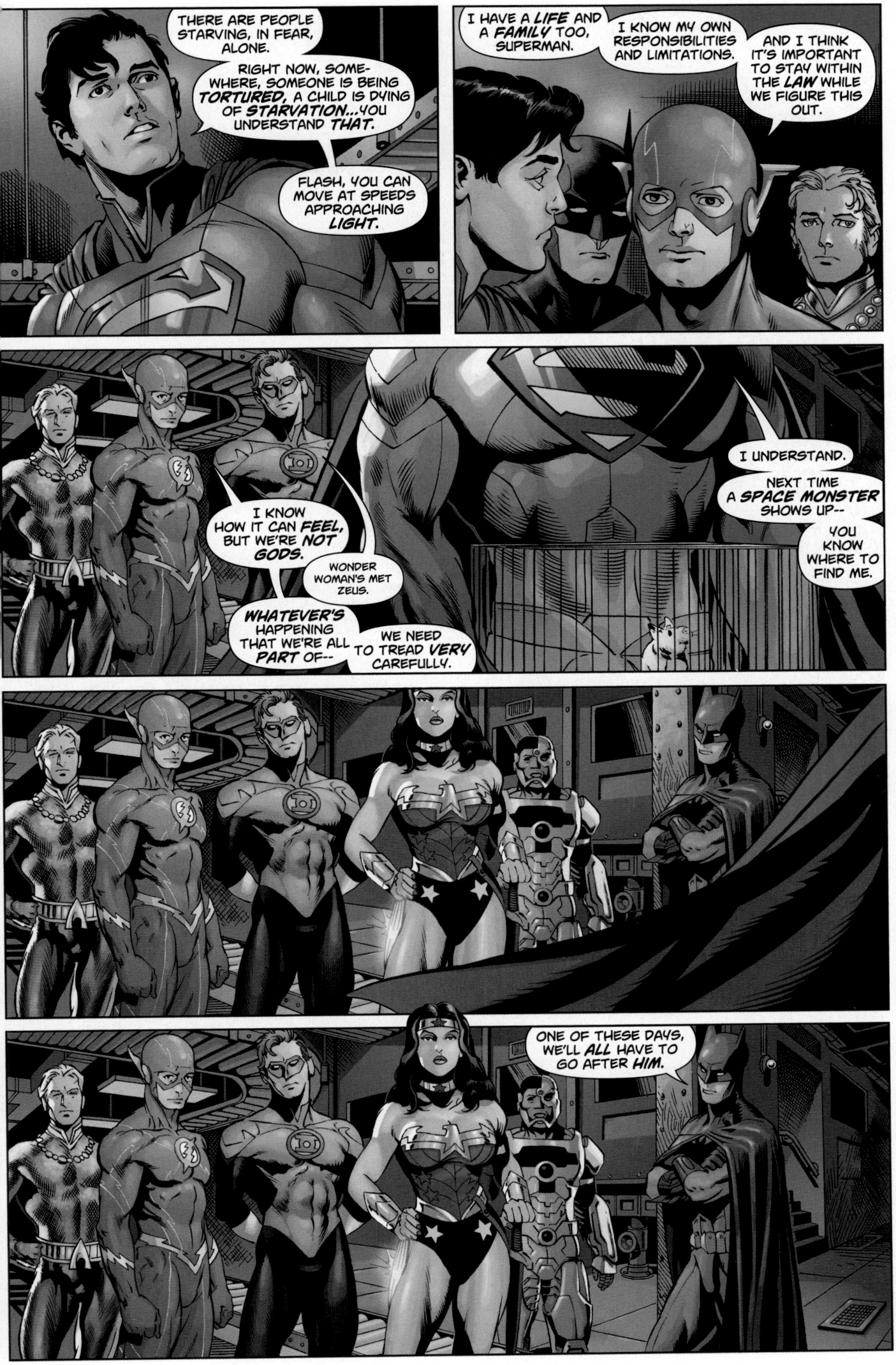
THERE ARE PEOPLE STARVING, IN FEAR, ALONE.
RIGHT NOW, SOME-WHERE, SOMEONE IS BEING TORTURED, A CHILD IS DYING OF STARVATION...YOU UNDERSTAND THAT.
FLASH, YOU CAN MOVE AT SPEEDS APPROACHING LIGHT.
I HAVE A LIFE AND A FAMILY TOO, SUPERMAN.
I KNOW MY OWN RESPONSIBILITIES AND LIMITATIONS.
AND I THINK IT'S IMPORTANT TO STAY WITHIN THE LAW WHILE WE FIGURE THIS OUT.
I KNOW HOW IT CAN FEEL, BUT WE'RE NOT GODS.
WONDER WOMAN'S MET ZEUS.
WHATEVER'S HAPPENING THAT WE'RE ALL PART OF--
WE NEED TO TREAD VERY CAREFULLY.
I UNDERSTAND.
NEXT TIME A SPACE MONSTER SHOWS UP--
YOU KNOW WHERE TO FIND ME.
ONE OF THESE DAYS, WE'LL ALL HAVE TO GO AFTER HIM.

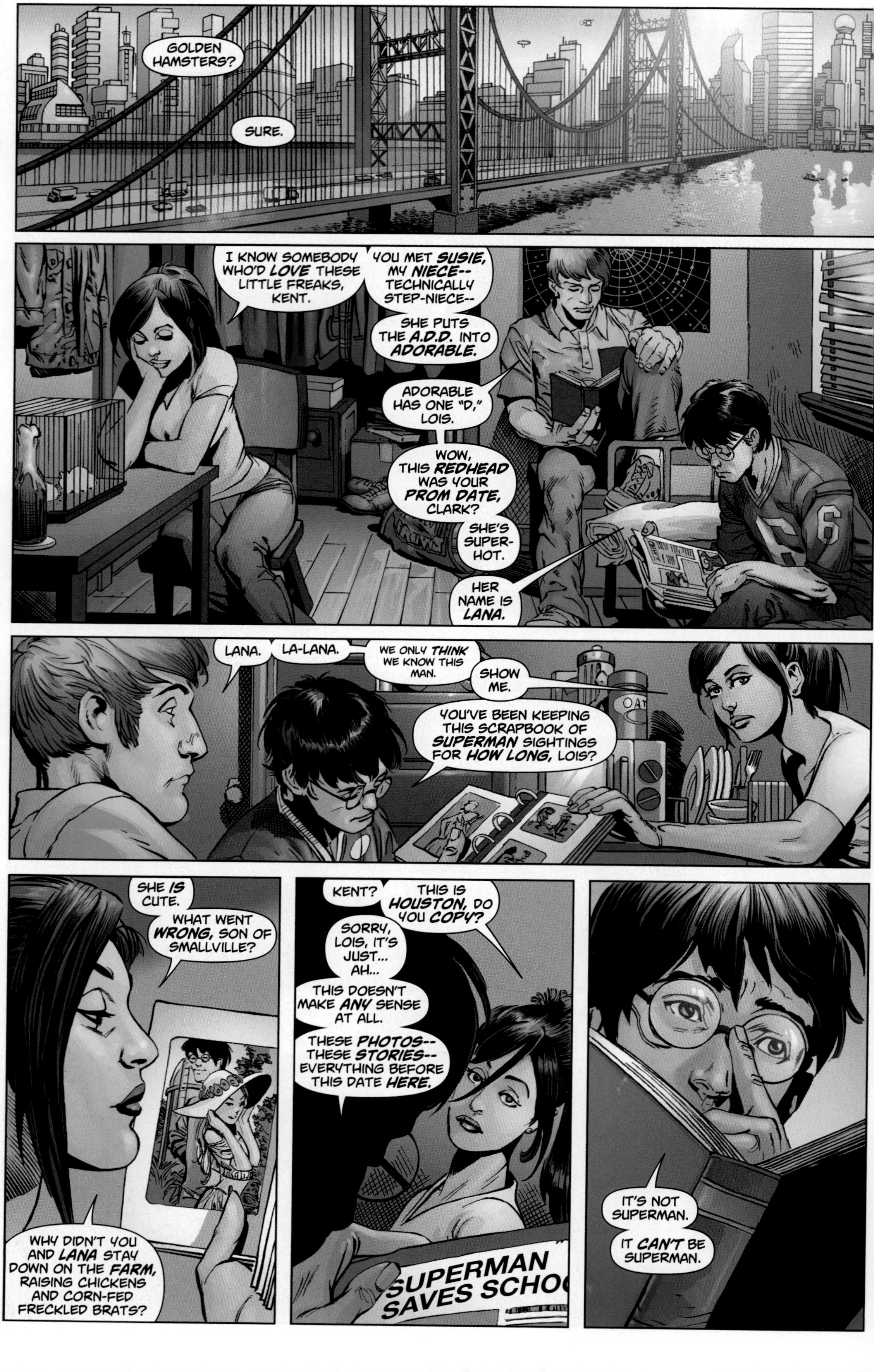
GOLDEN HAMSTERS?
SURE.
I KNOW SOMEBODY WHO'D LOVE THESE LITTLE FREAKS, KENT.
YOU MET SUSIE, MY NIECE-- TECHNICALLY STEP-NIECE--
SHE PUTS THE A.D.D. INTO ADORABLE.
ADORABLE HAS ONE "D," LOIS.
WOW, THIS REDHEAD WAS YOUR PROM DATE, CLARK?
SHE'S SUPER-HOT.
HER NAME IS LANA.
LANA.
LA-LANA.
WE ONLY THINK WE KNOW THIS MAN.
SHOW ME.
YOU'VE BEEN KEEPING THIS SCRAPBOOK OF SUPERMAN SIGHTINGS FOR HOW LONG, LOIS?
SHE IS CUTE.
WHAT WENT WRONG, SON OF SMALLVILLE?
WHY DIDN'T YOU AND LANA STAY DOWN ON THE FARM, RAISING CHICKENS AND CORN-FED FRECKLED BRATS?
KENT?
THIS IS HOUSTON, DO YOU COPY?
SORRY, LOIS, IT'S JUST... AH...
THIS DOESN'T MAKE ANY SENSE AT ALL.
THESE PHOTOS-- THESE STORIES-- EVERYTHING BEFORE THIS DATE HERE.
SUPERMAN SAVES SCHOO
IT'S NOT SUPERMAN.
IT CAN'T BE SUPERMAN.

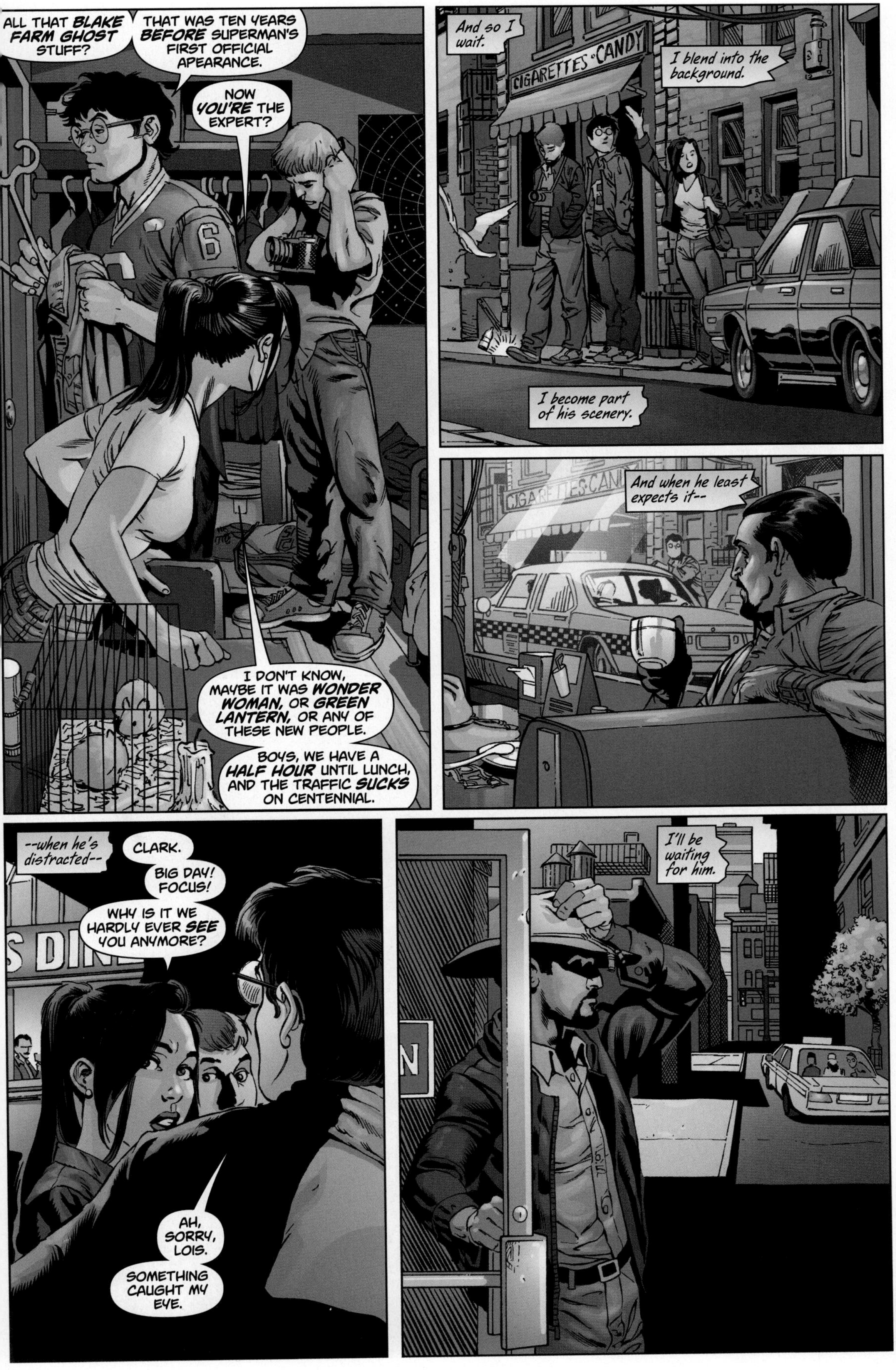
ALL THAT BLAKE FARM GHOST STUFF?
THAT WAS TEN YEARS BEFORE SUPERMAN'S FIRST OFFICIAL APEARANCE.
NOW YOU'RE THE EXPERT?
I DON'T KNOW, MAYBE IT WAS WONDER WOMAN, OR GREEN LANTERN, OR ANY OF THESE NEW PEOPLE.
BOYS, WE HAVE A HALF HOUR UNTIL LUNCH, AND THE TRAFFIC SUCKS ON CENTENNIAL.
And so I wait.
CIGARETTES CANDY
I blend into the background.
I become part of his scenery.
CIGARETTES CANDY
And when he least expects it--
--when he's distracted--
CLARK.
BIG DAY! FOCUS!
WHY IS IT WE HARDLY EVER SEE YOU ANYMORE?
AH, SORRY, LOIS.
SOMETHING CAUGHT MY EYE.
I'll be waiting for him.

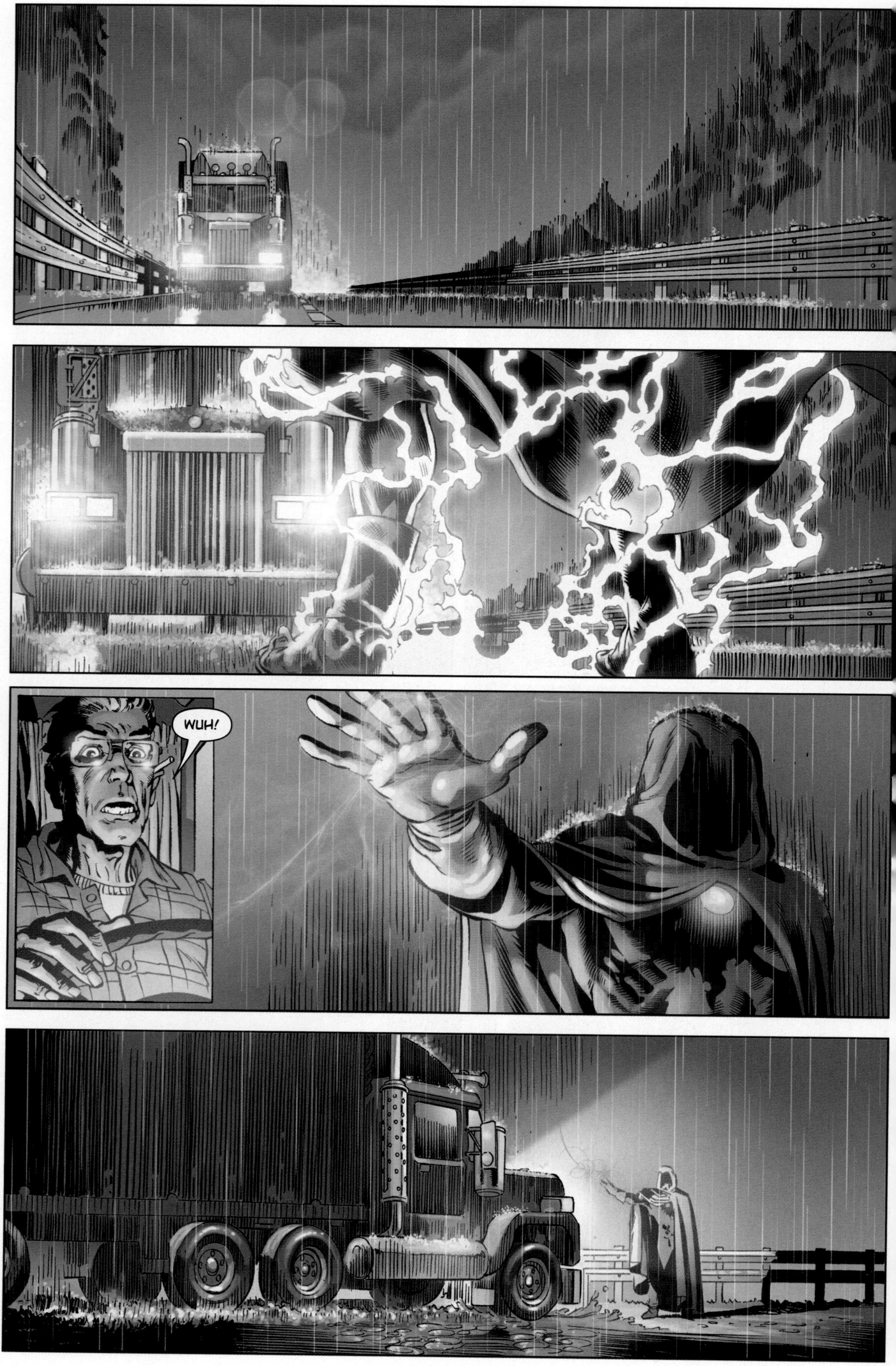
WUH!

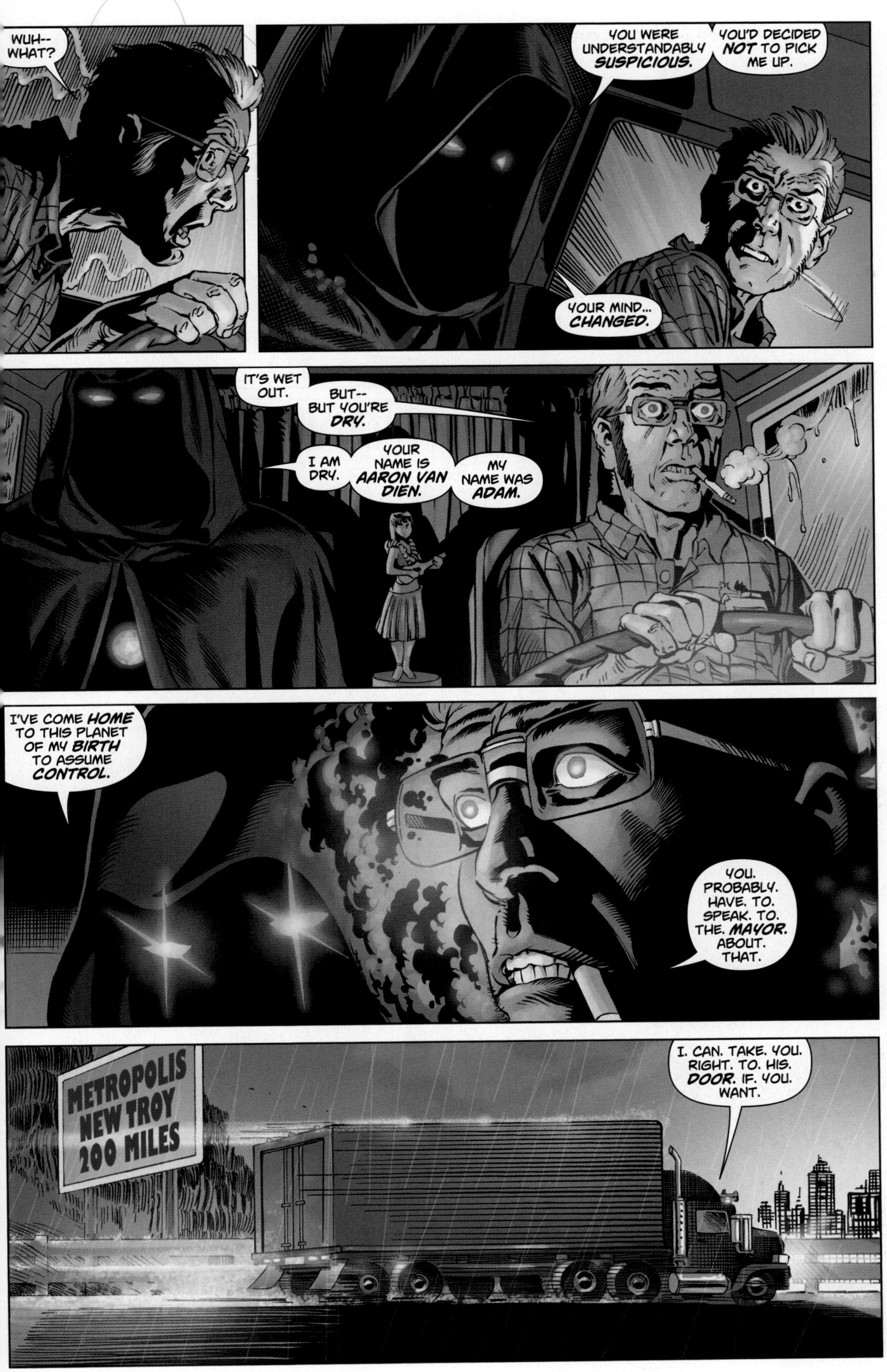
WUH--
WHAT?
YOU WERE UNDERSTANDABLY SUSPICIOUS.
YOU'D DECIDED NOT TO PICK ME UP.
YOUR MIND... CHANGED.
IT'S WET OUT.
BUT-- BUT YOU'RE DRY.
I AM DRY.
YOUR NAME IS AARON VAN DIEN.
MY NAME WAS ADAM.
I'VE COME HOME TO THIS PLANET OF MY BIRTH TO ASSUME CONTROL.
YOU. PROBABLY. HAVE. TO. SPEAK. TO. THE. MAYOR. ABOUT. THAT.
METROPOLIS
NEW TROY
200 MILES
I. CAN. TAKE. YOU. RIGHT. TO. HIS. DOOR. IF. YOU. WANT.

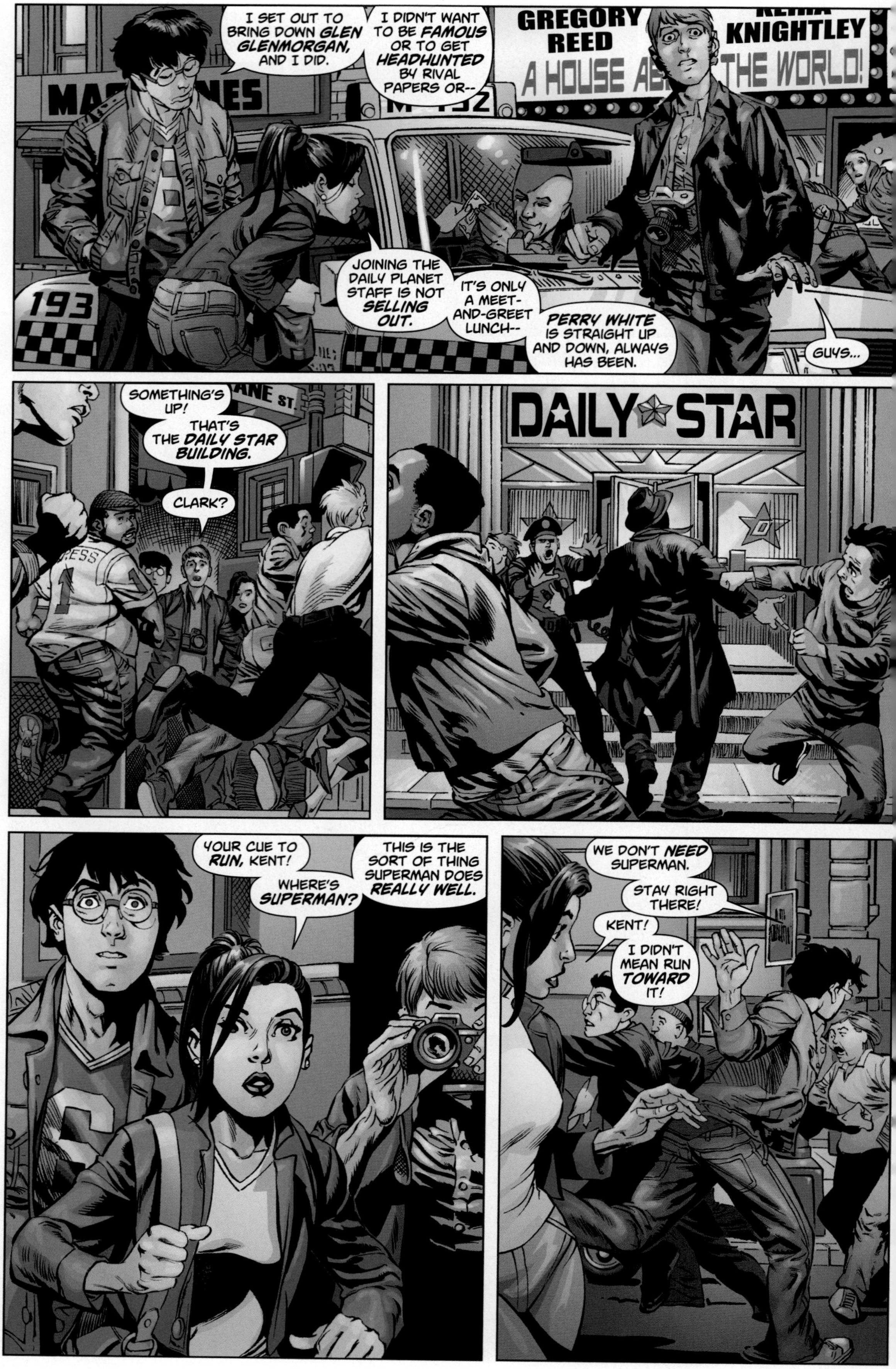
I SET OUT TO BRING DOWN GLEN GLENMORGAN, AND I DID.
I DIDN'T WANT TO BE FAMOUS OR TO GET HEADHUNTED BY RIVAL PAPERS OR--
GREGORY REED
KNIGHTLEY
A HOUSE AB THE WORLD!
MA NES
193
JOINING THE DAILY PLANET STAFF IS NOT SELLING OUT.
IT'S ONLY A MEET-AND-GREET LUNCH--
PERRY WHITE IS STRAIGHT UP AND DOWN, ALWAYS HAS BEEN.
GUYS...
SOMETHING'S UP!
THAT'S THE DAILY STAR BUILDING.
CLARK?
DAILY STAR
YOUR CUE TO RUN, KENT!
WHERE'S SUPERMAN?
THIS IS THE SORT OF THING SUPERMAN DOES REALLY WELL.
WE DON'T NEED SUPERMAN.
STAY RIGHT THERE!
KENT!
I DIDN'T MEAN RUN TOWARD IT!

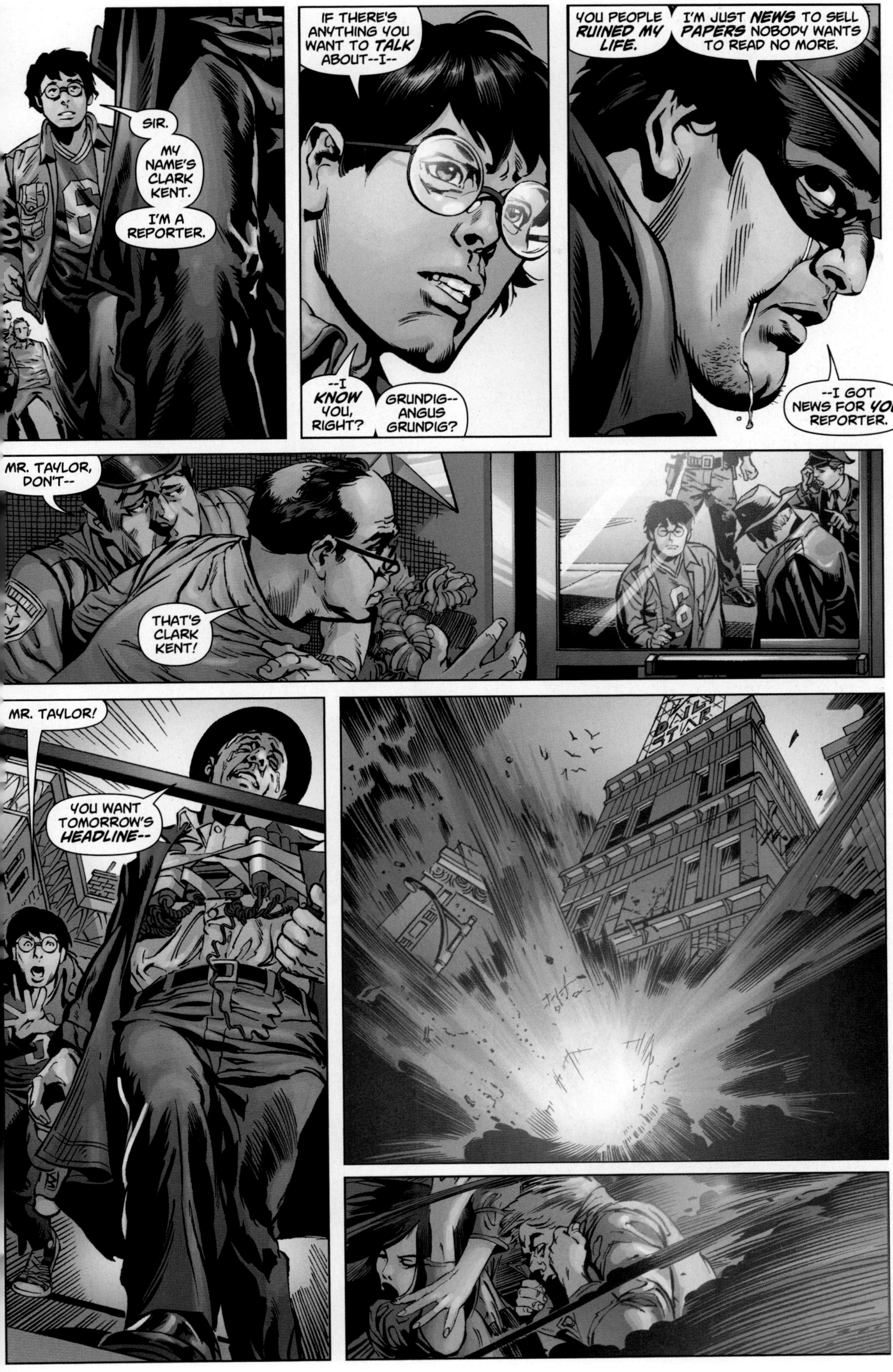
SIR.
MY NAME'S CLARK KENT.
I'M A REPORTER.
IF THERE'S ANYTHING YOU WANT TO TALK ABOUT--I--
--I KNOW YOU, RIGHT?
GRUNDIG-- ANGUS GRUNDIG?
YOU PEOPLE RUINED MY LIFE.
I'M JUST NEWS TO SELL PAPERS NOBODY WANTS TO READ NO MORE.
--I GOT NEWS FOR YOU, REPORTER.
MR. TAYLOR, DON'T--
THAT'S CLARK KENT!
MR. TAYLOR!
YOU WANT TOMORROW'S HEADLINE--

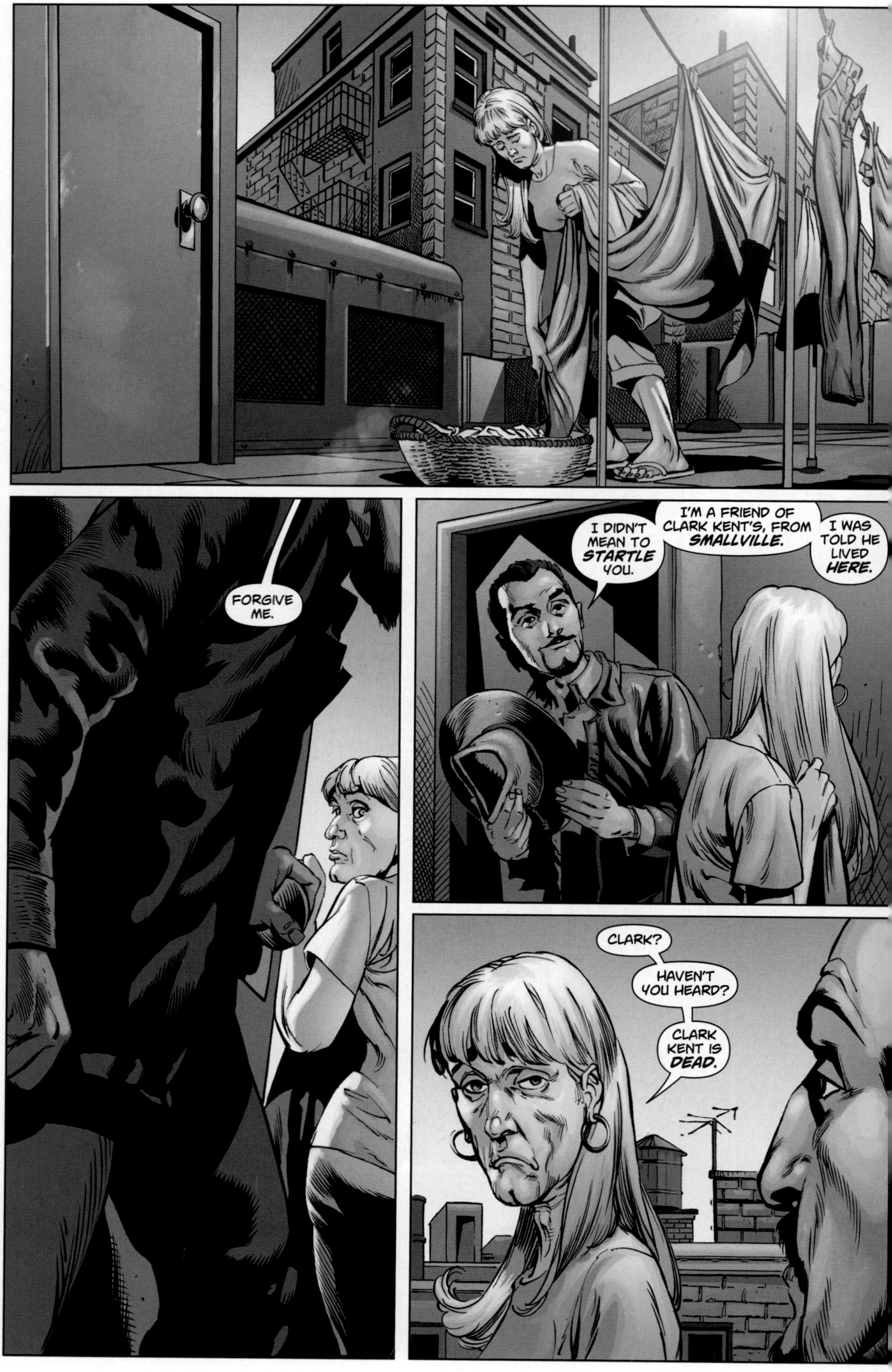
FORGIVE ME.
I DIDN'T MEAN TO STARTLE YOU.
I'M A FRIEND OF CLARK KENT'S, FROM SMALLVILLE.
I WAS TOLD HE LIVED HERE.
CLARK?
HAVEN'T YOU HEARD?
CLARK KENT IS DEAD.

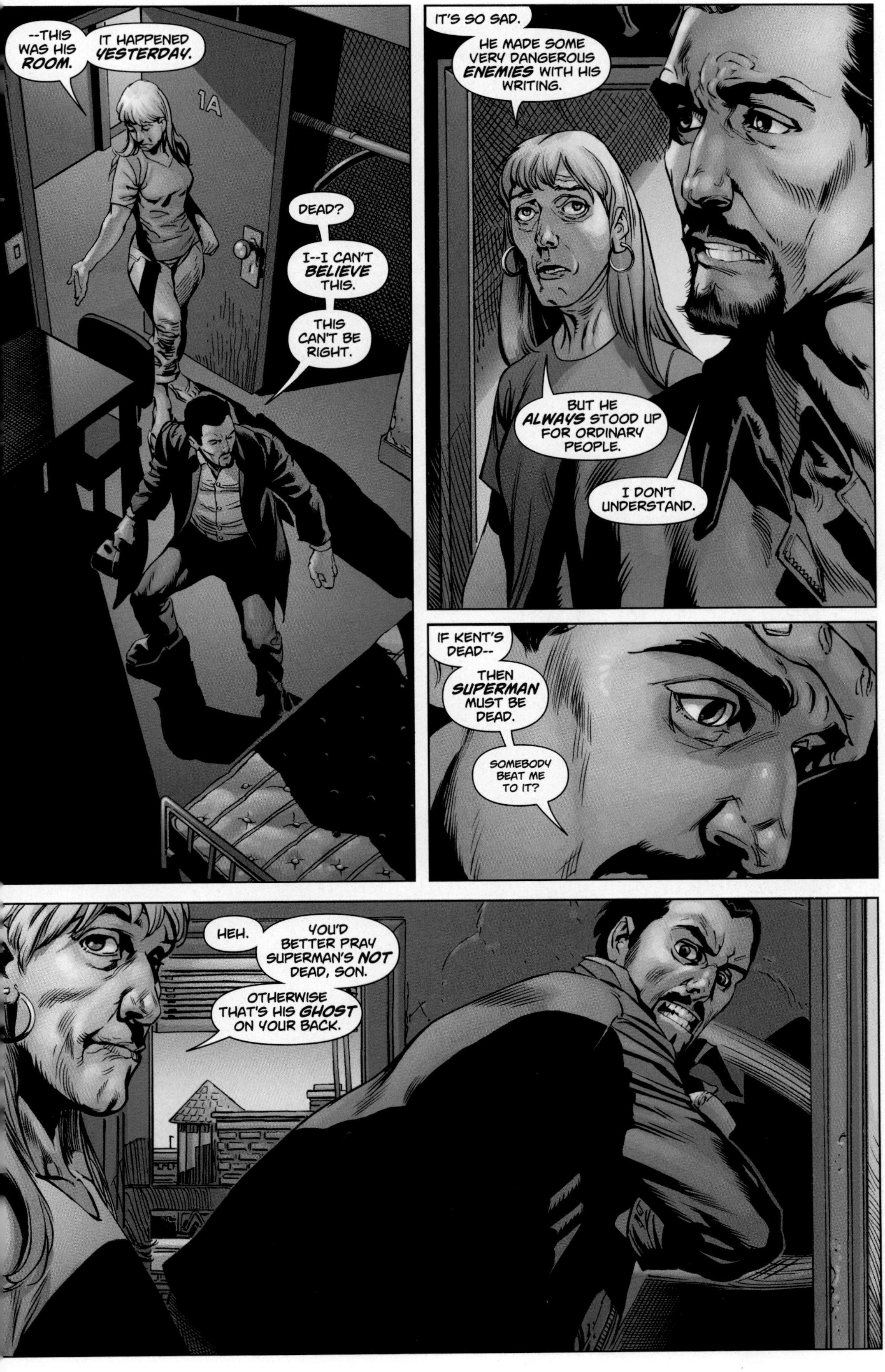
--THIS WAS HIS ROOM.
IT HAPPENED YESTERDAY.
1A
DEAD?
I--I CAN'T BELIEVE THIS.
THIS CAN'T BE RIGHT.
IT'S SO SAD.
HE MADE SOME VERY DANGEROUS ENEMIES WITH HIS WRITING.
BUT HE ALWAYS STOOD UP FOR ORDINARY PEOPLE.
I DON'T UNDERSTAND.
IF KENT'S DEAD--
THEN SUPERMAN MUST BE DEAD.
SOMEBODY BEAT ME TO IT?
HEH.
YOU'D BETTER PRAY SUPERMAN'S NOT DEAD, SON.
OTHERWISE THAT'S HIS GHOST ON YOUR BACK.

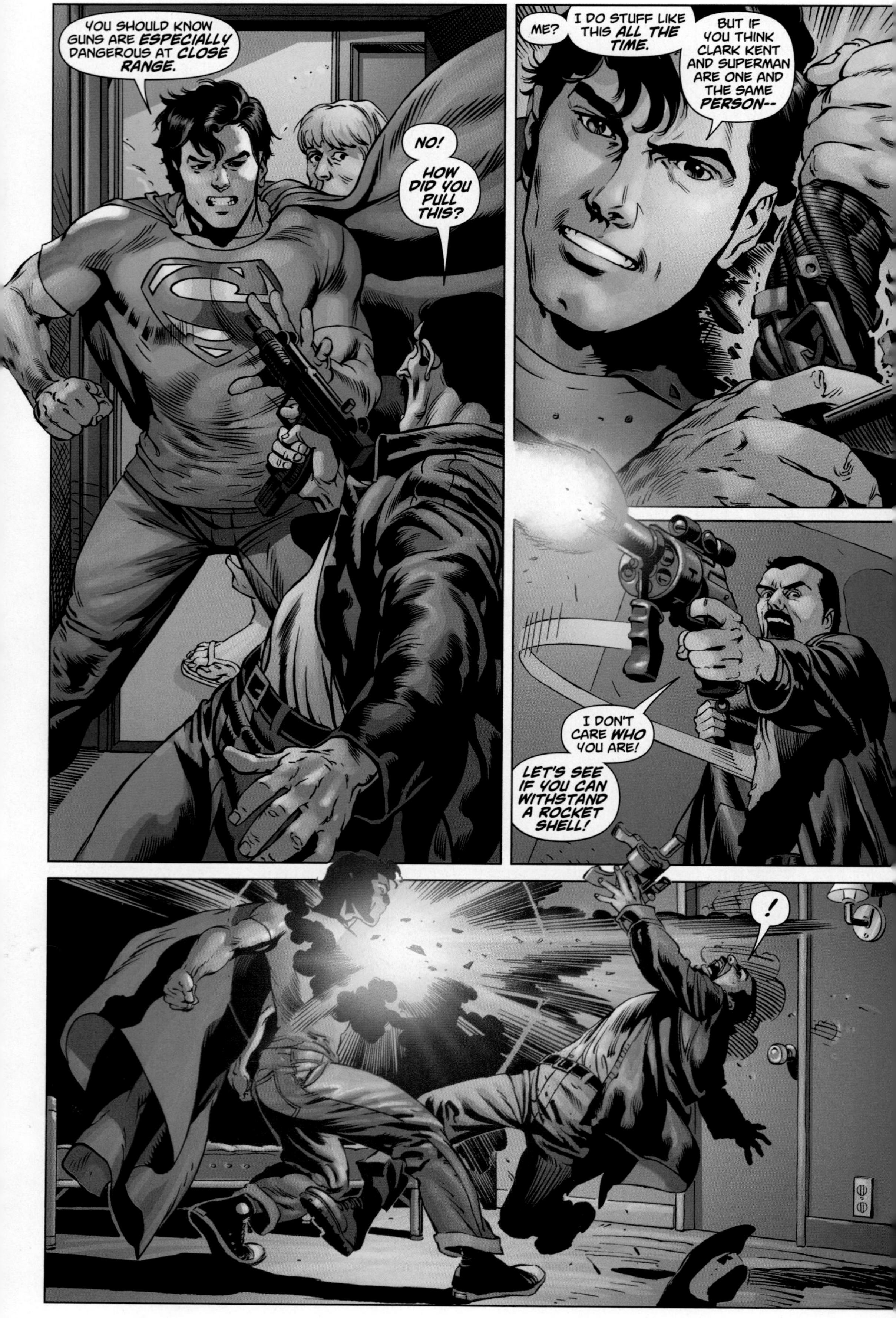
YOU SHOULD KNOW GUNS ARE ESPECIALLY DANGEROUS AT CLOSE RANGE.
NO!
HOW DID YOU PULL THIS?
ME?
I DO STUFF LIKE THIS ALL THE TIME.
BUT IF YOU THINK CLARK KENT AND SUPERMAN ARE ONE AND THE SAME PERSON--
I DON'T CARE WHO YOU ARE!
LET'S SEE IF YOU CAN WITHSTAND A ROCKET SHELL!
!

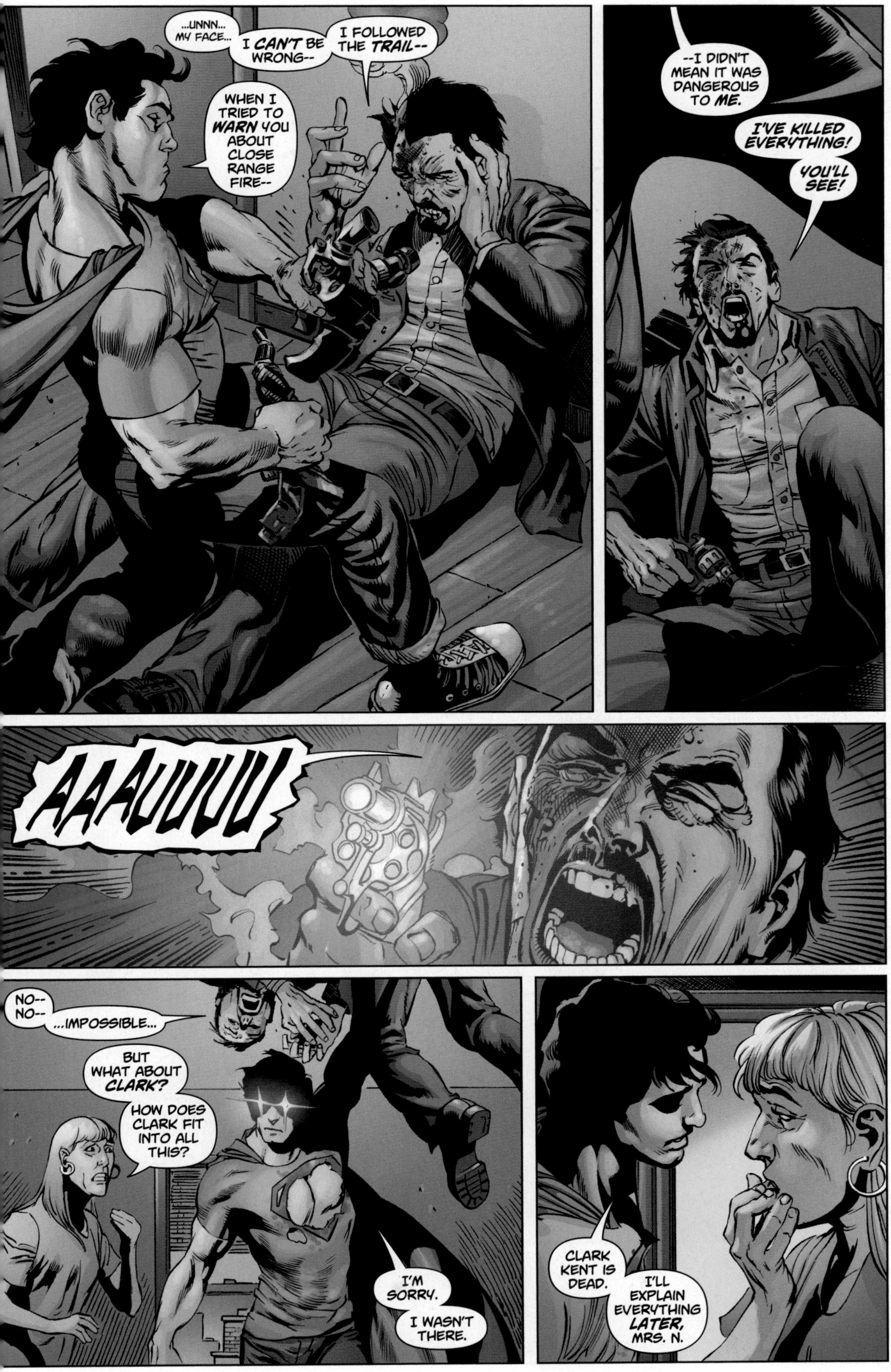
...UNNN... MY FACE...
I CAN'T BE WRONG--
I FOLLOWED THE TRAIL--
WHEN I TRIED TO WARN YOU ABOUT CLOSE RANGE FIRE--
--I DIDN'T MEAN IT WAS DANGEROUS TO ME.
I'VE KILLED EVERYTHING!
YOU'LL SEE!
AAAUUUUU
NO-- NO--
...IMPOSSIBLE...
BUT WHAT ABOUT CLARK?
HOW DOES CLARK FIT INTO ALL THIS?
I'M SORRY.
I WASN'T THERE.
CLARK KENT IS DEAD.
I'LL EXPLAIN EVERYTHING LATER, MRS. N.

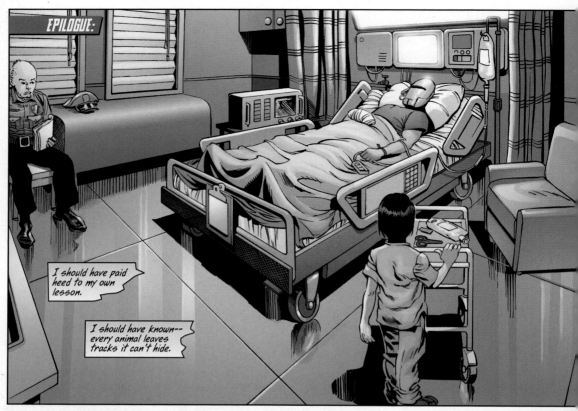

I should have paid heed to my own lesson.

I should have known-- every animal leaves tracks it can't hide.

Even me.

...I *KNOW* WHAT YOU WANT, MR. ZAROV.

I'M HERE TO TELL YOU IT *CAN* BE DONE, BUT NOT WITH LITTLE *TOY* GUNS.

UHH?

ME? I CAN PROVIDE YOU WITH WEAPONS--*STRONGER* WEAPONS FROM *OTHER* WORLDS.

I CAN MAKE YOU PART OF AN *ARMY* AGAINST SUPERMAN.

IT'S *SIMPLE.*

ALL YOU HAVE TO DO IS MAKE A *DEAL.*

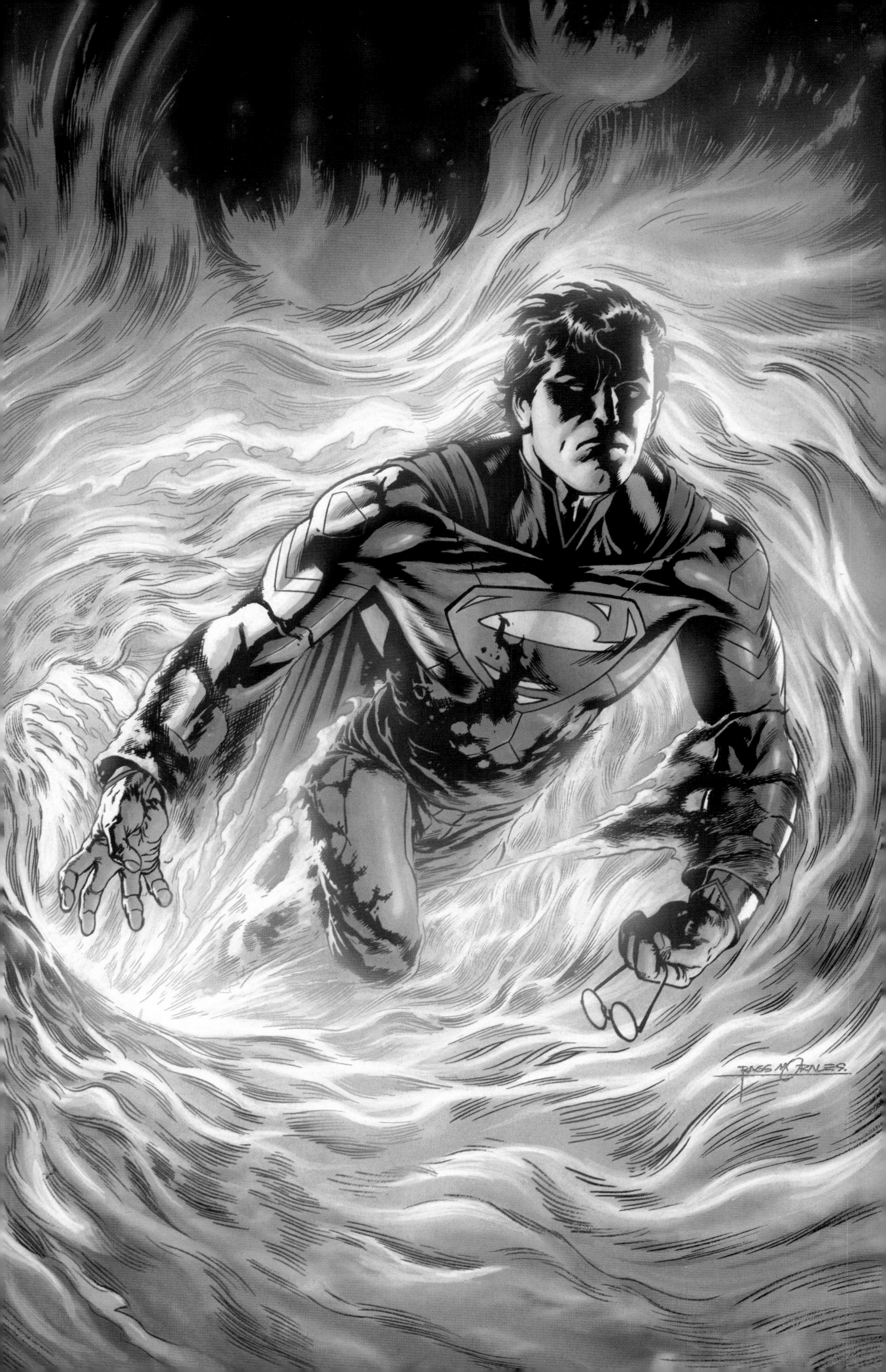

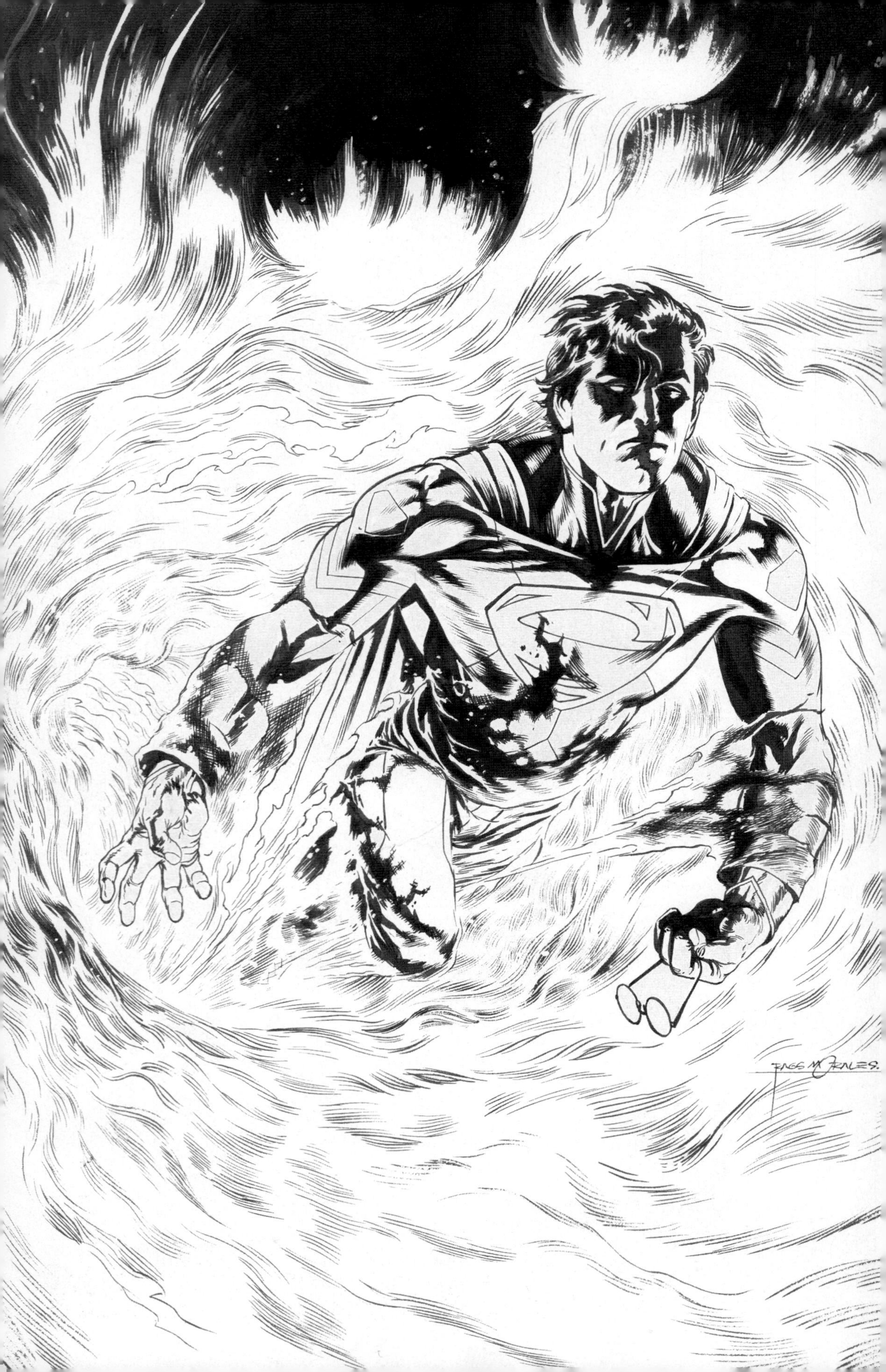

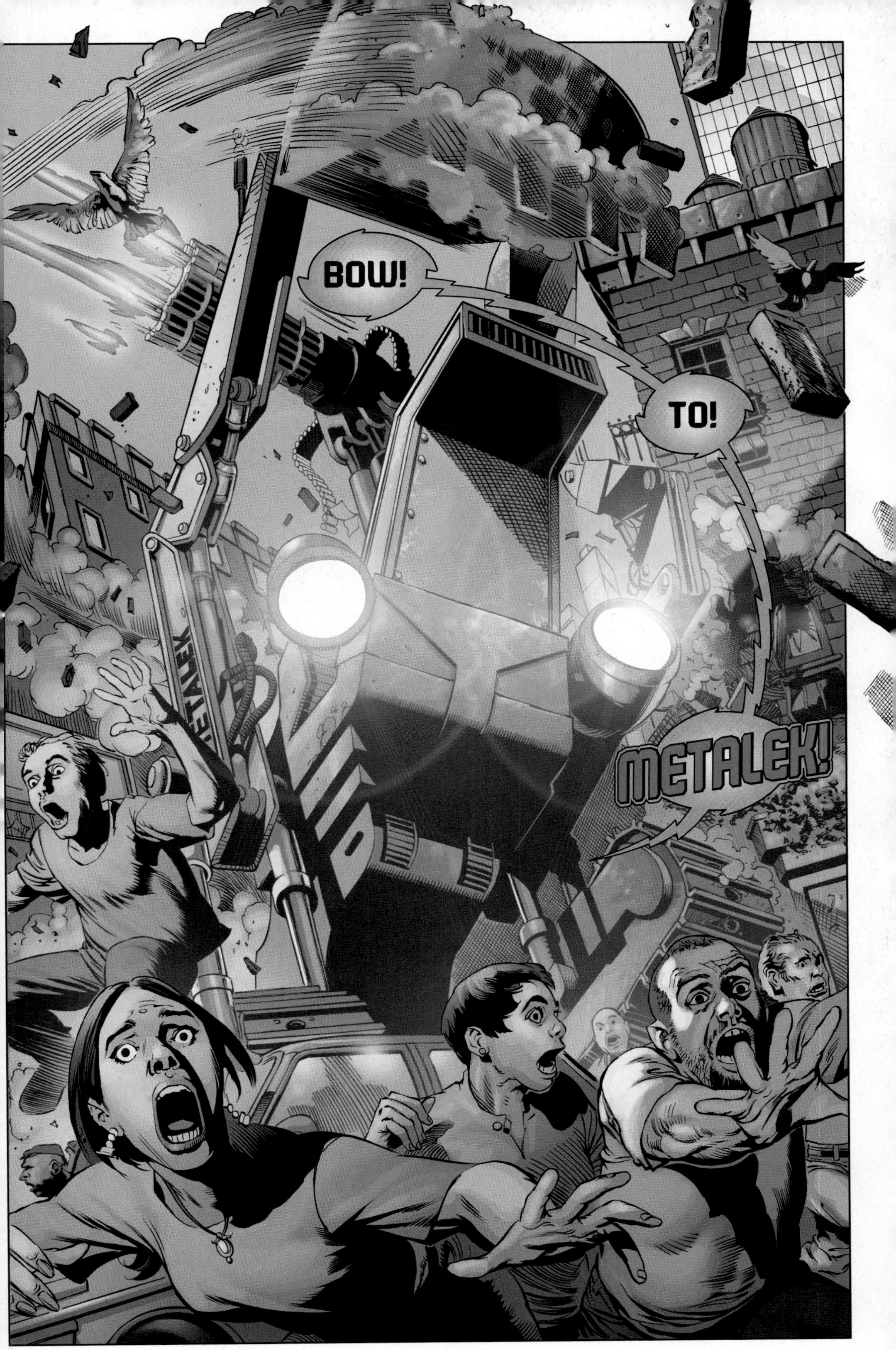
BOW!
TO!
METALEK!
METALEK

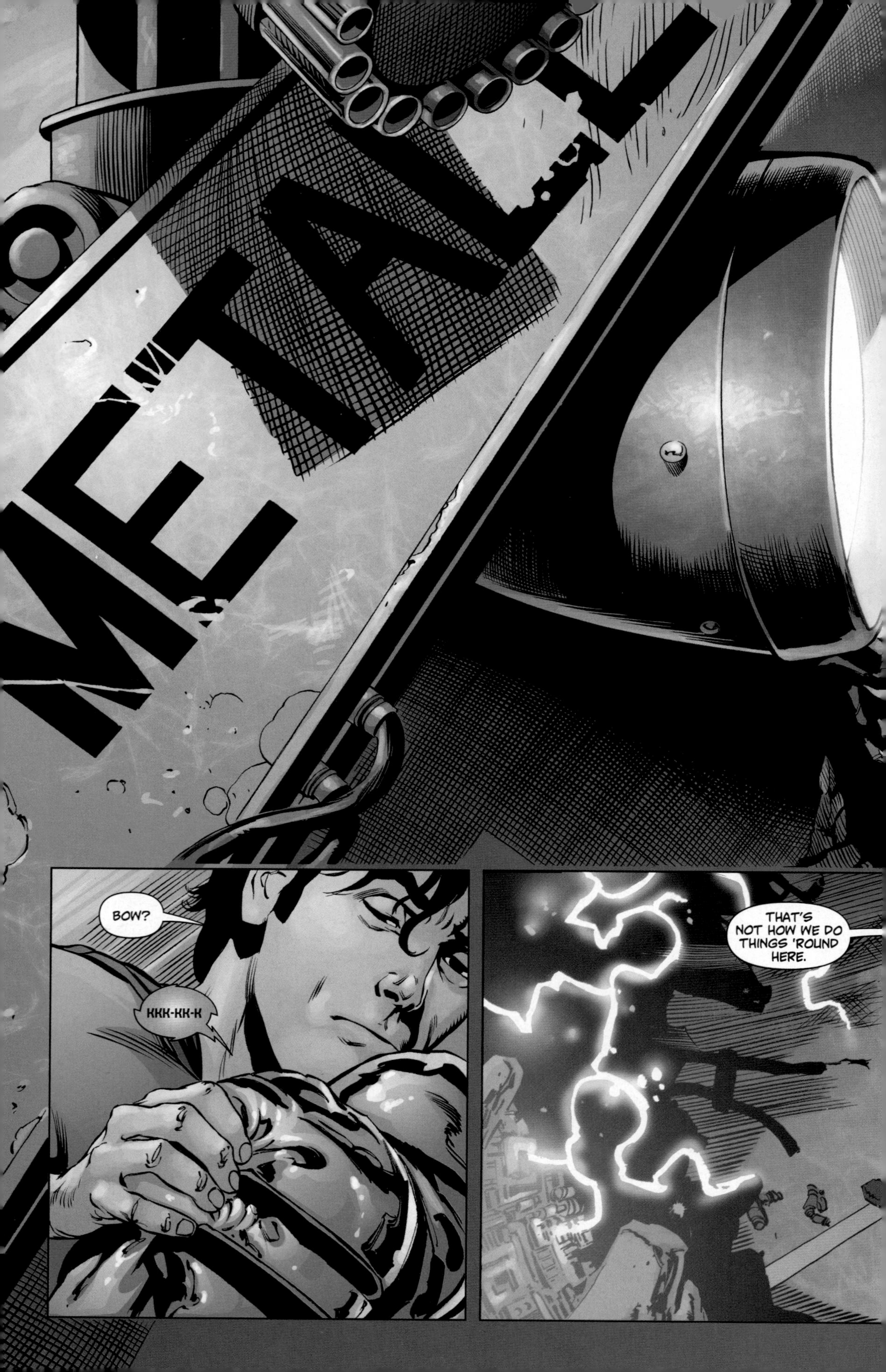
METAL
BOW?
KKK-KK-K
THAT'S NOT HOW WE DO THINGS 'ROUND HERE.

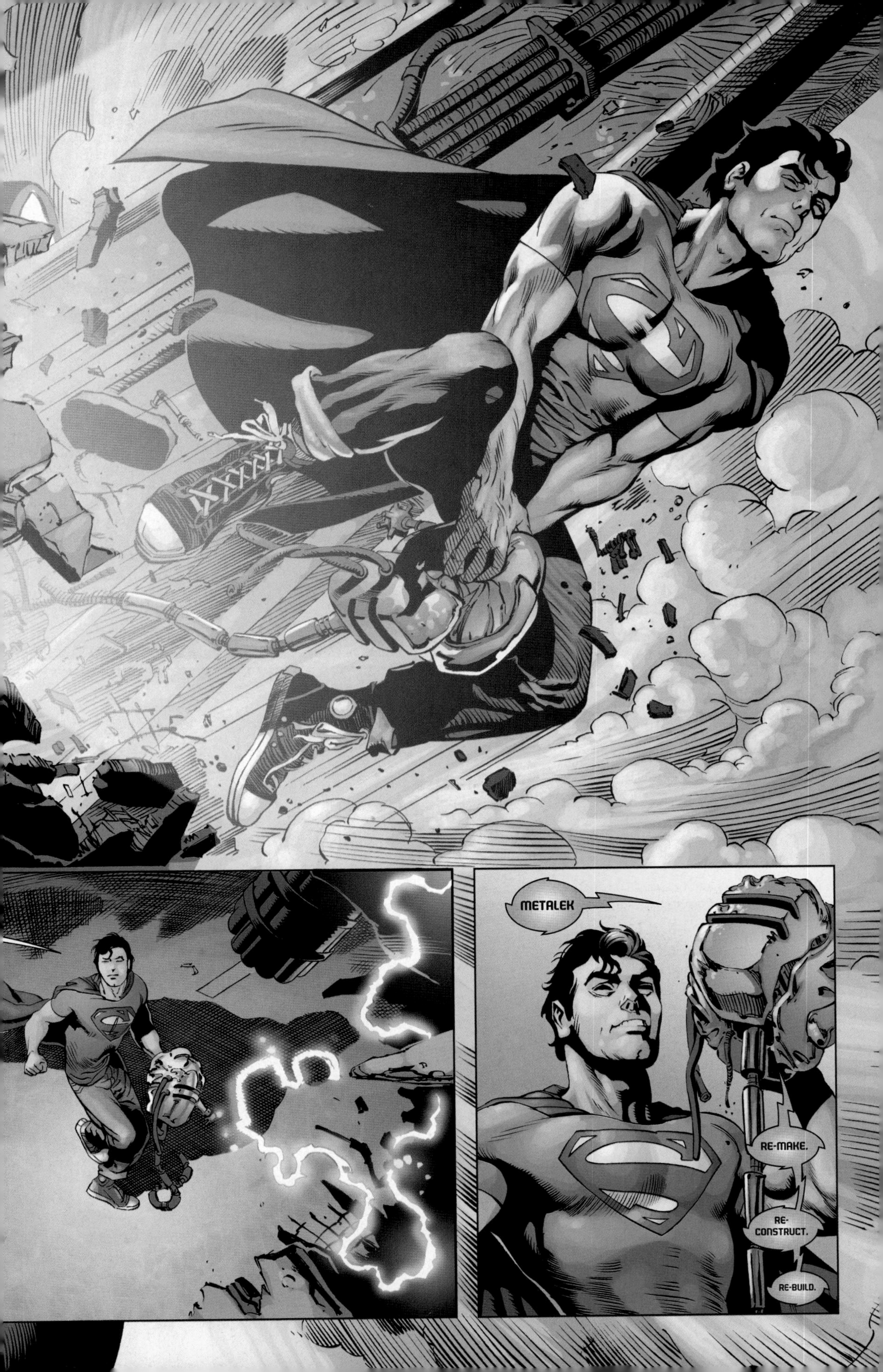
METALEK
RE-MAKE.
RE-CONSTRUCT.
RE-BUILD.

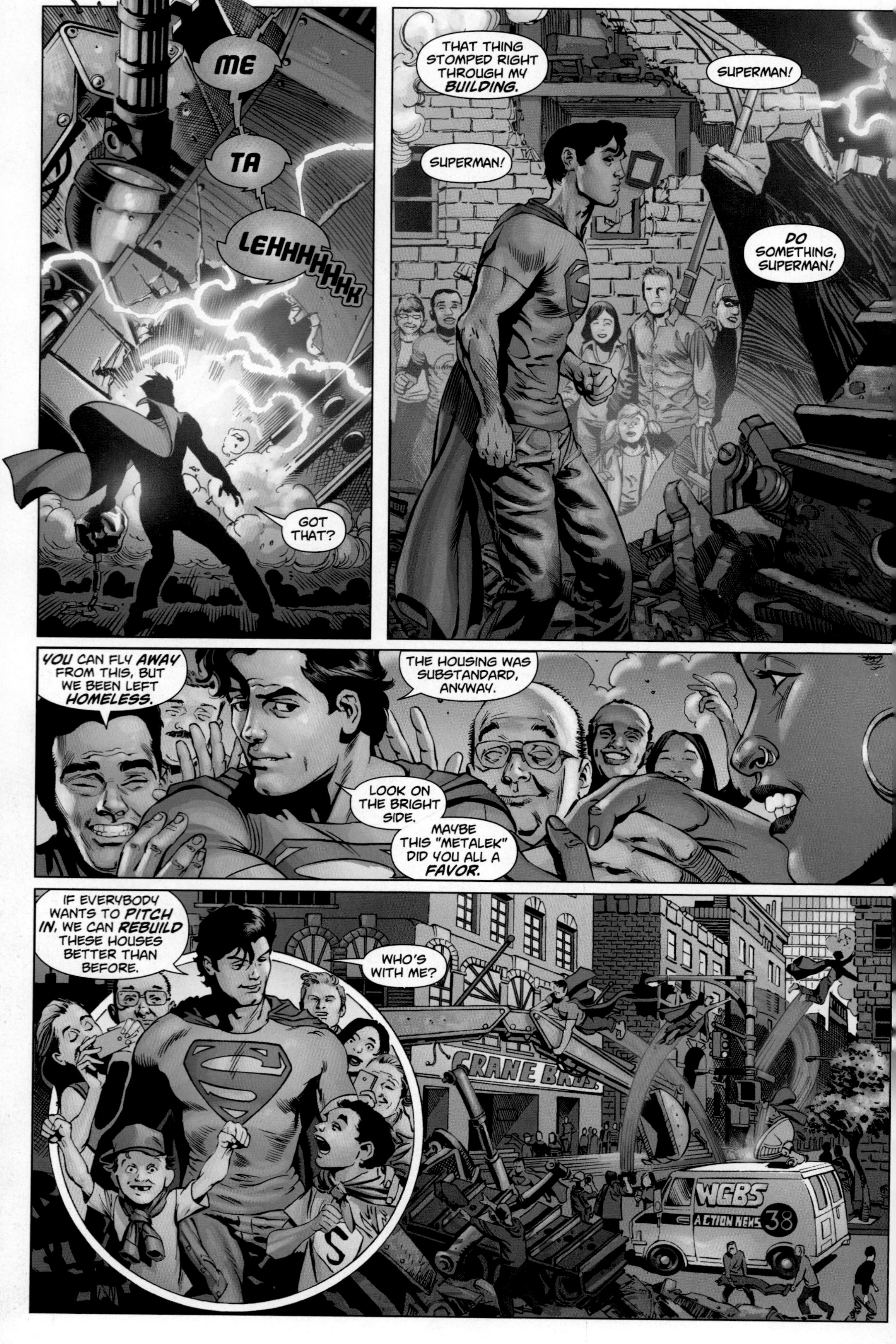
ME
TA
LEHHHHHHHK
GOT THAT?
THAT THING STOMPED RIGHT THROUGH MY BUILDING.
SUPERMAN!
SUPERMAN!
DO SOMETHING, SUPERMAN!
YOU CAN FLY AWAY FROM THIS, BUT WE BEEN LEFT HOMELESS.
THE HOUSING WAS SUBSTANDARD, ANYWAY.
LOOK ON THE BRIGHT SIDE.
MAYBE THIS "METALEK" DID YOU ALL A FAVOR.
IF EVERYBODY WANTS TO PITCH IN, WE CAN REBUILD THESE HOUSES BETTER THAN BEFORE.
WHO'S WITH ME?
CRANE BROS.
WGBS
ACTION NEWS 38

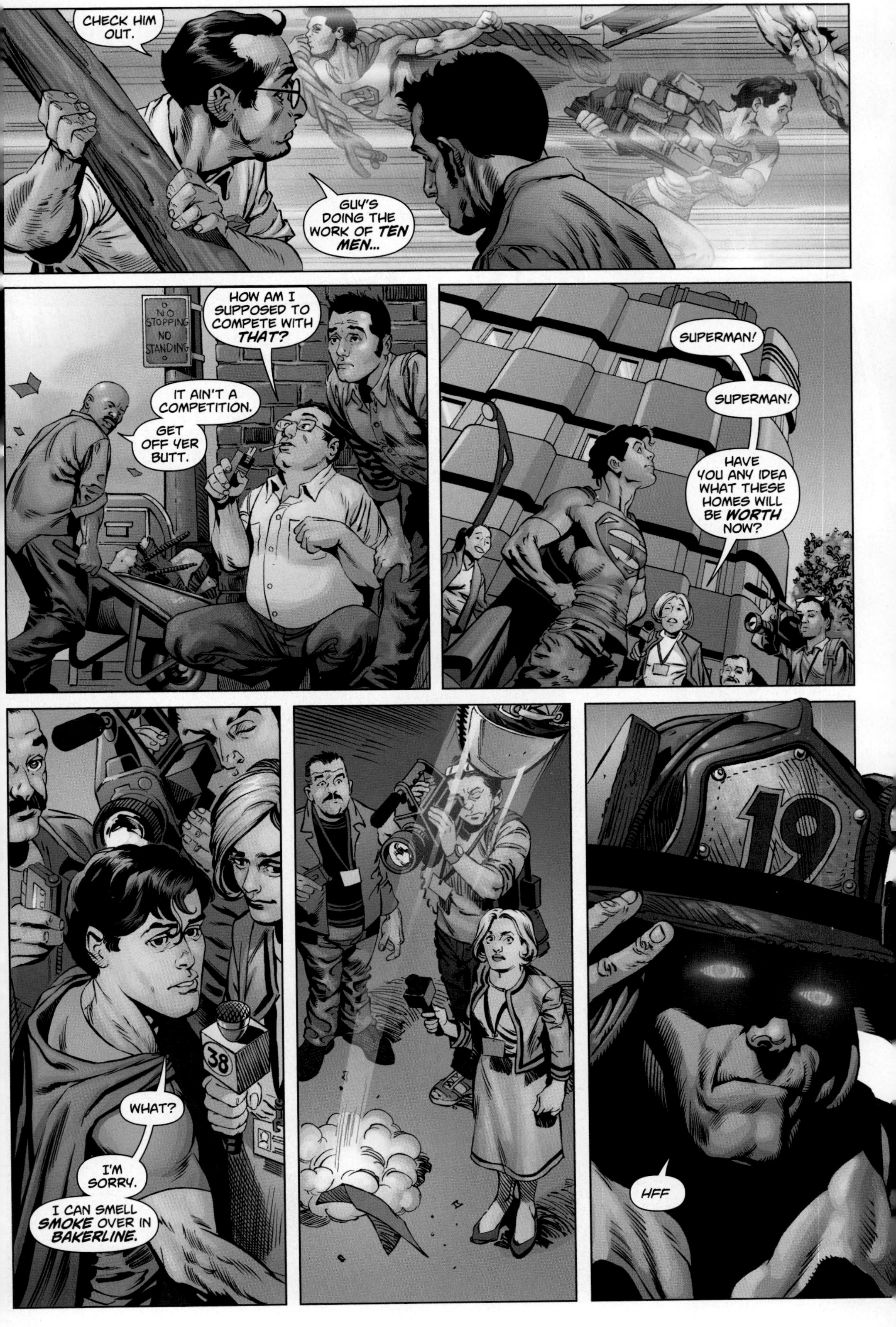
CHECK HIM OUT.
GUY'S DOING THE WORK OF TEN MEN...
NO STOPPING NO STANDING
HOW AM I SUPPOSED TO COMPETE WITH THAT?
IT AIN'T A COMPETITION.
GET OFF YER BUTT.
SUPERMAN!
SUPERMAN!
HAVE YOU ANY IDEA WHAT THESE HOMES WILL BE WORTH NOW?
38
WHAT?
I'M SORRY.
I CAN SMELL SMOKE OVER IN BAKERLINE.
19
HFF

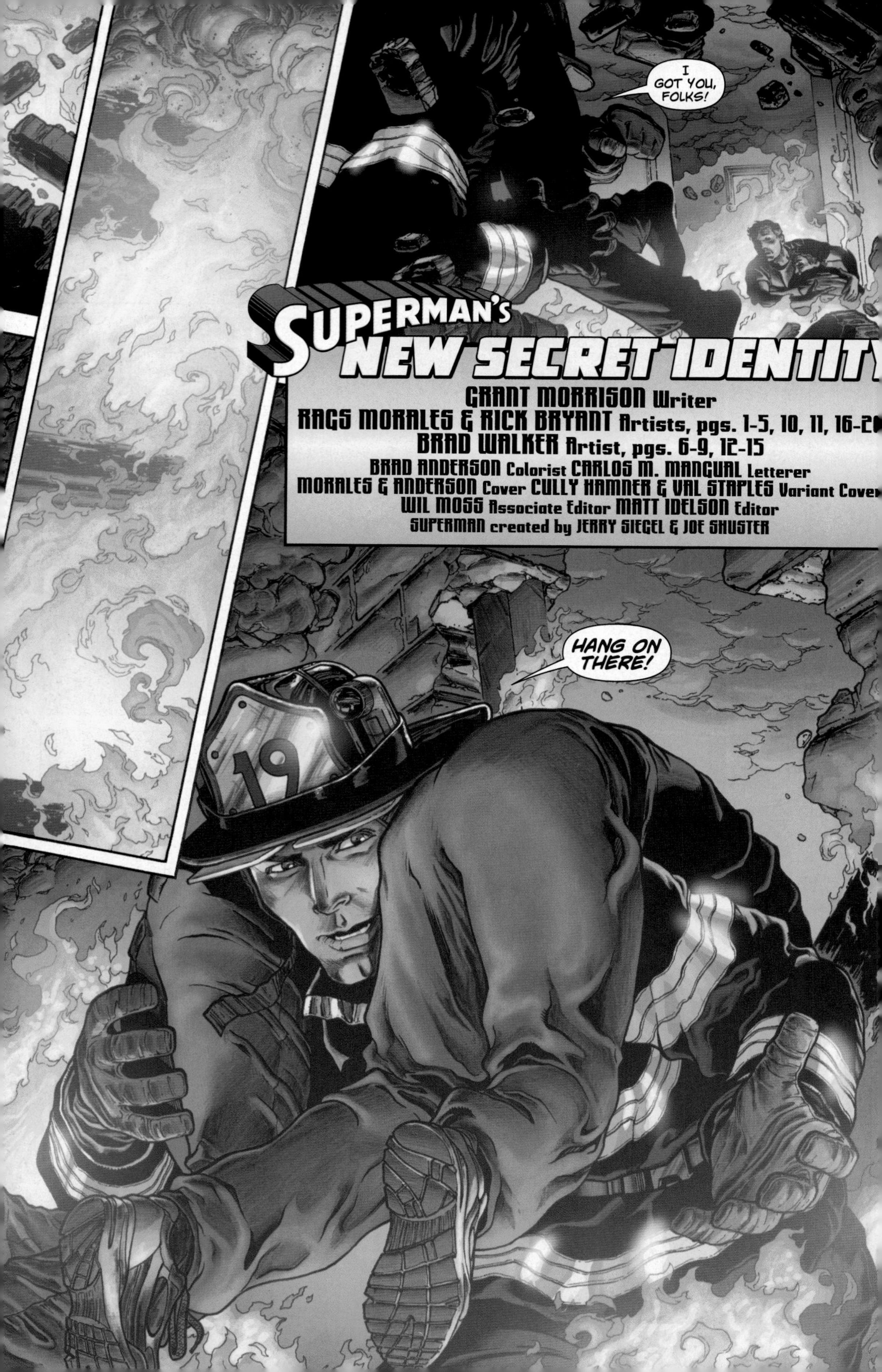
I GOT YOU, FOLKS!
SUPERMAN'S NEW SECRET IDENTITY
GRANT MORRISON Writer
RAGS MORALES & RICK BRYANT Artists, pgs. 1-5, 10, 11, 16-2
BRAD WALKER Artist, pgs. 6-9, 12-15
BRAD ANDERSON Colorist CARLOS M. MANGUAL Letterer
MORALES & ANDERSON Cover CULLY HAMNER & VAL STAPLES Variant Cove
WIL MOSS Associate Editor MATT IDELSON Editor
SUPERMAN created by JERRY SIEGEL & JOE SHUSTER
HANG ON THERE!

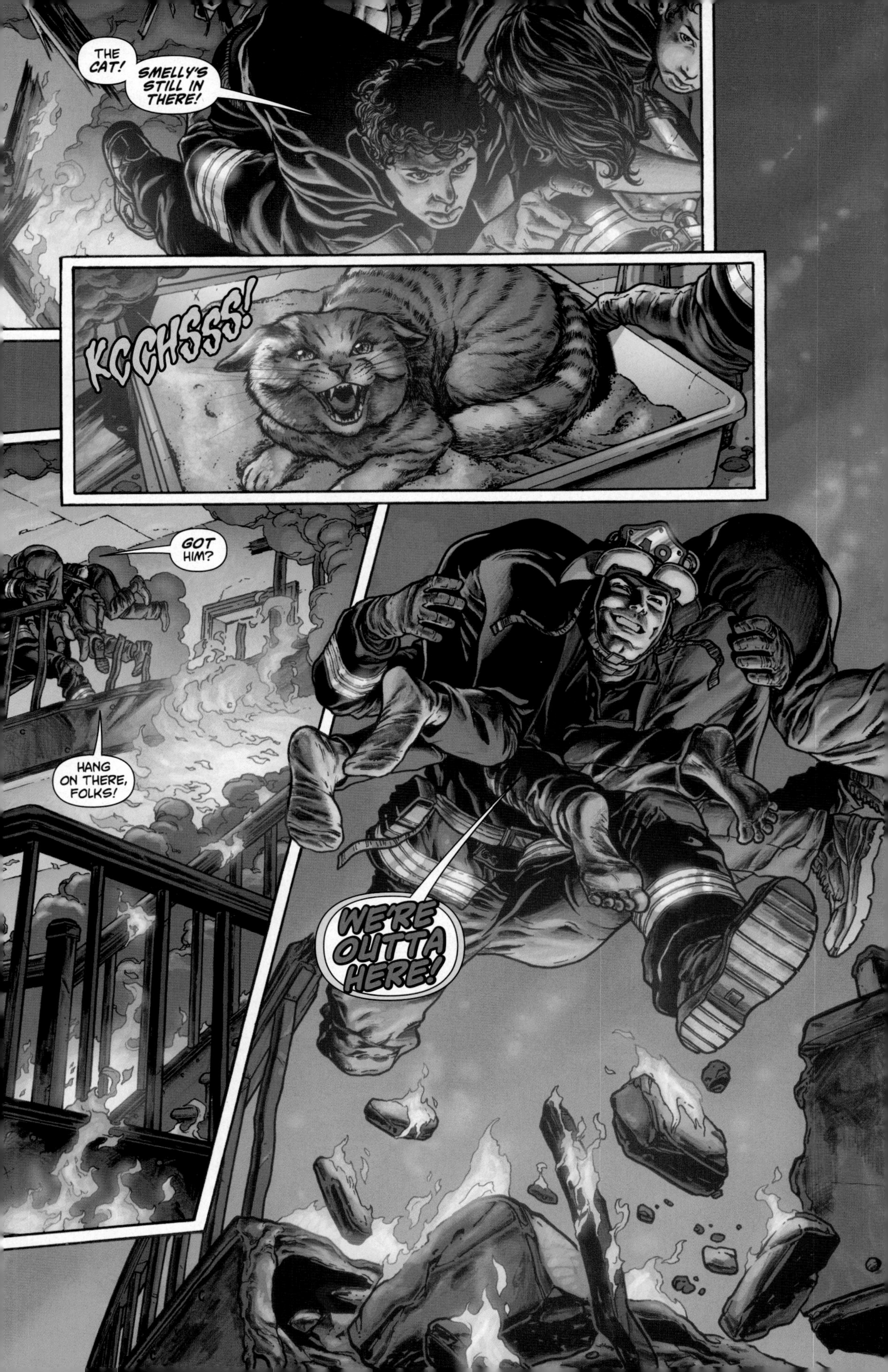
THE CAT!
SMELLY'S STILL IN THERE!
KCCHSSS!
GOT HIM?
HANG ON THERE, FOLKS!
WE'RE OUTTA HERE!

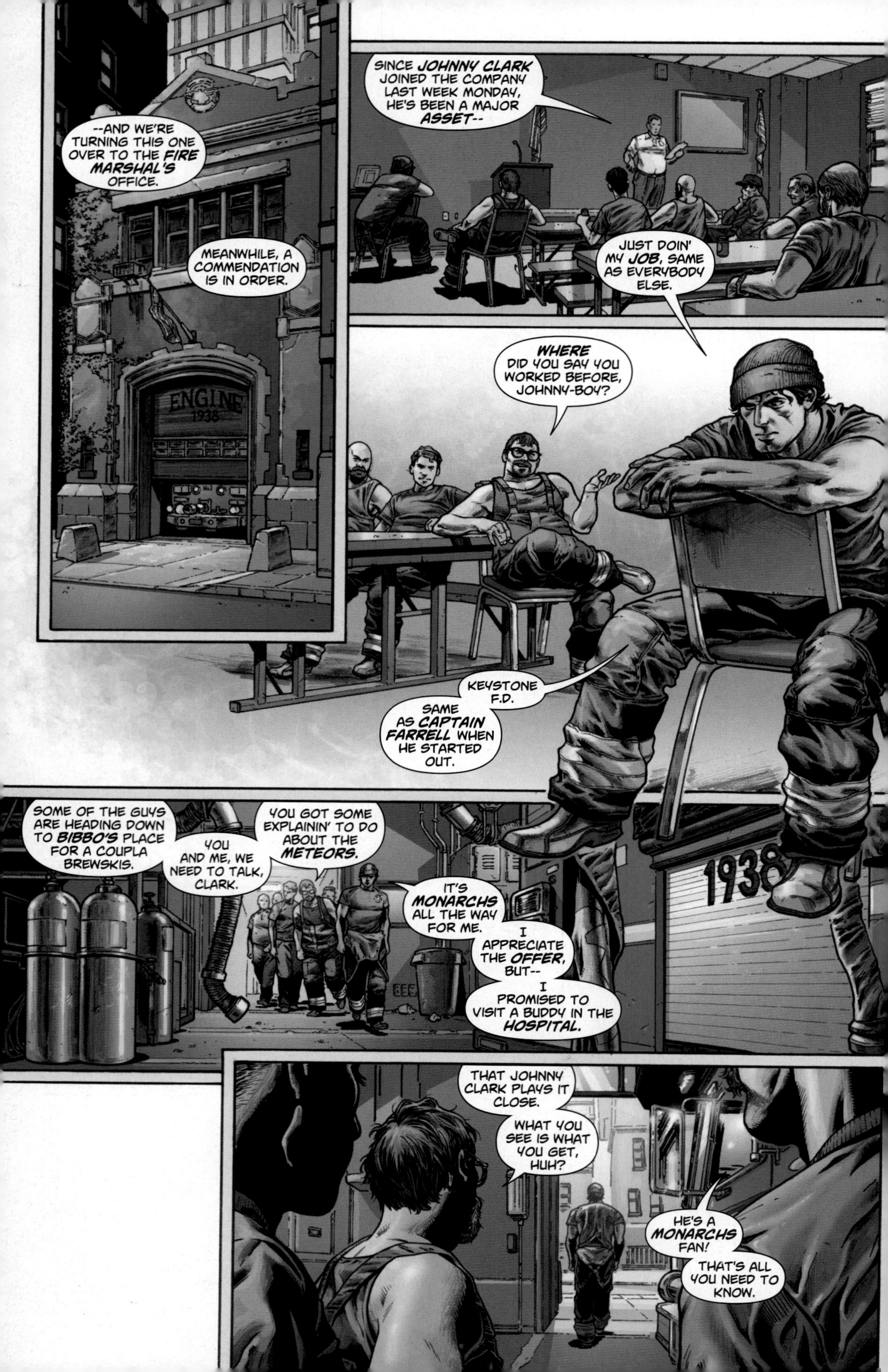
--AND WE'RE TURNING THIS ONE OVER TO THE FIRE MARSHAL'S OFFICE.
MEANWHILE, A COMMENDATION IS IN ORDER.
ENGINE 1938
SINCE JOHNNY CLARK JOINED THE COMPANY LAST WEEK MONDAY, HE'S BEEN A MAJOR ASSET--
JUST DOIN' MY JOB, SAME AS EVERYBODY ELSE.
WHERE DID YOU SAY YOU WORKED BEFORE, JOHNNY-BOY?
KEYSTONE F.D.
SAME AS CAPTAIN FARRELL WHEN HE STARTED OUT.
SOME OF THE GUYS ARE HEADING DOWN TO BIBBO'S PLACE FOR A COUPLA BREWSKIS.
YOU AND ME, WE NEED TO TALK, CLARK.
YOU GOT SOME EXPLAININ' TO DO ABOUT THE METEORS.
IT'S MONARCHS ALL THE WAY FOR ME.
I APPRECIATE THE OFFER, BUT--
I PROMISED TO VISIT A BUDDY IN THE HOSPITAL.
1938
THAT JOHNNY CLARK PLAYS IT CLOSE.
WHAT YOU SEE IS WHAT YOU GET, HUH?
HE'S A MONARCHS FAN!
THAT'S ALL YOU NEED TO KNOW.

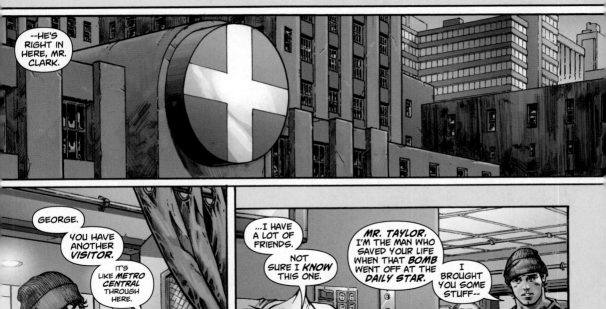

--HE'S RIGHT IN HERE, MR. CLARK.

GEORGE. YOU HAVE ANOTHER VISITOR.

IT'S LIKE METRO CENTRAL THROUGH HERE.

...I HAVE A LOT OF FRIENDS.

NOT SURE I KNOW THIS ONE.

MR. TAYLOR, I'M THE MAN WHO SAVED YOUR LIFE WHEN THAT BOMB WENT OFF AT THE DAILY STAR.

I BROUGHT YOU SOME STUFF--

YOU SHOULD HAVE SAVED THE KID. CLARK KENT. YOU SHOULD HAVE SAVED HIM INSTEAD OF ME.

...SIR, I...

I SHOULDA DIED--I'M AN OLD MAN, BUT THAT KID--

THAT KID WAS ONE OF THE BEST REPORTERS I'VE EVER KNOWN.

I PROMISED HIS PA I'D LOOK AFTER HIM.

THE POOR KID. THE WORLD JUST LOST ONE OF ITS GOOD GUYS.

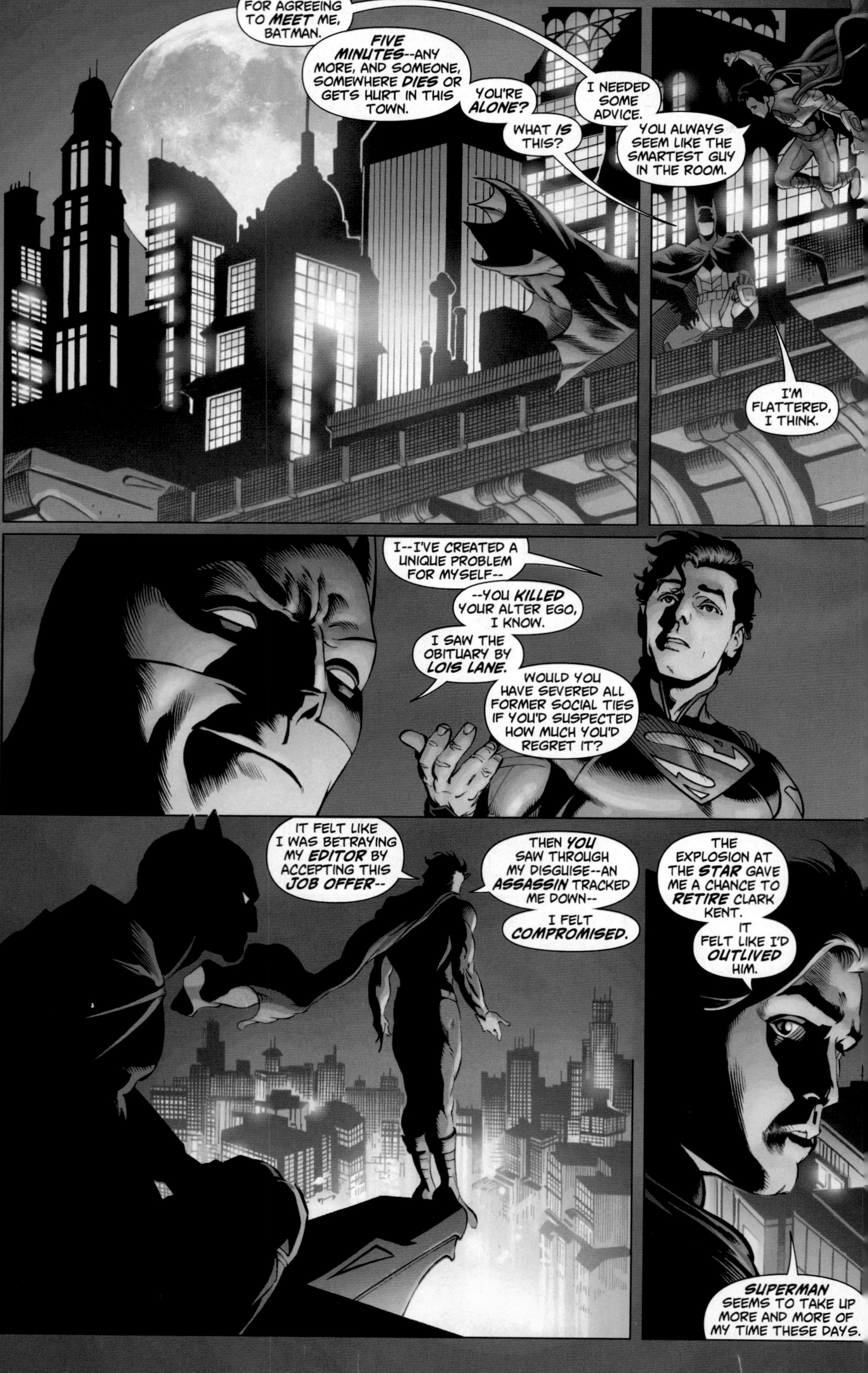
--THANKS FOR AGREEING TO MEET ME, BATMAN.
FIVE MINUTES--ANY MORE, AND SOMEONE, SOMEWHERE DIES OR GETS HURT IN THIS TOWN.
YOU'RE ALONE?
WHAT IS THIS?
I NEEDED SOME ADVICE.
YOU ALWAYS SEEM LIKE THE SMARTEST GUY IN THE ROOM.
I'M FLATTERED, I THINK.
I--I'VE CREATED A UNIQUE PROBLEM FOR MYSELF--
--YOU KILLED YOUR ALTER EGO, I KNOW.
I SAW THE OBITUARY BY LOIS LANE.
WOULD YOU HAVE SEVERED ALL FORMER SOCIAL TIES IF YOU'D SUSPECTED HOW MUCH YOU'D REGRET IT?
IT FELT LIKE I WAS BETRAYING MY EDITOR BY ACCEPTING THIS JOB OFFER--
THEN YOU SAW THROUGH MY DISGUISE--AN ASSASSIN TRACKED ME DOWN--
I FELT COMPROMISED.
THE EXPLOSION AT THE STAR GAVE ME A CHANCE TO RETIRE CLARK KENT.
IT FELT LIKE I'D OUTLIVED HIM.
SUPERMAN SEEMS TO TAKE UP MORE AND MORE OF MY TIME THESE DAYS.

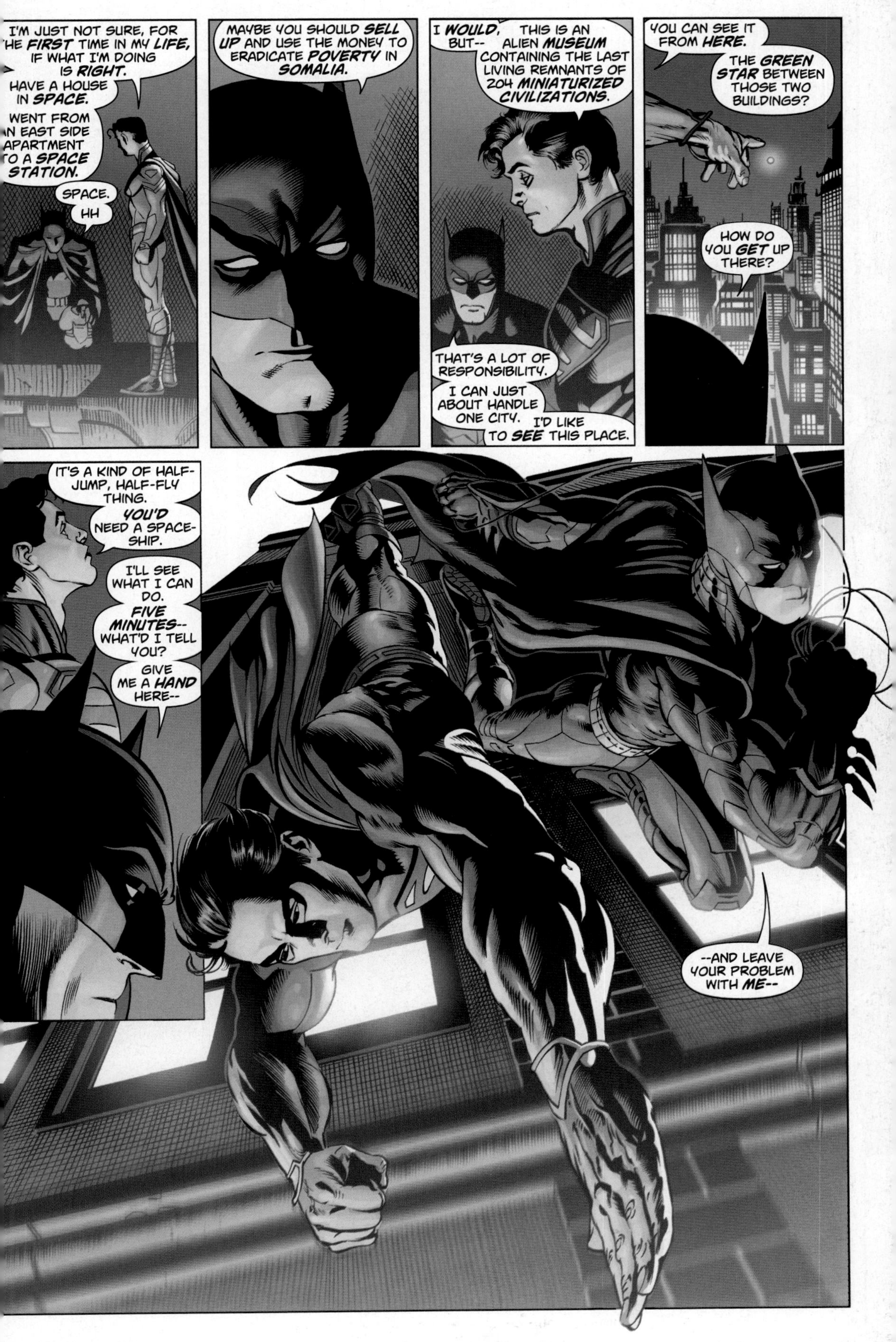
I'M JUST NOT SURE, FOR THE FIRST TIME IN MY LIFE, IF WHAT I'M DOING IS RIGHT.
HAVE A HOUSE IN SPACE.
WENT FROM AN EAST SIDE APARTMENT TO A SPACE STATION.
SPACE.
HH
MAYBE YOU SHOULD SELL UP AND USE THE MONEY TO ERADICATE POVERTY IN SOMALIA.
I WOULD, BUT--
THIS IS AN ALIEN MUSEUM CONTAINING THE LAST LIVING REMNANTS OF 204 MINIATURIZED CIVILIZATIONS.
THAT'S A LOT OF RESPONSIBILITY.
I CAN JUST ABOUT HANDLE ONE CITY.
I'D LIKE TO SEE THIS PLACE.
YOU CAN SEE IT FROM HERE.
THE GREEN STAR BETWEEN THOSE TWO BUILDINGS?
HOW DO YOU GET UP THERE?
IT'S A KIND OF HALF-JUMP, HALF-FLY THING.
YOU'D NEED A SPACE-SHIP.
I'LL SEE WHAT I CAN DO.
FIVE MINUTES-- WHAT'D I TELL YOU?
GIVE ME A HAND HERE--
--AND LEAVE YOUR PROBLEM WITH ME--

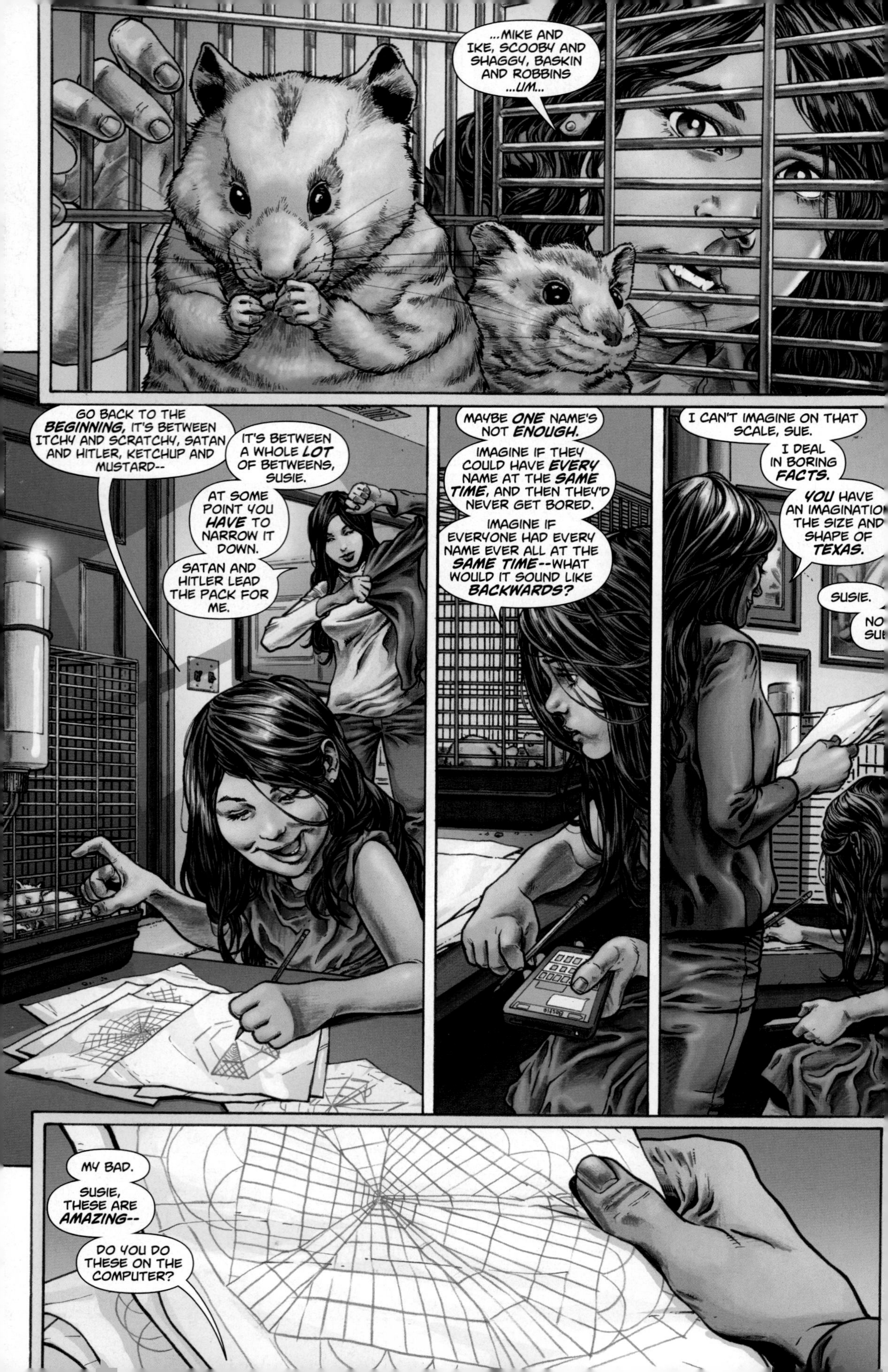
...MIKE AND IKE, SCOOBY AND SHAGGY, BASKIN AND ROBBINS ...UM...
GO BACK TO THE BEGINNING, IT'S BETWEEN ITCHY AND SCRATCHY, SATAN AND HITLER, KETCHUP AND MUSTARD--
IT'S BETWEEN A WHOLE LOT OF BETWEENS, SUSIE.
AT SOME POINT YOU HAVE TO NARROW IT DOWN.
SATAN AND HITLER LEAD THE PACK FOR ME.
MAYBE ONE NAME'S NOT ENOUGH.
IMAGINE IF THEY COULD HAVE EVERY NAME AT THE SAME TIME, AND THEN THEY'D NEVER GET BORED.
IMAGINE IF EVERYONE HAD EVERY NAME EVER ALL AT THE SAME TIME--WHAT WOULD IT SOUND LIKE BACKWARDS?
I CAN'T IMAGINE ON THAT SCALE, SUE.
I DEAL IN BORING FACTS.
SUSIE.
MY BAD.
SUSIE, THESE ARE AMAZING--
DO YOU DO THESE ON THE COMPUTER?

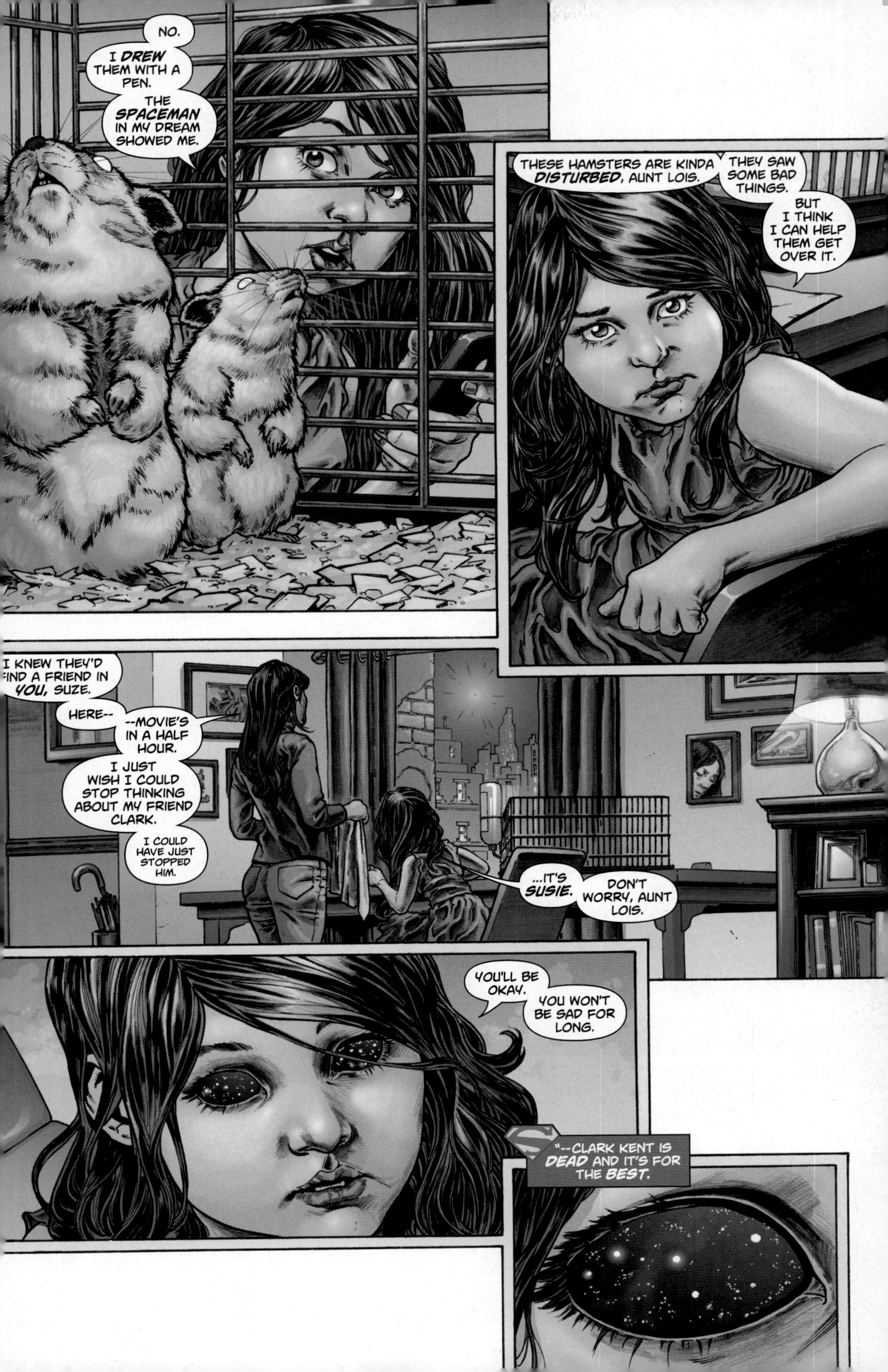
NO.
I DREW THEM WITH A PEN.
THE SPACEMAN IN MY DREAM SHOWED ME.
THESE HAMSTERS ARE KINDA DISTURBED, AUNT LOIS.
THEY SAW SOME BAD THINGS.
BUT I THINK I CAN HELP THEM GET OVER IT.
I KNEW THEY'D FIND A FRIEND IN YOU, SUZE.
HERE--
--MOVIE'S IN A HALF HOUR.
I JUST WISH I COULD STOP THINKING ABOUT MY FRIEND CLARK.
I COULD HAVE JUST STOPPED HIM.
...IT'S SUSIE.
DON'T WORRY, AUNT LOIS.
YOU'LL BE OKAY.
YOU WON'T BE SAD FOR LONG.
"--CLARK KENT IS DEAD AND IT'S FOR THE BEST.

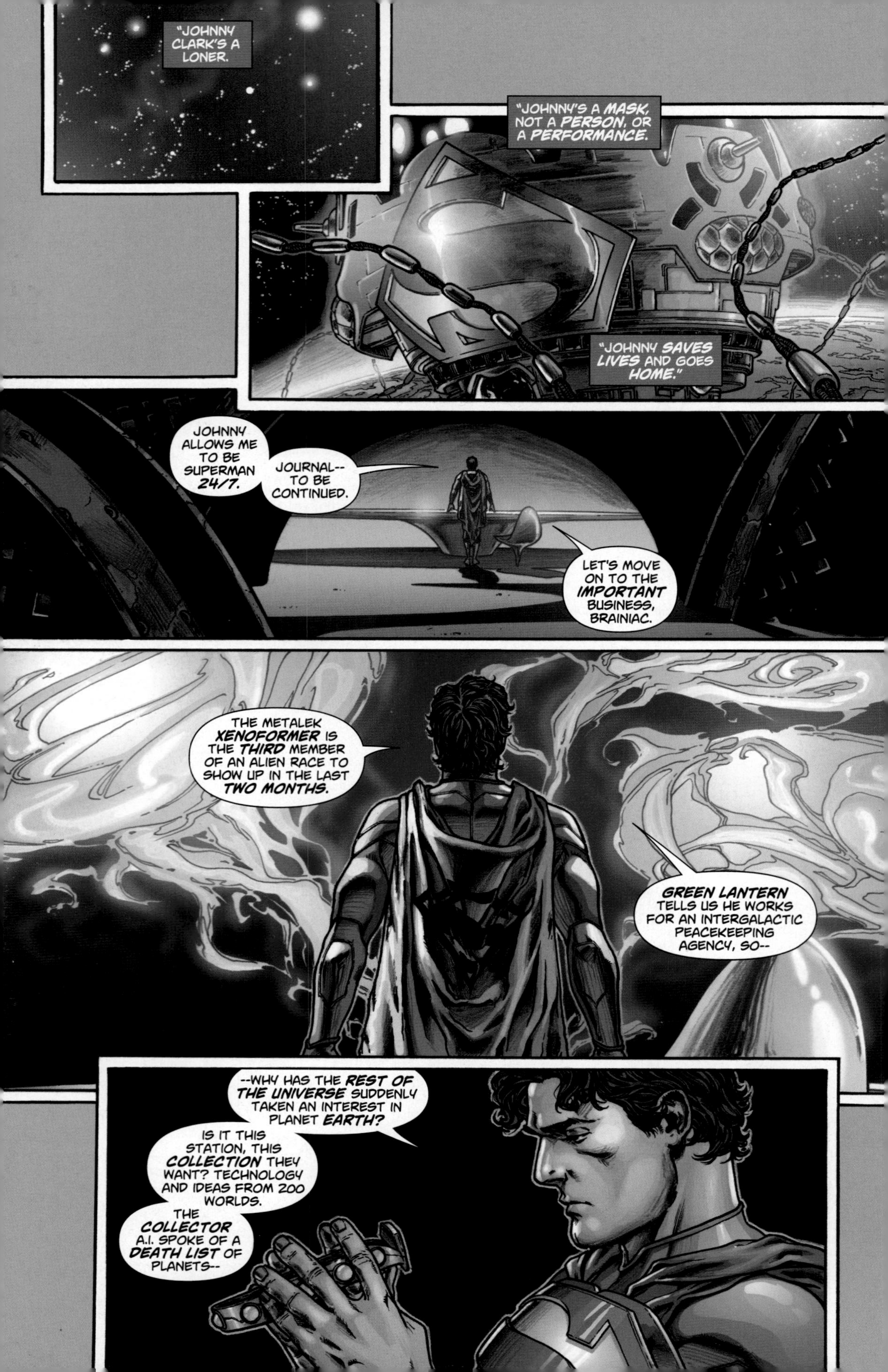
"JOHNNY CLARK'S A LONER.
"JOHNNY'S A MASK, NOT A PERSON, OR A PERFORMANCE.
"JOHNNY SAVES LIVES AND GOES HOME."
JOHNNY ALLOWS ME TO BE SUPERMAN 24/7.
JOURNAL-- TO BE CONTINUED.
LET'S MOVE ON TO THE IMPORTANT BUSINESS, BRAINIAC.
THE METALEK XENOFORMER IS THE THIRD MEMBER OF AN ALIEN RACE TO SHOW UP IN THE LAST TWO MONTHS.
GREEN LANTERN TELLS US HE WORKS FOR AN INTERGALACTIC PEACEKEEPING AGENCY, SO--
--WHY HAS THE REST OF THE UNIVERSE SUDDENLY TAKEN AN INTEREST IN PLANET EARTH?
IS IT THIS STATION, THIS COLLECTION THEY WANT? TECHNOLOGY AND IDEAS FROM 200 WORLDS.
THE COLLECTOR A.I. SPOKE OF A DEATH LIST OF PLANETS--

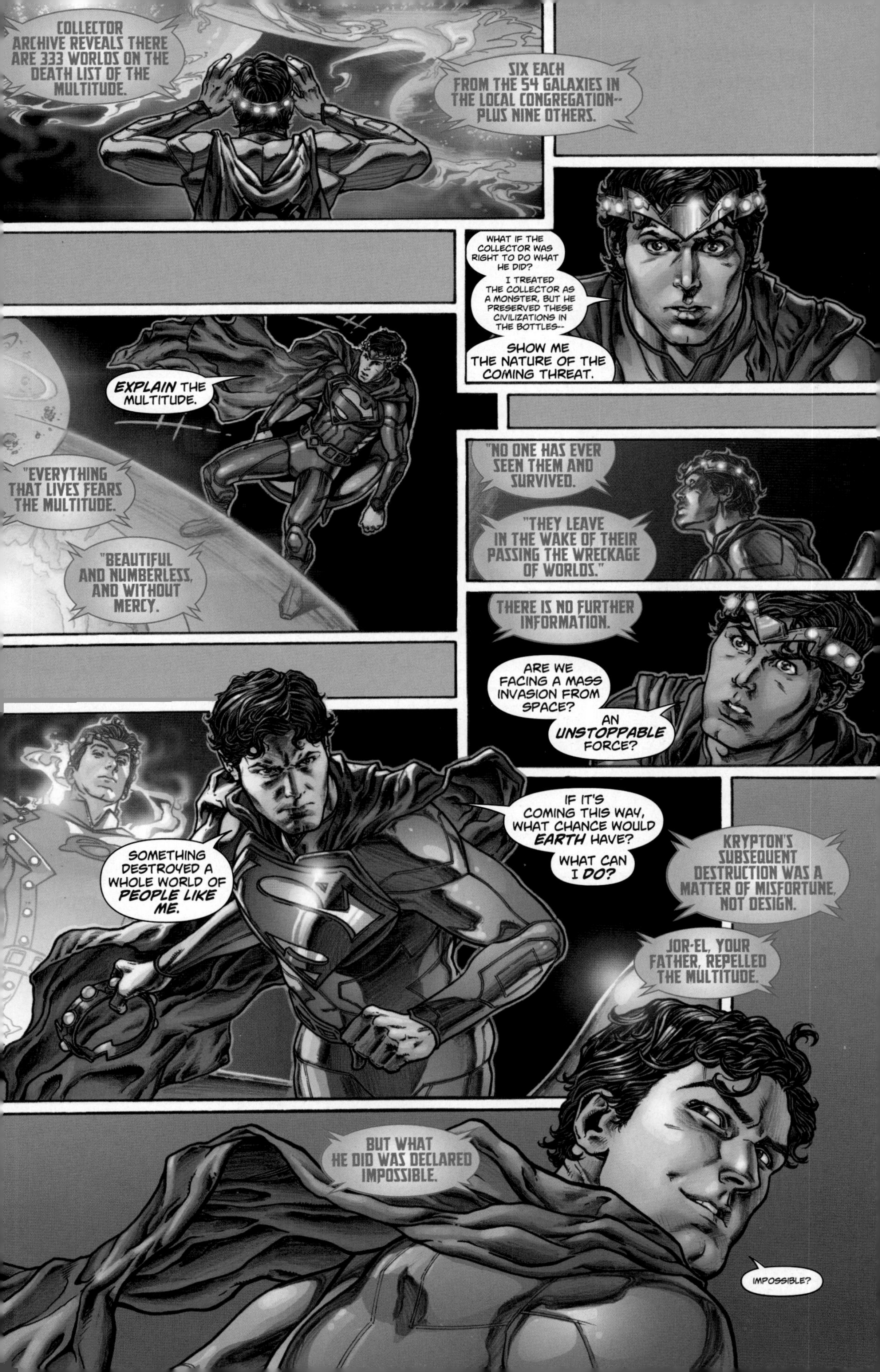
COLLECTOR ARCHIVE REVEALS THERE ARE 333 WORLDS ON THE DEATH LIST OF THE MULTITUDE.
SIX EACH FROM THE 54 GALAXIES IN THE LOCAL CONGREGATION-- PLUS NINE OTHERS.
WHAT IF THE COLLECTOR WAS RIGHT TO DO WHAT HE DID?
I TREATED THE COLLECTOR AS A MONSTER, BUT HE PRESERVED THESE CIVILIZATIONS IN THE BOTTLES--
SHOW ME THE NATURE OF THE COMING THREAT.
EXPLAIN THE MULTITUDE.
"EVERYTHING THAT LIVES FEARS THE MULTITUDE.
"BEAUTIFUL AND NUMBERLESS, AND WITHOUT MERCY.
"NO ONE HAS EVER SEEN THEM AND SURVIVED.
"THEY LEAVE IN THE WAKE OF THEIR PASSING THE WRECKAGE OF WORLDS."
THERE IS NO FURTHER INFORMATION.
ARE WE FACING A MASS INVASION FROM SPACE?
AN UNSTOPPABLE FORCE?
SOMETHING DESTROYED A WHOLE WORLD OF PEOPLE LIKE ME.
IF IT'S COMING THIS WAY, WHAT CHANCE WOULD EARTH HAVE?
WHAT CAN I DO?
KRYPTON'S SUBSEQUENT DESTRUCTION WAS A MATTER OF MISFORTUNE, NOT DESIGN.
JOR-EL, YOUR FATHER, REPELLED THE MULTITUDE.
BUT WHAT HE DID WAS DECLARED IMPOSSIBLE.
IMPOSSIBLE?

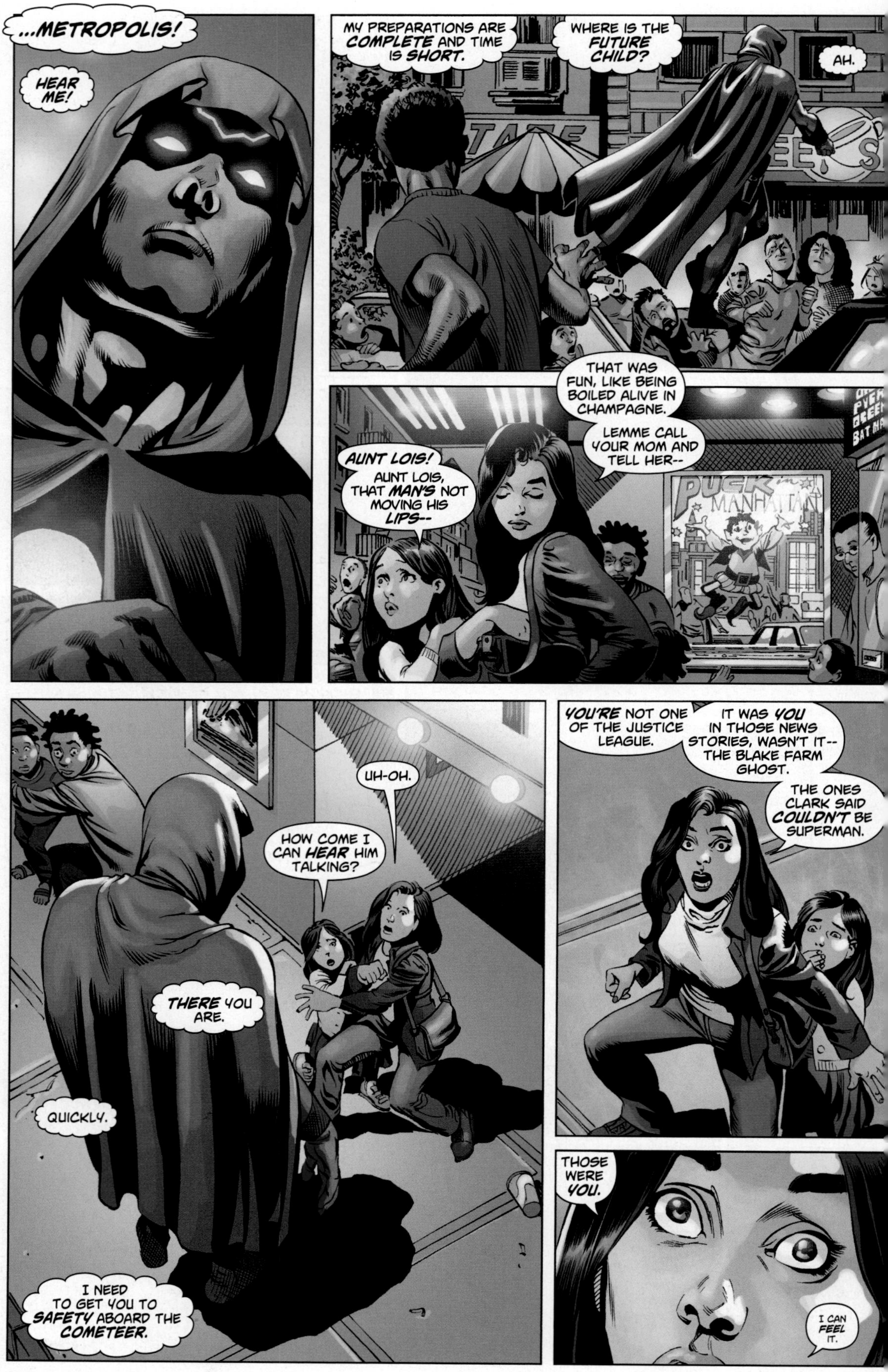
...METROPOLIS!
HEAR ME!
MY PREPARATIONS ARE COMPLETE AND TIME IS SHORT.
WHERE IS THE FUTURE CHILD?
AH.
THAT WAS FUN, LIKE BEING BOILED ALIVE IN CHAMPAGNE.
LEMME CALL YOUR MOM AND TELL HER--
AUNT LOIS!
AUNT LOIS, THAT MAN'S NOT MOVING HIS LIPS--
PUCK IN MANHATTAN
UH-OH.
HOW COME I CAN HEAR HIM TALKING?
THERE YOU ARE.
QUICKLY.
I NEED TO GET YOU TO SAFETY ABOARD THE COMETEER.
YOU'RE NOT ONE OF THE JUSTICE LEAGUE.
IT WAS YOU IN THOSE NEWS STORIES, WASN'T IT-- THE BLAKE FARM GHOST.
THE ONES CLARK SAID COULDN'T BE SUPERMAN.
THOSE WERE YOU.
I CAN FEEL IT.

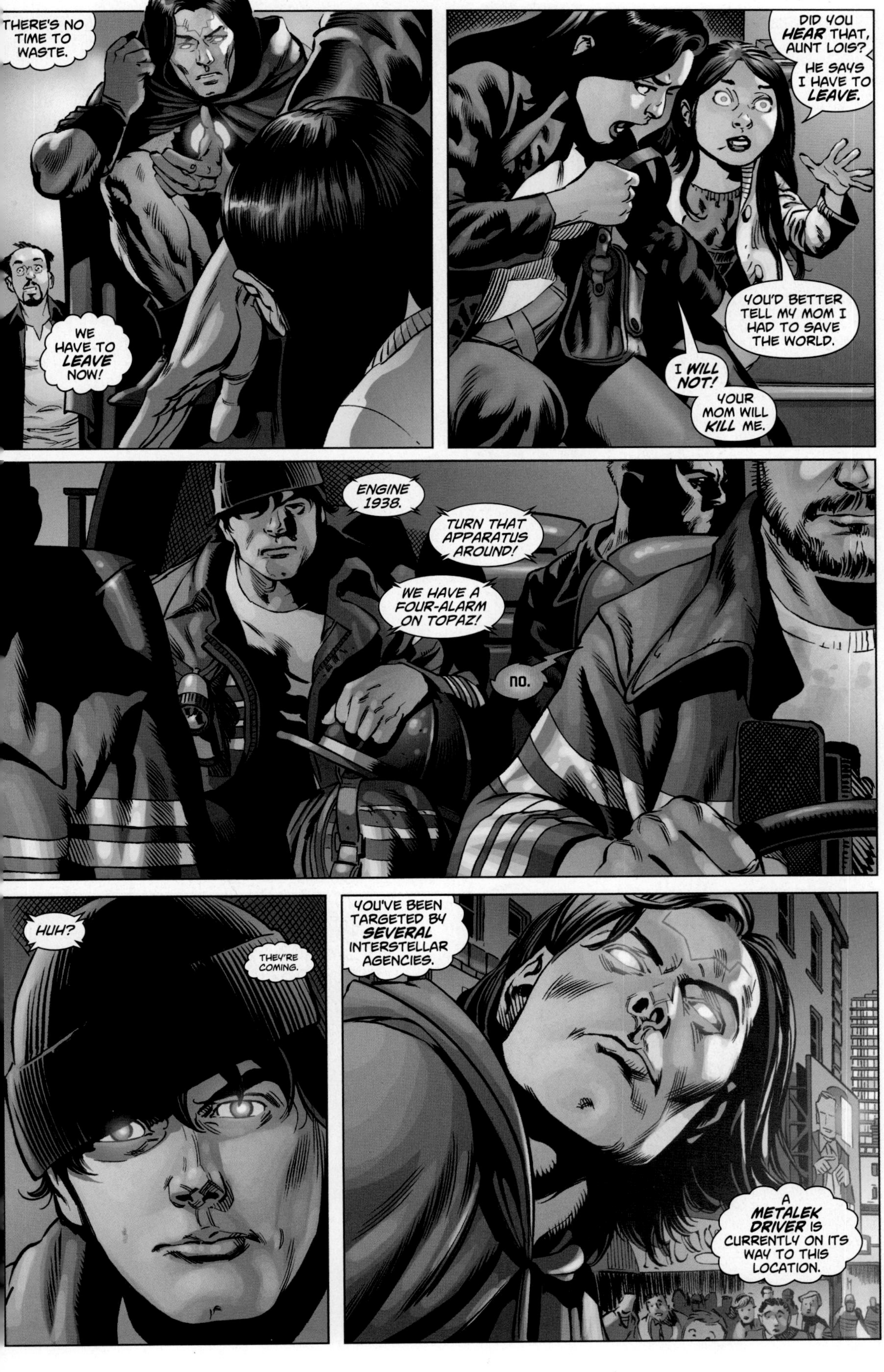
THERE'S NO TIME TO WASTE.
WE HAVE TO LEAVE NOW!
DID YOU HEAR THAT, AUNT LOIS?
HE SAYS I HAVE TO LEAVE.
YOU'D BETTER TELL MY MOM I HAD TO SAVE THE WORLD.
I WILL NOT!
YOUR MOM WILL KILL ME.
ENGINE 1938.
TURN THAT APPARATUS AROUND!
WE HAVE A FOUR-ALARM ON TOPAZ!
no.
HUH?
THEY'RE COMING.
YOU'VE BEEN TARGETED BY SEVERAL INTERSTELLAR AGENCIES.
A METALEK DRIVER IS CURRENTLY ON ITS WAY TO THIS LOCATION.

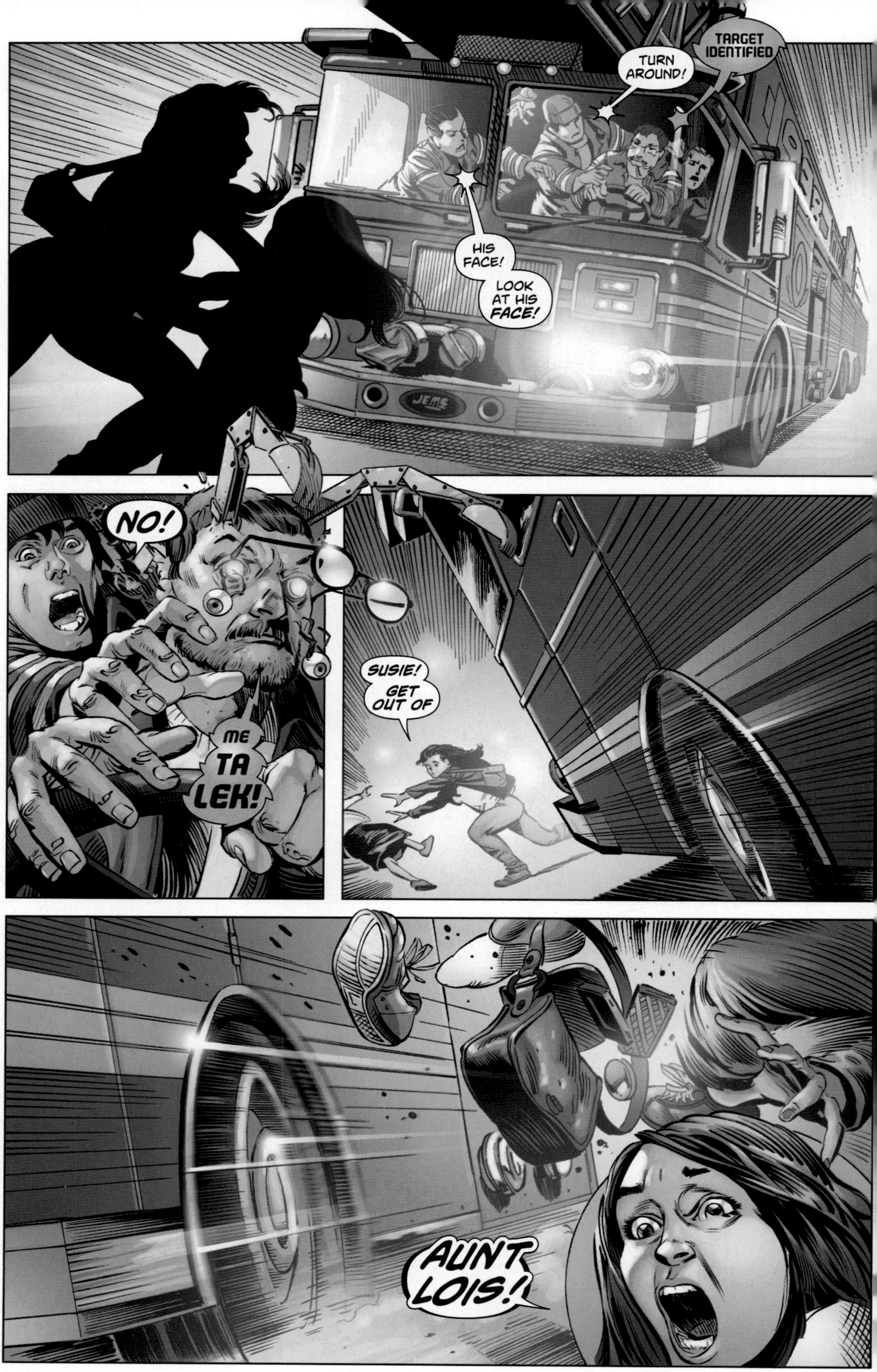
TARGET IDENTIFIED
TURN AROUND!
HIS FACE!
LOOK AT HIS FACE!
NO!
ME TA LEK!
SUSIE! GET OUT OF
AUNT LOIS!

...FEAR NOT. I *HAVE* HIM.

BUT *OTHERS* WILL COME.

YOU'RE THE *SPACEMAN!*

YOU WERE IN MY DREAM!

WHAT HAVE YOU DONE TO MY *AUNTIE LOIS?*

SHE BELONGS TO A SPECIES FACING *EXTINCTION,* BUT *YOU*--

YOU'RE *ONE OF US,* A *NUTANT.*

NEO SAPIENS-- BORN *ONE HUNDRED THOUSAND YEARS AHEAD* OF OUR TIME TO PREPARE THE WAY AND *INHERIT* THE EARTH...

I *KNOW* YOU'VE ALWAYS FELT SPECIAL, SUSIE.

I'M HERE TO *PROTECT* YOU AND ALLOW THAT POTENTIAL TO *FLOURISH.*

YOU'RE NOT *ALONE,* SUSIE.

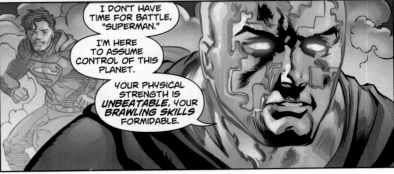

I DON'T HAVE TIME FOR BATTLE, "SUPERMAN."

I'M HERE TO *ASSUME CONTROL* OF THIS PLANET.

YOUR PHYSICAL STRENGTH IS *UNBEATABLE,* YOUR *BRAWLING SKILLS* FORMIDABLE.

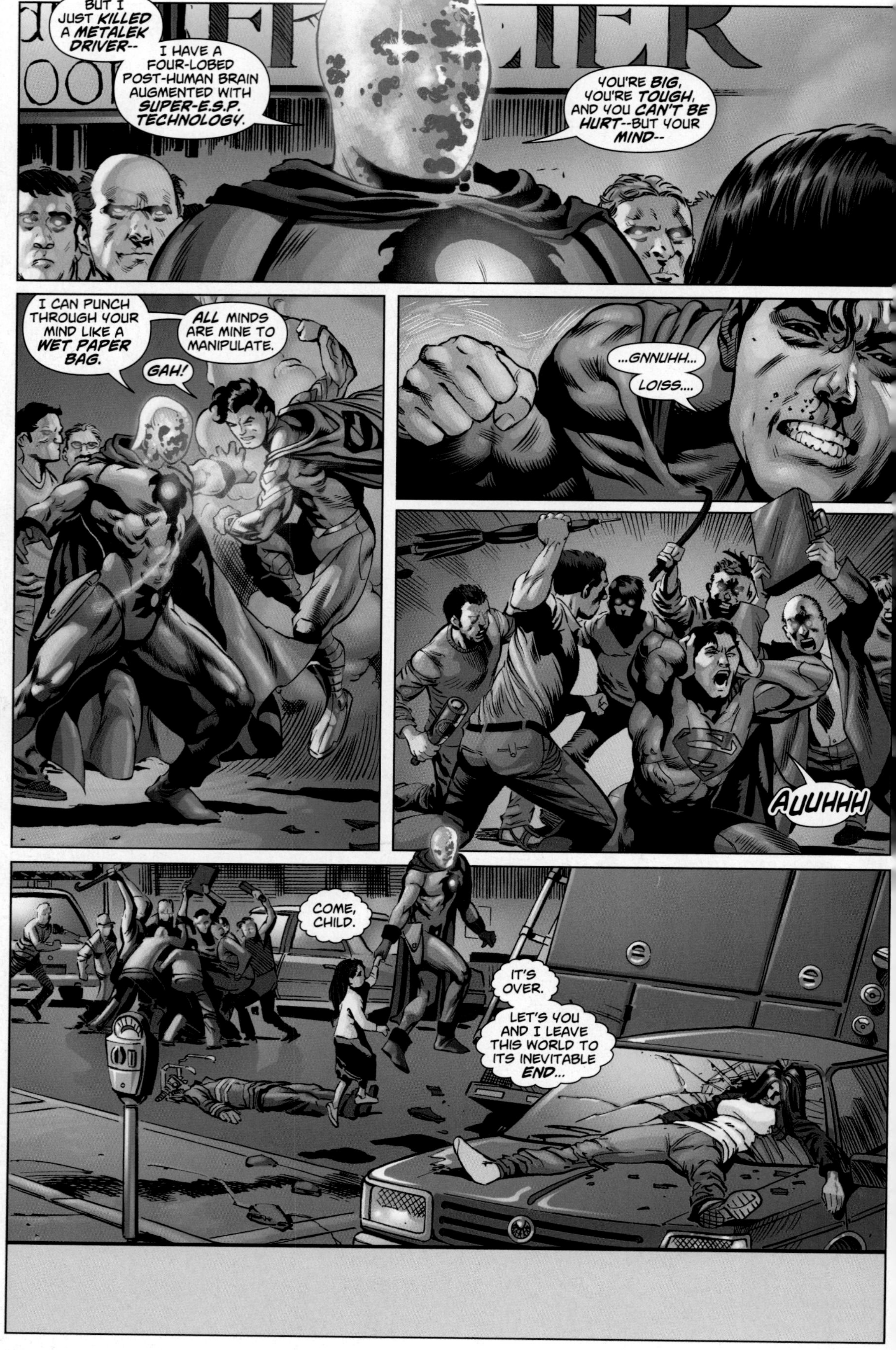

BUT I JUST KILLED A METALEK DRIVER--
I HAVE A FOUR-LOBED POST-HUMAN BRAIN AUGMENTED WITH SUPER-E.S.P. TECHNOLOGY.
YOU'RE BIG, YOU'RE TOUGH, AND YOU CAN'T BE HURT--BUT YOUR MIND--
I CAN PUNCH THROUGH YOUR MIND LIKE A WET PAPER BAG.
ALL MINDS ARE MINE TO MANIPULATE.
GAH!
...GNNUHH...
LOISS....
AUUHHH
COME, CHILD.
IT'S OVER.
LET'S YOU AND I LEAVE THIS WORLD TO ITS INEVITABLE END...

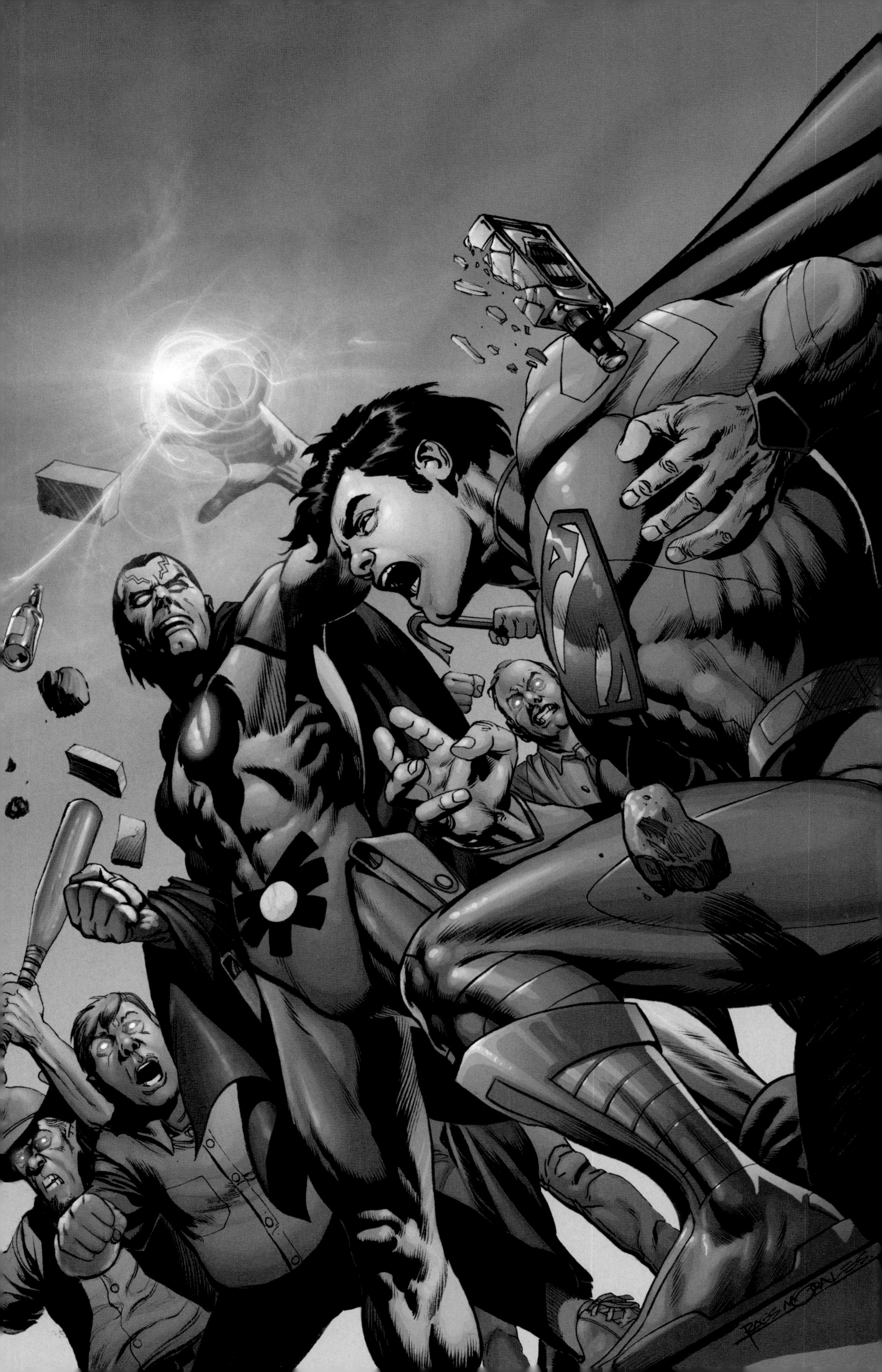

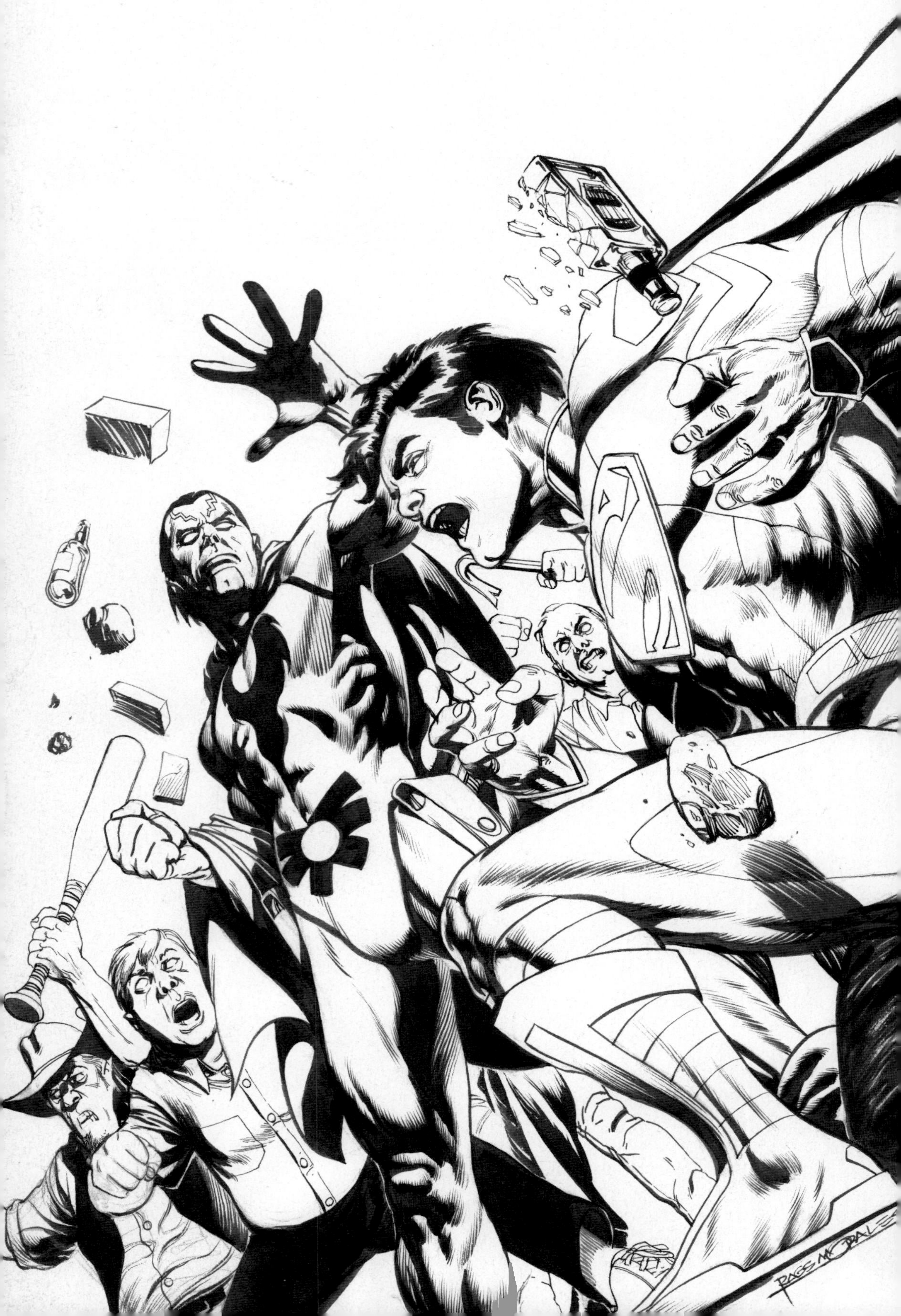

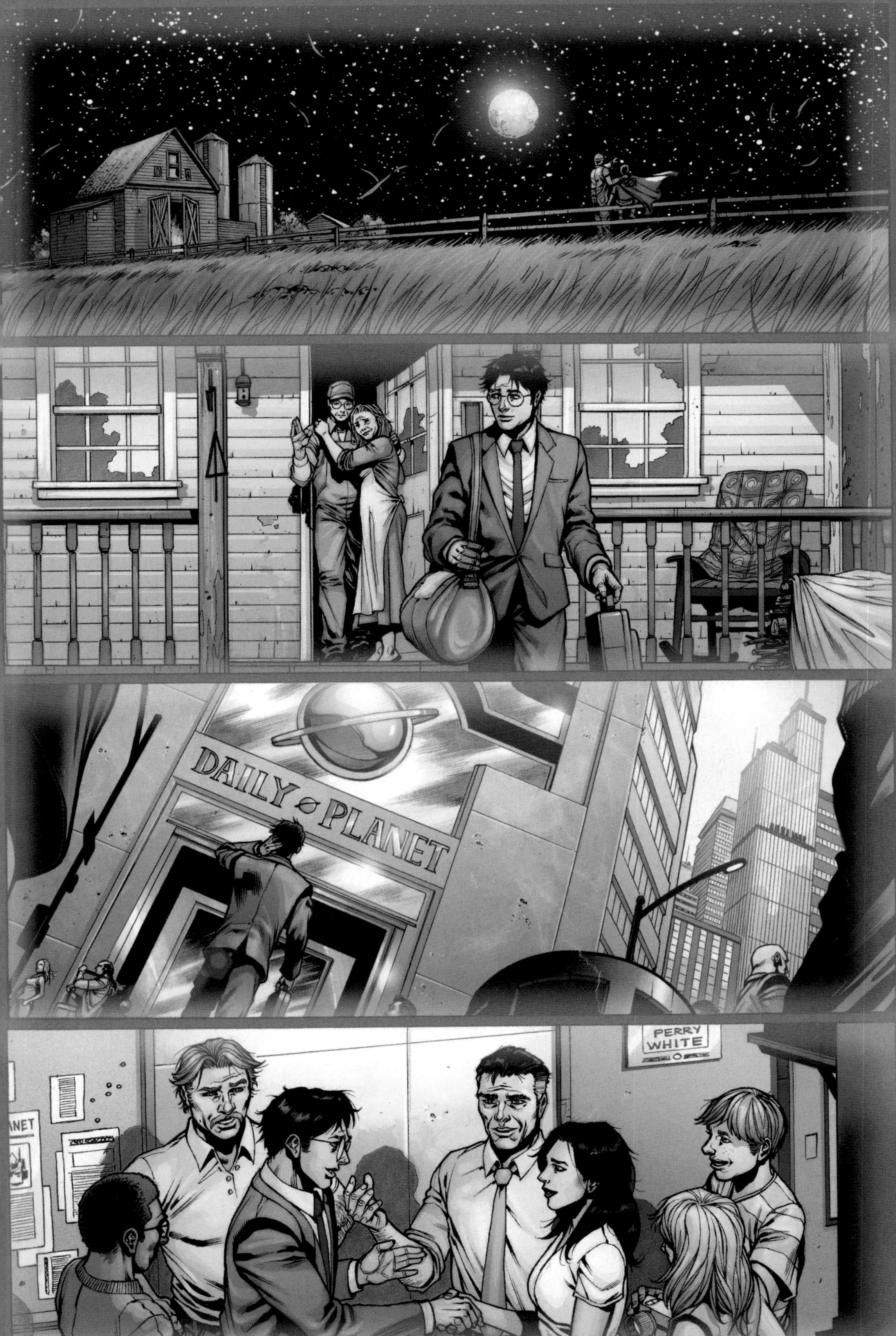
DAILY PLANET
PERRY WHITE

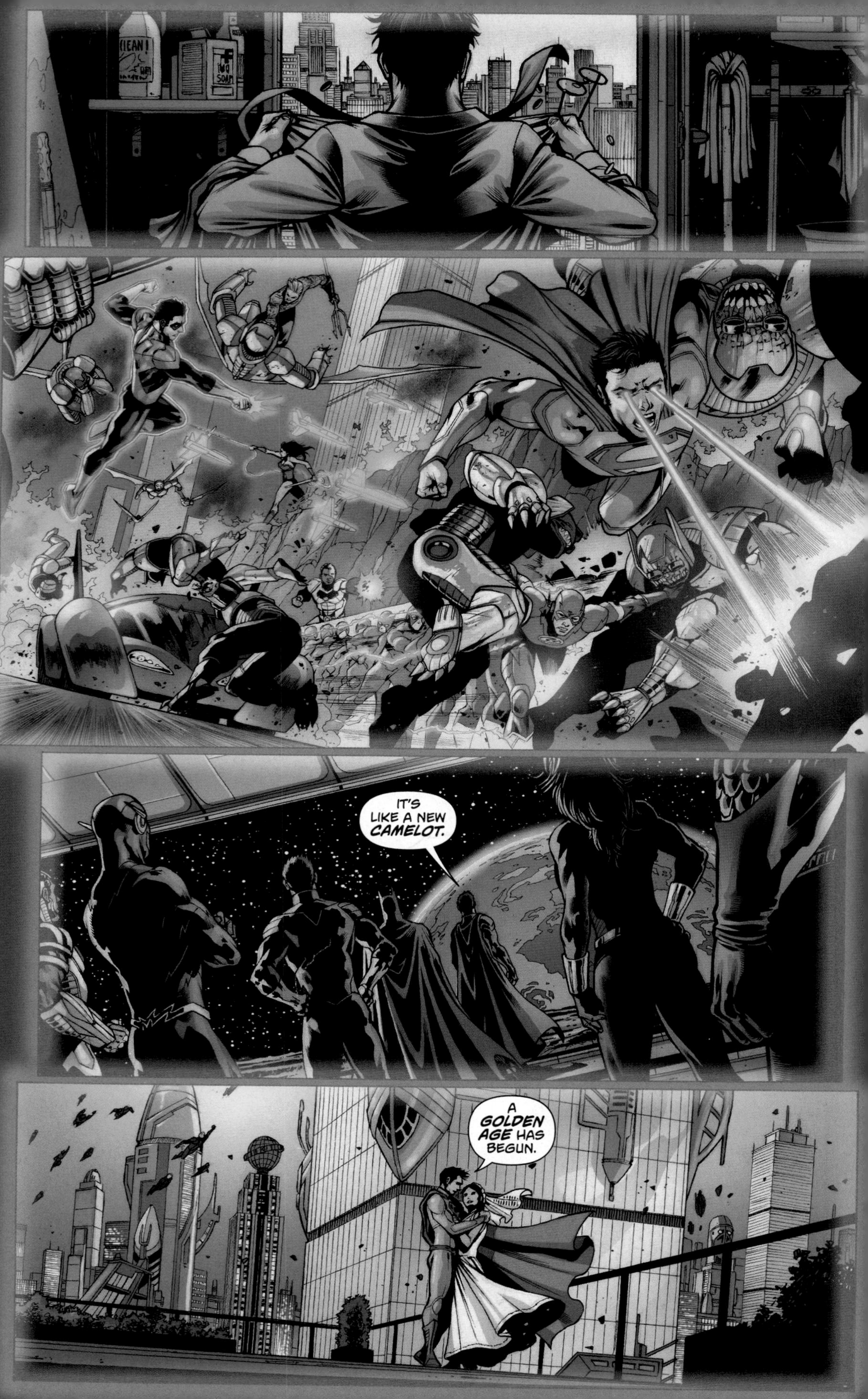

IT'S LIKE A NEW CAMELOT.
A GOLDEN AGE HAS BEGUN.

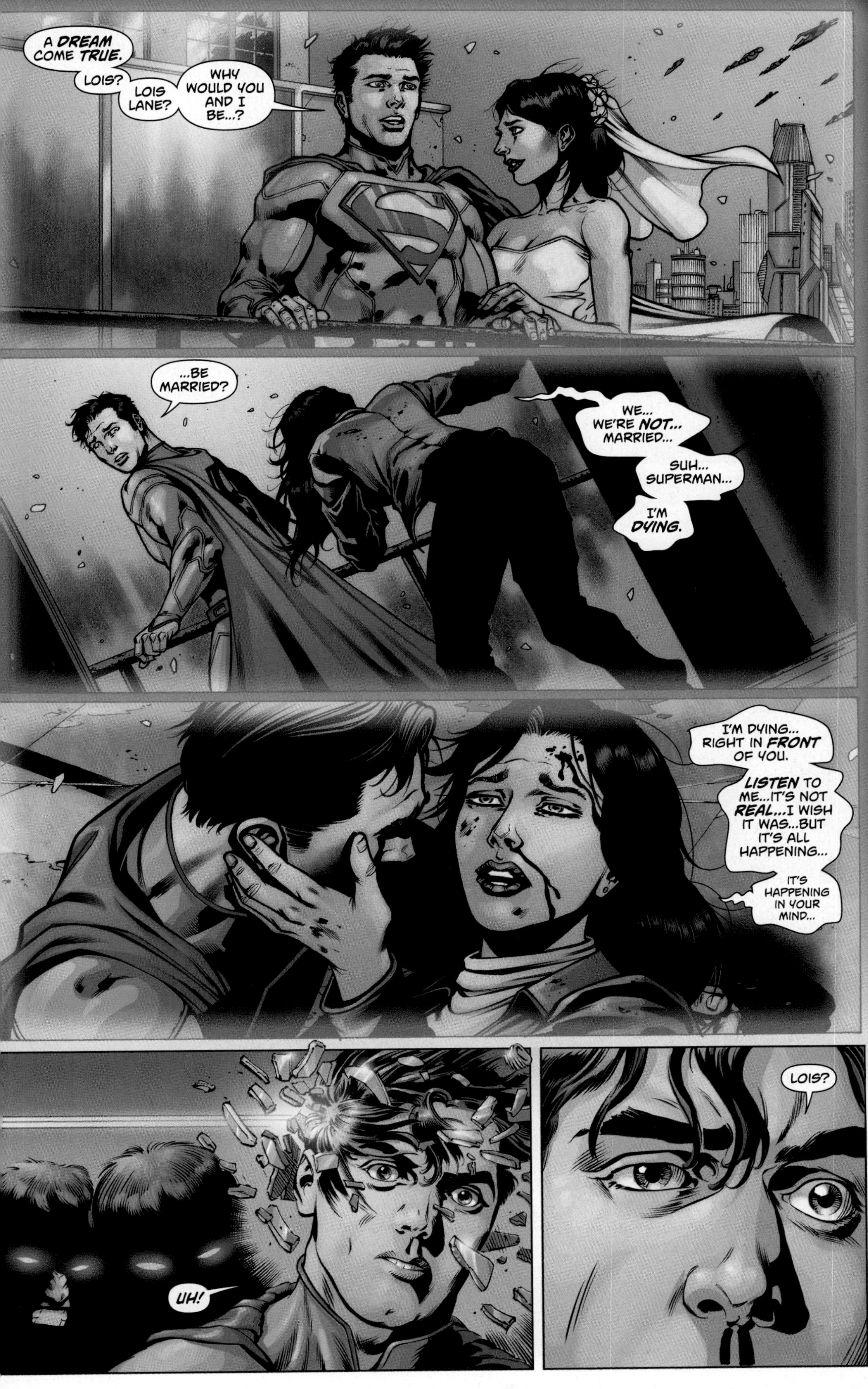
A DREAM COME TRUE.
LOIS?
LOIS LANE?
WHY WOULD YOU AND I BE...?
...BE MARRIED?
WE... WE'RE NOT... MARRIED...
SUH... SUPERMAN...
I'M DYING.
I'M DYING... RIGHT IN FRONT OF YOU.
LISTEN TO ME...IT'S NOT REAL...I WISH IT WAS...BUT IT'S ALL HAPPENING...
IT'S HAPPENING IN YOUR MIND...
UH!
LOIS?

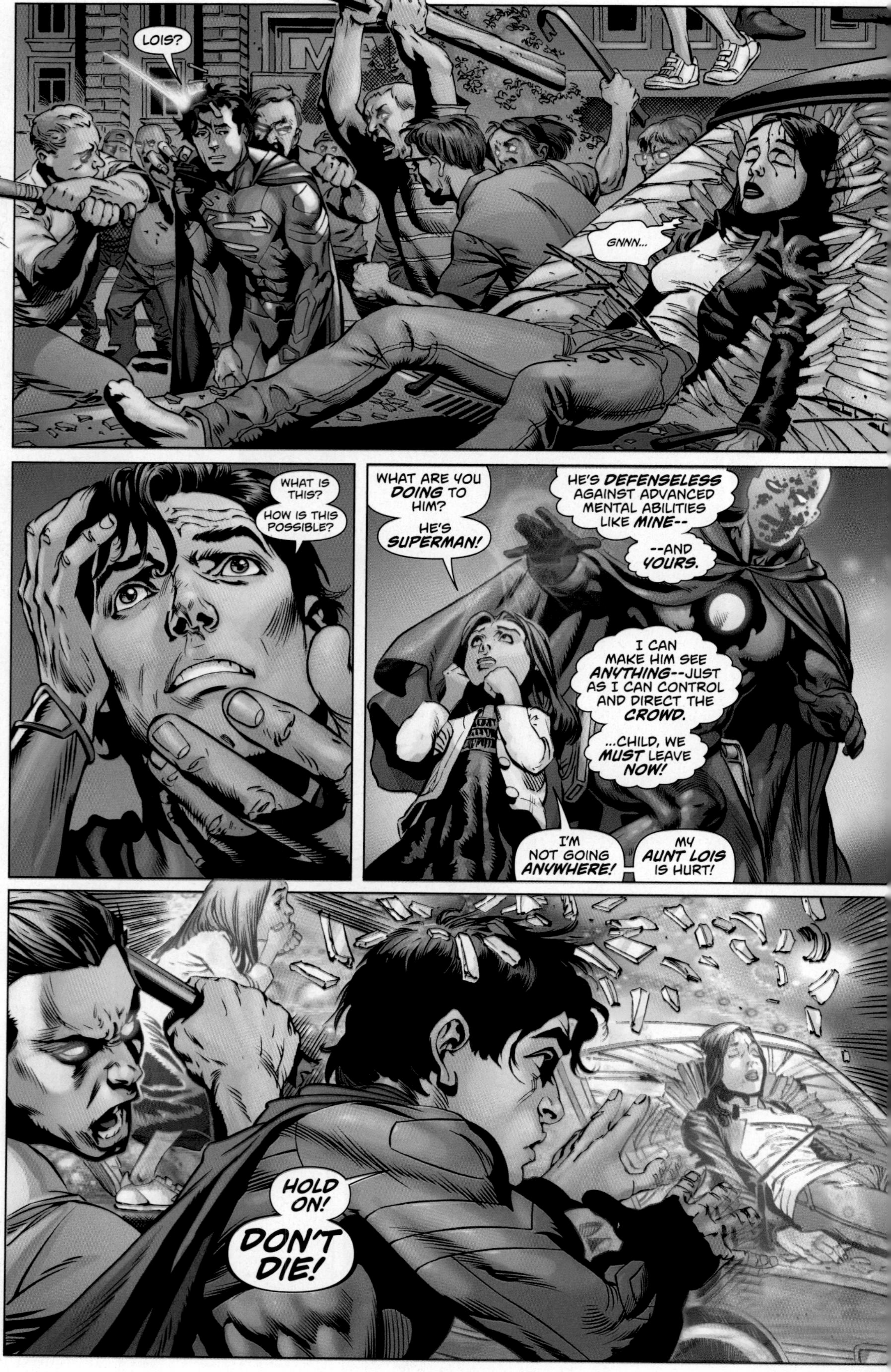
LOIS?
GNNN...
WHAT IS THIS?
HOW IS THIS POSSIBLE?
WHAT ARE YOU DOING TO HIM?
HE'S SUPERMAN!
HE'S DEFENSELESS AGAINST ADVANCED MENTAL ABILITIES LIKE MINE--
--AND YOURS.
I CAN MAKE HIM SEE ANYTHING--JUST AS I CAN CONTROL AND DIRECT THE CROWD.
...CHILD, WE MUST LEAVE NOW!
I'M NOT GOING ANYWHERE!
MY AUNT LOIS IS HURT!
HOLD ON!
DON'T DIE!

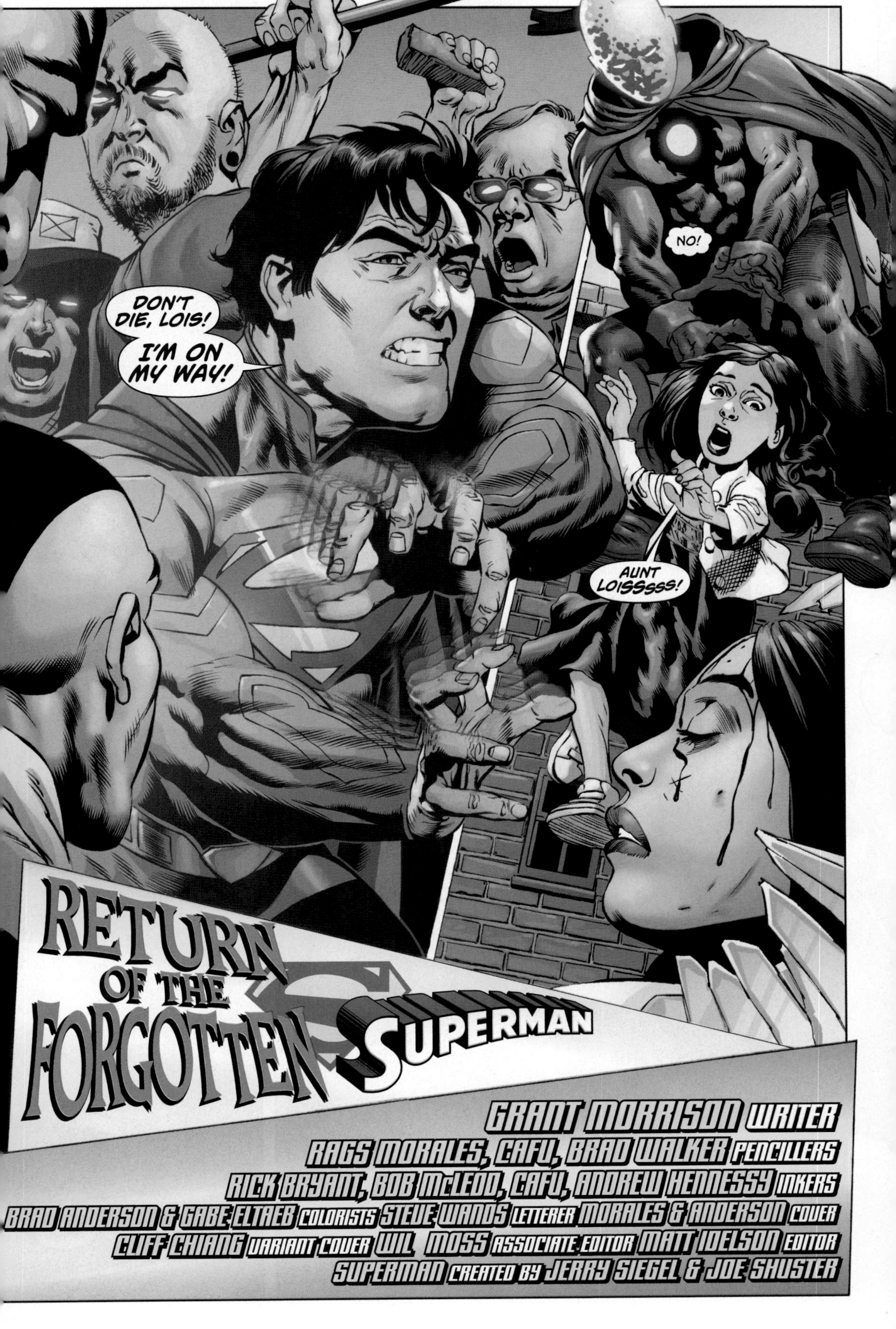
NO!
DON'T DIE, LOIS! I'M ON MY WAY!
AUNT LOISSSSS!
RETURN OF THE FORGOTTEN
SUPERMAN
GRANT MORRISON WRITER
RAGS MORALES, CAFU, BRAD WALKER PENCILLERS
RICK BRYANT, BOB McLEOD, CAFU, ANDREW HENNESSY INKERS
BRAD ANDERSON & GABE ELTAEB COLORISTS STEVE WANDS LETTERER MORALES & ANDERSON COVER
CLIFF CHIANG VARIANT COVER WIL MOSS ASSOCIATE EDITOR MATT IDELSON EDITOR
SUPERMAN CREATED BY JERRY SIEGEL & JOE SHUSTER

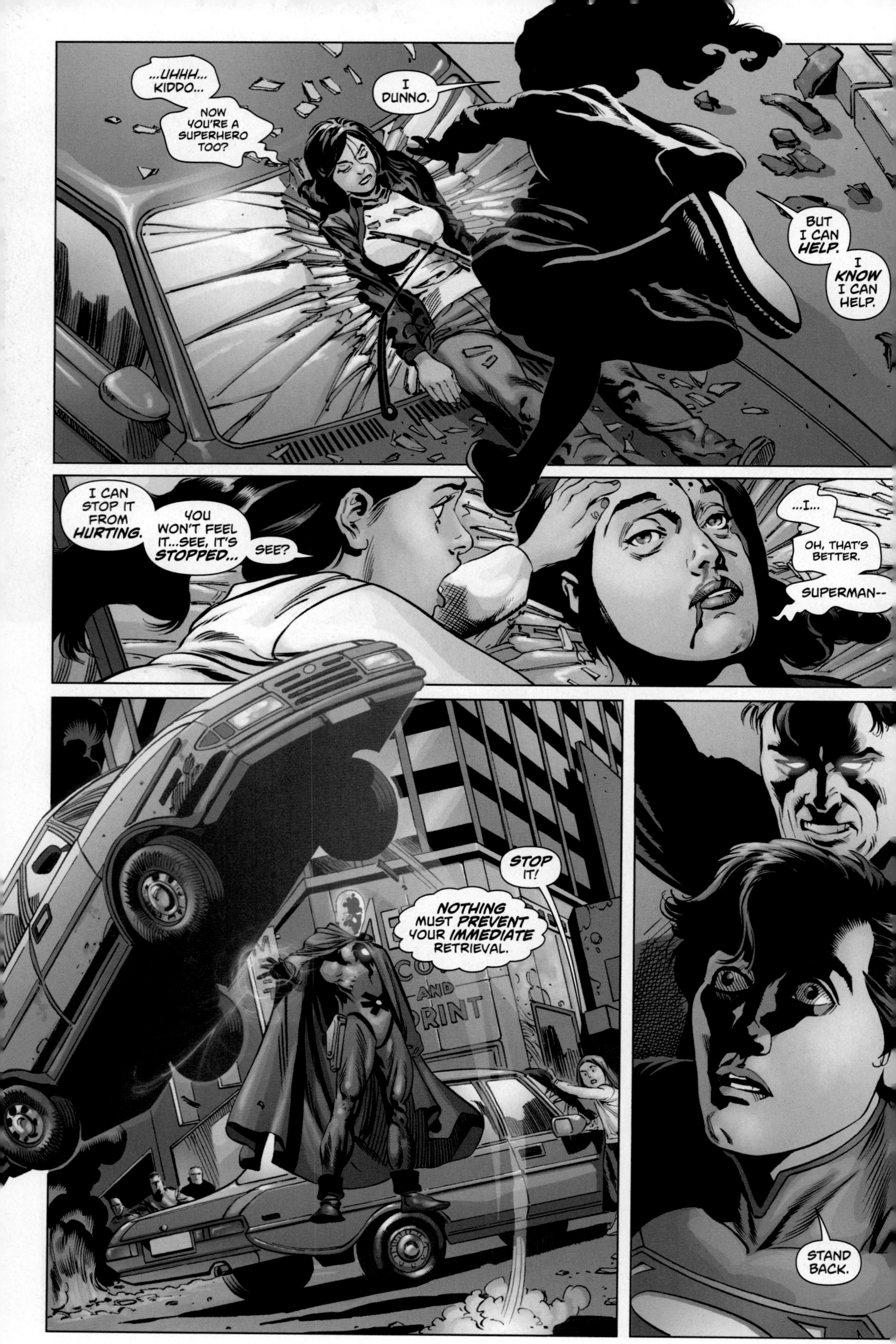
...UHHH... KIDDO...
NOW YOU'RE A SUPERHERO TOO?
I DUNNO.
BUT I CAN HELP.
I KNOW I CAN HELP.
I CAN STOP IT FROM HURTING.
YOU WON'T FEEL IT...SEE, IT'S STOPPED...
SEE?
...I...
OH, THAT'S BETTER.
SUPERMAN--
STOP IT!
NOTHING MUST PREVENT YOUR IMMEDIATE RETRIEVAL.
STAND BACK.

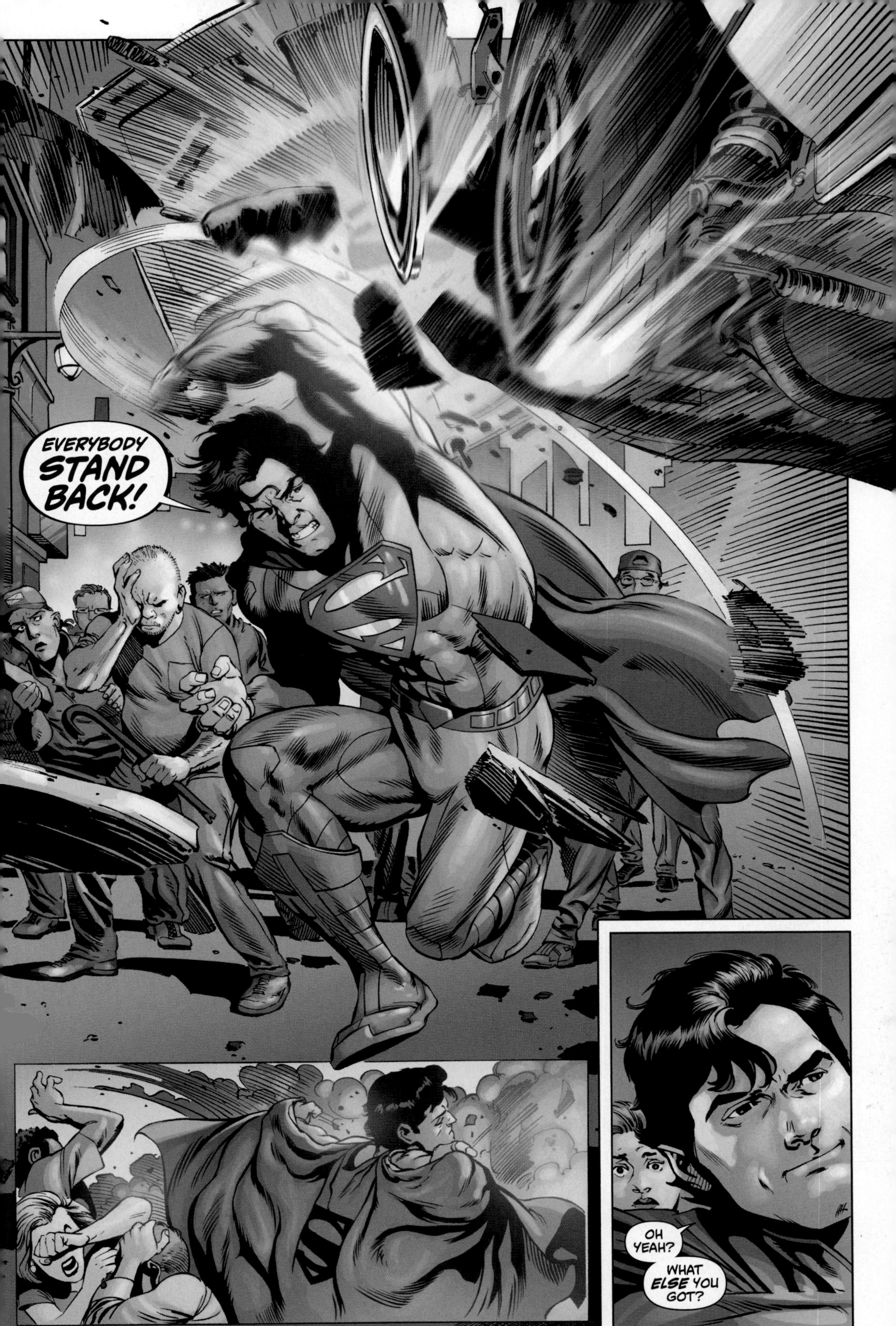
EVERYBODY STAND BACK!
OH YEAH?
WHAT ELSE YOU GOT?

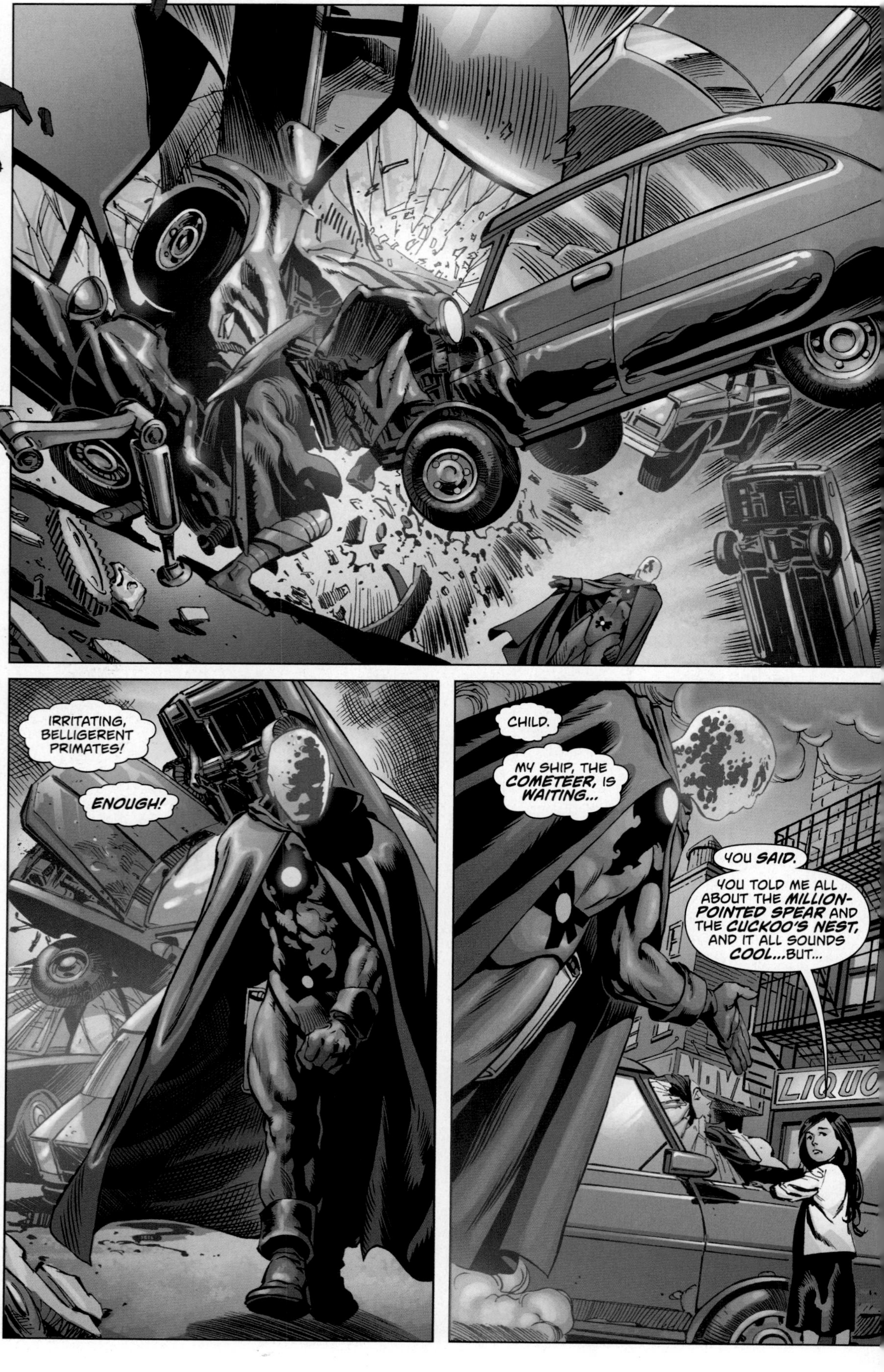
IRRITATING, BELLIGERENT PRIMATES!
ENOUGH!
CHILD.
MY SHIP, THE COMETEER, IS WAITING...
YOU SAID.
YOU TOLD ME ALL ABOUT THE MILLION-POINTED SPEAR AND THE CUCKOO'S NEST, AND IT ALL SOUNDS COOL...BUT...
NOVA
LIQU

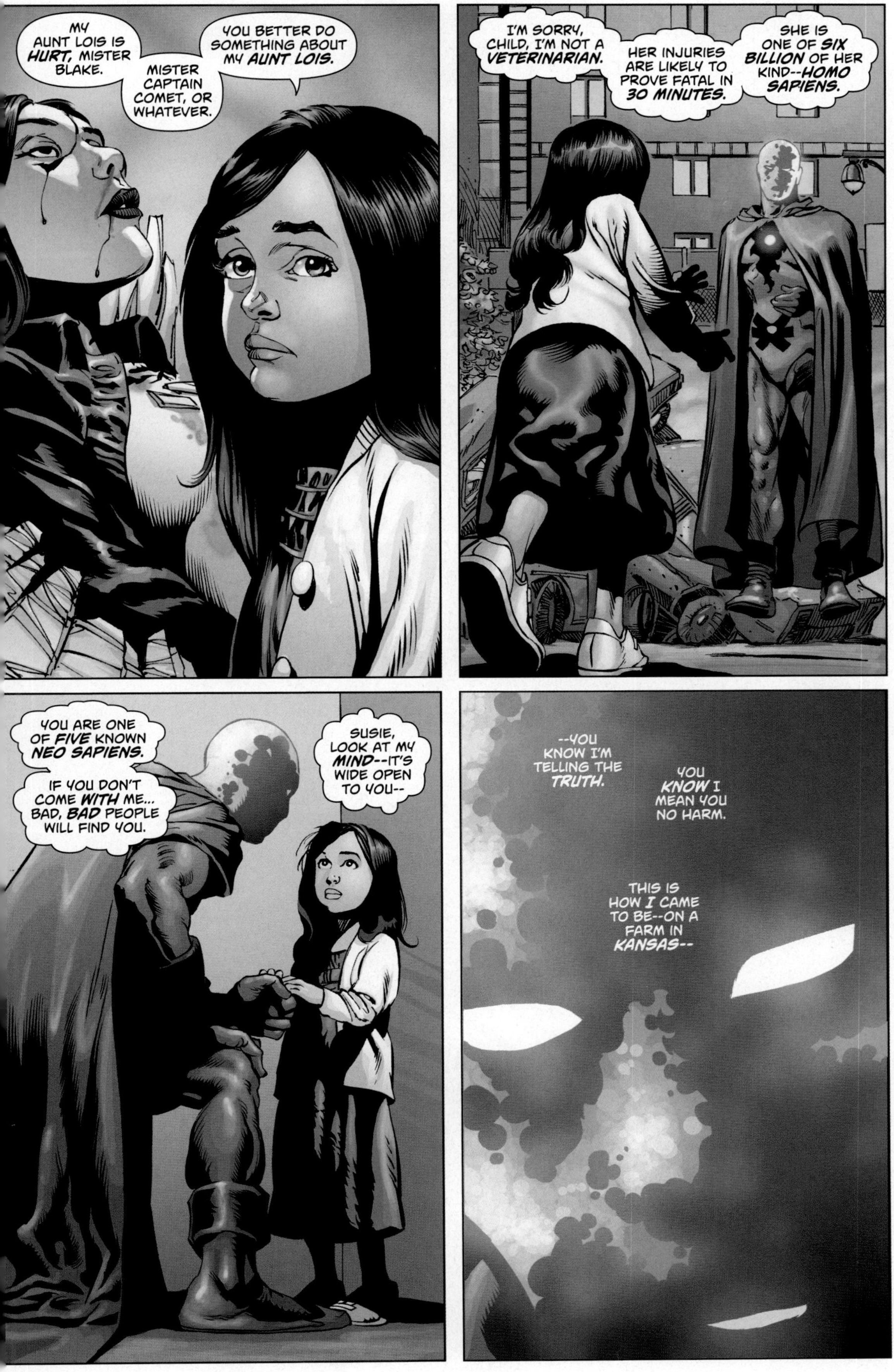
MY AUNT LOIS IS HURT, MISTER BLAKE.
MISTER CAPTAIN COMET, OR WHATEVER.
YOU BETTER DO SOMETHING ABOUT MY AUNT LOIS.
I'M SORRY, CHILD, I'M NOT A VETERINARIAN.
HER INJURIES ARE LIKELY TO PROVE FATAL IN 30 MINUTES.
SHE IS ONE OF SIX BILLION OF HER KIND--HOMO SAPIENS.
YOU ARE ONE OF FIVE KNOWN NEO SAPIENS.
IF YOU DON'T COME WITH ME... BAD, BAD PEOPLE WILL FIND YOU.
SUSIE, LOOK AT MY MIND--IT'S WIDE OPEN TO YOU--
--YOU KNOW I'M TELLING THE TRUTH.
YOU KNOW I MEAN YOU NO HARM.
THIS IS HOW I CAME TO BE--ON A FARM IN KANSAS--

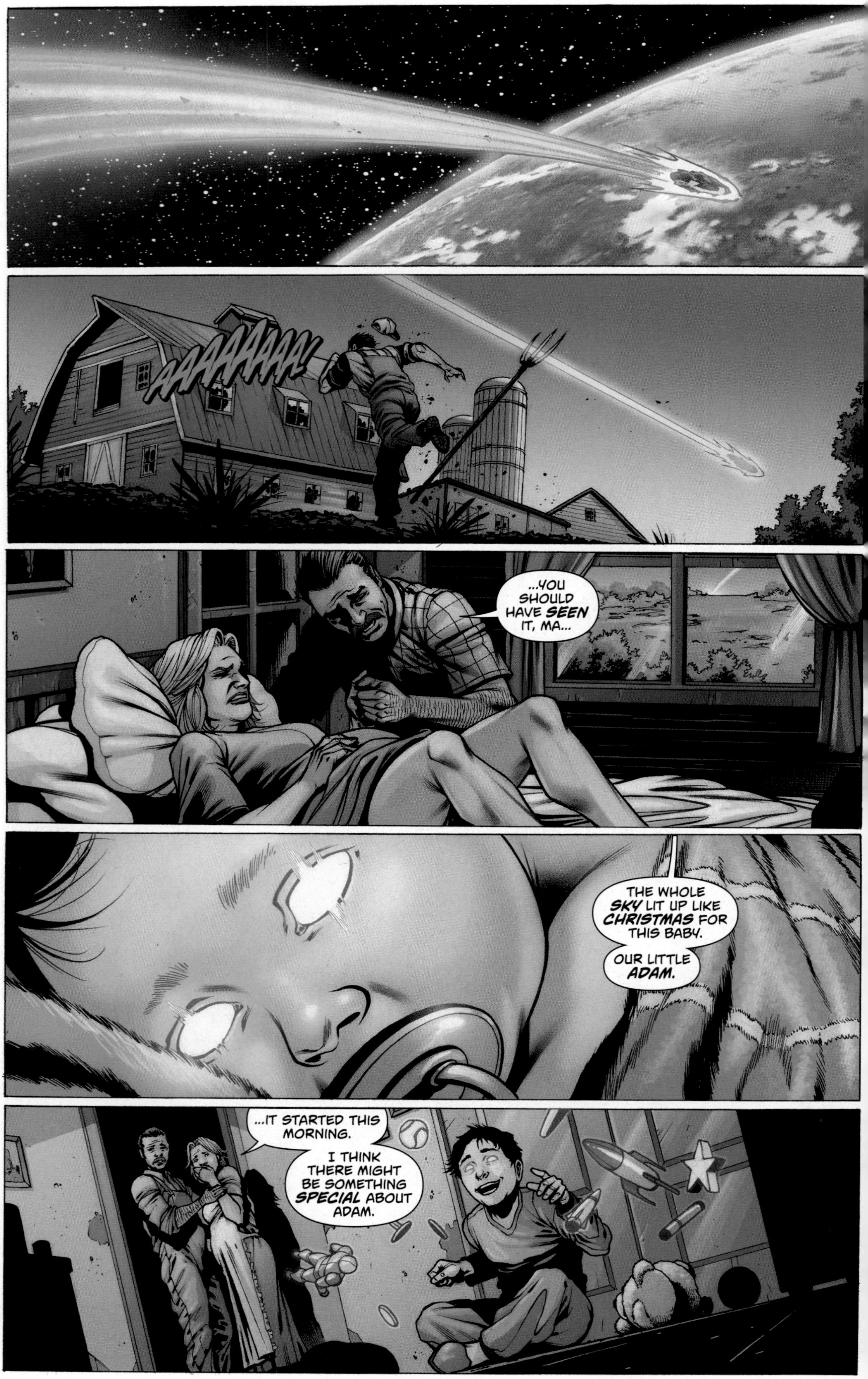
AAAAAAAA!
...YOU SHOULD HAVE SEEN IT, MA...
THE WHOLE SKY LIT UP LIKE CHRISTMAS FOR THIS BABY.
OUR LITTLE ADAM.
...IT STARTED THIS MORNING.
I THINK THERE MIGHT BE SOMETHING SPECIAL ABOUT ADAM.

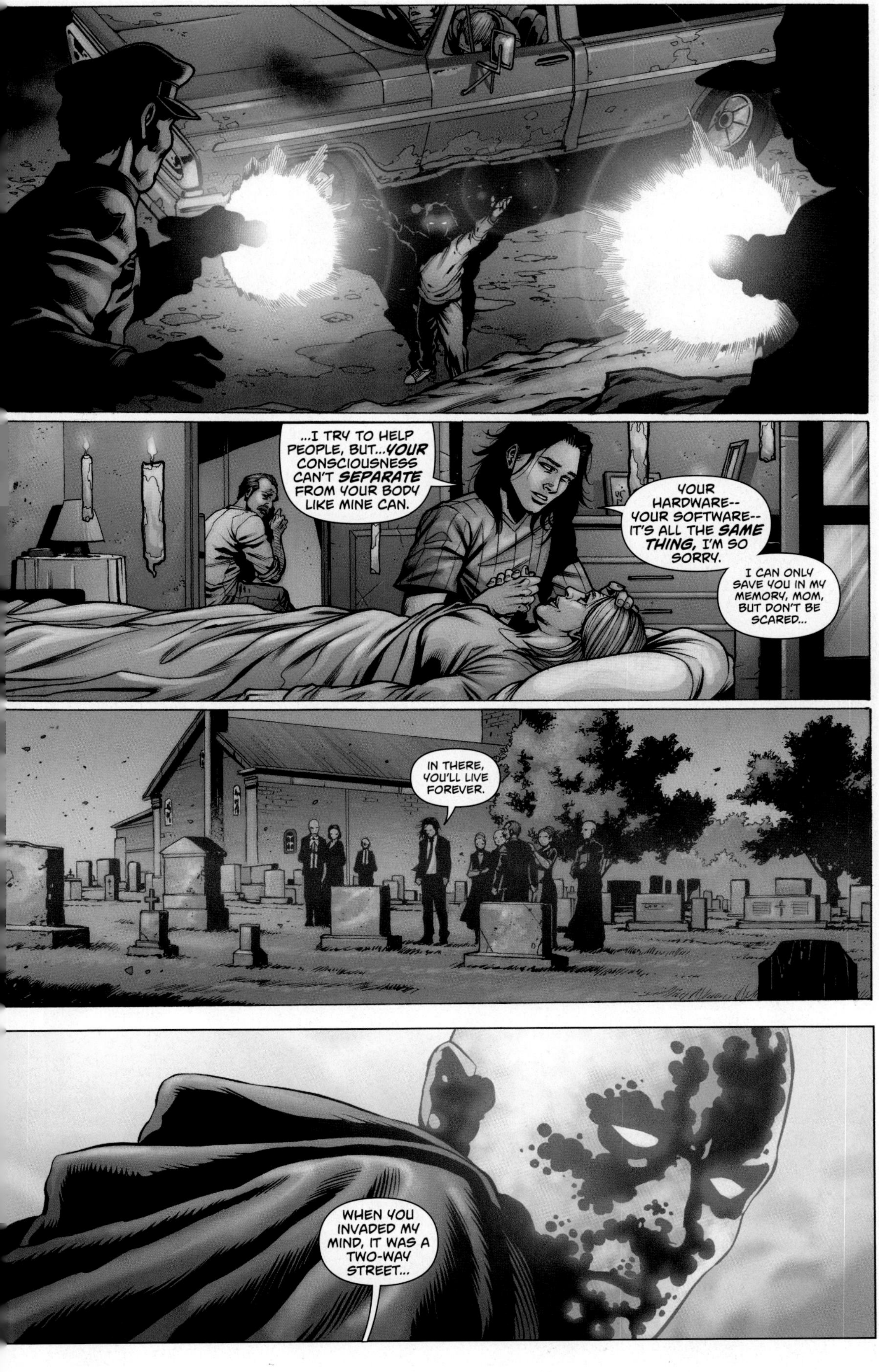

...I TRY TO HELP PEOPLE, BUT...YOUR CONSCIOUSNESS CAN'T SEPARATE FROM YOUR BODY LIKE MINE CAN.
YOUR HARDWARE--YOUR SOFTWARE--IT'S ALL THE SAME THING, I'M SO SORRY.
I CAN ONLY SAVE YOU IN MY MEMORY, MOM, BUT DON'T BE SCARED...
IN THERE, YOU'LL LIVE FOREVER.
WHEN YOU INVADED MY MIND, IT WAS A TWO-WAY STREET...

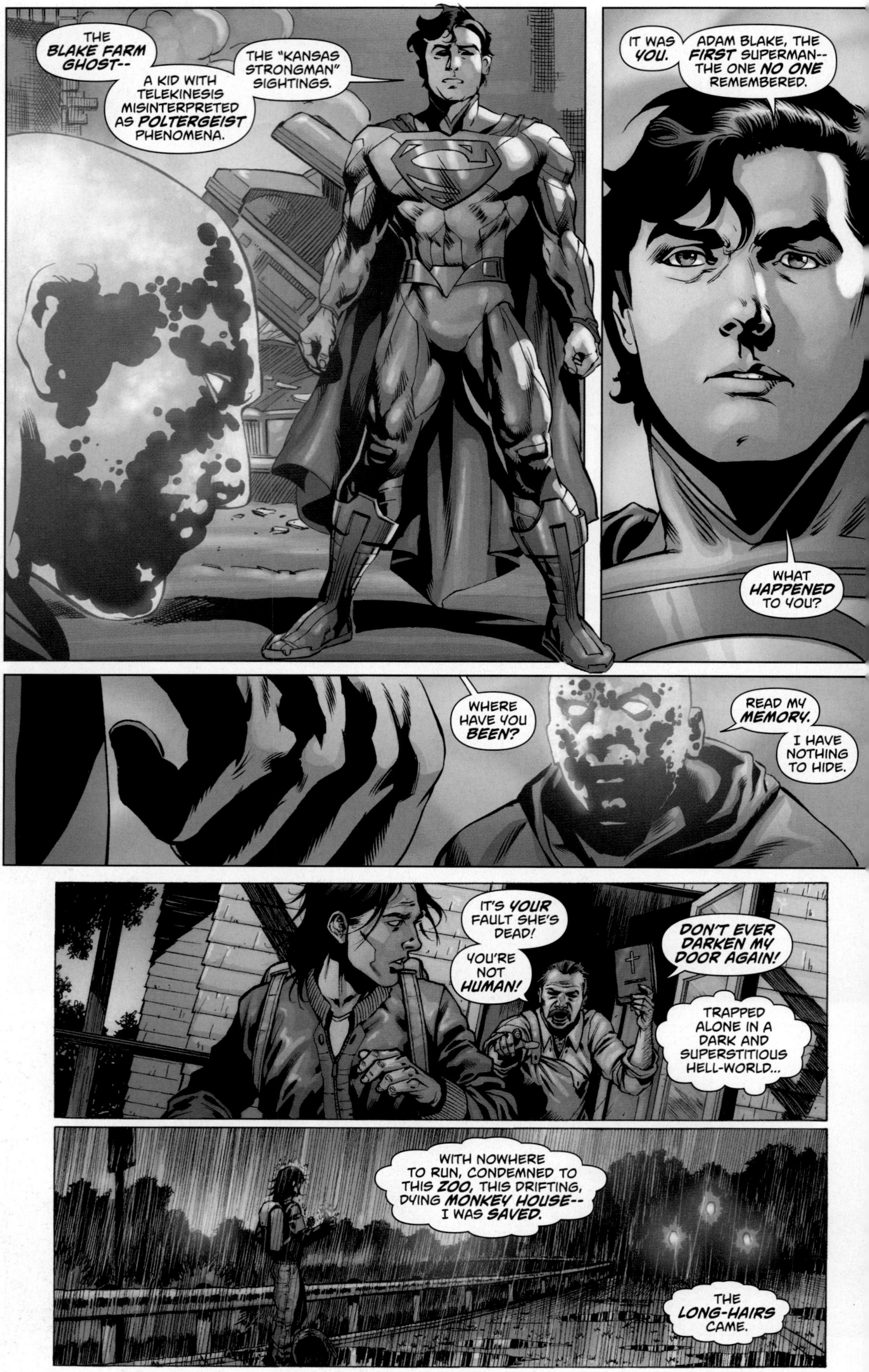
THE BLAKE FARM GHOST--
A KID WITH TELEKINESIS MISINTERPRETED AS POLTERGEIST PHENOMENA.
THE "KANSAS STRONGMAN" SIGHTINGS.
IT WAS YOU.
ADAM BLAKE, THE FIRST SUPERMAN-- THE ONE NO ONE REMEMBERED.
WHAT HAPPENED TO YOU?
WHERE HAVE YOU BEEN?
READ MY MEMORY.
I HAVE NOTHING TO HIDE.
IT'S YOUR FAULT SHE'S DEAD!
YOU'RE NOT HUMAN!
DON'T EVER DARKEN MY DOOR AGAIN!
TRAPPED ALONE IN A DARK AND SUPERSTITIOUS HELL-WORLD...
WITH NOWHERE TO RUN, CONDEMNED TO THIS ZOO, THIS DRIFTING, DYING MONKEY HOUSE-- I WAS SAVED.
THE LONG-HAIRS CAME.

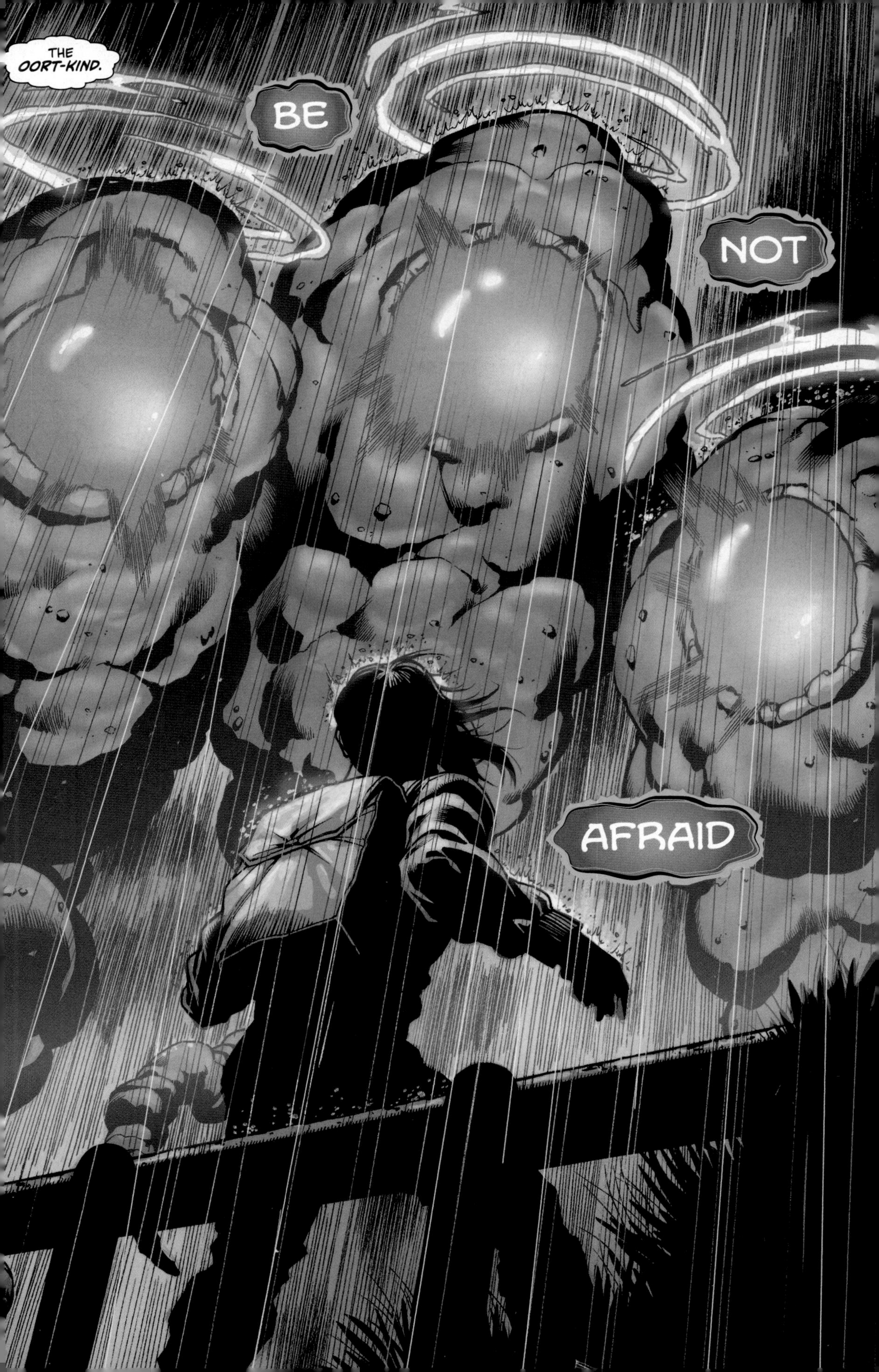
THE OORT-KIND.
BE
NOT
AFRAID

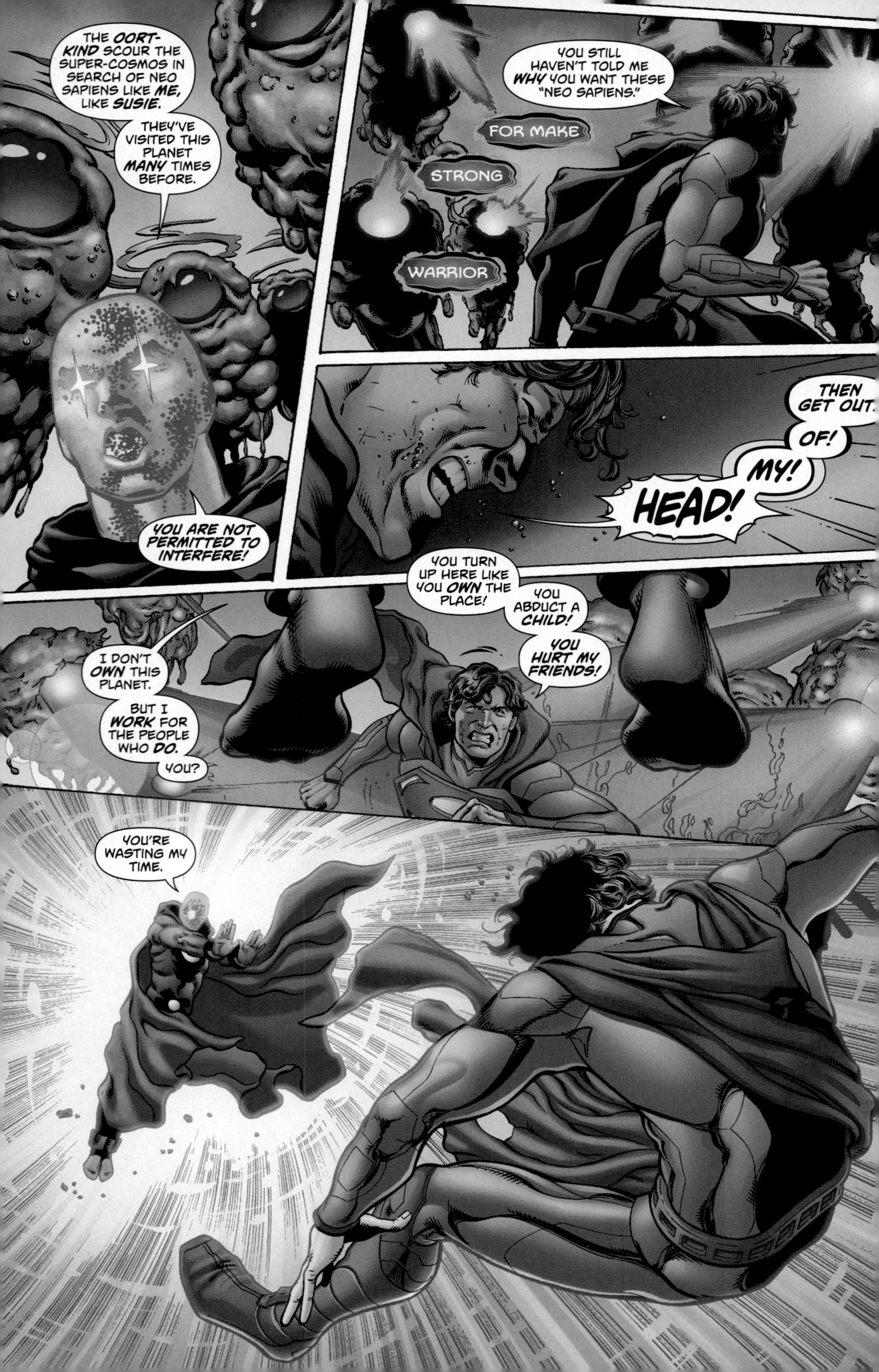
THE OORT-KIND SCOUR THE SUPER-COSMOS IN SEARCH OF NEO SAPIENS LIKE ME, LIKE SUSIE.
THEY'VE VISITED THIS PLANET MANY TIMES BEFORE.
YOU ARE NOT PERMITTED TO INTERFERE!
YOU STILL HAVEN'T TOLD ME WHY YOU WANT THESE "NEO SAPIENS."
FOR MAKE
STRONG
WARRIOR
THEN GET OUT.
OF!
MY!
HEAD!
YOU TURN UP HERE LIKE YOU OWN THE PLACE!
YOU ABDUCT A CHILD!
YOU HURT MY FRIENDS!
I DON'T OWN THIS PLANET.
BUT I WORK FOR THE PEOPLE WHO DO.
YOU?
YOU'RE WASTING MY TIME.

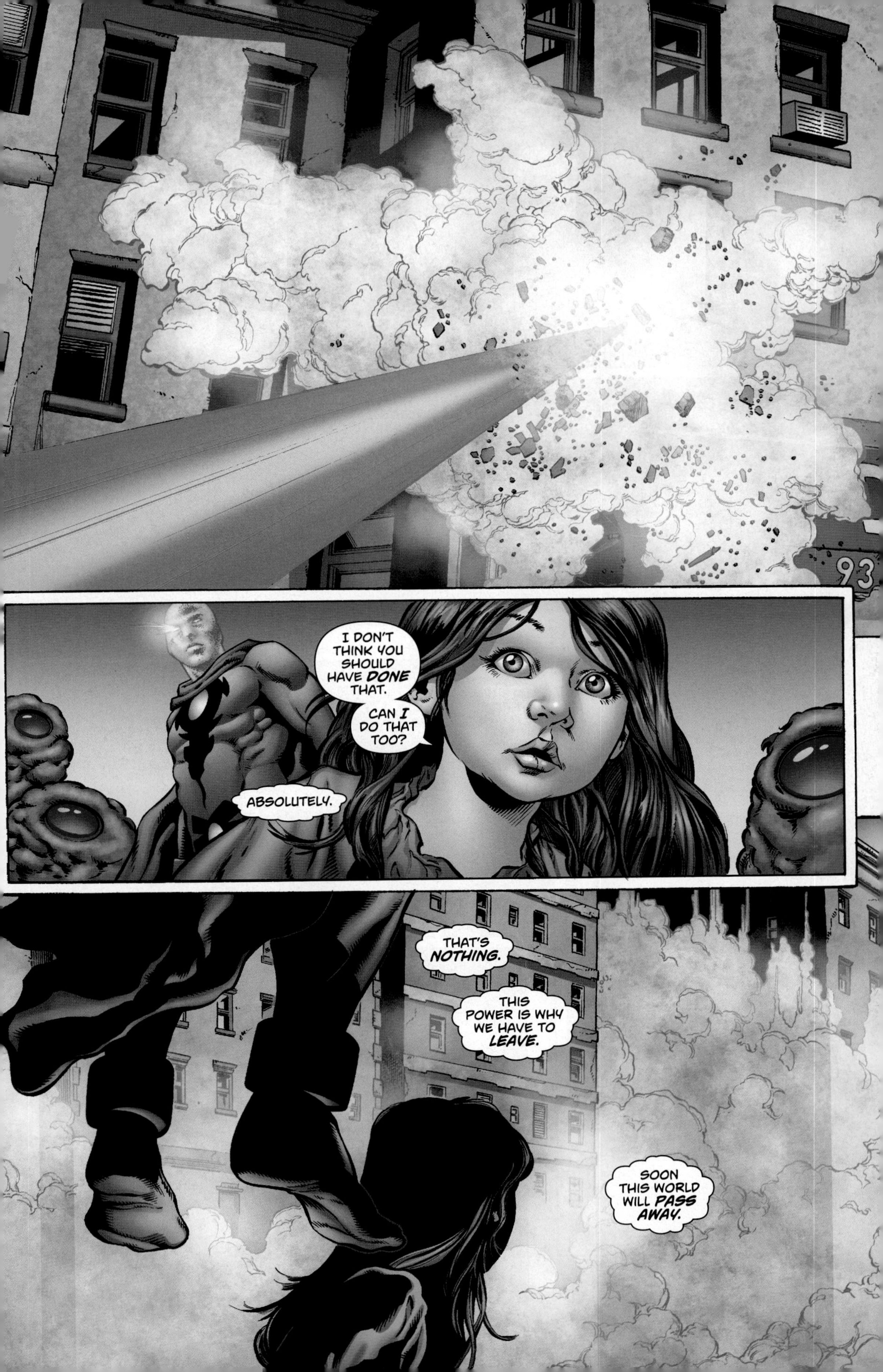
93
I DON'T THINK YOU SHOULD HAVE DONE THAT.
CAN I DO THAT TOO?
ABSOLUTELY.
THAT'S NOTHING.
THIS POWER IS WHY WE HAVE TO LEAVE.
SOON THIS WORLD WILL PASS AWAY.

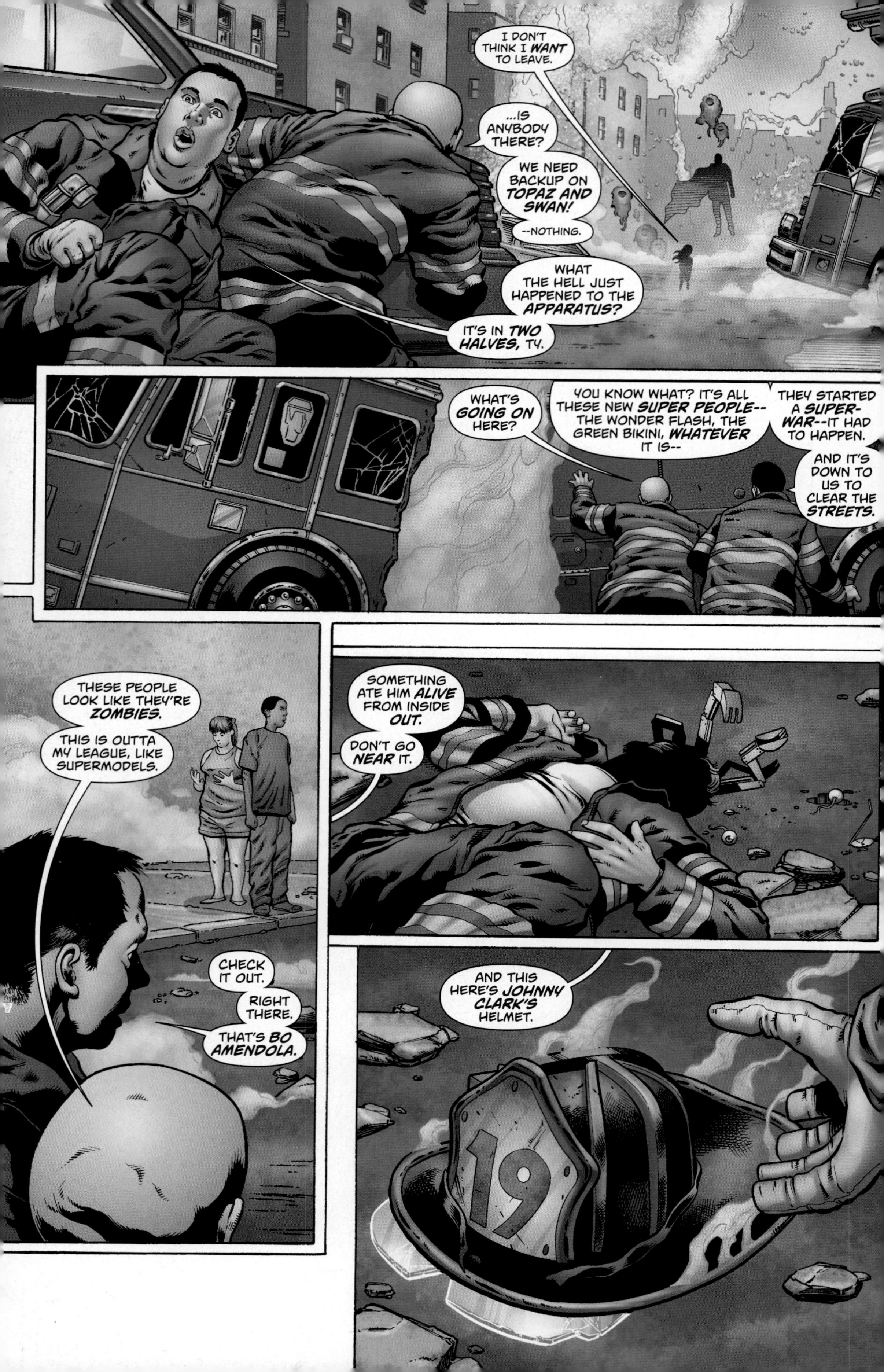
I DON'T THINK I WANT TO LEAVE.
...IS ANYBODY THERE?
WE NEED BACKUP ON TOPAZ AND SWAN!
--NOTHING.
WHAT THE HELL JUST HAPPENED TO THE APPARATUS?
IT'S IN TWO HALVES, TY.
WHAT'S GOING ON HERE?
YOU KNOW WHAT? IT'S ALL THESE NEW SUPER PEOPLE-- THE WONDER FLASH, THE GREEN BIKINI, WHATEVER IT IS--
THEY STARTED A SUPER-WAR--IT HAD TO HAPPEN.
AND IT'S DOWN TO US TO CLEAR THE STREETS.
THESE PEOPLE LOOK LIKE THEY'RE ZOMBIES.
THIS IS OUTTA MY LEAGUE, LIKE SUPERMODELS.
CHECK IT OUT.
RIGHT THERE.
THAT'S BO AMENDOLA.
SOMETHING ATE HIM ALIVE FROM INSIDE OUT.
DON'T GO NEAR IT.
AND THIS HERE'S JOHNNY CLARK'S HELMET.
19

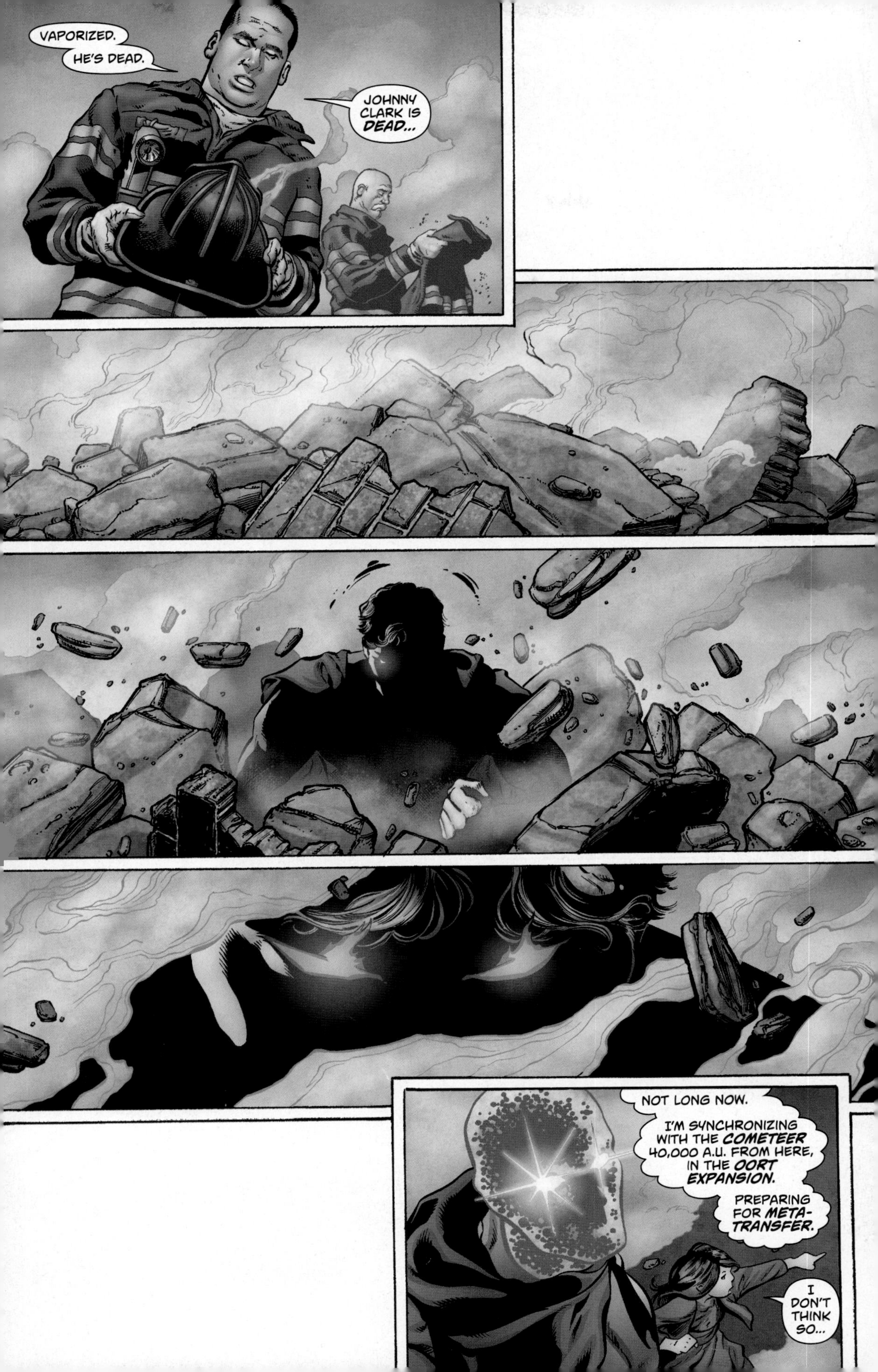

VAPORIZED.
HE'S DEAD.
JOHNNY CLARK IS DEAD...
NOT LONG NOW.
I'M SYNCHRONIZING WITH THE COMETEER 40,000 A.U. FROM HERE, IN THE OORT EXPANSION.
PREPARING FOR META-TRANSFER.
I DON'T THINK SO...

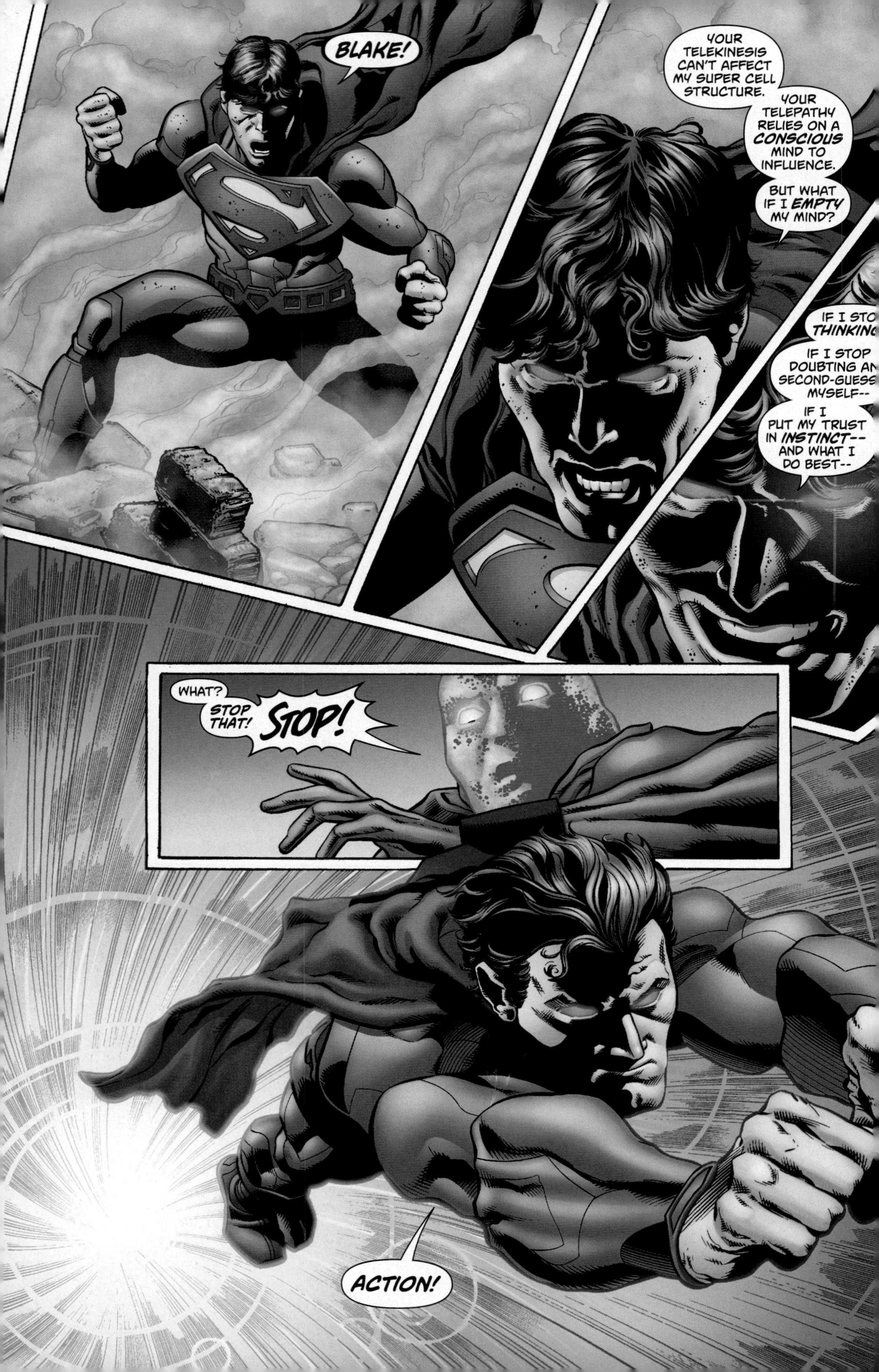
BLAKE!
YOUR TELEKINESIS CAN'T AFFECT MY SUPER CELL STRUCTURE.
YOUR TELEPATHY RELIES ON A CONSCIOUS MIND TO INFLUENCE.
BUT WHAT IF I EMPTY MY MIND?
IF I STOP THINKING
IF I STOP DOUBTING AND SECOND-GUESS MYSELF--
IF I PUT MY TRUST IN INSTINCT--
AND WHAT I DO BEST--
WHAT?
STOP THAT!
STOP!
ACTION!

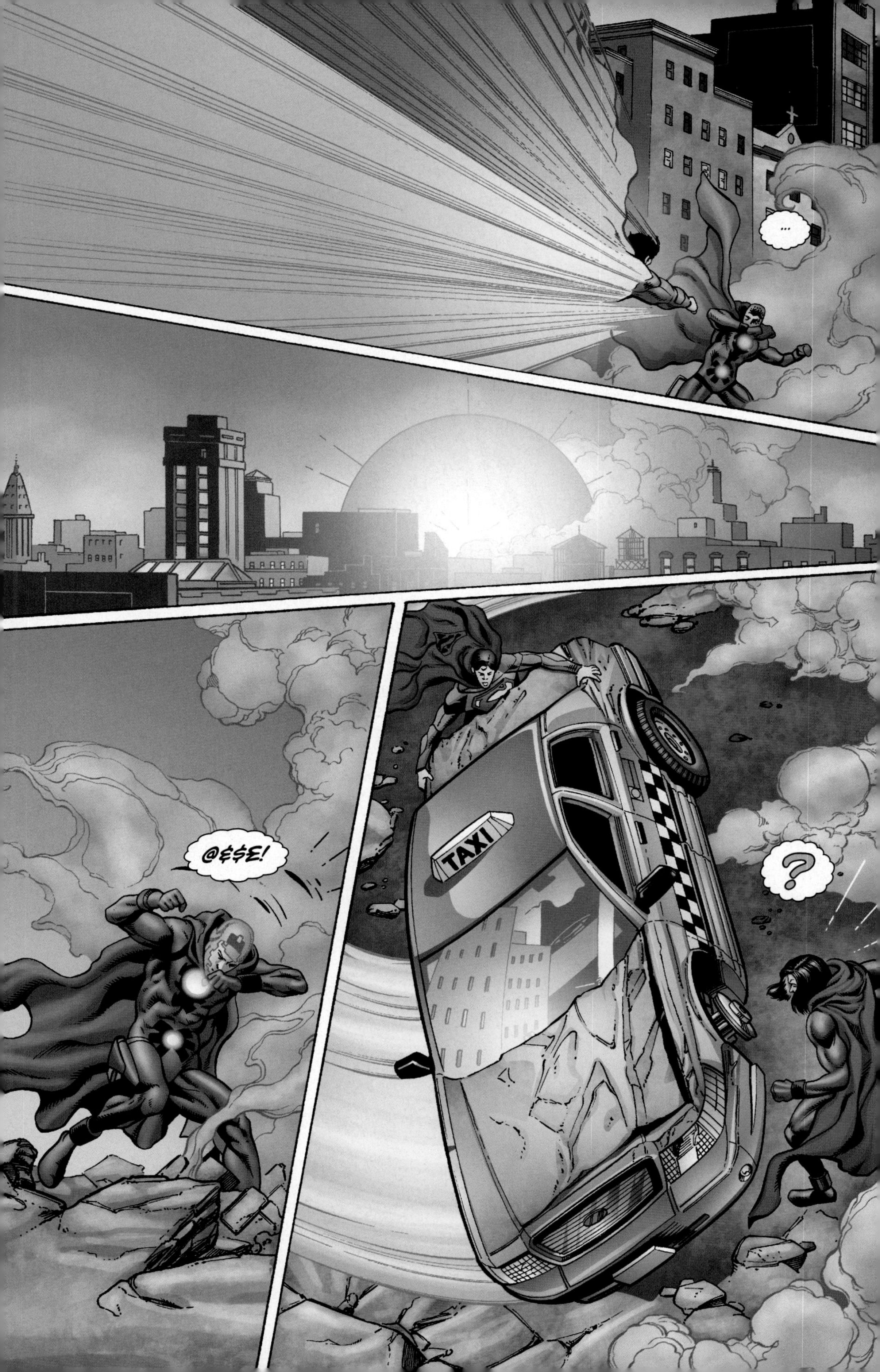
...
@¢$£!
?

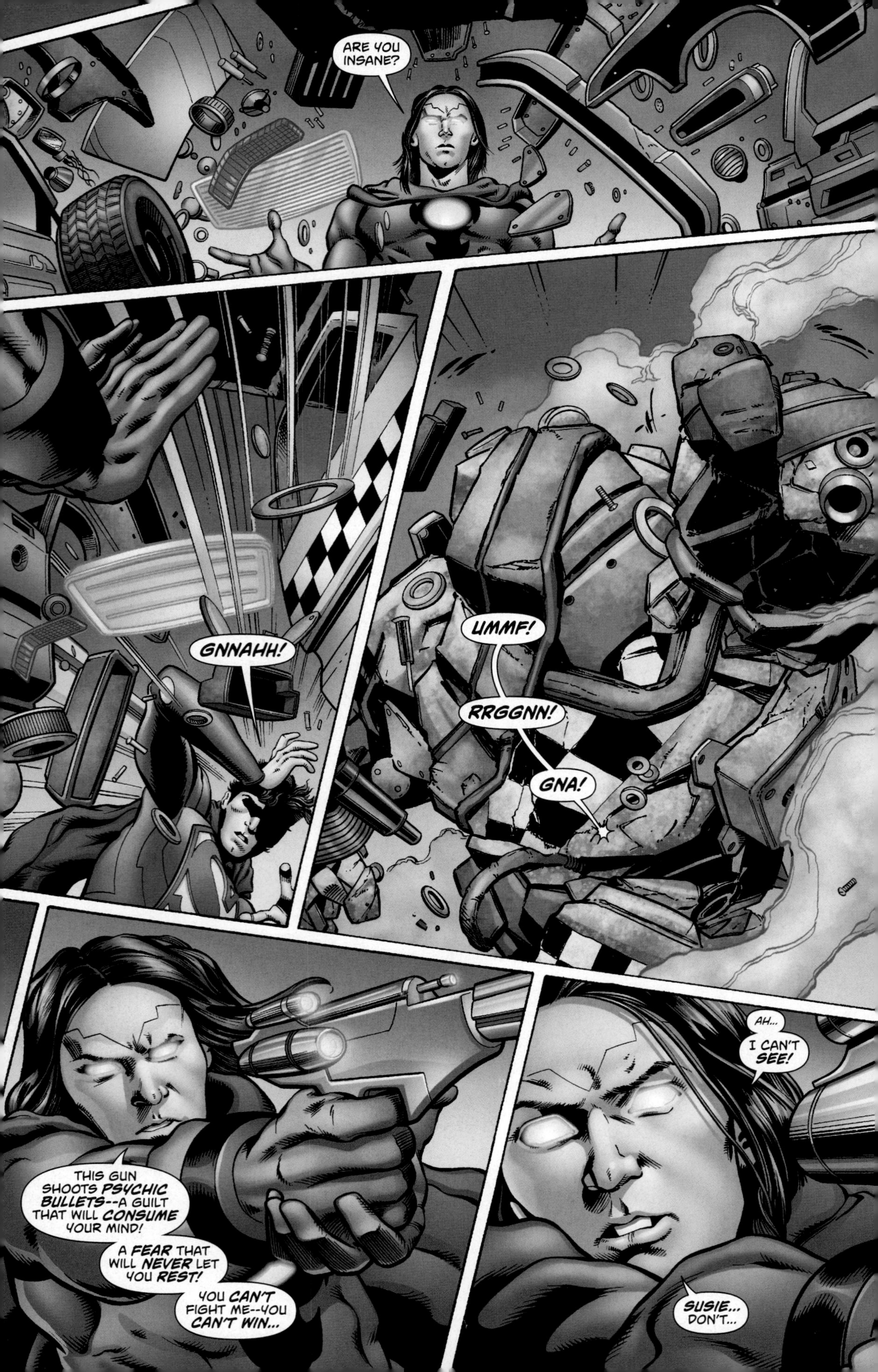
ARE YOU INSANE?
GNNAHH!
UMMF!
RRGGNN!
GNA!
THIS GUN SHOOTS PSYCHIC BULLETS--A GUILT THAT WILL CONSUME YOUR MIND!
A FEAR THAT WILL NEVER LET YOU REST!
YOU CAN'T FIGHT ME--YOU CAN'T WIN...
AH...
I CAN'T SEE!
SUSIE... DON'T...

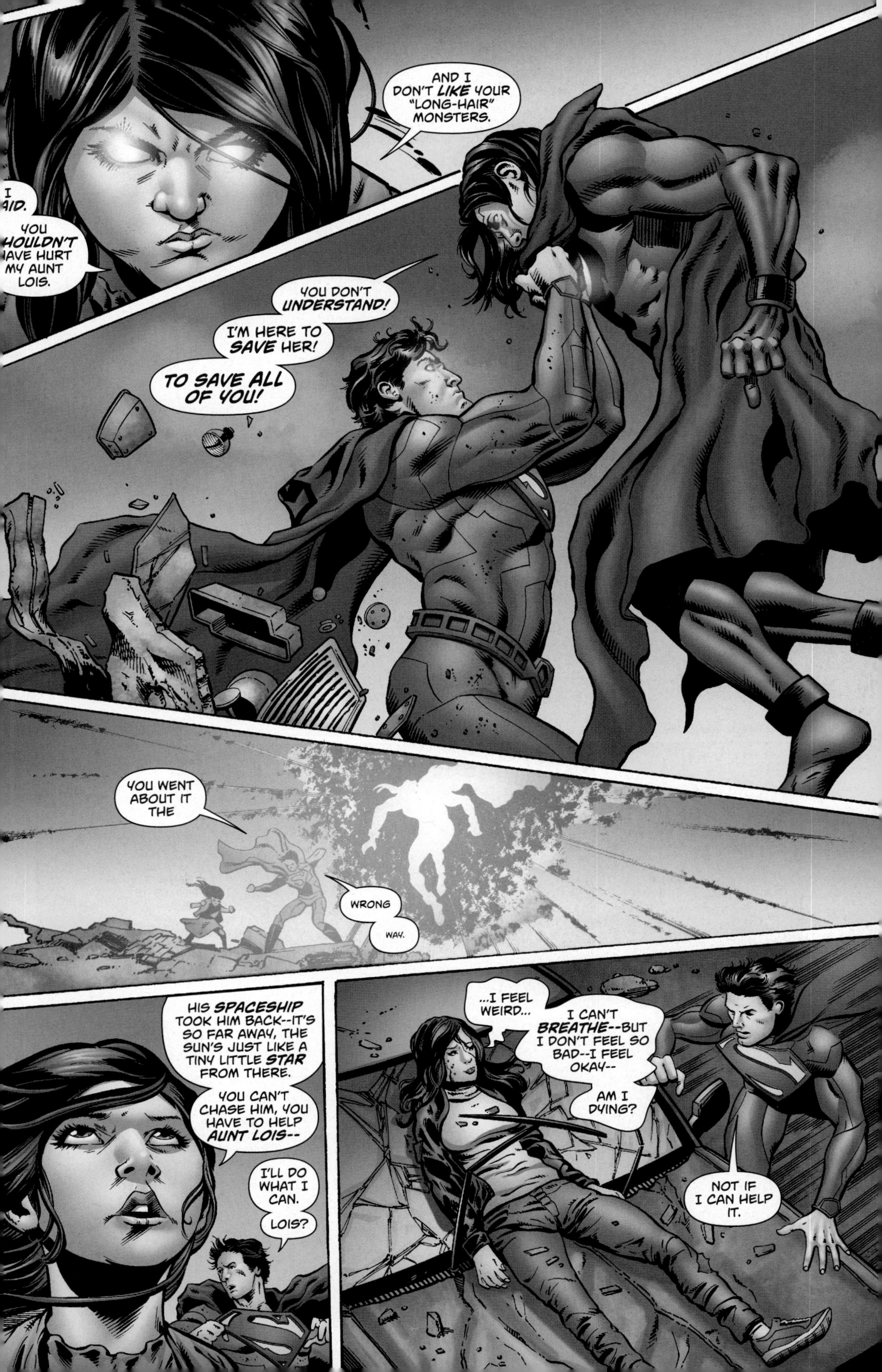
AND I DON'T LIKE YOUR "LONG-HAIR" MONSTERS.
I AID.
YOU HOULDN'T AVE HURT MY AUNT LOIS.
YOU DON'T UNDERSTAND!
I'M HERE TO SAVE HER!
TO SAVE ALL OF YOU!
YOU WENT ABOUT IT THE
WRONG
WAY.
HIS SPACESHIP TOOK HIM BACK--IT'S SO FAR AWAY, THE SUN'S JUST LIKE A TINY LITTLE STAR FROM THERE.
YOU CAN'T CHASE HIM, YOU HAVE TO HELP AUNT LOIS--
I'LL DO WHAT I CAN.
LOIS?
...I FEEL WEIRD...
I CAN'T BREATHE--BUT I DON'T FEEL SO BAD--I FEEL OKAY--
AM I DYING?
NOT IF I CAN HELP IT.

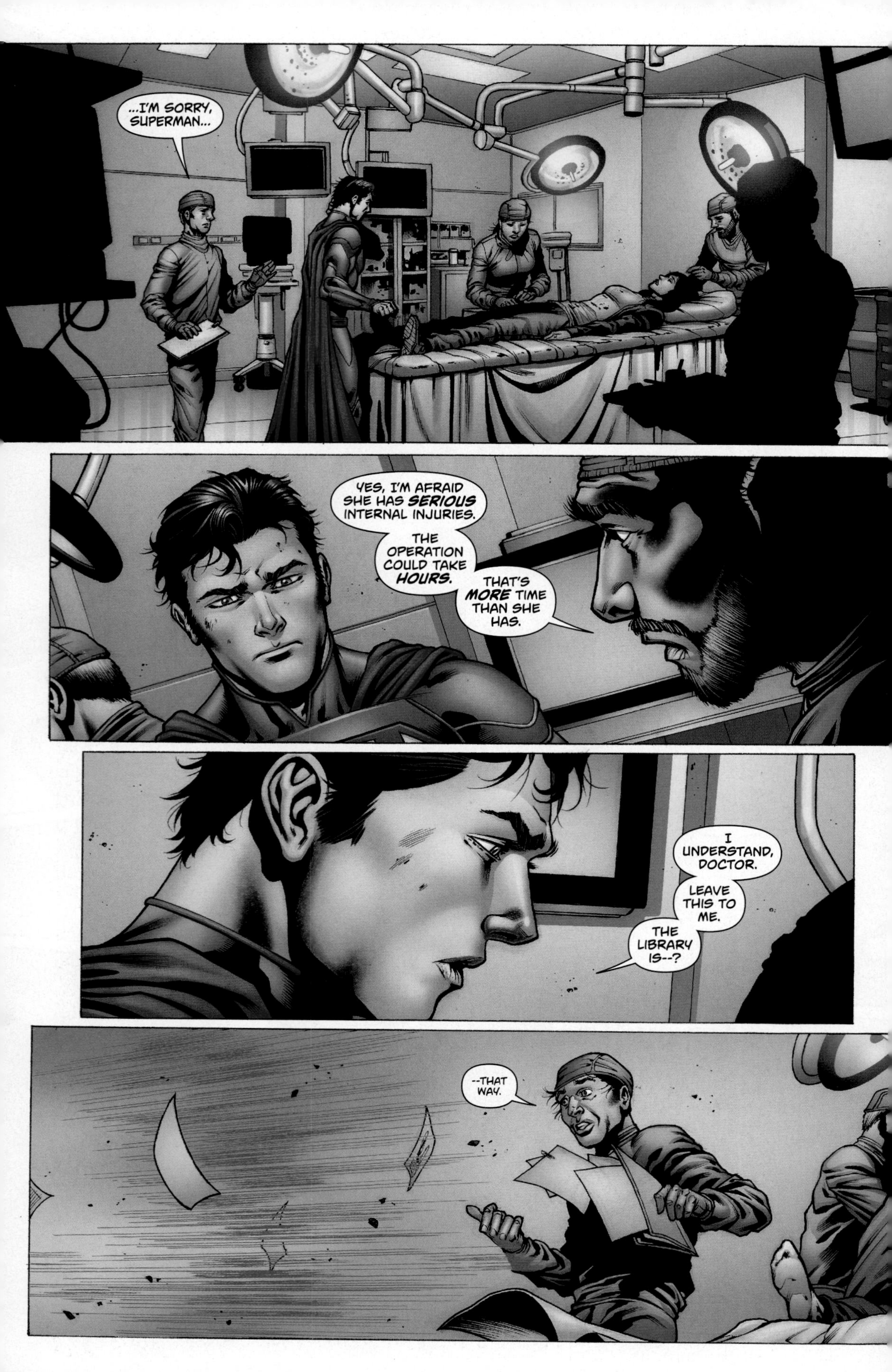
...I'M SORRY, SUPERMAN...
YES, I'M AFRAID SHE HAS SERIOUS INTERNAL INJURIES.
THE OPERATION COULD TAKE HOURS.
THAT'S MORE TIME THAN SHE HAS.
I UNDERSTAND, DOCTOR.
LEAVE THIS TO ME.
THE LIBRARY IS--?
--THAT WAY.

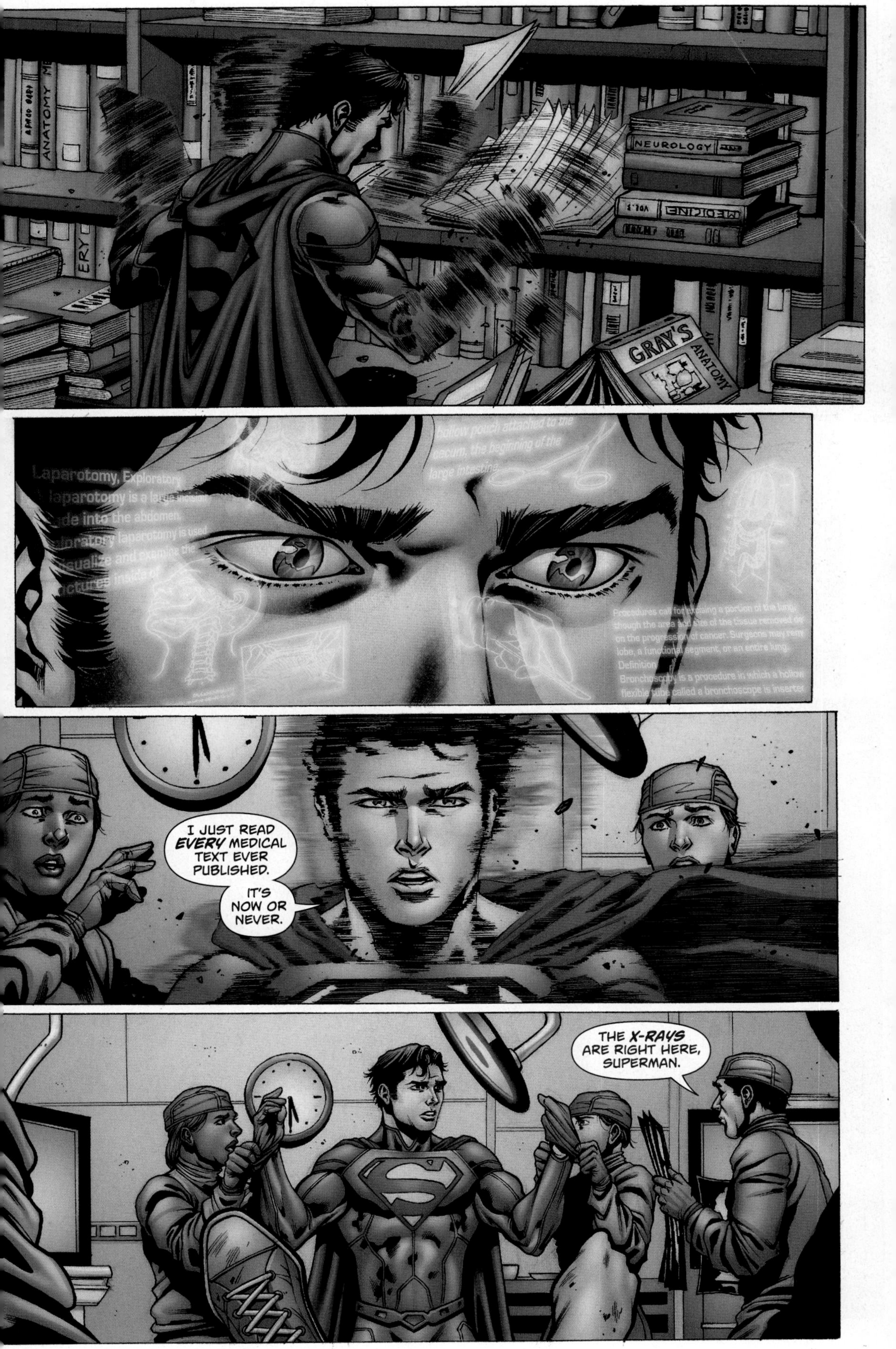

ANATOMY
NEUROLOGY
GRAY'S ANATOMY
Laparotomy, Exploratory
large intestine
I JUST READ *EVERY* MEDICAL TEXT EVER PUBLISHED.
IT'S NOW OR NEVER.
THE *X-RAYS* ARE RIGHT HERE, SUPERMAN.

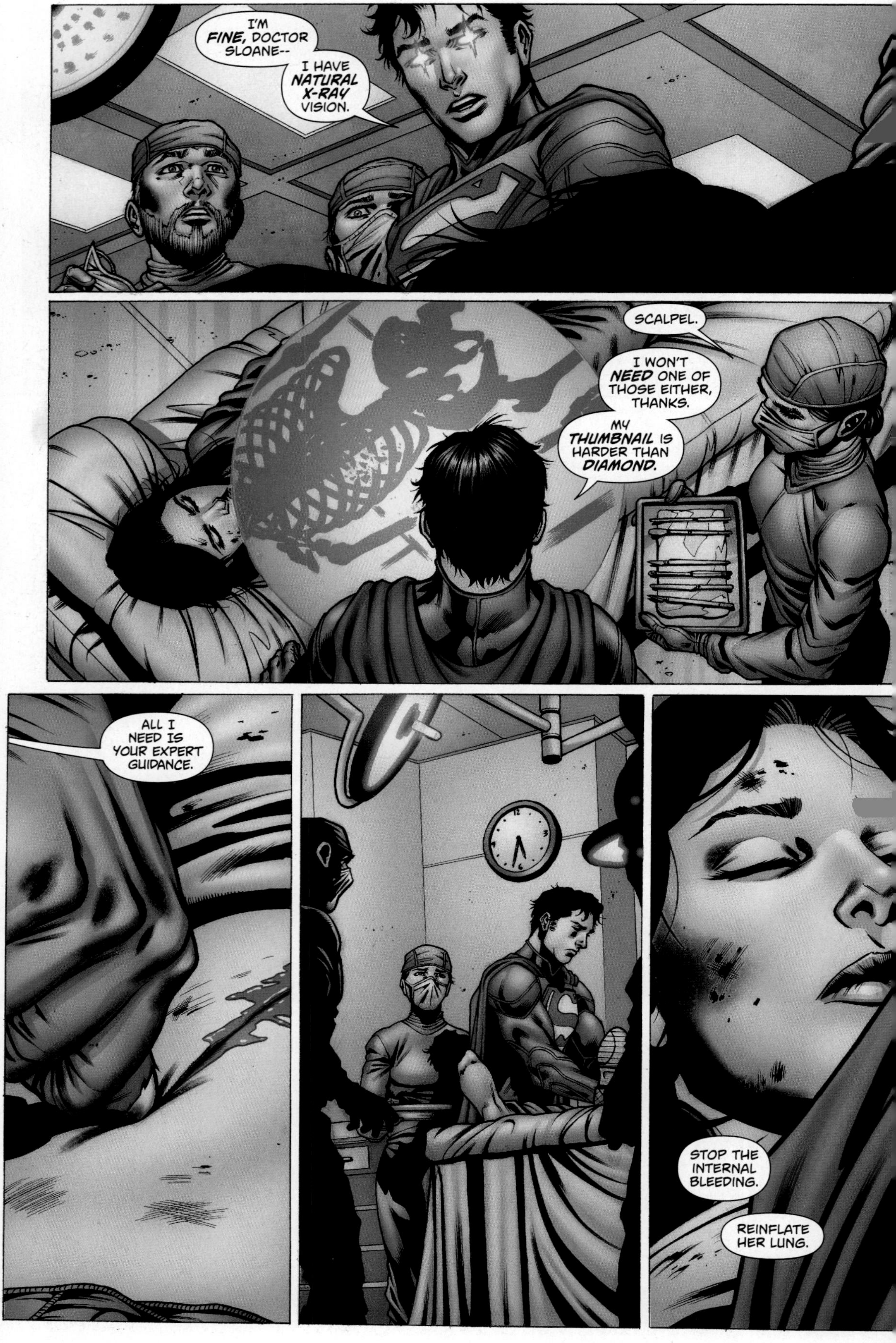

I'M FINE, DOCTOR SLOANE--
I HAVE NATURAL X-RAY VISION.
SCALPEL.
I WON'T NEED ONE OF THOSE EITHER, THANKS.
MY THUMBNAIL IS HARDER THAN DIAMOND.
ALL I NEED IS YOUR EXPERT GUIDANCE.
STOP THE INTERNAL BLEEDING.
REINFLATE HER LUNG.

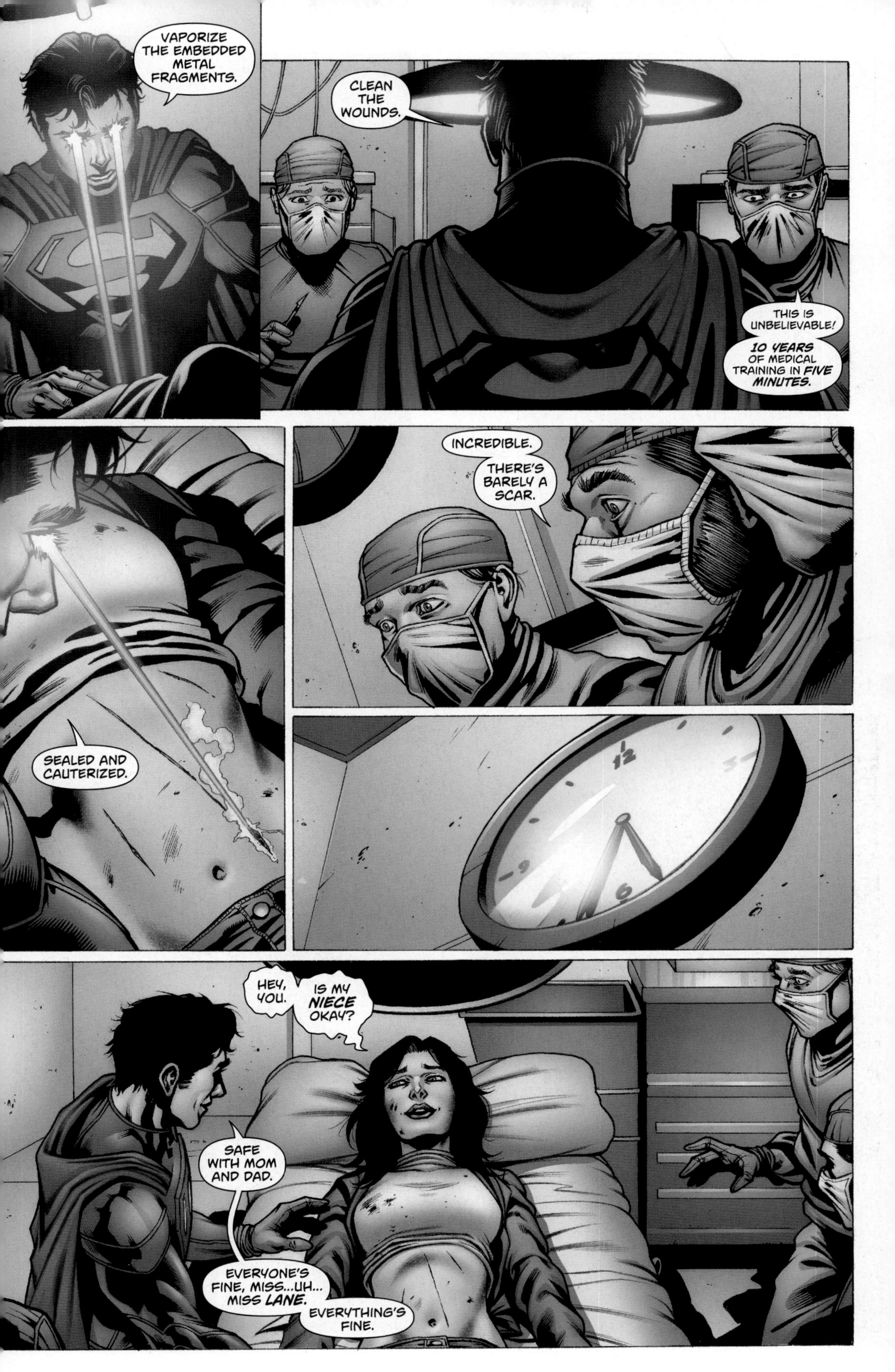
VAPORIZE THE EMBEDDED METAL FRAGMENTS.
CLEAN THE WOUNDS.
THIS IS UNBELIEVABLE!
10 YEARS OF MEDICAL TRAINING IN FIVE MINUTES.
SEALED AND CAUTERIZED.
INCREDIBLE.
THERE'S BARELY A SCAR.
HEY, YOU.
IS MY NIECE OKAY?
SAFE WITH MOM AND DAD.
EVERYONE'S FINE, MISS...UH... MISS LANE.
EVERYTHING'S FINE.

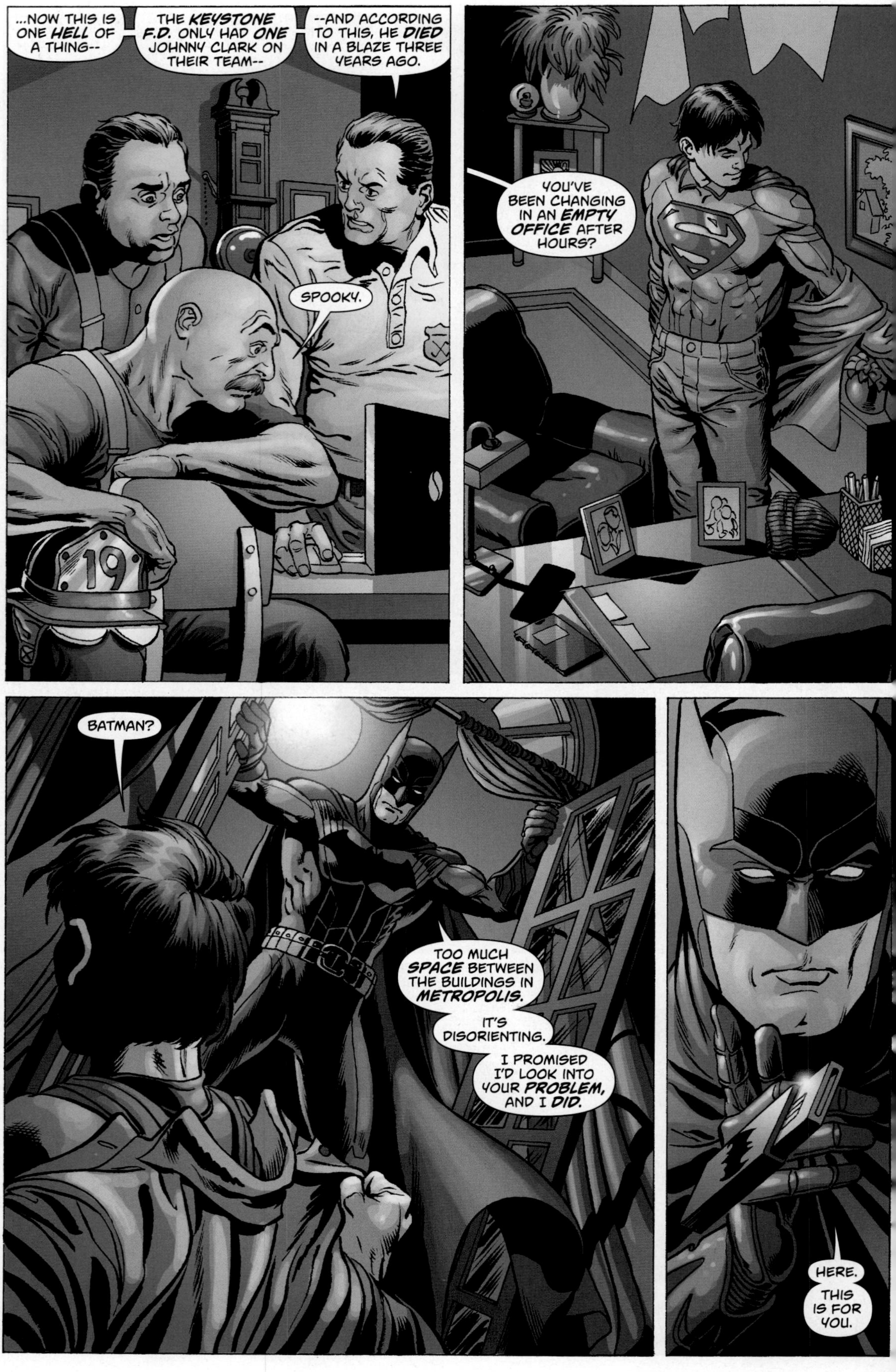
...NOW THIS IS ONE HELL OF A THING--
THE KEYSTONE F.D. ONLY HAD ONE JOHNNY CLARK ON THEIR TEAM--
--AND ACCORDING TO THIS, HE DIED IN A BLAZE THREE YEARS AGO.
SPOOKY.
YOU'VE BEEN CHANGING IN AN EMPTY OFFICE AFTER HOURS?
BATMAN?
TOO MUCH SPACE BETWEEN THE BUILDINGS IN METROPOLIS.
IT'S DISORIENTING.
I PROMISED I'D LOOK INTO YOUR PROBLEM, AND I DID.
HERE.
THIS IS FOR YOU.

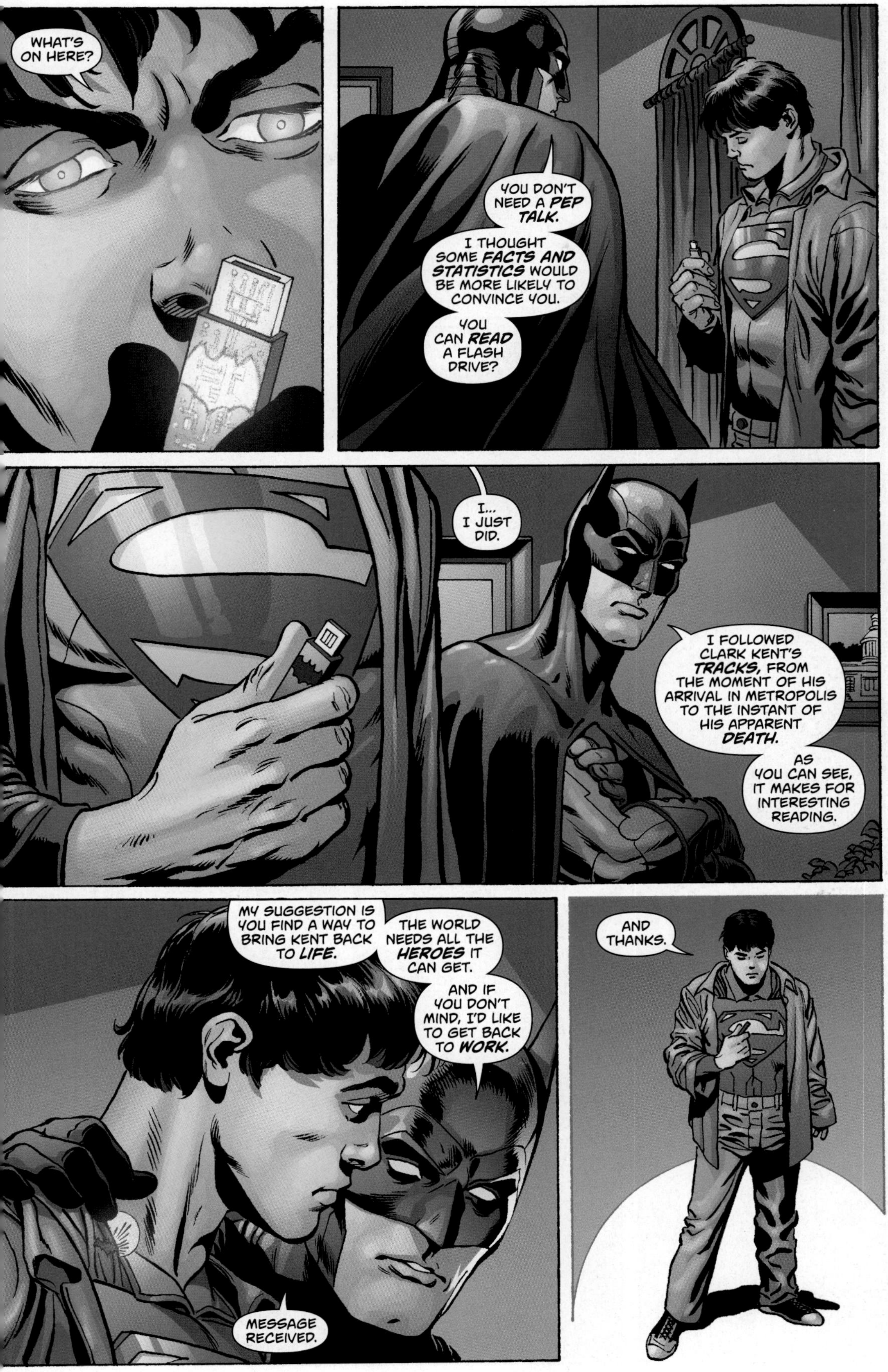
WHAT'S ON HERE?
YOU DON'T NEED A PEP TALK.
I THOUGHT SOME FACTS AND STATISTICS WOULD BE MORE LIKELY TO CONVINCE YOU.
YOU CAN READ A FLASH DRIVE?
I... I JUST DID.
I FOLLOWED CLARK KENT'S TRACKS, FROM THE MOMENT OF HIS ARRIVAL IN METROPOLIS TO THE INSTANT OF HIS APPARENT DEATH.
AS YOU CAN SEE, IT MAKES FOR INTERESTING READING.
MY SUGGESTION IS YOU FIND A WAY TO BRING KENT BACK TO LIFE.
THE WORLD NEEDS ALL THE HEROES IT CAN GET.
AND IF YOU DON'T MIND, I'D LIKE TO GET BACK TO WORK.
MESSAGE RECEIVED.
AND THANKS.

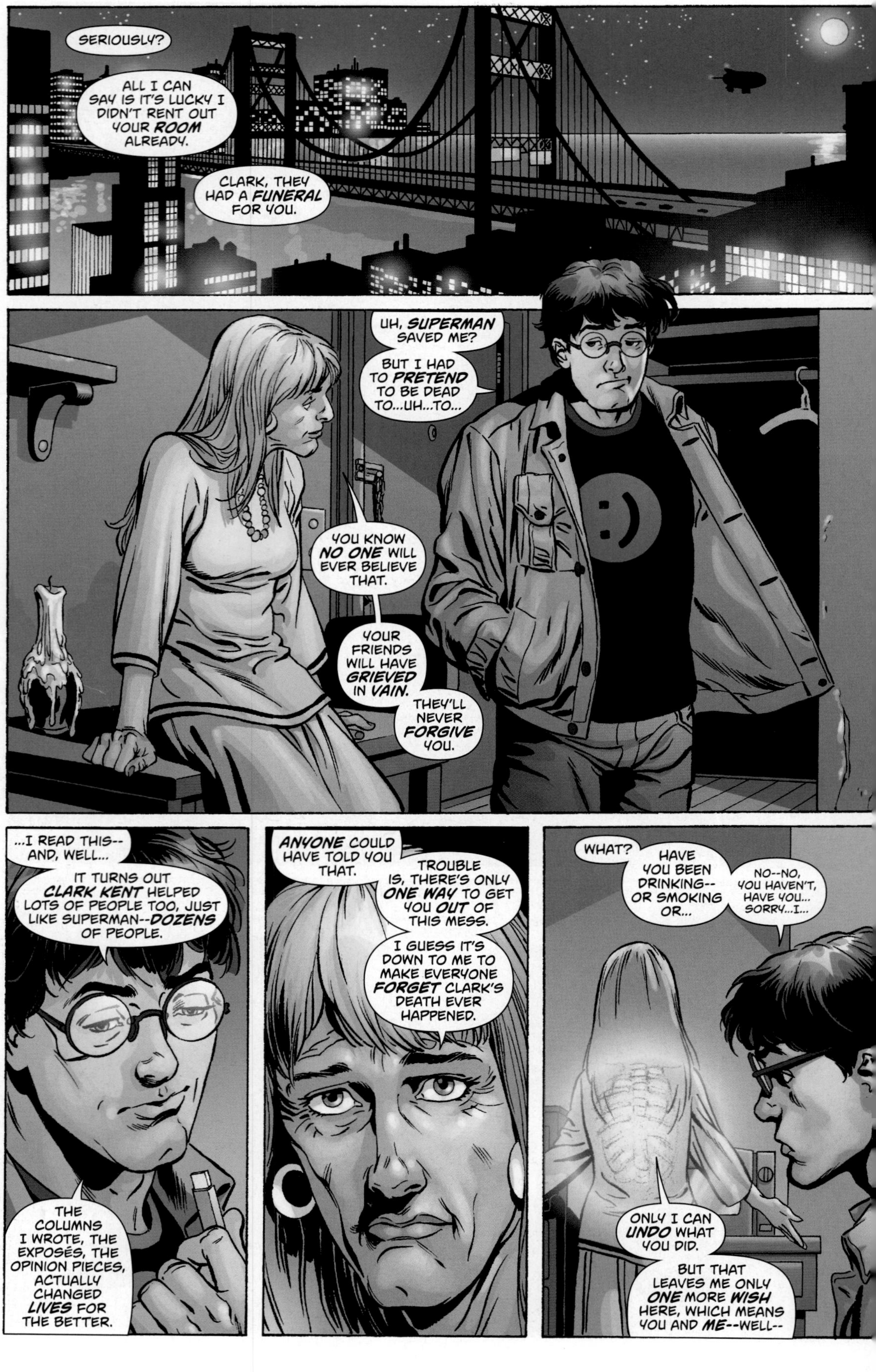
SERIOUSLY?
ALL I CAN SAY IS IT'S LUCKY I DIDN'T RENT OUT YOUR ROOM ALREADY.
CLARK, THEY HAD A FUNERAL FOR YOU.
UH, SUPERMAN SAVED ME?
BUT I HAD TO PRETEND TO BE DEAD TO...UH...TO...
YOU KNOW NO ONE WILL EVER BELIEVE THAT.
YOUR FRIENDS WILL HAVE GRIEVED IN VAIN.
THEY'LL NEVER FORGIVE YOU.
...I READ THIS-- AND, WELL...
IT TURNS OUT CLARK KENT HELPED LOTS OF PEOPLE TOO, JUST LIKE SUPERMAN--DOZENS OF PEOPLE.
THE COLUMNS I WROTE, THE EXPOSÉS, THE OPINION PIECES, ACTUALLY CHANGED LIVES FOR THE BETTER.
ANYONE COULD HAVE TOLD YOU THAT.
TROUBLE IS, THERE'S ONLY ONE WAY TO GET YOU OUT OF THIS MESS.
I GUESS IT'S DOWN TO ME TO MAKE EVERYONE FORGET CLARK'S DEATH EVER HAPPENED.
WHAT?
HAVE YOU BEEN DRINKING-- OR SMOKING OR...
NO--NO, YOU HAVEN'T, HAVE YOU... SORRY...I...
ONLY I CAN UNDO WHAT YOU DID.
BUT THAT LEAVES ME ONLY ONE MORE WISH HERE, WHICH MEANS YOU AND ME--WELL--

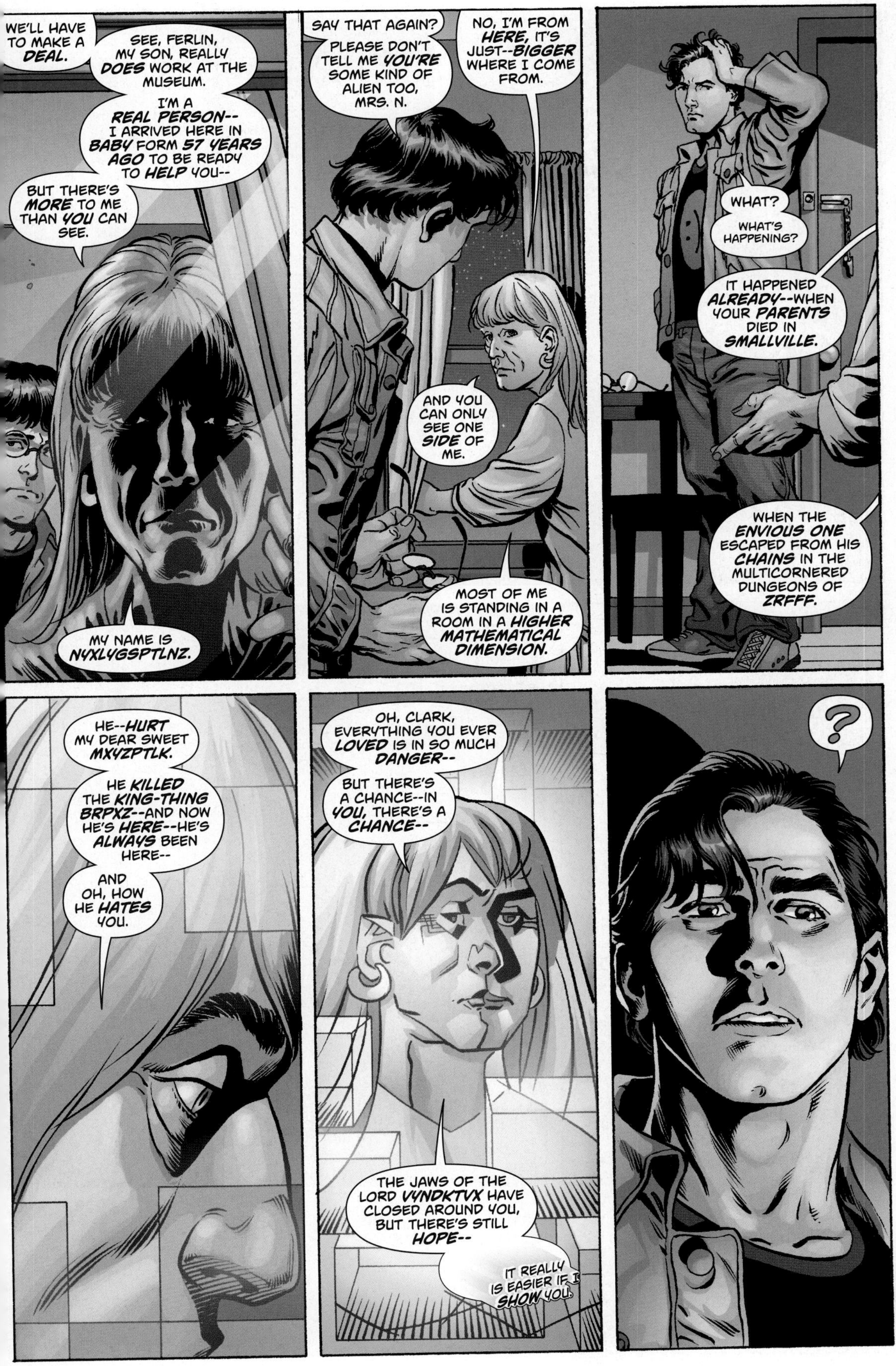
WE'LL HAVE TO MAKE A DEAL.
SEE, FERLIN, MY SON, REALLY DOES WORK AT THE MUSEUM.
I'M A REAL PERSON-- I ARRIVED HERE IN BABY FORM 57 YEARS AGO TO BE READY TO HELP YOU--
BUT THERE'S MORE TO ME THAN YOU CAN SEE.
MY NAME IS NYXLYGSPTLNZ.
SAY THAT AGAIN?
PLEASE DON'T TELL ME YOU'RE SOME KIND OF ALIEN TOO, MRS. N.
NO, I'M FROM HERE, IT'S JUST--BIGGER WHERE I COME FROM.
AND YOU CAN ONLY SEE ONE SIDE OF ME.
MOST OF ME IS STANDING IN A ROOM IN A HIGHER MATHEMATICAL DIMENSION.
WHAT?
WHAT'S HAPPENING?
IT HAPPENED ALREADY--WHEN YOUR PARENTS DIED IN SMALLVILLE.
WHEN THE ENVIOUS ONE ESCAPED FROM HIS CHAINS IN THE MULTICORNERED DUNGEONS OF ZRFFF.
HE--HURT MY DEAR SWEET MXYZPTLK.
HE KILLED THE KING-THING BRPXZ--AND NOW HE'S HERE--HE'S ALWAYS BEEN HERE--
AND OH, HOW HE HATES YOU.
OH, CLARK, EVERYTHING YOU EVER LOVED IS IN SO MUCH DANGER--
BUT THERE'S A CHANCE--IN YOU, THERE'S A CHANCE--
THE JAWS OF THE LORD VYNDKTVX HAVE CLOSED AROUND YOU, BUT THERE'S STILL HOPE--
IT REALLY IS EASIER IF I SHOW YOU.
?

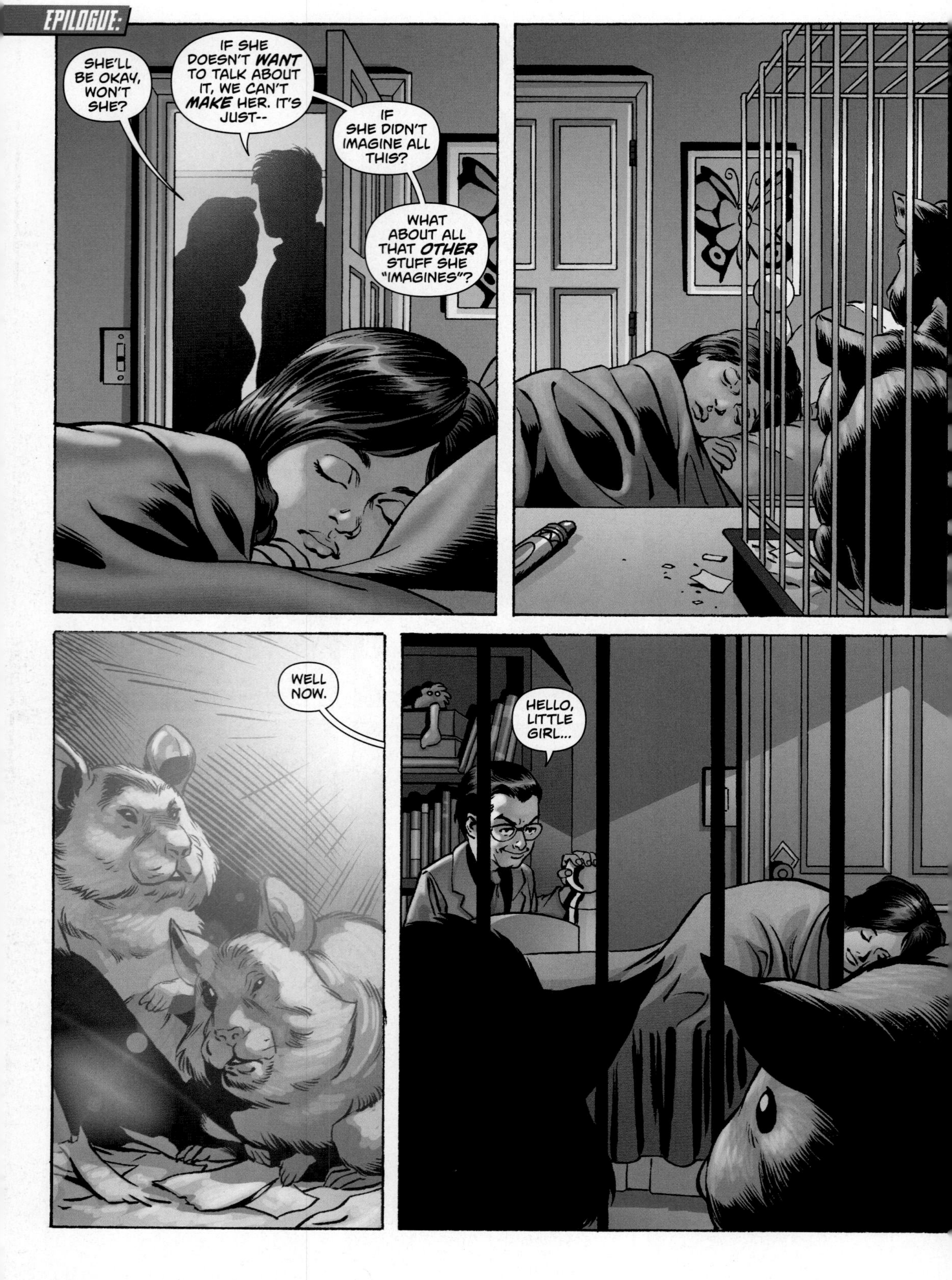
EPILOGUE:
SHE'LL BE OKAY, WON'T SHE?
IF SHE DOESN'T WANT TO TALK ABOUT IT, WE CAN'T MAKE HER. IT'S JUST--
IF SHE DIDN'T IMAGINE ALL THIS?
WHAT ABOUT ALL THAT OTHER STUFF SHE "IMAGINES"?
WELL NOW.
HELLO, LITTLE GIRL...

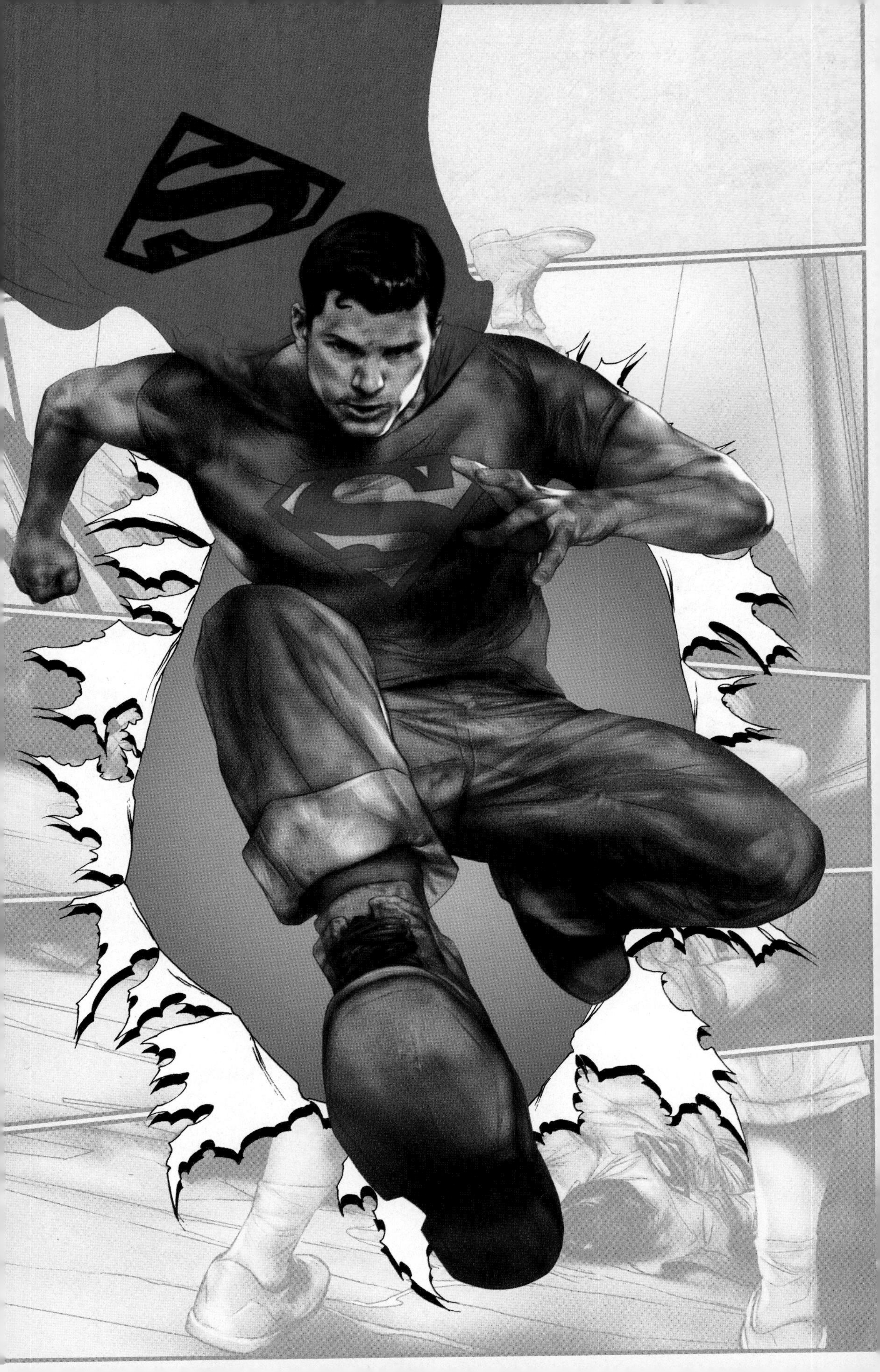

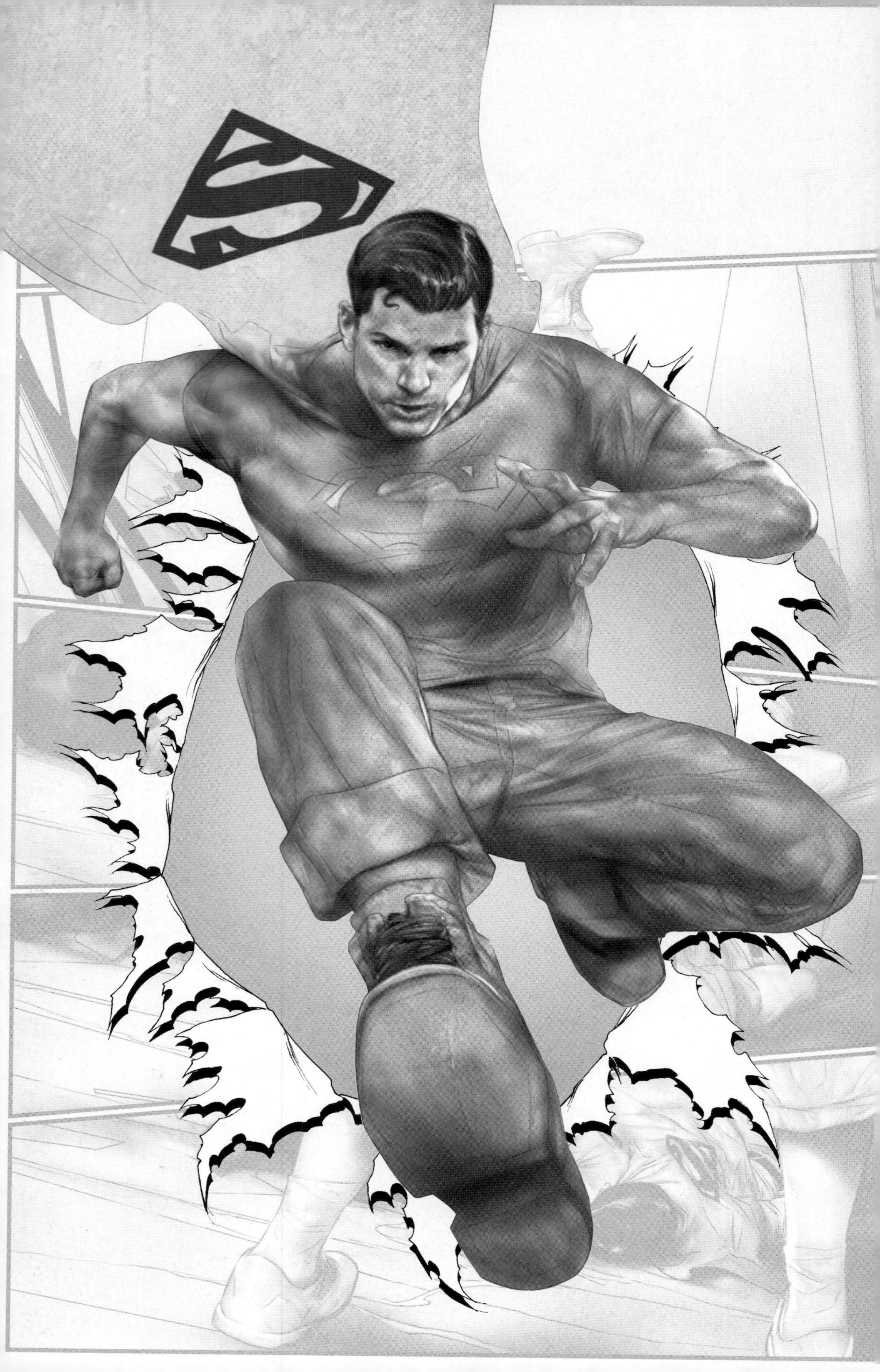

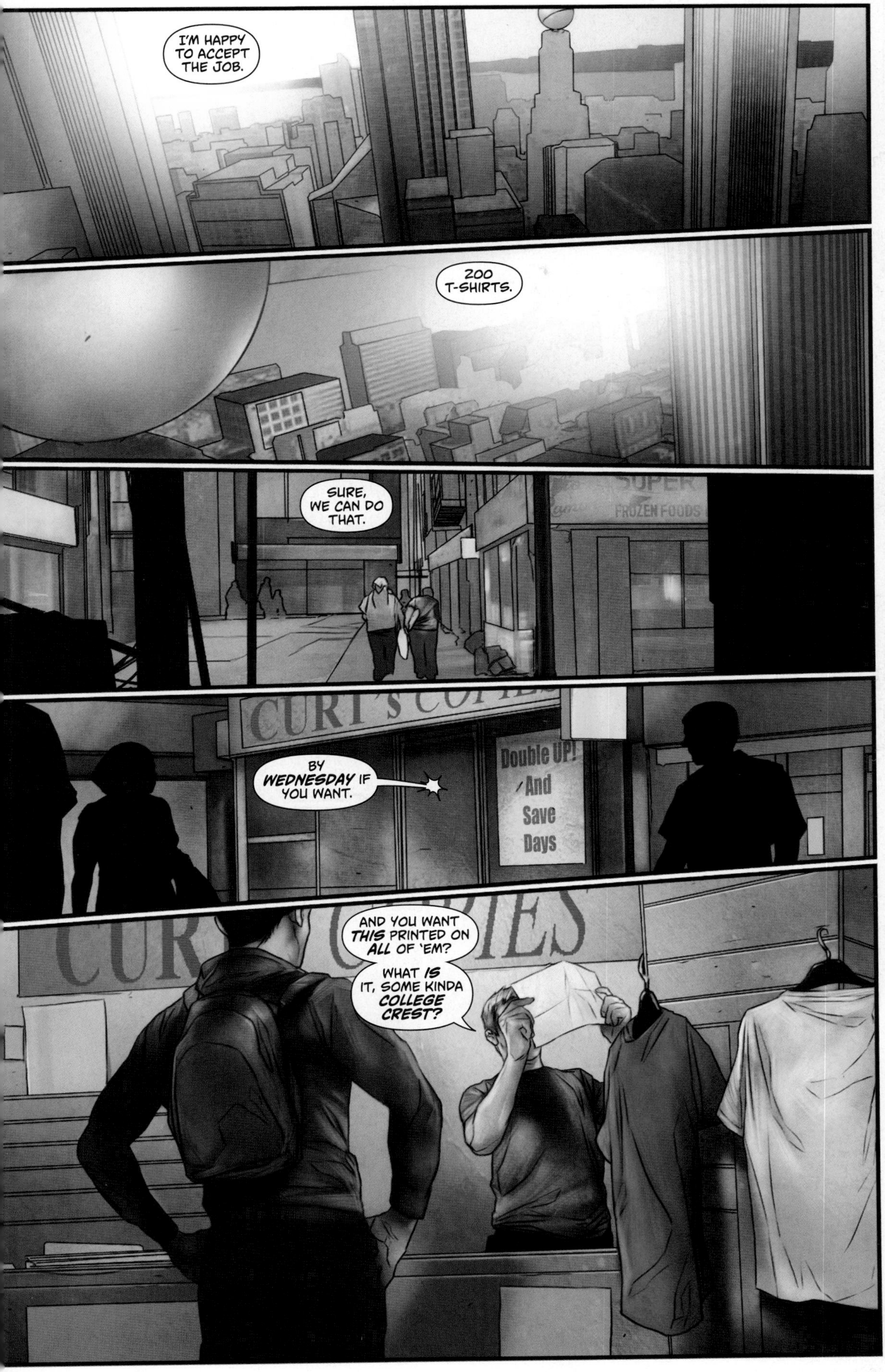
I'M HAPPY TO ACCEPT THE JOB.
200 T-SHIRTS.
SURE, WE CAN DO THAT.
SUPER
FROZEN FOODS
CURT'S COPIES
BY WEDNESDAY IF YOU WANT.
Double UP! And Save Days
AND YOU WANT THIS PRINTED ON ALL OF 'EM?
WHAT IS IT, SOME KINDA COLLEGE CREST?

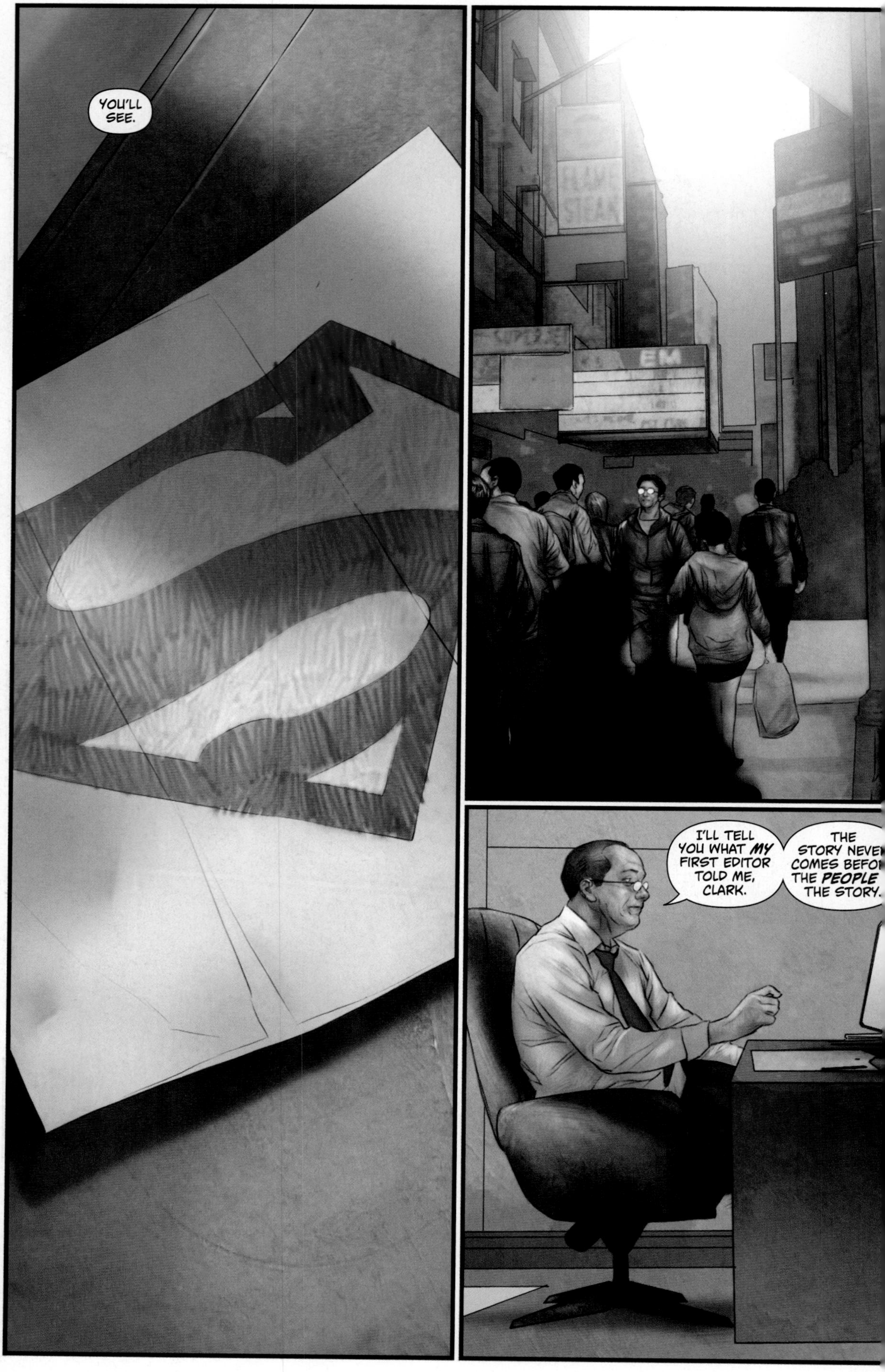
YOU'LL SEE.
I'LL TELL YOU WHAT *MY* FIRST EDITOR TOLD ME, CLARK.
THE STORY NEVE COMES BEFO THE *PEOPLE* THE STORY.

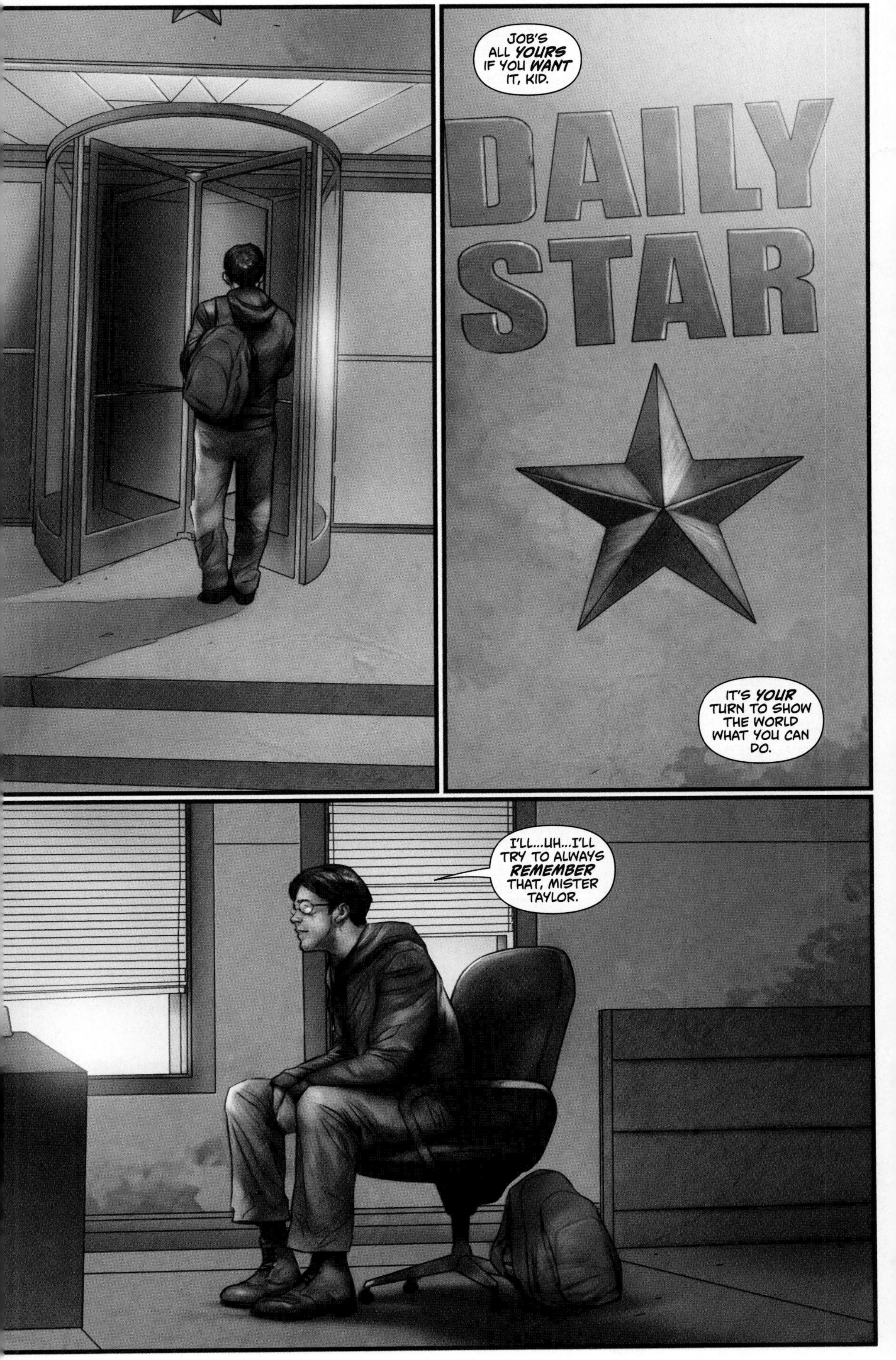
JOB'S ALL YOURS IF YOU WANT IT, KID.
DAILY STAR
IT'S YOUR TURN TO SHOW THE WORLD WHAT YOU CAN DO.
I'LL...UH...I'LL TRY TO ALWAYS REMEMBER THAT, MISTER TAYLOR.

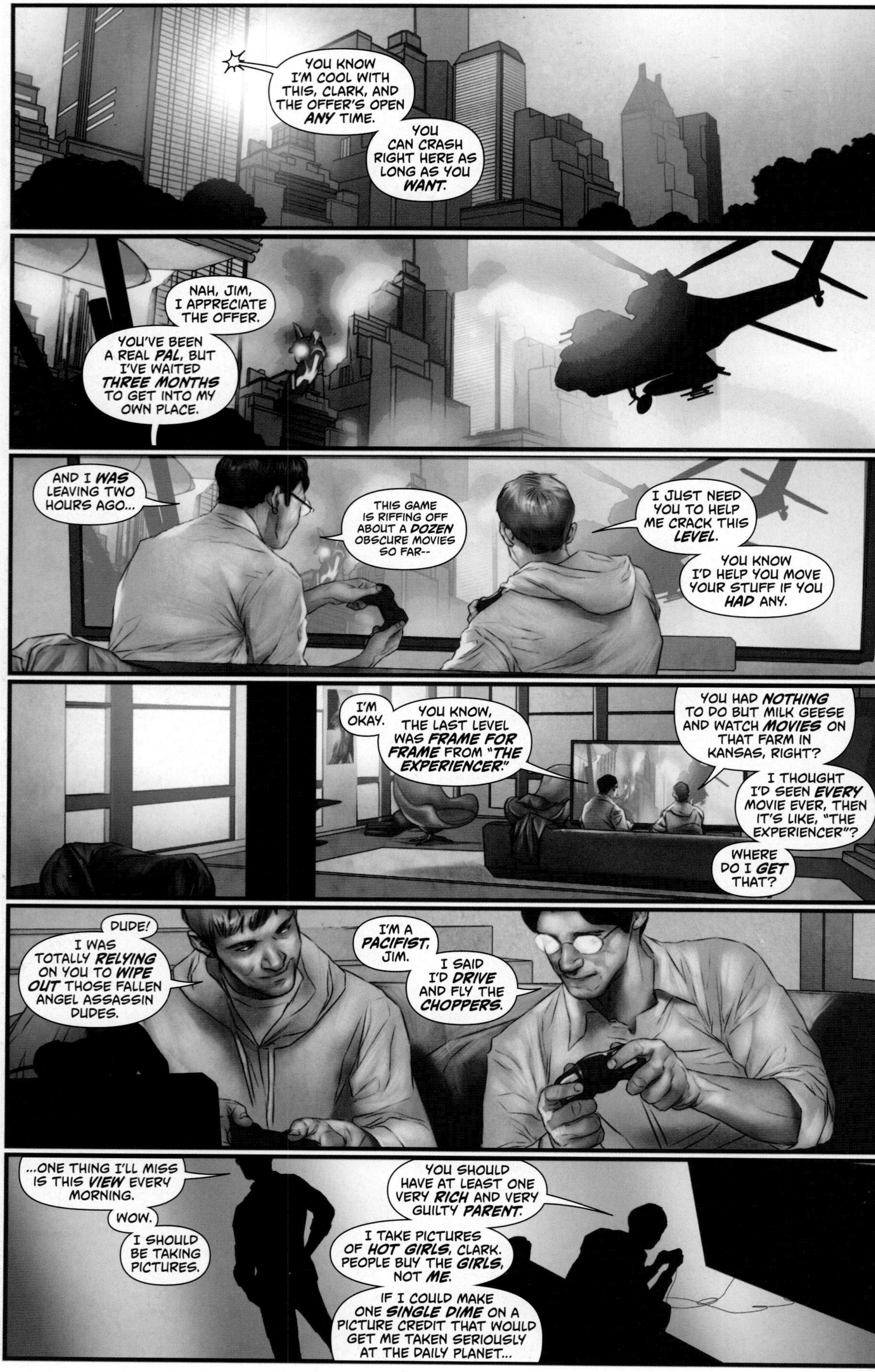
YOU KNOW I'M COOL WITH THIS, CLARK, AND THE OFFER'S OPEN ANY TIME.
YOU CAN CRASH RIGHT HERE AS LONG AS YOU WANT.
NAH, JIM, I APPRECIATE THE OFFER.
YOU'VE BEEN A REAL PAL, BUT I'VE WAITED THREE MONTHS TO GET INTO MY OWN PLACE.
AND I WAS LEAVING TWO HOURS AGO...
THIS GAME IS RIFFING OFF ABOUT A DOZEN OBSCURE MOVIES SO FAR--
I JUST NEED YOU TO HELP ME CRACK THIS LEVEL.
YOU KNOW I'D HELP YOU MOVE YOUR STUFF IF YOU HAD ANY.
I'M OKAY.
YOU KNOW, THE LAST LEVEL WAS FRAME FOR FRAME FROM "THE EXPERIENCER."
YOU HAD NOTHING TO DO BUT MILK GEESE AND WATCH MOVIES ON THAT FARM IN KANSAS, RIGHT?
I THOUGHT I'D SEEN EVERY MOVIE EVER, THEN IT'S LIKE, "THE EXPERIENCER"?
WHERE DO I GET THAT?
DUDE!
I WAS TOTALLY RELYING ON YOU TO WIPE OUT THOSE FALLEN ANGEL ASSASSIN DUDES.
I'M A PACIFIST, JIM.
I SAID I'D DRIVE AND FLY THE CHOPPERS.
...ONE THING I'LL MISS IS THIS VIEW EVERY MORNING.
WOW.
I SHOULD BE TAKING PICTURES.
YOU SHOULD HAVE AT LEAST ONE VERY RICH AND VERY GUILTY PARENT.
I TAKE PICTURES OF HOT GIRLS, CLARK. PEOPLE BUY THE GIRLS, NOT ME.
IF I COULD MAKE ONE SINGLE DIME ON A PICTURE CREDIT THAT WOULD GET ME TAKEN SERIOUSLY AT THE DAILY PLANET...

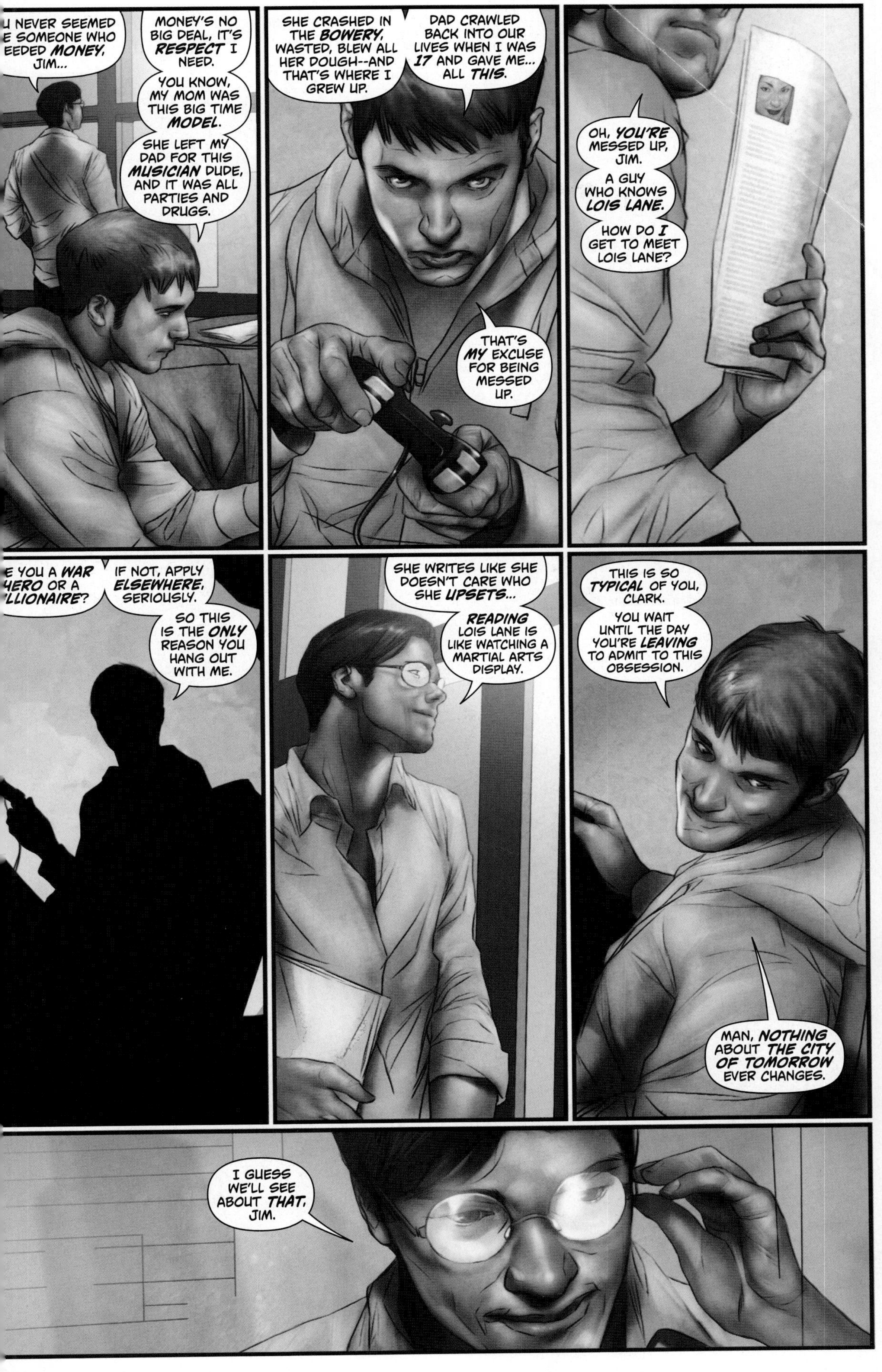
U NEVER SEEMED E SOMEONE WHO EEDED MONEY, JIM...
MONEY'S NO BIG DEAL, IT'S RESPECT I NEED.
YOU KNOW, MY MOM WAS THIS BIG TIME MODEL.
SHE LEFT MY DAD FOR THIS MUSICIAN DUDE, AND IT WAS ALL PARTIES AND DRUGS.
SHE CRASHED IN THE BOWERY, WASTED, BLEW ALL HER DOUGH--AND THAT'S WHERE I GREW UP.
DAD CRAWLED BACK INTO OUR LIVES WHEN I WAS 17 AND GAVE ME... ALL THIS.
THAT'S MY EXCUSE FOR BEING MESSED UP.
OH, YOU'RE MESSED UP, JIM.
A GUY WHO KNOWS LOIS LANE.
HOW DO I GET TO MEET LOIS LANE?
E YOU A WAR HERO OR A LLIONAIRE?
IF NOT, APPLY ELSEWHERE, SERIOUSLY.
SO THIS IS THE ONLY REASON YOU HANG OUT WITH ME.
SHE WRITES LIKE SHE DOESN'T CARE WHO SHE UPSETS...
READING LOIS LANE IS LIKE WATCHING A MARTIAL ARTS DISPLAY.
THIS IS SO TYPICAL OF YOU, CLARK.
YOU WAIT UNTIL THE DAY YOU'RE LEAVING TO ADMIT TO THIS OBSESSION.
MAN, NOTHING ABOUT THE CITY OF TOMORROW EVER CHANGES.
I GUESS WE'LL SEE ABOUT THAT, JIM.

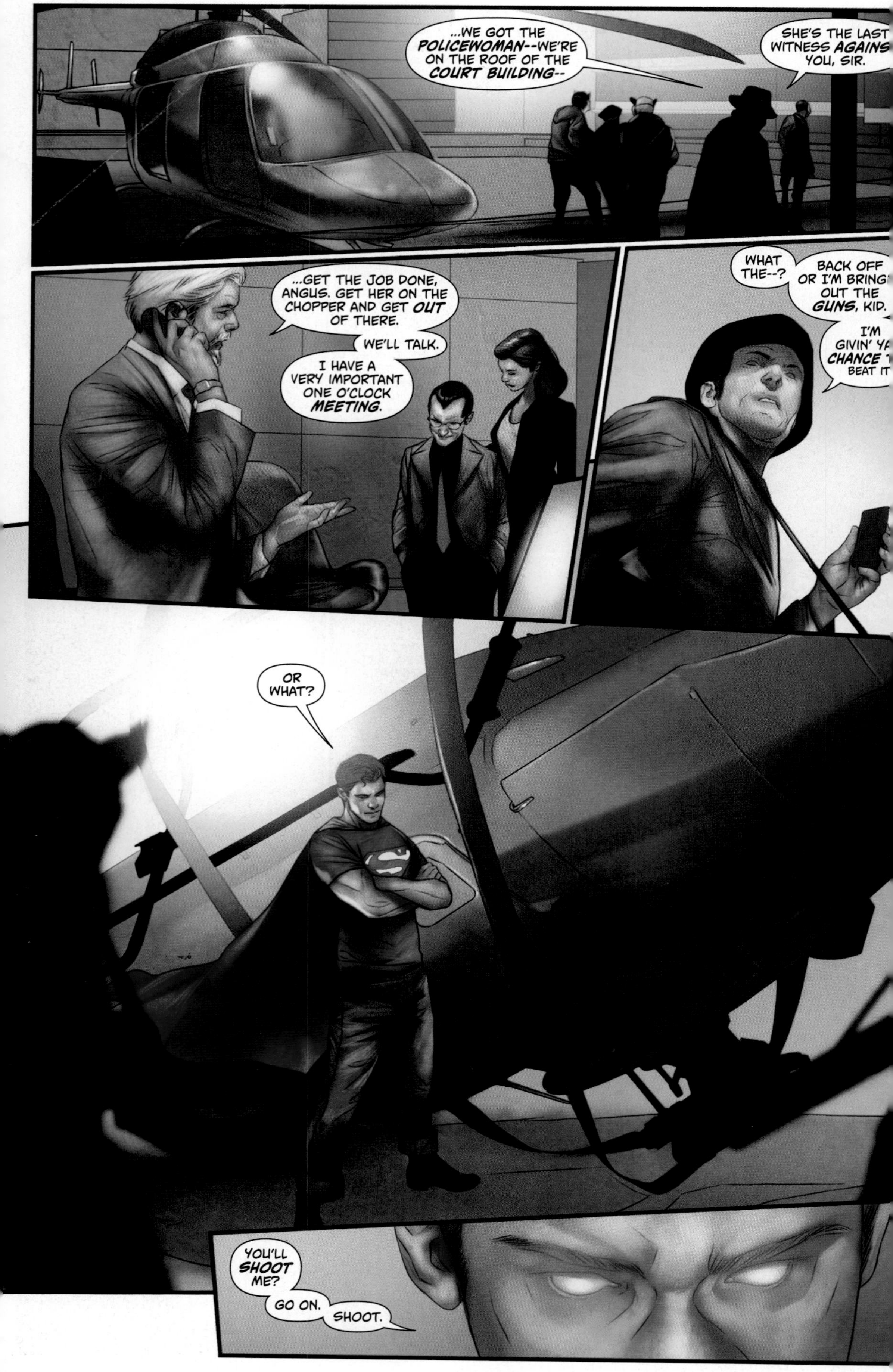
...WE GOT THE POLICEWOMAN--WE'RE ON THE ROOF OF THE COURT BUILDING--
SHE'S THE LAST WITNESS AGAINS YOU, SIR.
...GET THE JOB DONE, ANGUS. GET HER ON THE CHOPPER AND GET OUT OF THERE.
WE'LL TALK.
I HAVE A VERY IMPORTANT ONE O'CLOCK MEETING.
WHAT THE--?
BACK OFF OR I'M BRING OUT THE GUNS, KID.
I'M GIVIN' YA CHANCE T BEAT IT
OR WHAT?
YOU'LL SHOOT ME?
GO ON.
SHOOT.

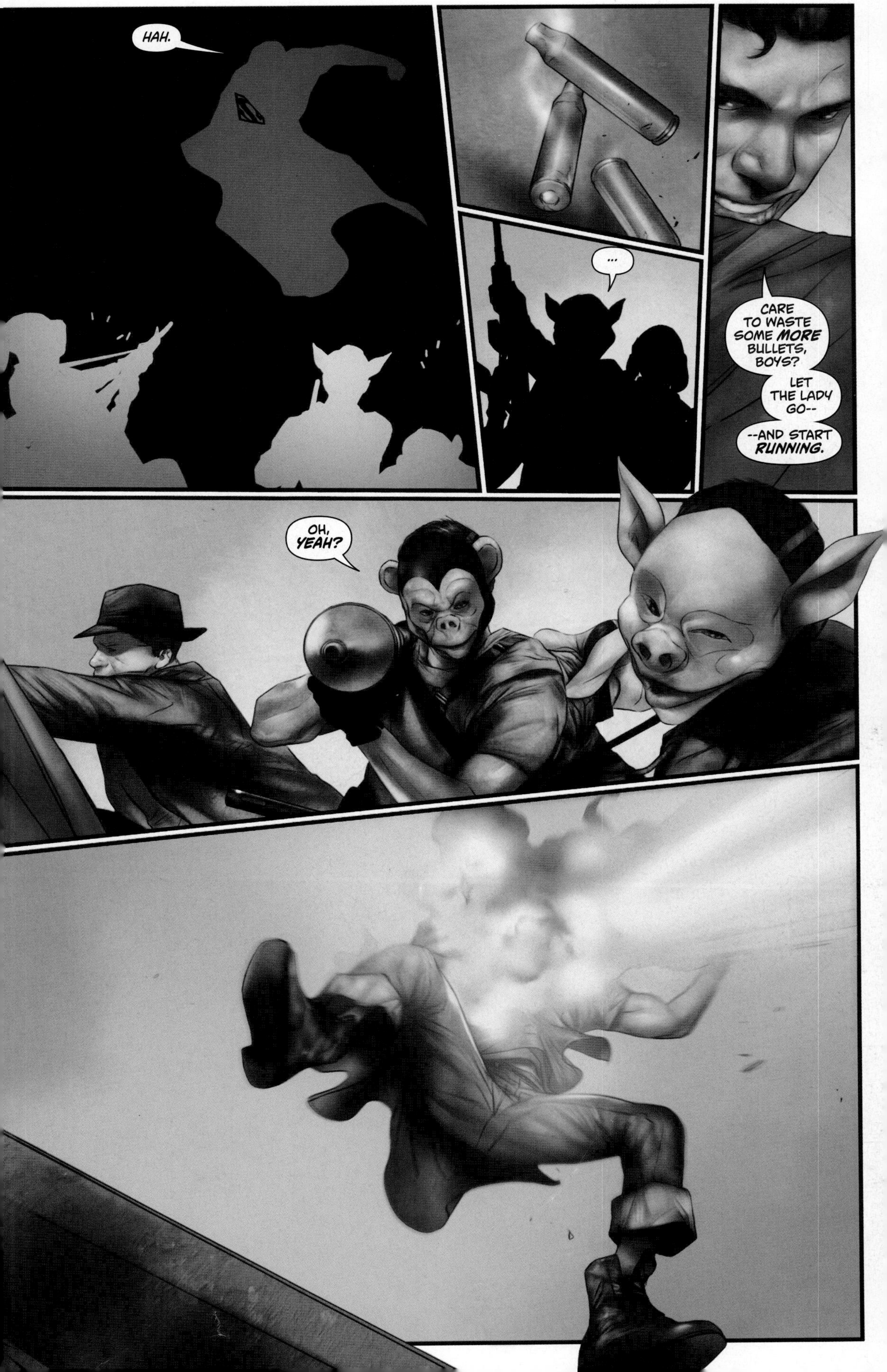
HAH.
...
CARE TO WASTE SOME MORE BULLETS, BOYS?
LET THE LADY GO--
--AND START RUNNING.
OH, YEAH?

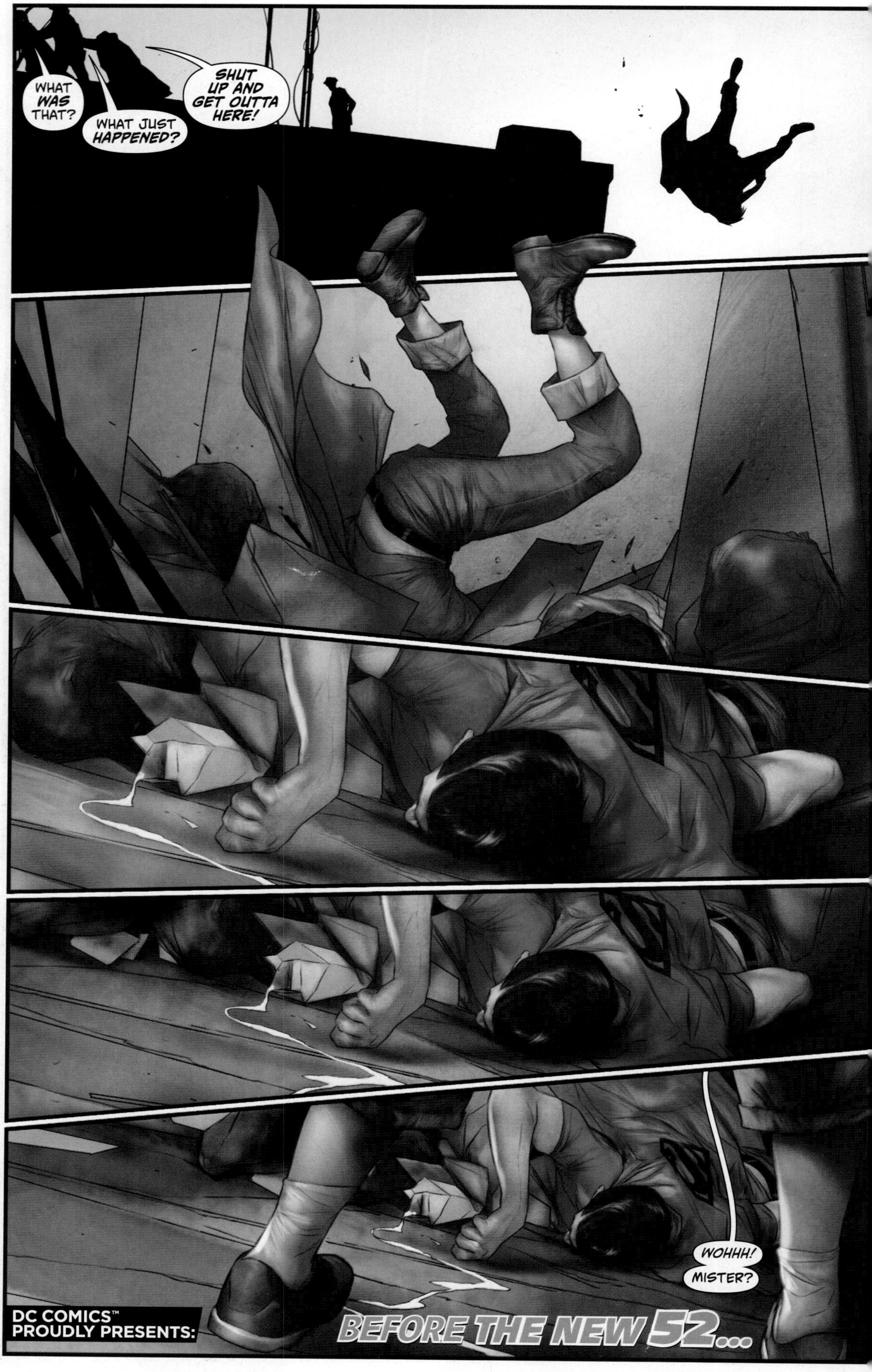
WHAT WAS THAT?
WHAT JUST HAPPENED?
SHUT UP AND GET OUTTA HERE!
WOHHH! MISTER?
DC COMICS™ PROUDLY PRESENTS:
BEFORE THE NEW 52...

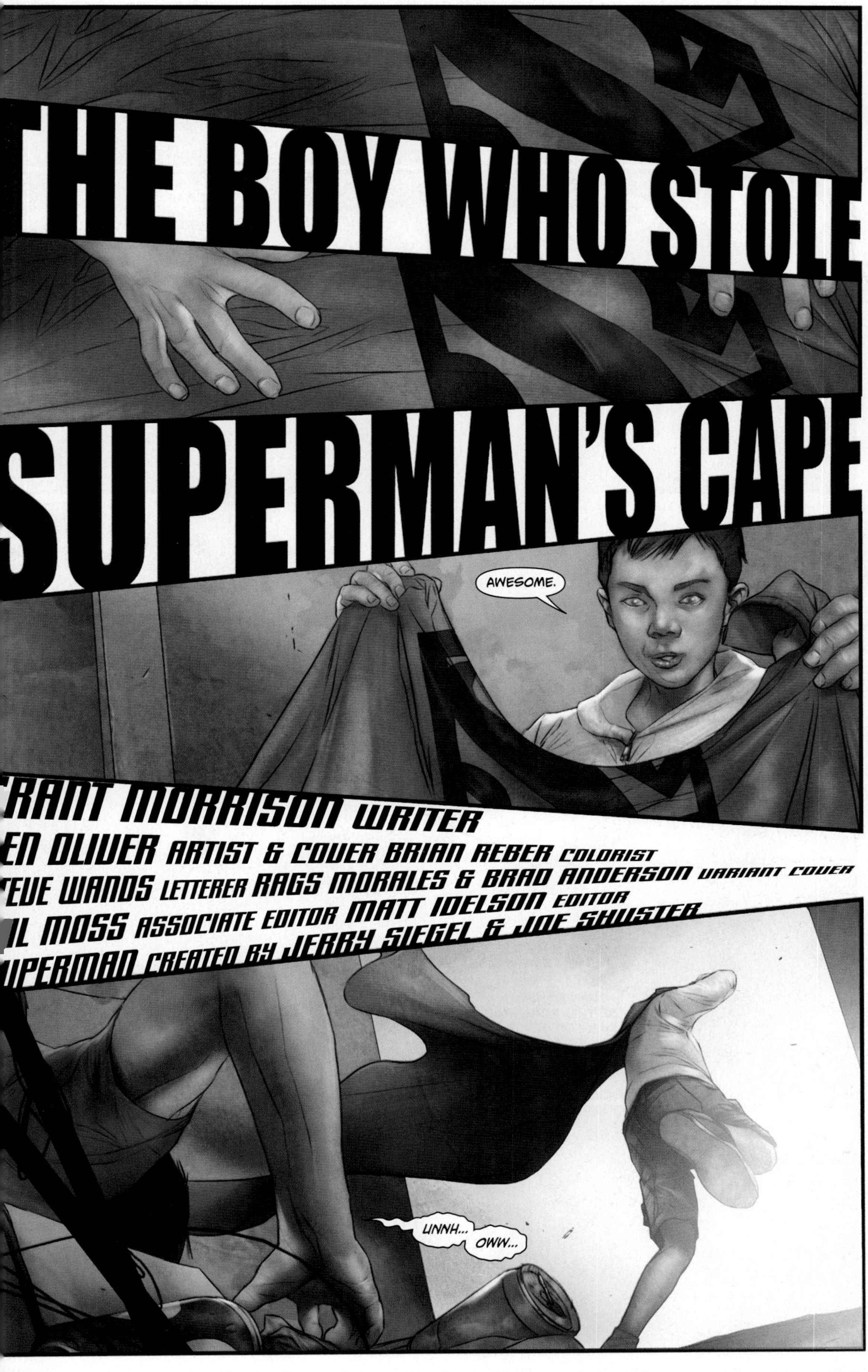
THE BOY WHO STOLE
SUPERMAN'S CAPE
AWESOME.
RANT MORRISON WRITER
EN OLIVER ARTIST & COVER BRIAN REBER COLORIST
EVE WANDS LETTERER RAGS MORALES & BRAD ANDERSON VARIANT COVER
IL MOSS ASSOCIATE EDITOR MATT IDELSON EDITOR
UPERMAN CREATED BY JERRY SIEGEL & JOE SHUSTER
UNNH... OWW...

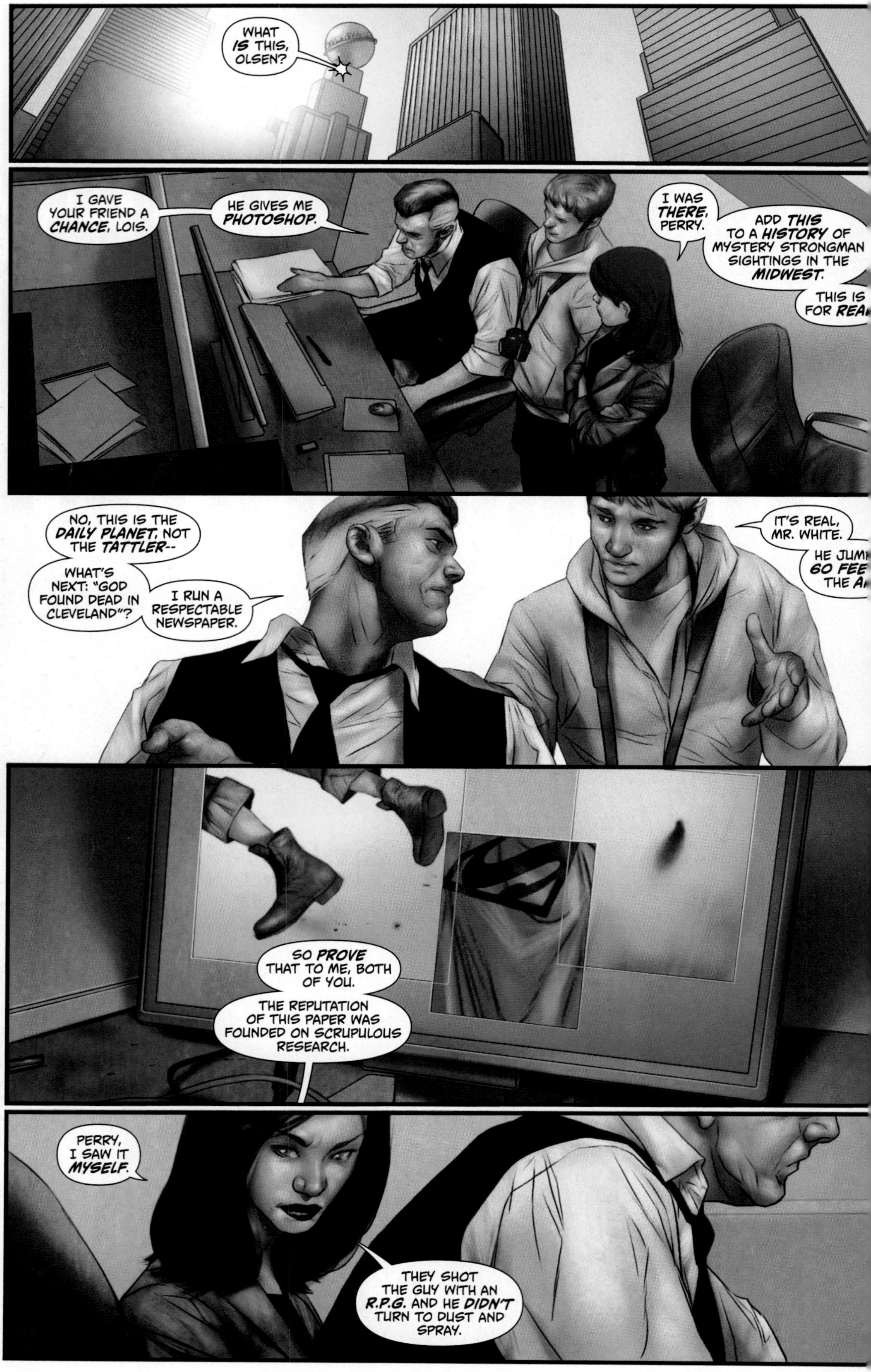
WHAT IS THIS, OLSEN?
I GAVE YOUR FRIEND A CHANCE, LOIS.
HE GIVES ME PHOTOSHOP.
I WAS THERE, PERRY.
ADD THIS TO A HISTORY OF MYSTERY STRONGMAN SIGHTINGS IN THE MIDWEST.
NO, THIS IS THE DAILY PLANET, NOT THE TATTLER--
WHAT'S NEXT: "GOD FOUND DEAD IN CLEVELAND"?
I RUN A RESPECTABLE NEWSPAPER.
IT'S REAL, MR. WHITE.
SO PROVE THAT TO ME, BOTH OF YOU.
THE REPUTATION OF THIS PAPER WAS FOUNDED ON SCRUPULOUS RESEARCH.
PERRY, I SAW IT MYSELF.
THEY SHOT THE GUY WITH AN R.P.G. AND HE DIDN'T TURN TO DUST AND SPRAY.

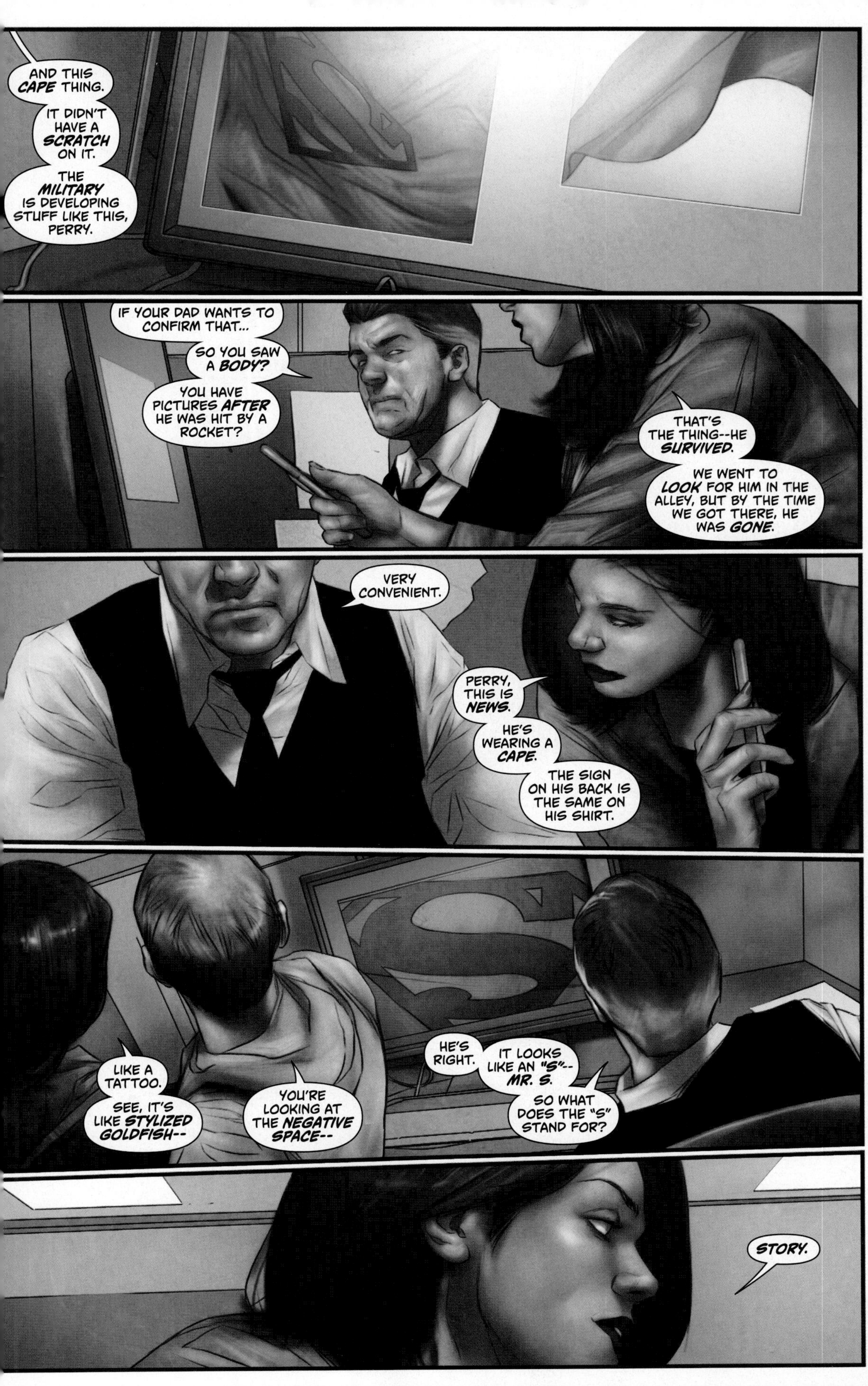
AND THIS CAPE THING.
IT DIDN'T HAVE A SCRATCH ON IT.
THE MILITARY IS DEVELOPING STUFF LIKE THIS, PERRY.
IF YOUR DAD WANTS TO CONFIRM THAT...
SO YOU SAW A BODY?
YOU HAVE PICTURES AFTER HE WAS HIT BY A ROCKET?
THAT'S THE THING--HE SURVIVED.
WE WENT TO LOOK FOR HIM IN THE ALLEY, BUT BY THE TIME WE GOT THERE, HE WAS GONE.
VERY CONVENIENT.
PERRY, THIS IS NEWS.
HE'S WEARING A CAPE.
THE SIGN ON HIS BACK IS THE SAME ON HIS SHIRT.
LIKE A TATTOO.
SEE, IT'S LIKE STYLIZED GOLDFISH--
YOU'RE LOOKING AT THE NEGATIVE SPACE--
HE'S RIGHT.
IT LOOKS LIKE AN "S"-- MR. S.
SO WHAT DOES THE "S" STAND FOR?
STORY.

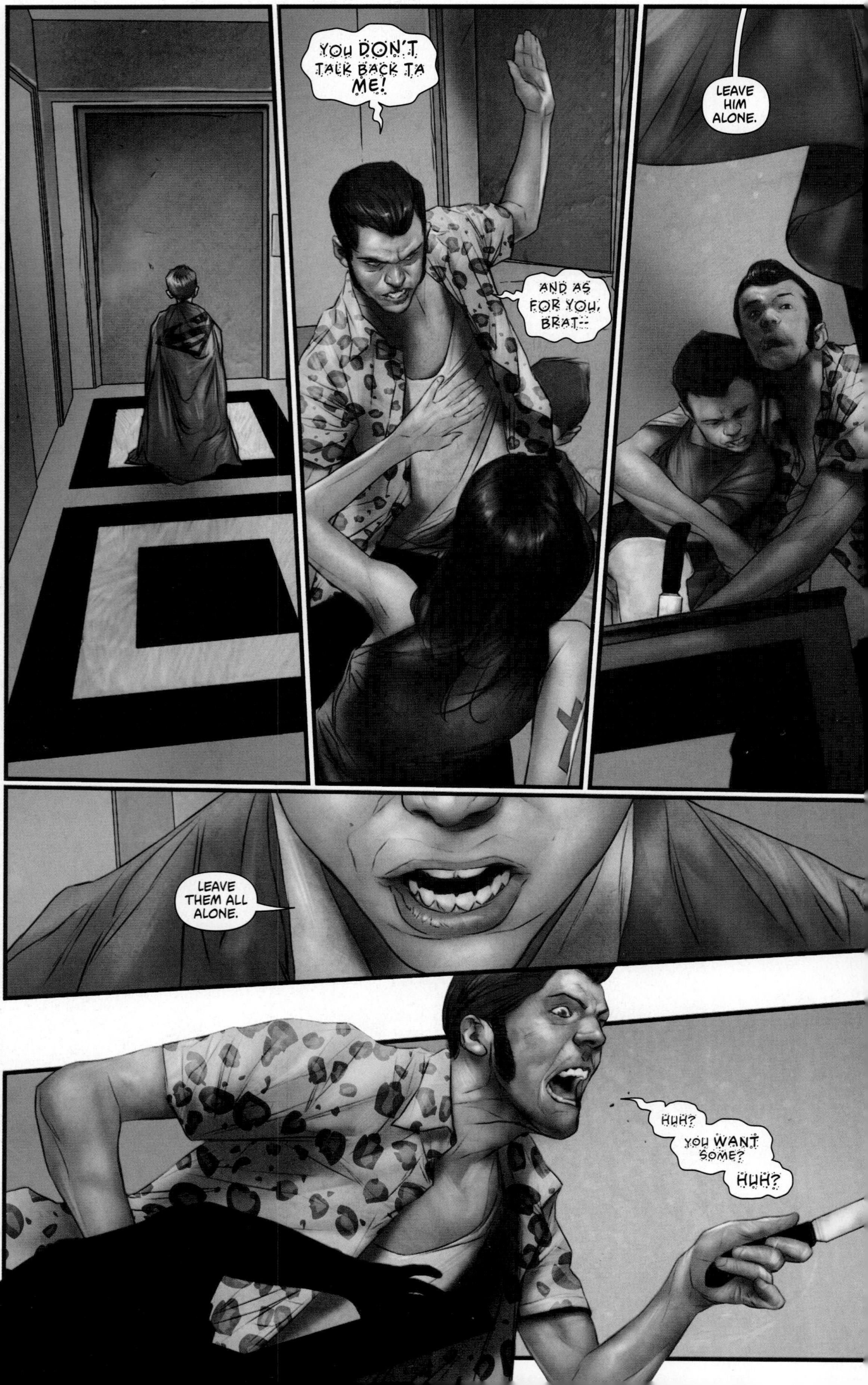
YOU DON'T TALK BACK TA ME!
AND AS FOR YOU, BRAT--
LEAVE HIM ALONE.
LEAVE THEM ALL ALONE.
HUH?
YOU WANT SOME?
HUH?

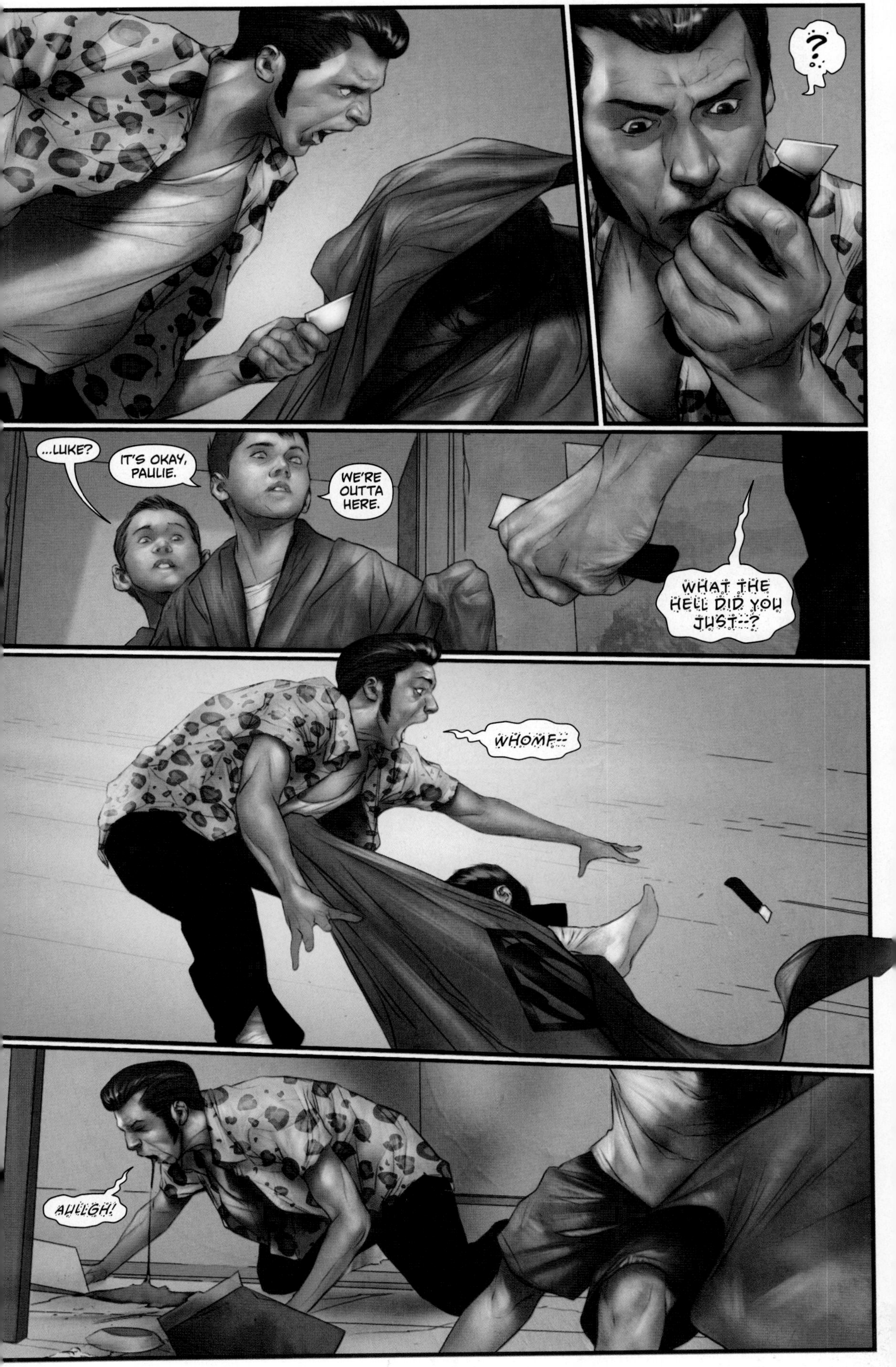
?
...LUKE?
IT'S OKAY, PAULIE.
WE'RE OUTTA HERE.
WHAT THE HELL DID YOU JUST--?
WHOMF--
AULLGH!

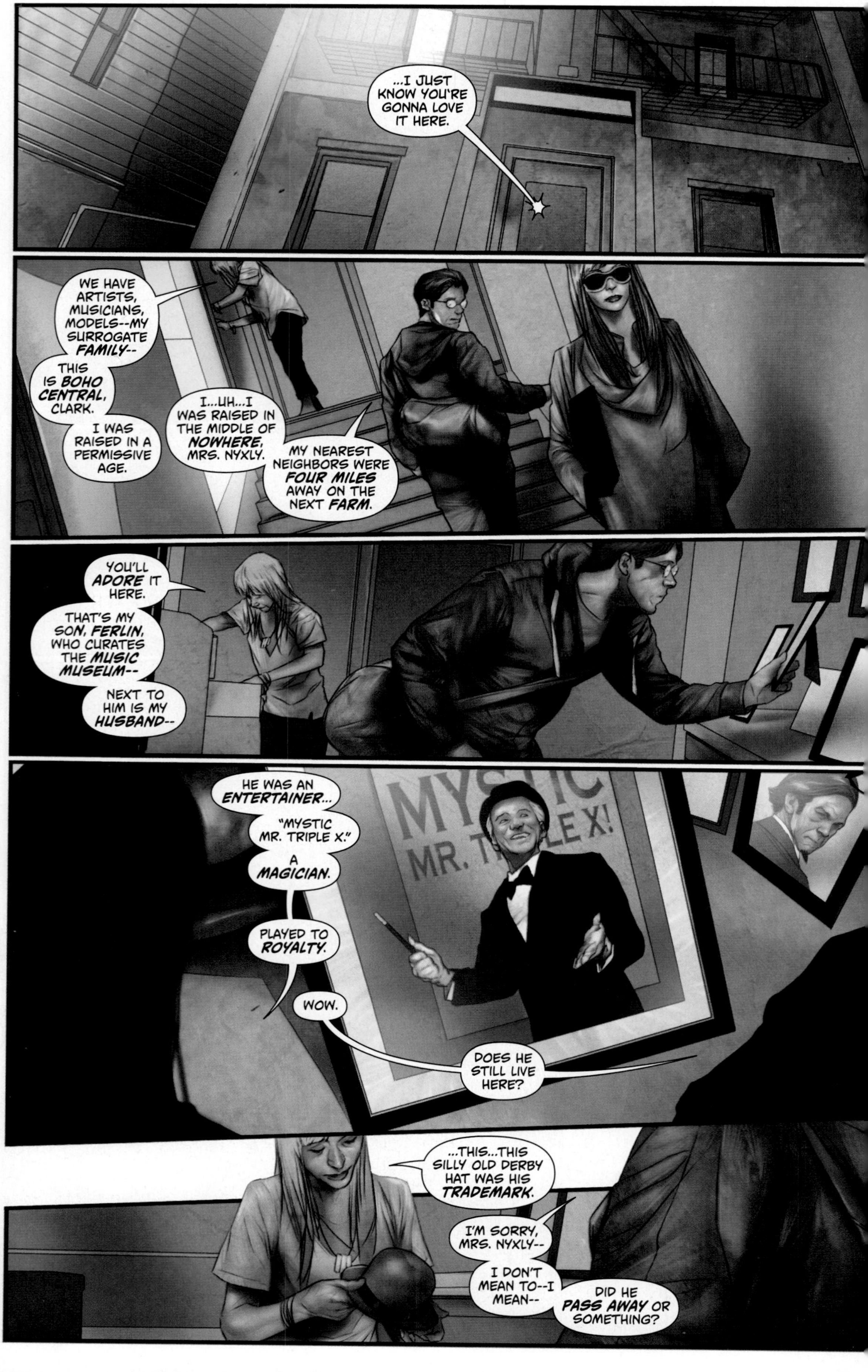

...I JUST KNOW YOU'RE GONNA LOVE IT HERE.
WE HAVE ARTISTS, MUSICIANS, MODELS--MY SURROGATE FAMILY--
THIS IS BOHO CENTRAL, CLARK.
I WAS RAISED IN A PERMISSIVE AGE.
I...UH...I WAS RAISED IN THE MIDDLE OF NOWHERE, MRS. NYXLY.
MY NEAREST NEIGHBORS WERE FOUR MILES AWAY ON THE NEXT FARM.
YOU'LL ADORE IT HERE.
THAT'S MY SON, FERLIN, WHO CURATES THE MUSIC MUSEUM--
NEXT TO HIM IS MY HUSBAND--
MYSTIC MR. TR LE X!
HE WAS AN ENTERTAINER...
"MYSTIC MR. TRIPLE X."
A MAGICIAN.
PLAYED TO ROYALTY.
WOW.
DOES HE STILL LIVE HERE?
...THIS...THIS SILLY OLD DERBY HAT WAS HIS TRADEMARK.
I'M SORRY, MRS. NYXLY--
I DON'T MEAN TO--I MEAN--
DID HE PASS AWAY OR SOMETHING?

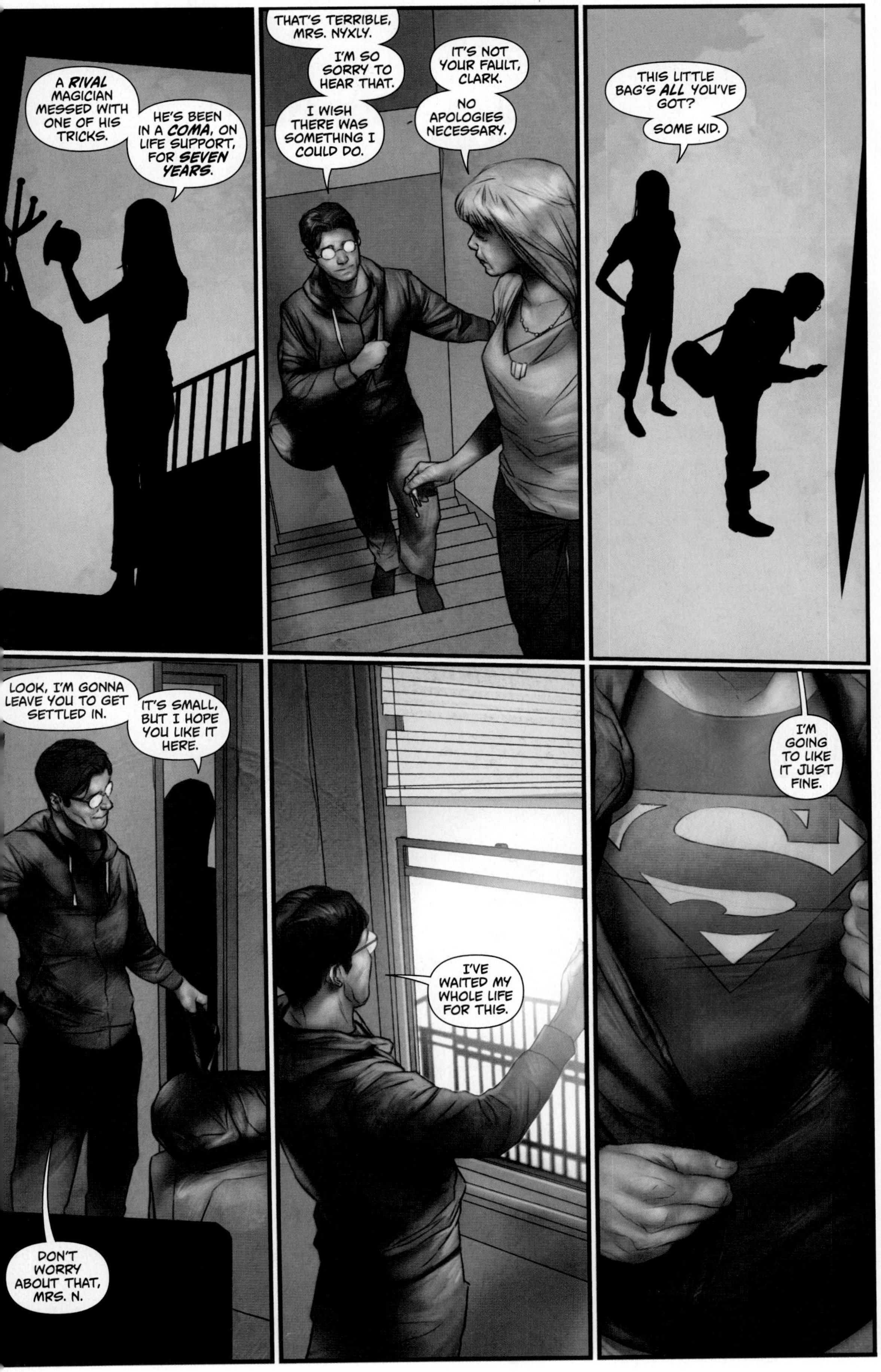
A RIVAL MAGICIAN MESSED WITH ONE OF HIS TRICKS.
HE'S BEEN IN A COMA, ON LIFE SUPPORT, FOR SEVEN YEARS.
THAT'S TERRIBLE, MRS. NYXLY.
I'M SO SORRY TO HEAR THAT.
I WISH THERE WAS SOMETHING I COULD DO.
IT'S NOT YOUR FAULT, CLARK.
NO APOLOGIES NECESSARY.
THIS LITTLE BAG'S ALL YOU'VE GOT?
SOME KID.
LOOK, I'M GONNA LEAVE YOU TO GET SETTLED IN.
IT'S SMALL, BUT I HOPE YOU LIKE IT HERE.
DON'T WORRY ABOUT THAT, MRS. N.
I'VE WAITED MY WHOLE LIFE FOR THIS.
I'M GOING TO LIKE IT JUST FINE.

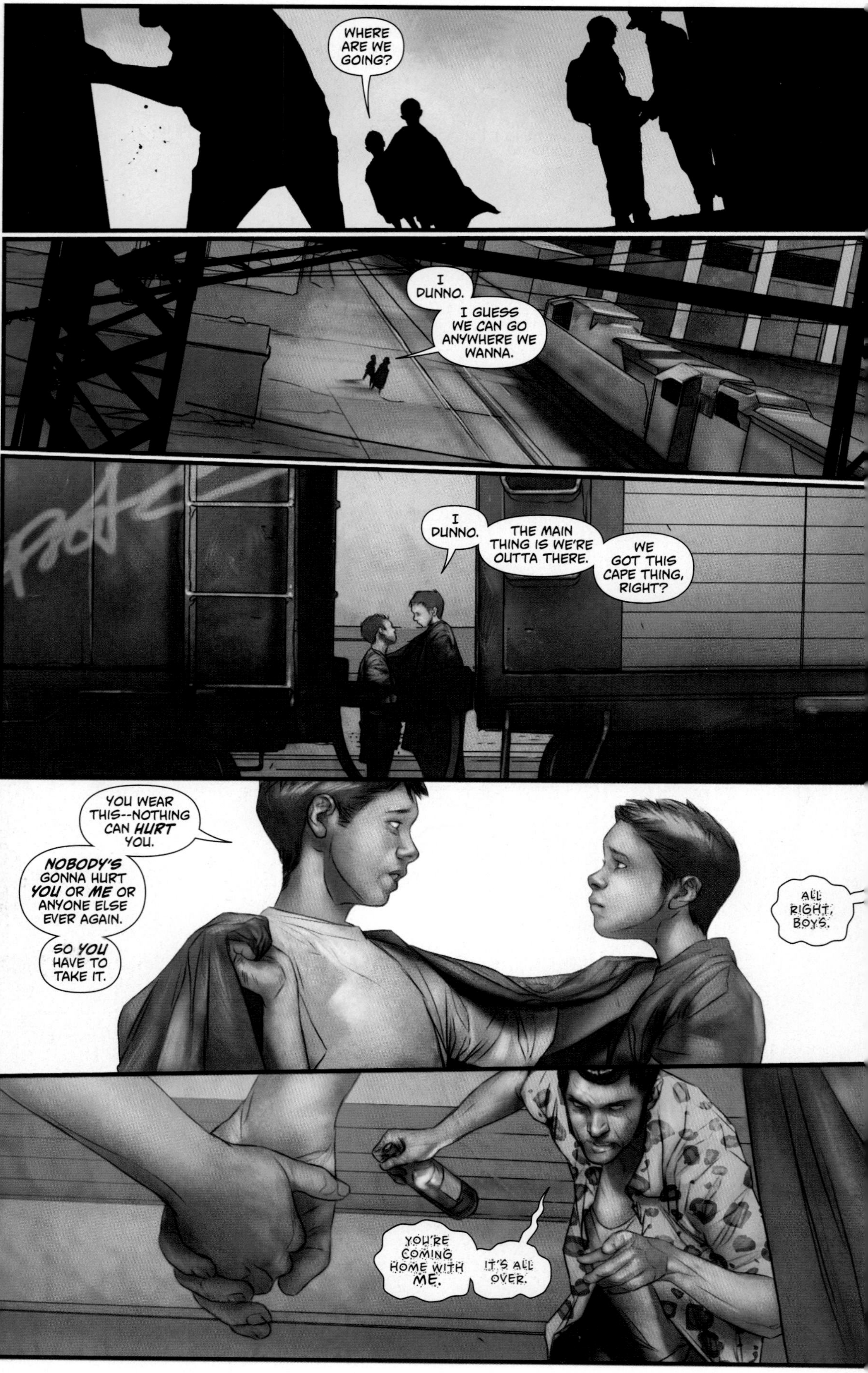
WHERE ARE WE GOING?
I DUNNO.
I GUESS WE CAN GO ANYWHERE WE WANNA.
I DUNNO.
THE MAIN THING IS WE'RE OUTTA THERE.
WE GOT THIS CAPE THING, RIGHT?
YOU WEAR THIS--NOTHING CAN HURT YOU.
NOBODY'S GONNA HURT YOU OR ME OR ANYONE ELSE EVER AGAIN.
SO YOU HAVE TO TAKE IT.
ALL RIGHT, BOYS.
YOU'RE COMING HOME WITH ME.
IT'S ALL OVER.

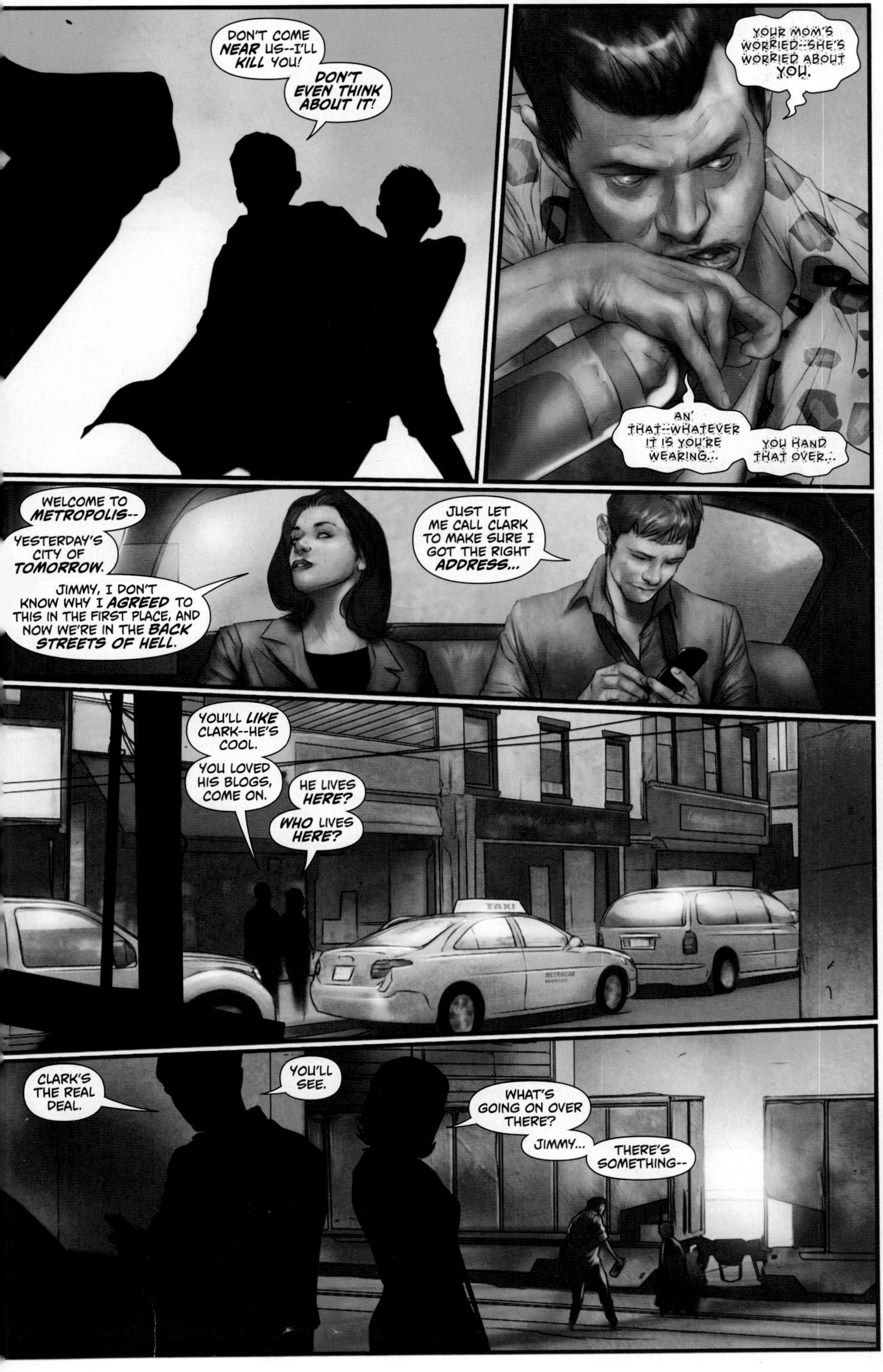
DON'T COME NEAR US--I'LL KILL YOU!
DON'T EVEN THINK ABOUT IT!
YOUR MOM'S WORRIED--SHE'S WORRIED ABOUT YOU.
AN' THAT--WHATEVER IT IS YOU'RE WEARING...
YOU HAND THAT OVER...
WELCOME TO METROPOLIS--
YESTERDAY'S CITY OF TOMORROW.
JIMMY, I DON'T KNOW WHY I AGREED TO THIS IN THE FIRST PLACE, AND NOW WE'RE IN THE BACK STREETS OF HELL.
JUST LET ME CALL CLARK TO MAKE SURE I GOT THE RIGHT ADDRESS...
YOU'LL LIKE CLARK--HE'S COOL.
YOU LOVED HIS BLOGS, COME ON.
HE LIVES HERE?
WHO LIVES HERE?
TAXI
METROCAB
CLARK'S THE REAL DEAL.
YOU'LL SEE.
WHAT'S GOING ON OVER THERE?
JIMMY...
THERE'S SOMETHING--

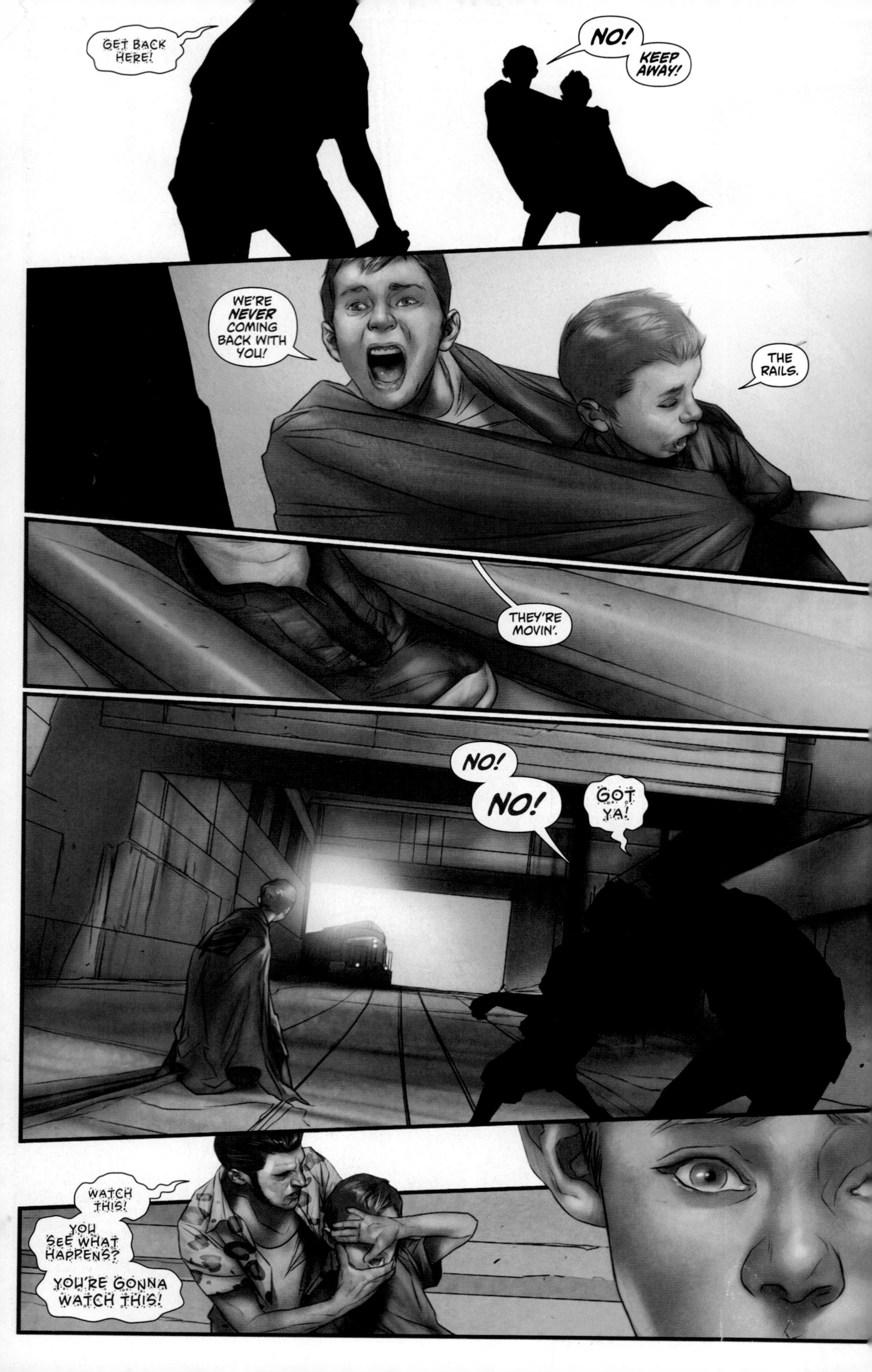
GET BACK HERE!
NO!
KEEP AWAY!
WE'RE *NEVER* COMING BACK WITH YOU!
THE RAILS.
THEY'RE MOVIN'.
NO!
NO!
GOT YA!
WATCH THIS!
YOU SEE WHAT HAPPENS?
YOU'RE GONNA WATCH THIS!

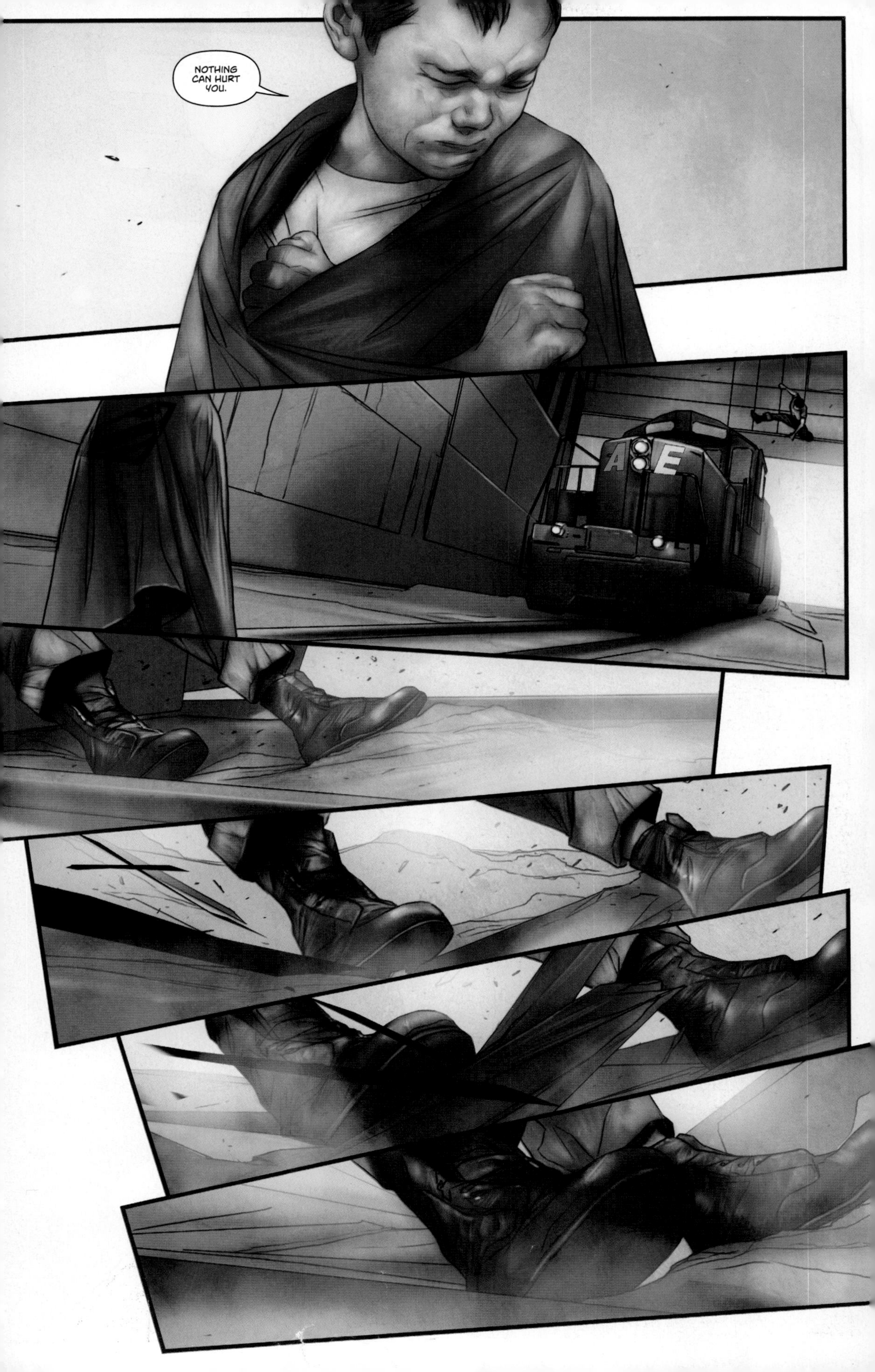
NOTHING CAN HURT YOU.
A E

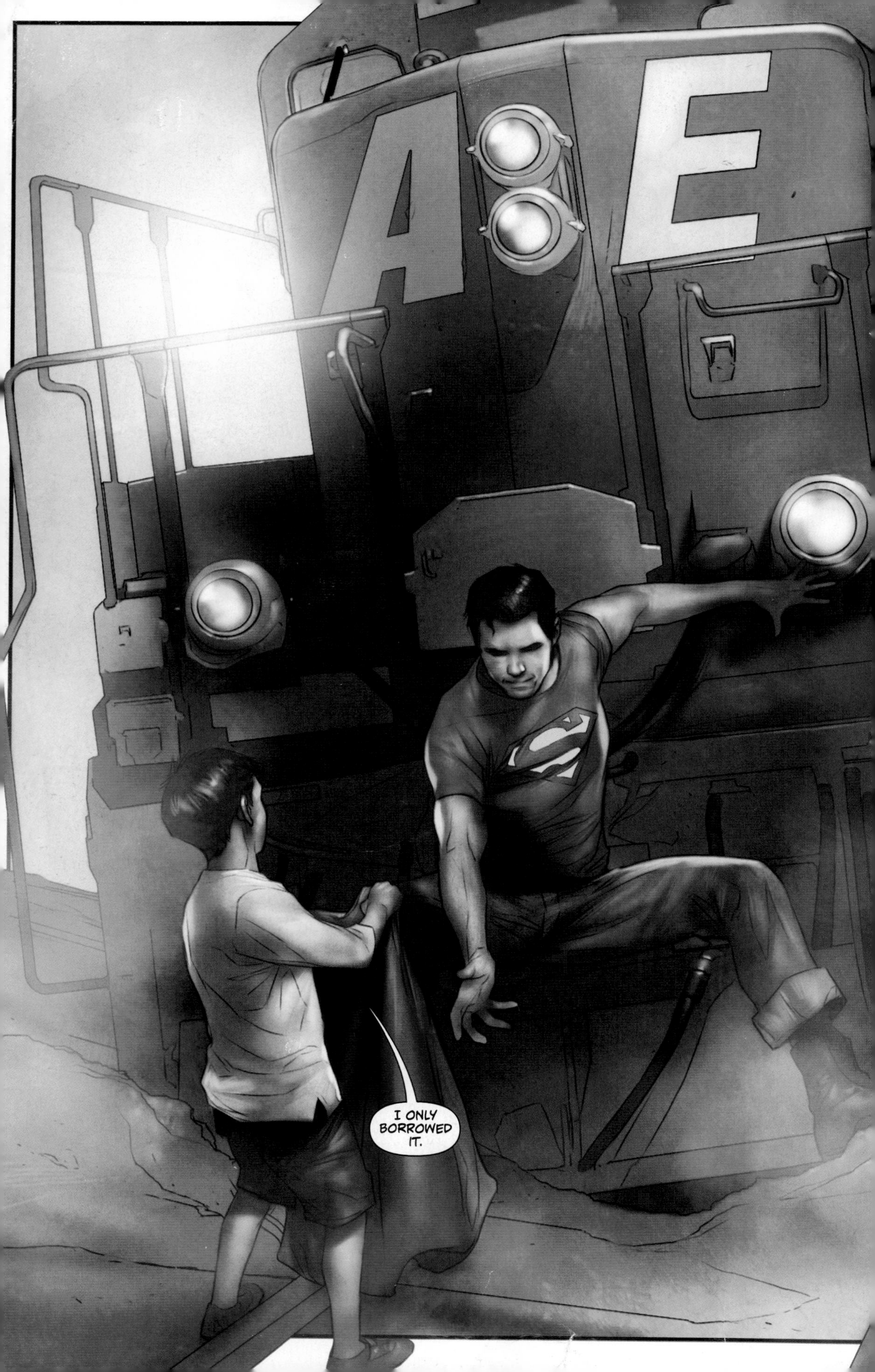
I ONLY BORROWED IT.

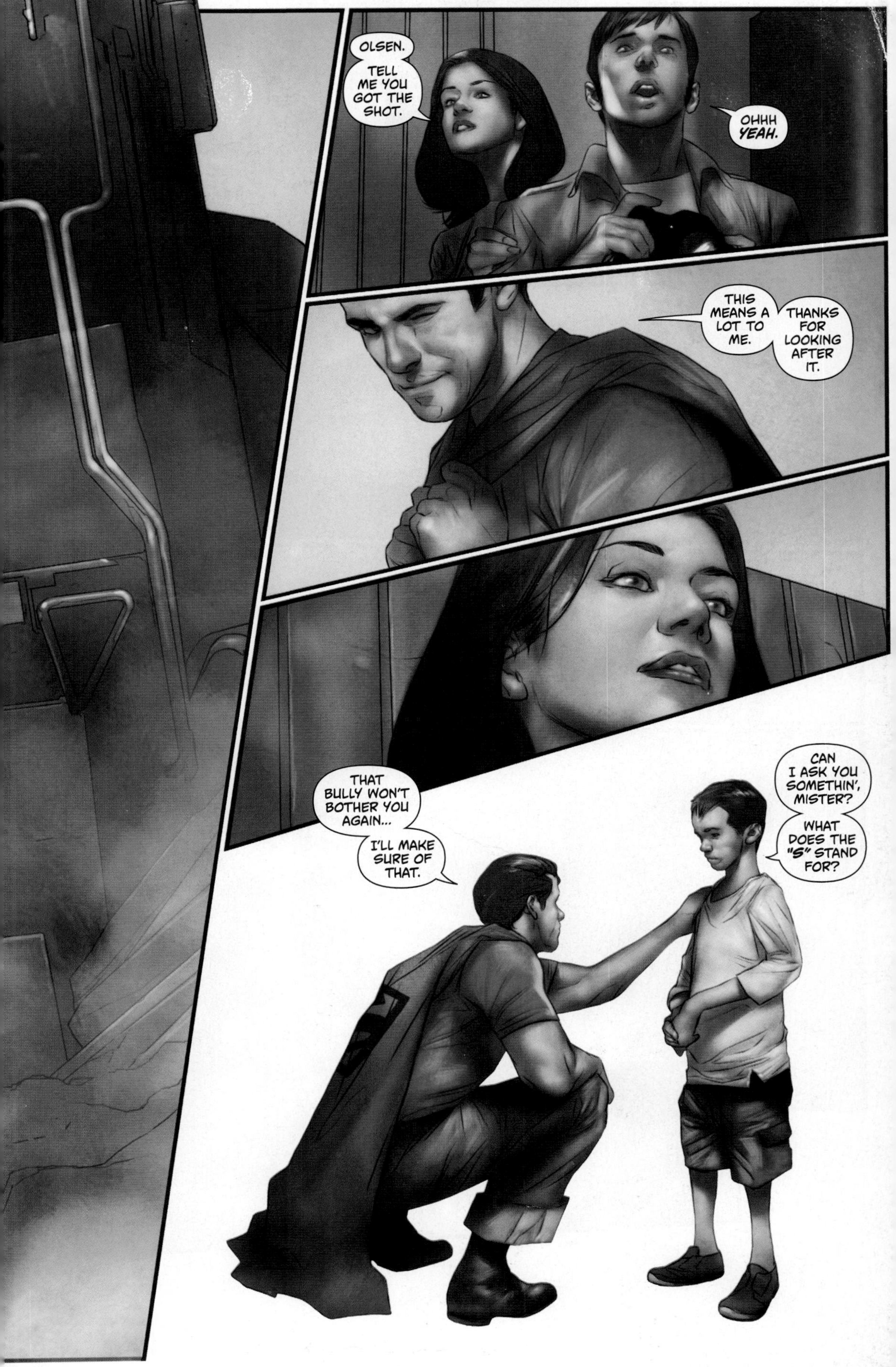
OLSEN.
TELL ME YOU GOT THE SHOT.
OHHH *YEAH.*
THIS MEANS A LOT TO ME.
THANKS FOR LOOKING AFTER IT.
THAT BULLY WON'T BOTHER YOU AGAIN...
I'LL MAKE SURE OF THAT.
CAN I ASK YOU SOMETHIN', MISTER?
WHAT DOES THE *"S"* STAND FOR?

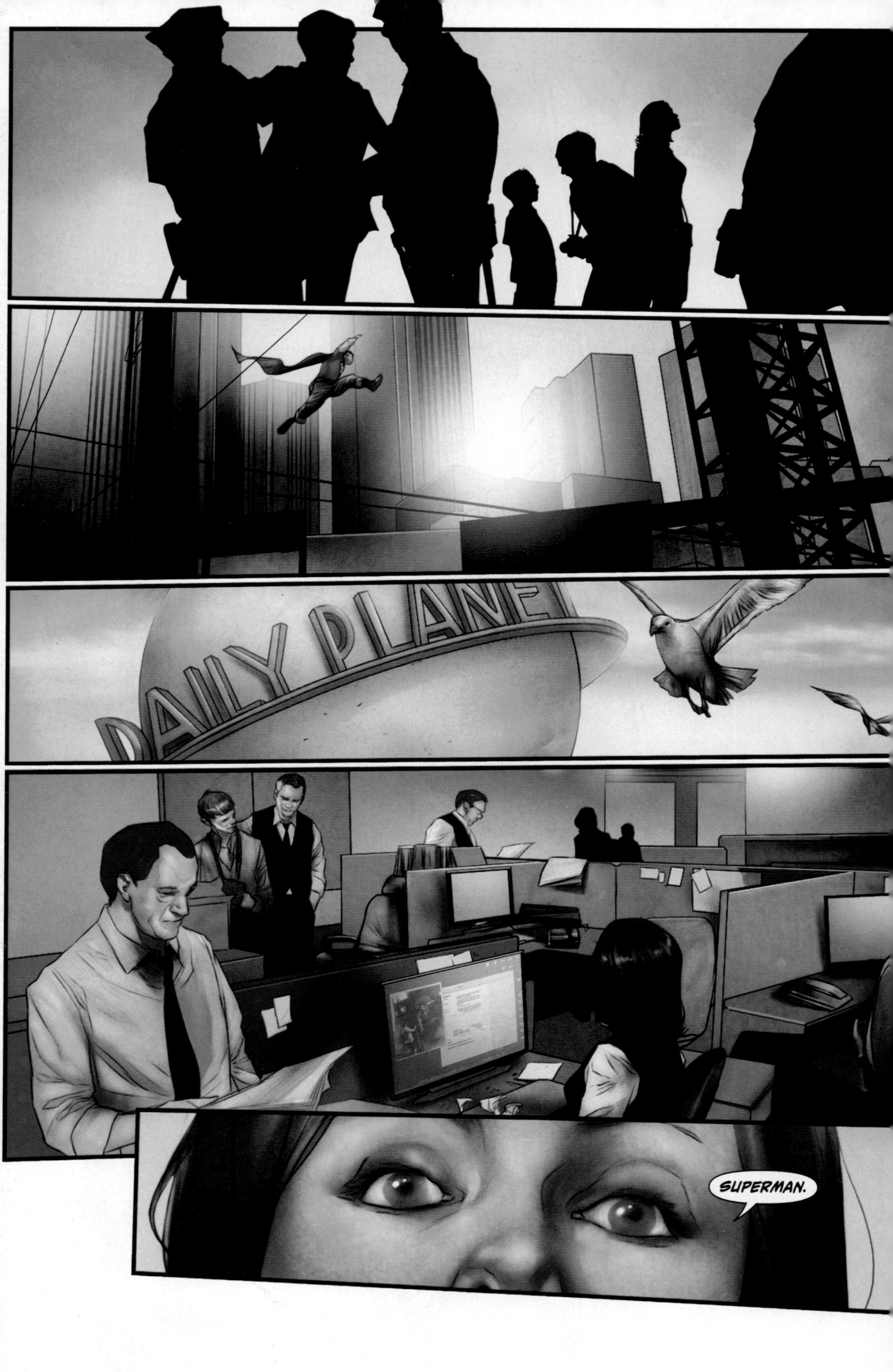
DAILY PLANET
SUPERMAN.

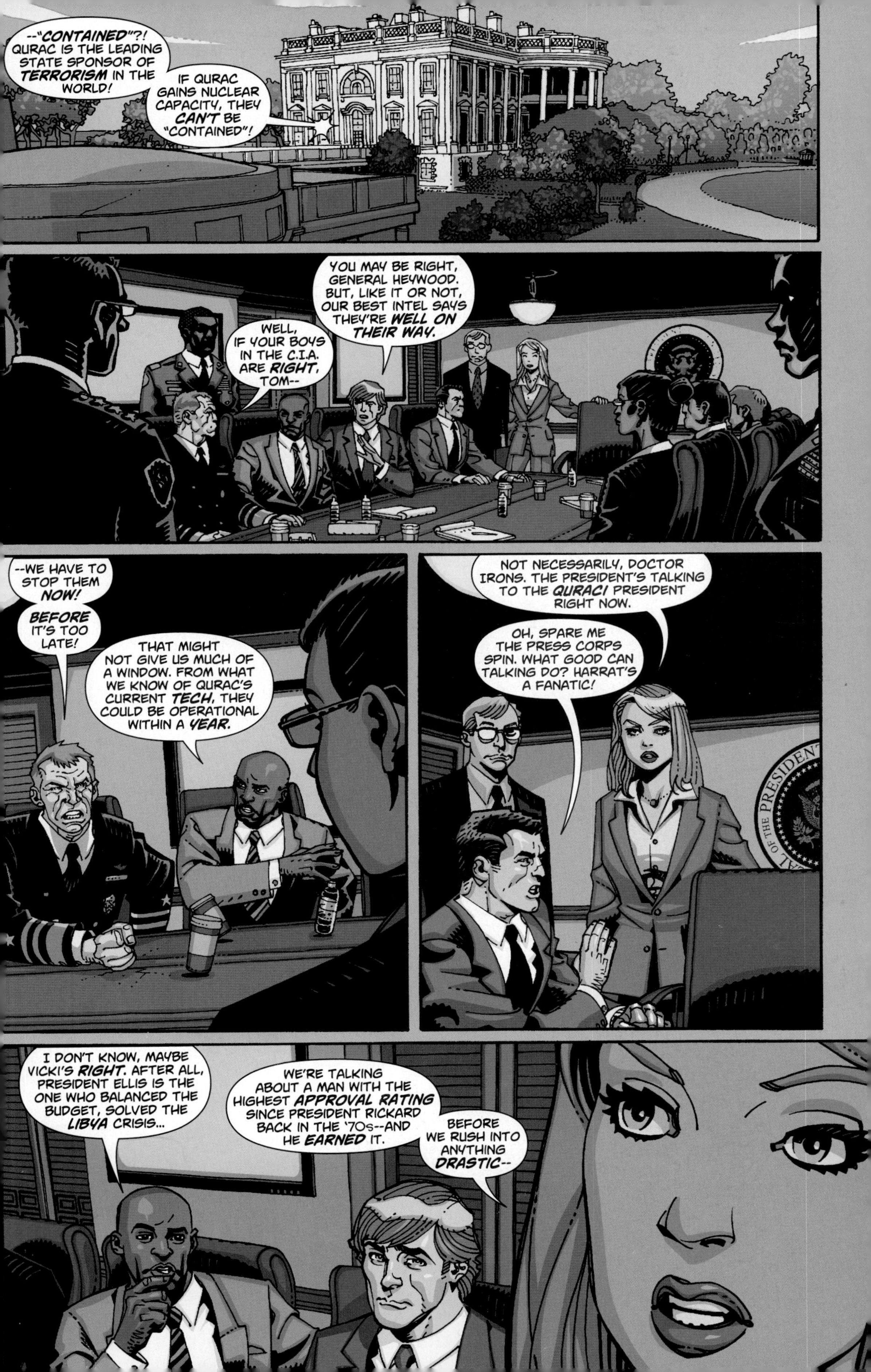
--"CONTAINED"?! QURAC IS THE LEADING STATE SPONSOR OF TERRORISM IN THE WORLD!
IF QURAC GAINS NUCLEAR CAPACITY, THEY CAN'T BE "CONTAINED"!
YOU MAY BE RIGHT, GENERAL HEYWOOD. BUT, LIKE IT OR NOT, OUR BEST INTEL SAYS THEY'RE WELL ON THEIR WAY.
WELL, IF YOUR BOYS IN THE C.I.A. ARE RIGHT, TOM--
--WE HAVE TO STOP THEM NOW!
BEFORE IT'S TOO LATE!
THAT MIGHT NOT GIVE US MUCH OF A WINDOW. FROM WHAT WE KNOW OF QURAC'S CURRENT TECH, THEY COULD BE OPERATIONAL WITHIN A YEAR.
NOT NECESSARILY, DOCTOR IRONS. THE PRESIDENT'S TALKING TO THE QURACI PRESIDENT RIGHT NOW.
OH, SPARE ME THE PRESS CORPS SPIN. WHAT GOOD CAN TALKING DO? HARRAT'S A FANATIC!
I DON'T KNOW, MAYBE VICKI'S RIGHT. AFTER ALL, PRESIDENT ELLIS IS THE ONE WHO BALANCED THE BUDGET, SOLVED THE LIBYA CRISIS...
WE'RE TALKING ABOUT A MAN WITH THE HIGHEST APPROVAL RATING SINCE PRESIDENT RICKARD BACK IN THE '70s--AND HE EARNED IT.
BEFORE WE RUSH INTO ANYTHING DRASTIC--

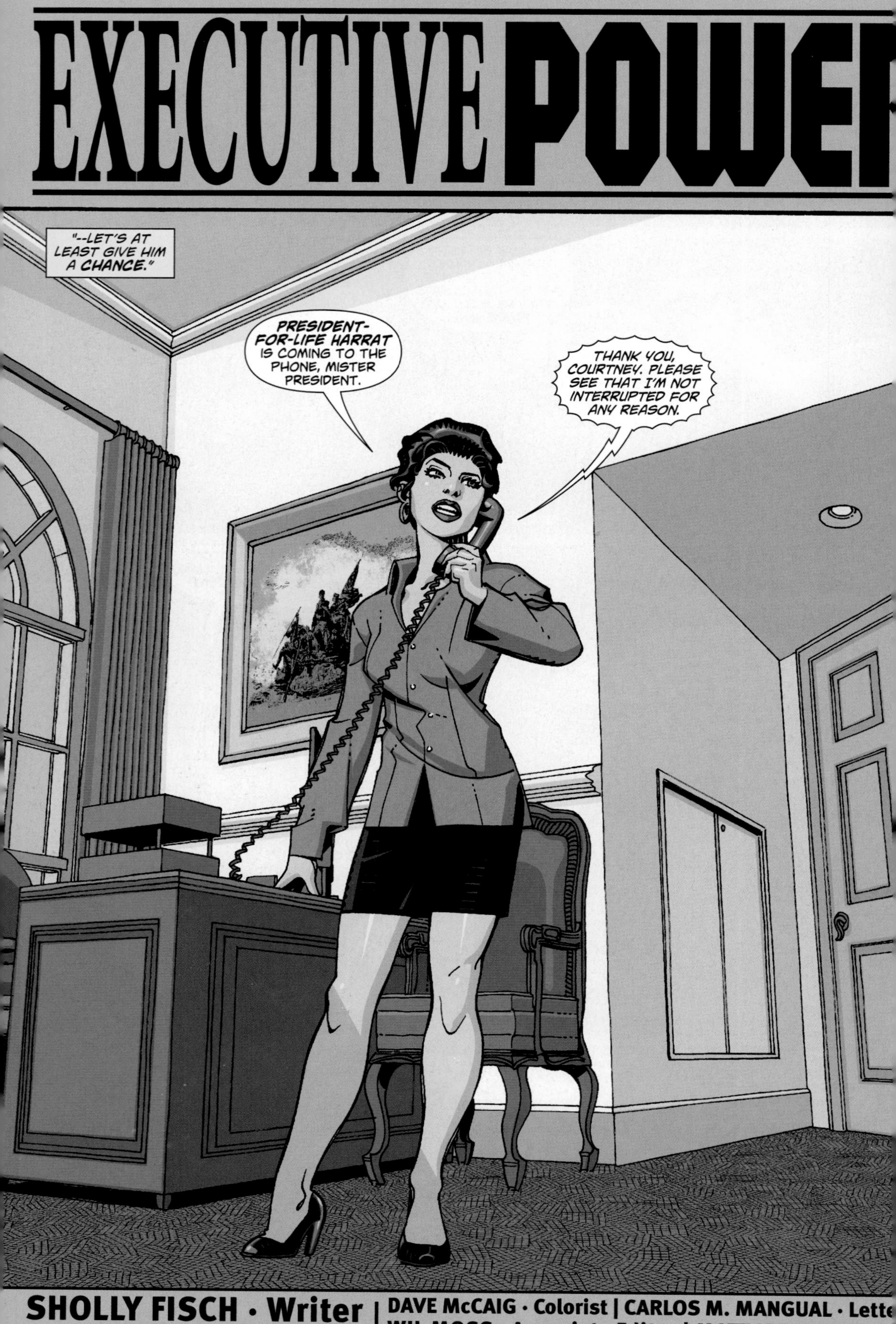
EXECUTIVE POWE
"--LET'S AT LEAST GIVE HIM A CHANCE."
PRESIDENT-FOR-LIFE HARRAT IS COMING TO THE PHONE, MISTER PRESIDENT.
THANK YOU, COURTNEY. PLEASE SEE THAT I'M NOT INTERRUPTED FOR ANY REASON.
SHOLLY FISCH • Writer
CULLY HAMNER • Artist
DAVE McCAIG • Colorist | CARLOS M. MANGUAL • Lette
WIL MOSS • Associate Editor | MATT IDELSON • Edi
SUPERMAN created by JERRY SIEGEL & JOE SHUS

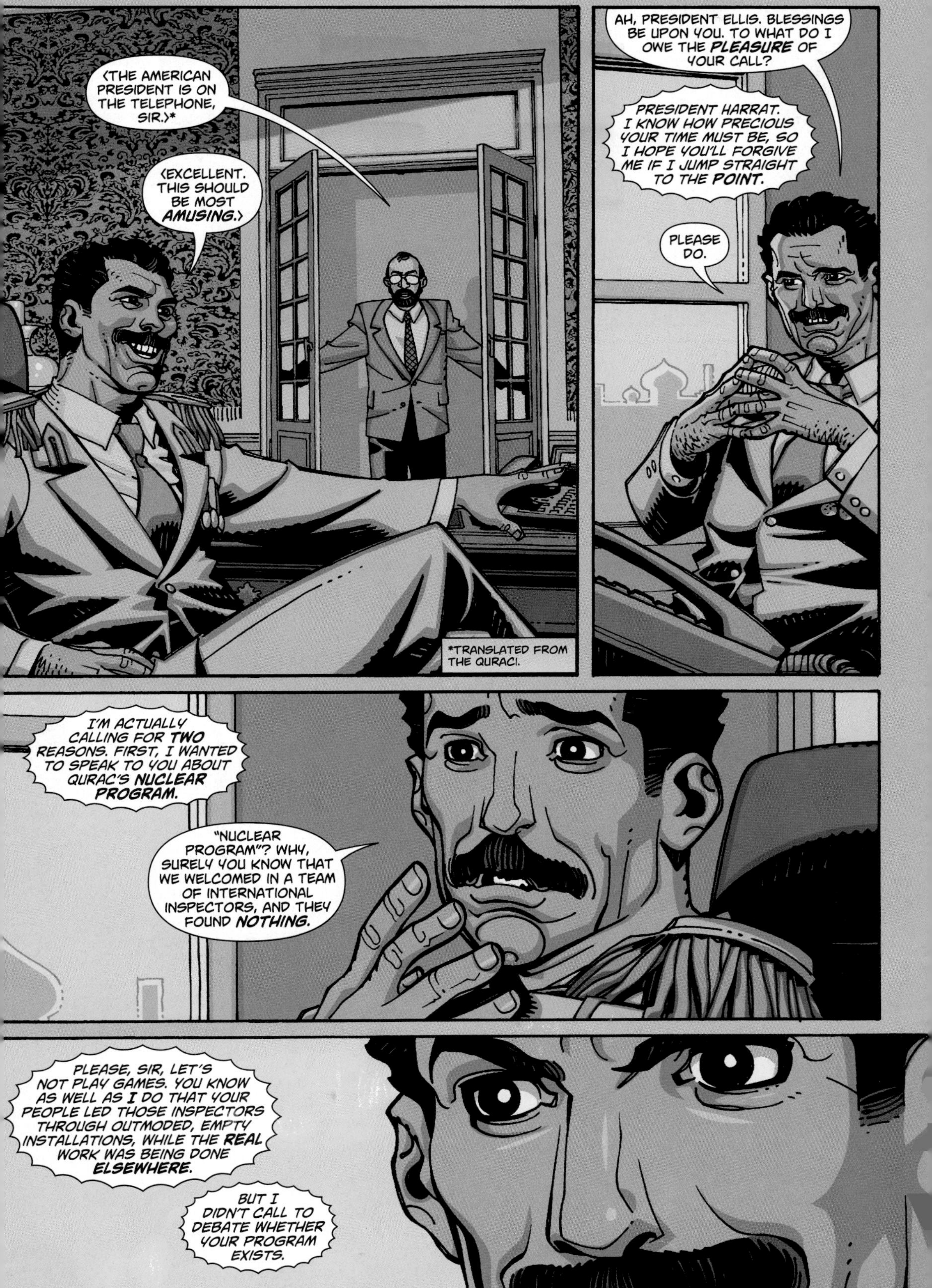

<THE AMERICAN PRESIDENT IS ON THE TELEPHONE, SIR.>*
<EXCELLENT. THIS SHOULD BE MOST AMUSING.>
*TRANSLATED FROM THE QURACI.
AH, PRESIDENT ELLIS. BLESSINGS BE UPON YOU. TO WHAT DO I OWE THE PLEASURE OF YOUR CALL?
PRESIDENT HARRAT. I KNOW HOW PRECIOUS YOUR TIME MUST BE, SO I HOPE YOU'LL FORGIVE ME IF I JUMP STRAIGHT TO THE POINT.
PLEASE DO.
I'M ACTUALLY CALLING FOR TWO REASONS. FIRST, I WANTED TO SPEAK TO YOU ABOUT QURAC'S NUCLEAR PROGRAM.
"NUCLEAR PROGRAM"? WHY, SURELY YOU KNOW THAT WE WELCOMED IN A TEAM OF INTERNATIONAL INSPECTORS, AND THEY FOUND NOTHING.
PLEASE, SIR, LET'S NOT PLAY GAMES. YOU KNOW AS WELL AS I DO THAT YOUR PEOPLE LED THOSE INSPECTORS THROUGH OUTMODED, EMPTY INSTALLATIONS, WHILE THE REAL WORK WAS BEING DONE ELSEWHERE.
BUT I DIDN'T CALL TO DEBATE WHETHER YOUR PROGRAM EXISTS.
NO?

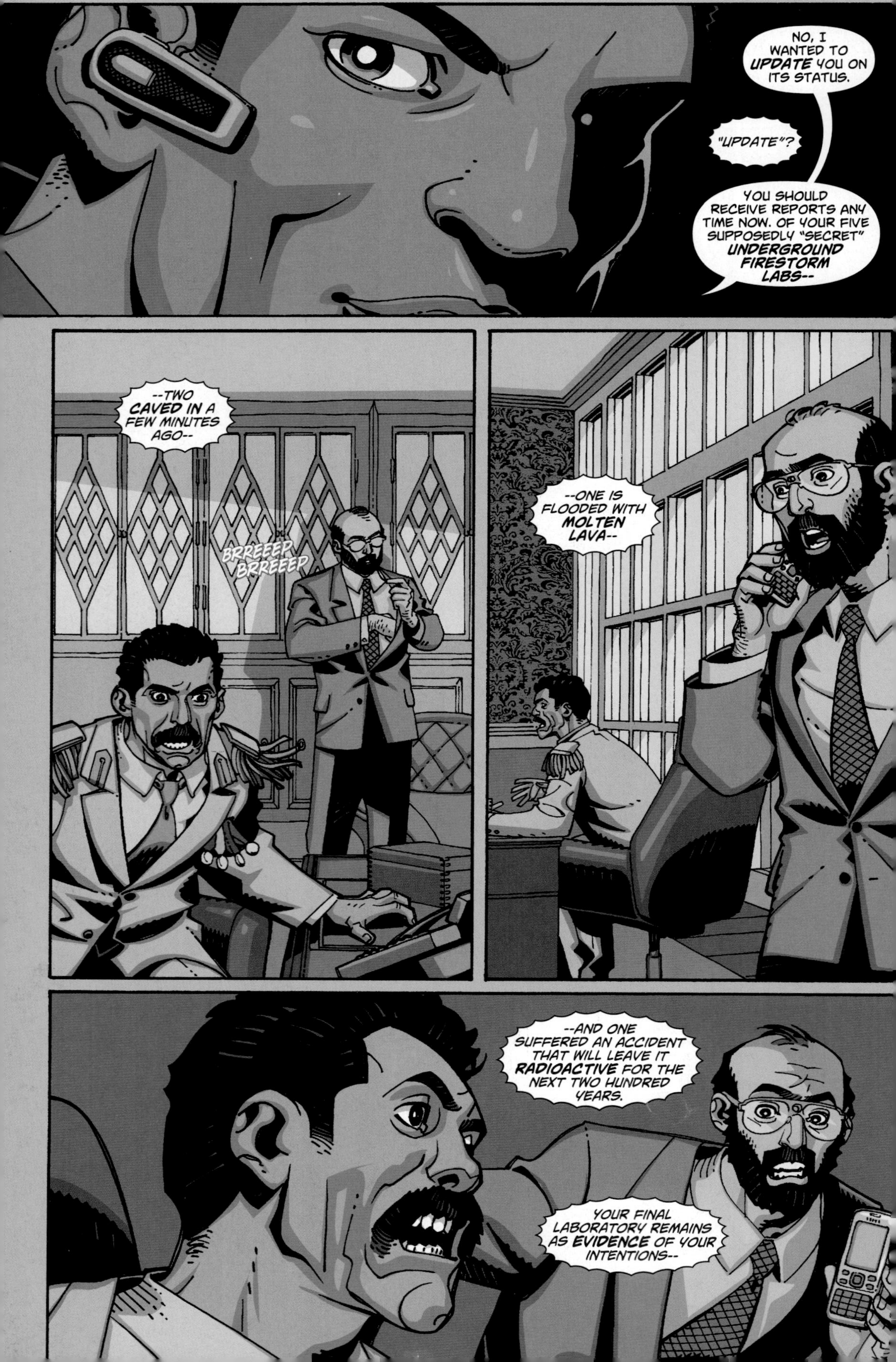
NO, I WANTED TO UPDATE YOU ON ITS STATUS.
"UPDATE"?
YOU SHOULD RECEIVE REPORTS ANY TIME NOW. OF YOUR FIVE SUPPOSEDLY "SECRET" UNDERGROUND FIRESTORM LABS--
--TWO CAVED IN A FEW MINUTES AGO--
BRREEEP BRREEEP
--ONE IS FLOODED WITH MOLTEN LAVA--
--AND ONE SUFFERED AN ACCIDENT THAT WILL LEAVE IT RADIOACTIVE FOR THE NEXT TWO HUNDRED YEARS.
YOUR FINAL LABORATORY REMAINS AS EVIDENCE OF YOUR INTENTIONS--

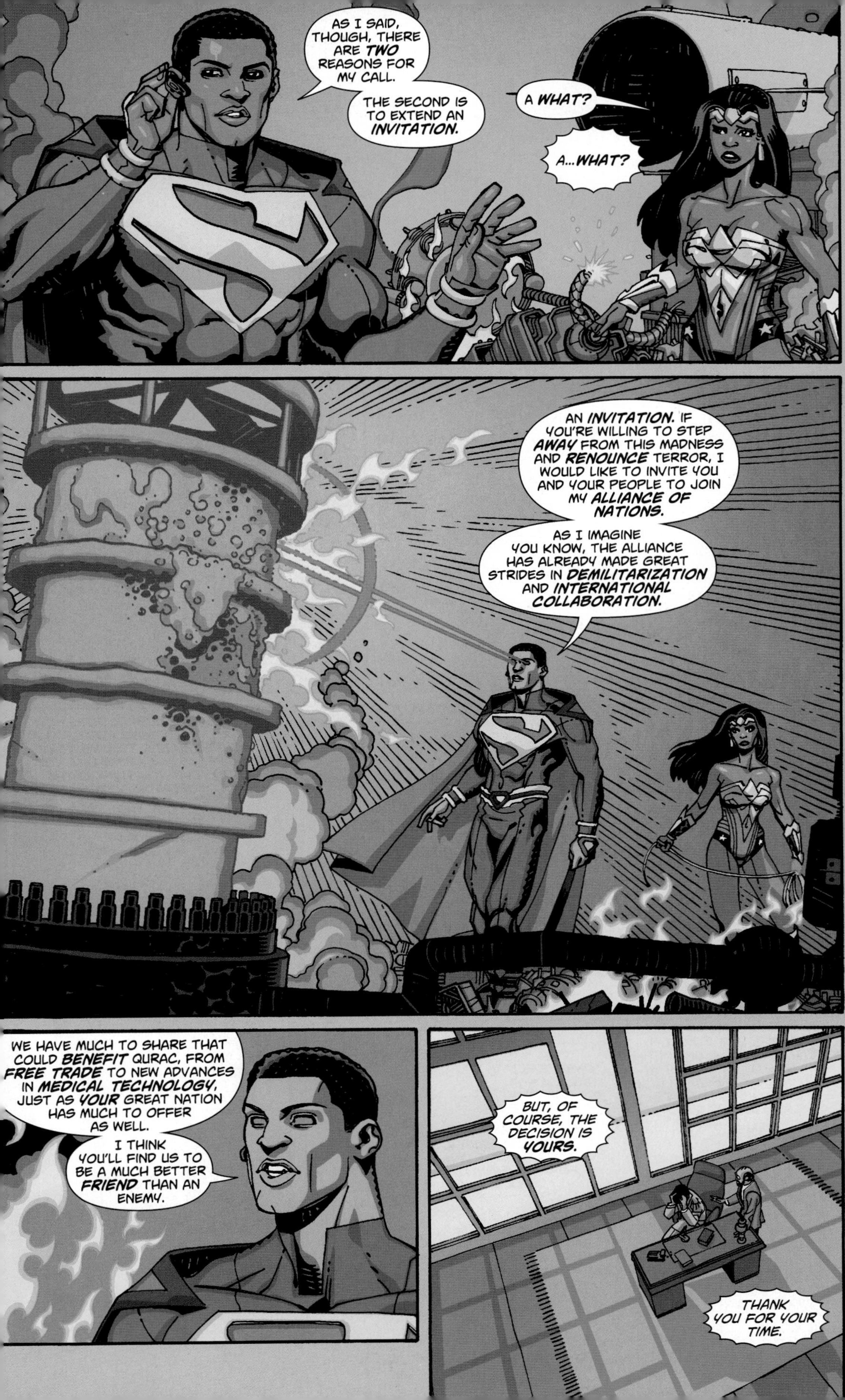
AS I SAID, THOUGH, THERE ARE TWO REASONS FOR MY CALL.
THE SECOND IS TO EXTEND AN INVITATION.
A WHAT?
A...WHAT?
AN INVITATION. IF YOU'RE WILLING TO STEP AWAY FROM THIS MADNESS AND RENOUNCE TERROR, I WOULD LIKE TO INVITE YOU AND YOUR PEOPLE TO JOIN MY ALLIANCE OF NATIONS.
AS I IMAGINE YOU KNOW, THE ALLIANCE HAS ALREADY MADE GREAT STRIDES IN DEMILITARIZATION AND INTERNATIONAL COLLABORATION.
WE HAVE MUCH TO SHARE THAT COULD BENEFIT QURAC, FROM FREE TRADE TO NEW ADVANCES IN MEDICAL TECHNOLOGY, JUST AS YOUR GREAT NATION HAS MUCH TO OFFER AS WELL.
I THINK YOU'LL FIND US TO BE A MUCH BETTER FRIEND THAN AN ENEMY.
BUT, OF COURSE, THE DECISION IS YOURS.
THANK YOU FOR YOUR TIME.

AND THAT'S THAT. I'D BETTER GET BACK BEFORE SOMEONE REALIZES I'M NOT IN MY *OFFICE*.

BRAINIAC CAN ONLY COVER FOR ME FOR SO LONG.

YOU TRULY ARE A FASCINATING MASS OF *CONTRADICTIONS*, CAL.

WELL, I HAD TO OFFER HARRAT A *CHANCE*...

NO, I MEANT ALL OF THIS *SUBTERFUGE*, CONCEALING YOUR ACTIONS.

AS SUPERMAN, YOU STAND FOR *TRUTH* AND *JUSTICE*. YET YOU HAVE NO PROBLEM *LYING* TO THE ENTIRE WORLD ABOUT WHAT YOU DO AND WHO YOU ARE.

MY *SECRET IDENTITY*? THAT'S NOTHING NEW IN *OUR* LINE OF WORK, NUBIA.

TRUE. BUT YOU MUST REALIZE THAT IT MEANS SOMETHING *DIFFERENT* FOR YOU NOW.

WHEN YOU TOOK OFFICE, YOU SWORE TO *UPHOLD* YOUR NATION'S LAWS.

I CANNOT *IMAGINE* HOW MANY INTERNATIONAL LAWS WE'VE VIOLATED TODAY.

WHAT, YOU THINK I SHOULD HAVE *LET* HARRAT HAVE NUCLEAR WEAPONS?

DON'T BE RIDICULOUS. THE MAN'S A *MADMAN*.

HOWEVER, YOU HAVE SET *YOURSELF* OUTSIDE THE LAW AS WELL.

--*CALVIN ELLIS'* ACTIONS NOW AFFECT EVEN MORE PEOPLE THAN *SUPERMAN'S*. TELL ME, WHAT HAPPENS WHEN, ONE DAY, YOU DO WHAT YOU THINK IS THE "GREATER GOOD"--

--BUT THE WORLD SEES IT *DIFFERENTLY*?

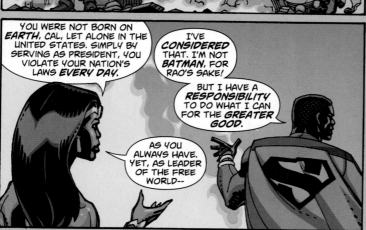

YOU WERE NOT BORN ON *EARTH*, CAL, LET ALONE IN THE UNITED STATES. SIMPLY BY SERVING AS PRESIDENT, YOU VIOLATE YOUR NATION'S LAWS *EVERY DAY*.

I'VE *CONSIDERED* THAT. I'M NOT *BATMAN*, FOR RAO'S SAKE!

BUT I HAVE A *RESPONSIBILITY* TO DO WHAT I CAN FOR THE *GREATER GOOD*.

AS YOU ALWAYS HAVE. YET, AS LEADER OF THE FREE WORLD--

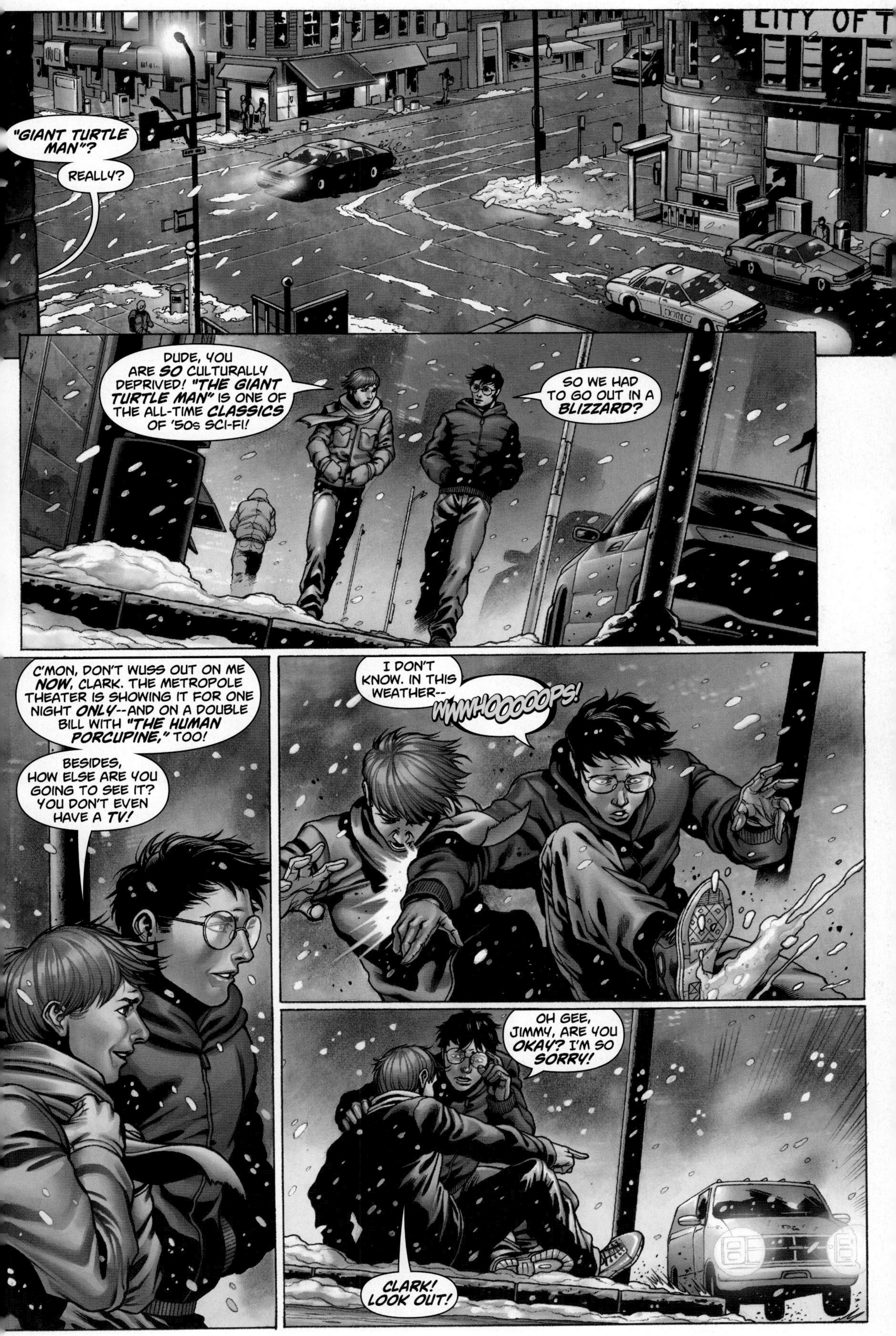

"GIANT TURTLE MAN"?
REALLY?
DUDE, YOU ARE SO CULTURALLY DEPRIVED! "THE GIANT TURTLE MAN" IS ONE OF THE ALL-TIME CLASSICS OF '50s SCI-FI!
SO WE HAD TO GO OUT IN A BLIZZARD?
C'MON, DON'T WUSS OUT ON ME NOW, CLARK. THE METROPOLE THEATER IS SHOWING IT FOR ONE NIGHT ONLY--AND ON A DOUBLE BILL WITH "THE HUMAN PORCUPINE," TOO!
BESIDES, HOW ELSE ARE YOU GOING TO SEE IT? YOU DON'T EVEN HAVE A TV!
I DON'T KNOW. IN THIS WEATHER--
WWWHOOOOOPS!
OH GEE, JIMMY, ARE YOU OKAY? I'M SO SORRY!
CLARK! LOOK OUT!

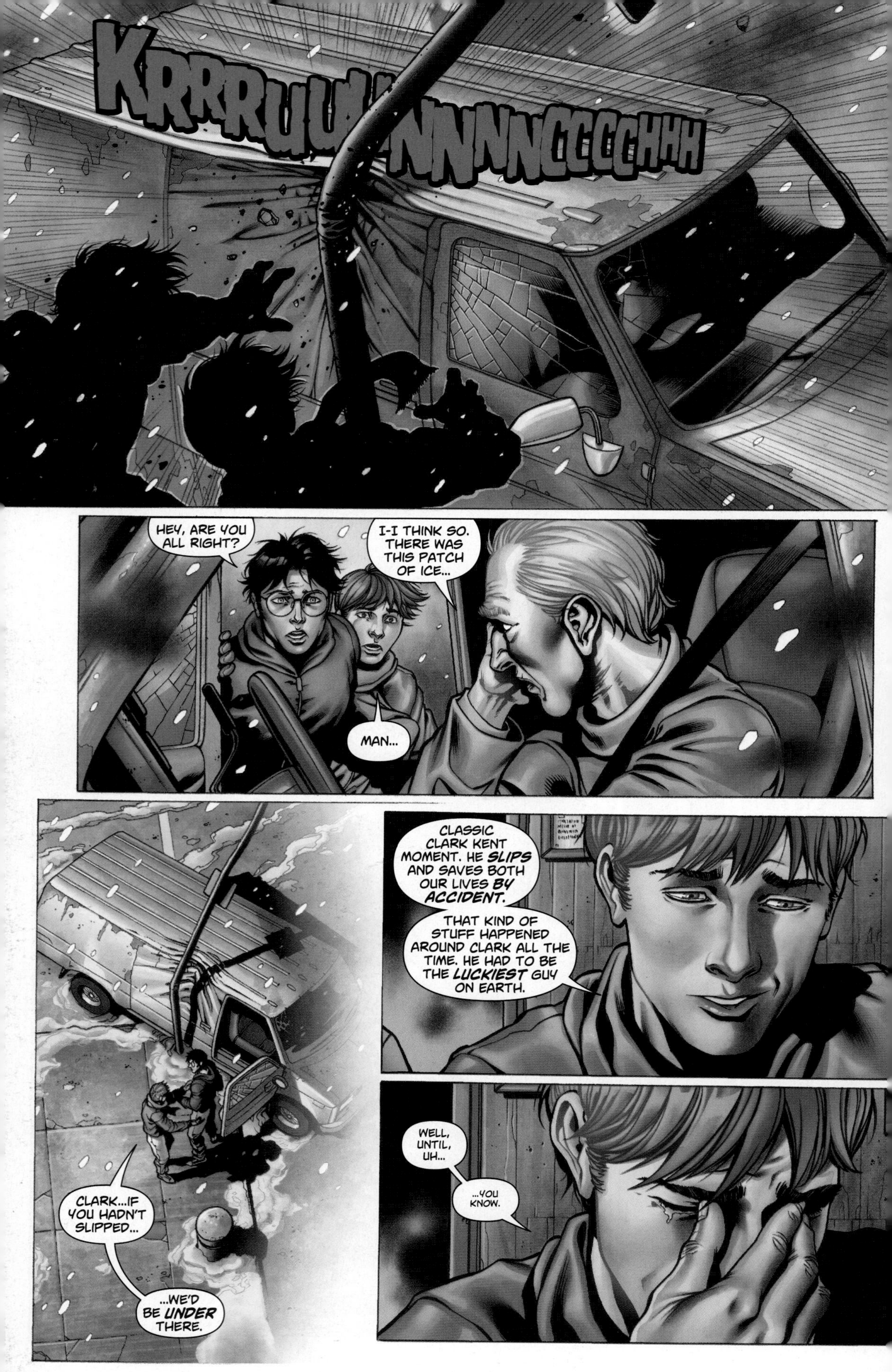
KRRRUUUNNNNCCCCHHH
HEY, ARE YOU ALL RIGHT?
I-I THINK SO. THERE WAS THIS PATCH OF ICE...
MAN...
CLARK...IF YOU HADN'T SLIPPED...
...WE'D BE UNDER THERE.
CLASSIC CLARK KENT MOMENT. HE SLIPS AND SAVES BOTH OUR LIVES BY ACCIDENT.
THAT KIND OF STUFF HAPPENED AROUND CLARK ALL THE TIME. HE HAD TO BE THE LUCKIEST GUY ON EARTH.
WELL, UNTIL, UH...
...YOU KNOW.

IT'S OKAY, JIM.

YOU KNOW, METROPOLIS NEWSMEN--YES, LOIS, AND NEWS*WOMEN*, TOO--HAVE BEEN GATHERING HERE AT SWAN'S TAVERN FOR NEARLY TWO HUNDRED YEARS.

I'VE LOST COUNT OF THE NUMBER OF TIMES I'VE SAT AT THAT BAR. BUT IT'S ALWAYS *HARDEST* WHEN WE GET TOGETHER--

--TO SAY *GOODBYE* TO ONE OF OUR OWN.

ABSENT FRIENDS

HOLLY FISCH - Writer CAFU - Artist
Y DAVID RAMOS - Colorist CARLOS M. MANGUAL - Letterer
IL MOSS - Associate Editor MATT IDELSON - Editor
IPERMAN created by JERRY SIEGEL & JOE SHUSTER

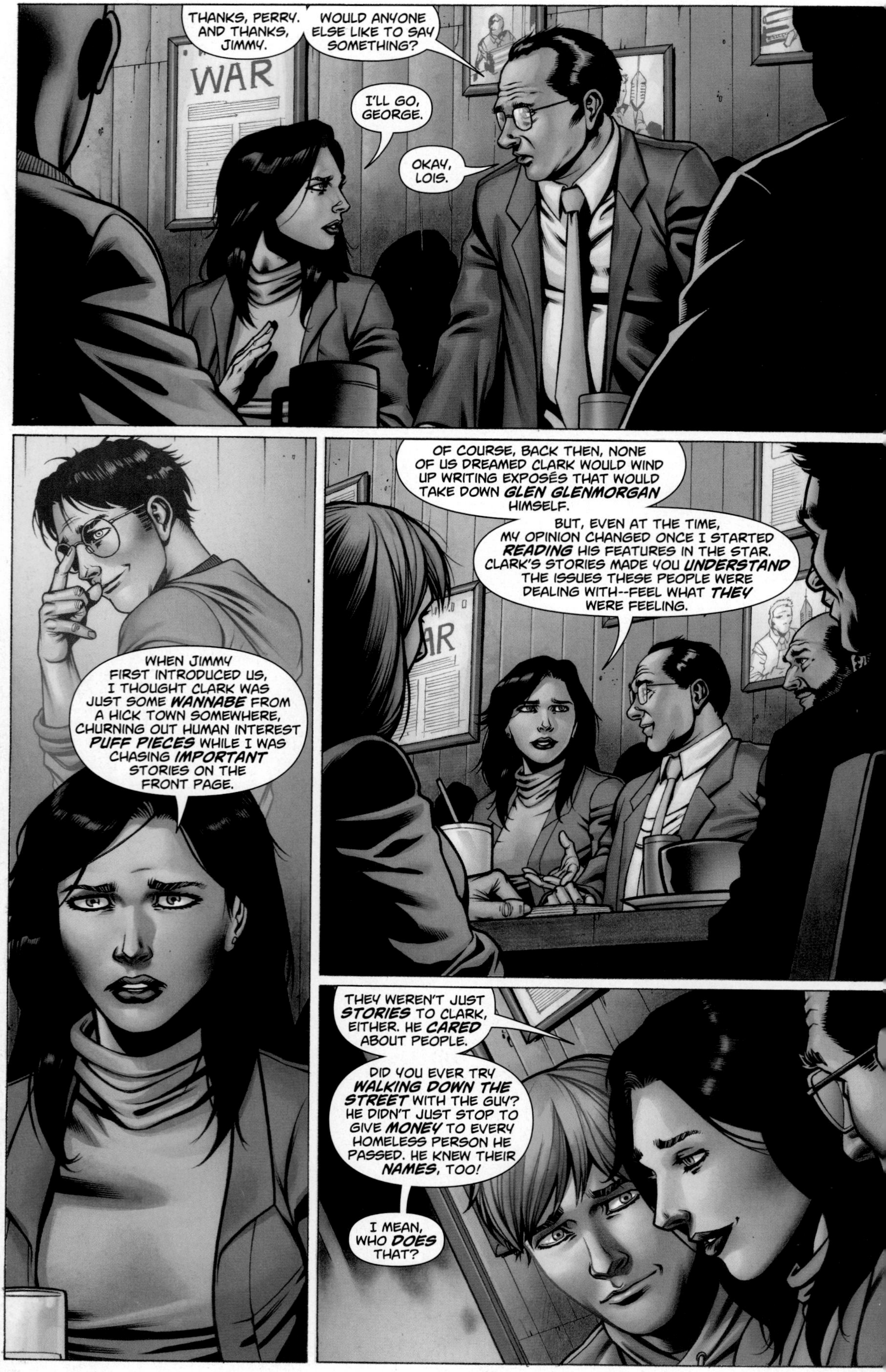

THANKS, PERRY. AND THANKS, JIMMY.
WOULD ANYONE ELSE LIKE TO SAY SOMETHING?
WAR
I'LL GO, GEORGE.
OKAY, LOIS.
WHEN JIMMY FIRST INTRODUCED US, I THOUGHT CLARK WAS JUST SOME WANNABE FROM A HICK TOWN SOMEWHERE, CHURNING OUT HUMAN INTEREST PUFF PIECES WHILE I WAS CHASING IMPORTANT STORIES ON THE FRONT PAGE.
OF COURSE, BACK THEN, NONE OF US DREAMED CLARK WOULD WIND UP WRITING EXPOSÉS THAT WOULD TAKE DOWN GLEN GLENMORGAN HIMSELF.
BUT, EVEN AT THE TIME, MY OPINION CHANGED ONCE I STARTED READING HIS FEATURES IN THE STAR. CLARK'S STORIES MADE YOU UNDERSTAND THE ISSUES THESE PEOPLE WERE DEALING WITH--FEEL WHAT THEY WERE FEELING.
THEY WEREN'T JUST STORIES TO CLARK, EITHER. HE CARED ABOUT PEOPLE.
DID YOU EVER TRY WALKING DOWN THE STREET WITH THE GUY? HE DIDN'T JUST STOP TO GIVE MONEY TO EVERY HOMELESS PERSON HE PASSED. HE KNEW THEIR NAMES, TOO!
I MEAN, WHO DOES THAT?

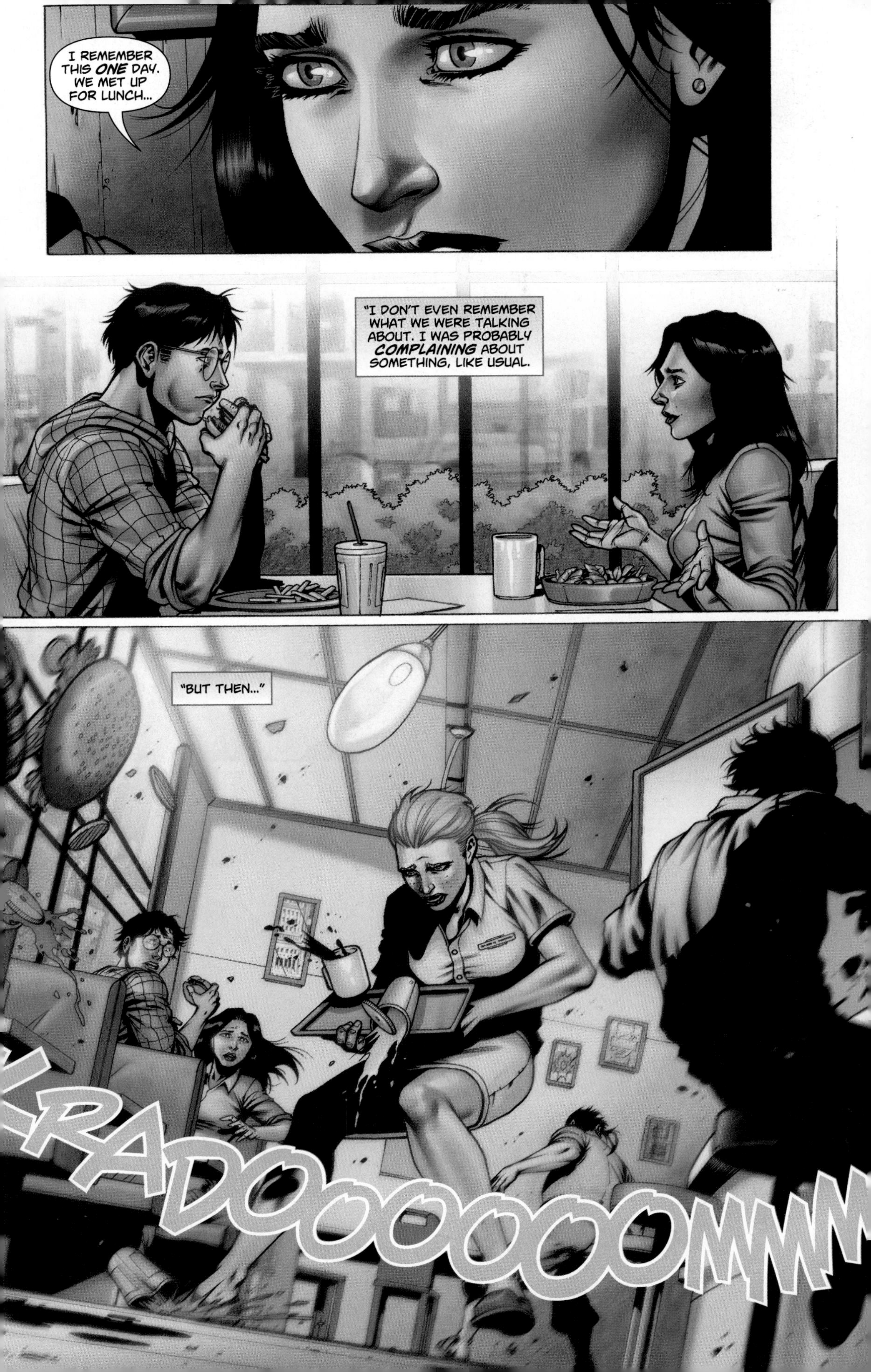
I REMEMBER THIS ONE DAY. WE MET UP FOR LUNCH...
"I DON'T EVEN REMEMBER WHAT WE WERE TALKING ABOUT. I WAS PROBABLY COMPLAINING ABOUT SOMETHING, LIKE USUAL.
"BUT THEN..."
KRADOOOOOOMMM

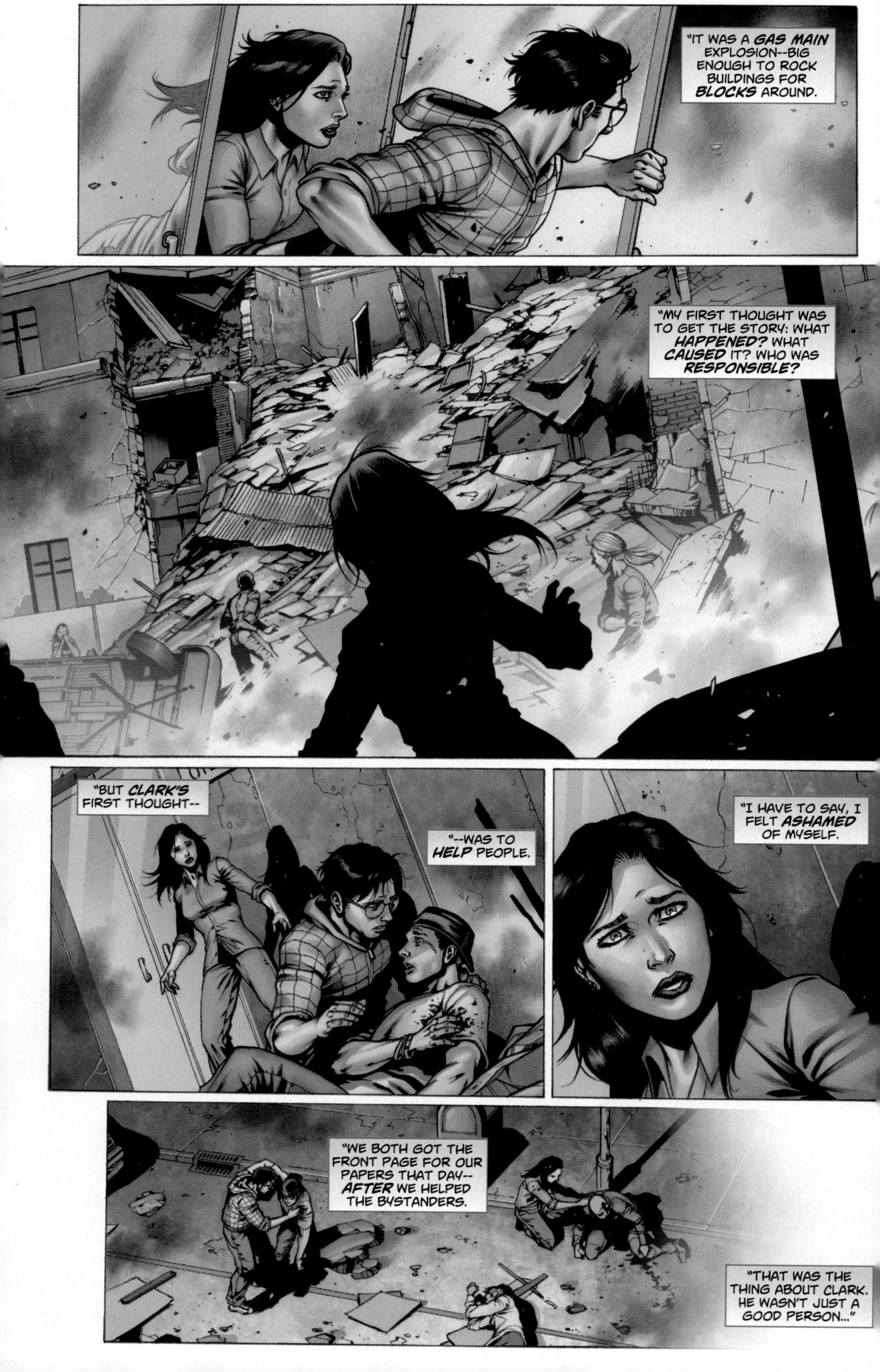
"IT WAS A GAS MAIN EXPLOSION--BIG ENOUGH TO ROCK BUILDINGS FOR BLOCKS AROUND.
"MY FIRST THOUGHT WAS TO GET THE STORY: WHAT HAPPENED? WHAT CAUSED IT? WHO WAS RESPONSIBLE?
"BUT CLARK'S FIRST THOUGHT--
"--WAS TO HELP PEOPLE.
"I HAVE TO SAY, I FELT ASHAMED OF MYSELF.
"WE BOTH GOT THE FRONT PAGE FOR OUR PAPERS THAT DAY--AFTER WE HELPED THE BYSTANDERS.
"THAT WAS THE THING ABOUT CLARK. HE WASN'T JUST A GOOD PERSON..."

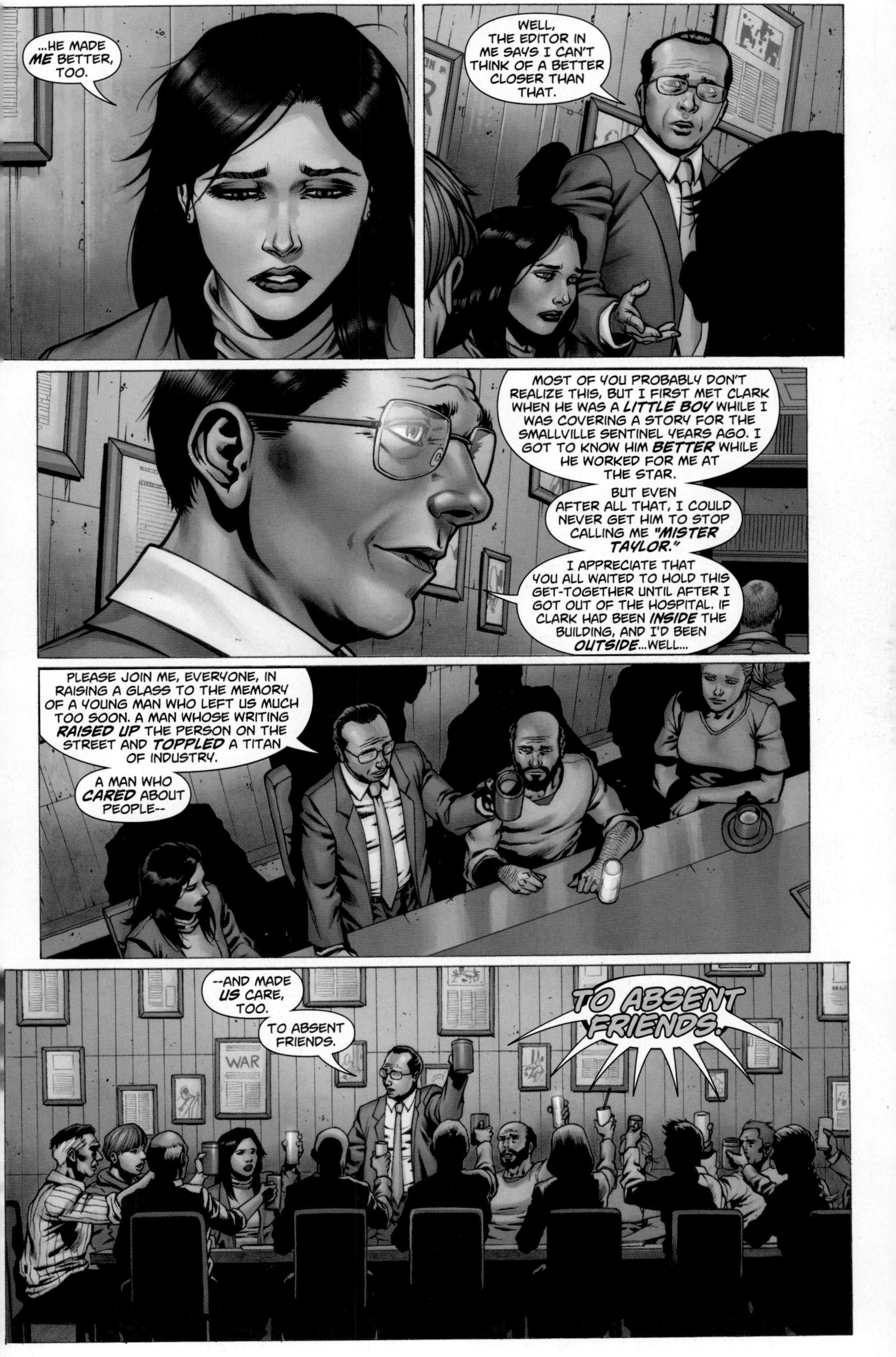
...HE MADE ME BETTER, TOO.
WELL, THE EDITOR IN ME SAYS I CAN'T THINK OF A BETTER CLOSER THAN THAT.
MOST OF YOU PROBABLY DON'T REALIZE THIS, BUT I FIRST MET CLARK WHEN HE WAS A LITTLE BOY WHILE I WAS COVERING A STORY FOR THE SMALLVILLE SENTINEL YEARS AGO. I GOT TO KNOW HIM BETTER WHILE HE WORKED FOR ME AT THE STAR.
BUT EVEN AFTER ALL THAT, I COULD NEVER GET HIM TO STOP CALLING ME "MISTER TAYLOR."
I APPRECIATE THAT YOU ALL WAITED TO HOLD THIS GET-TOGETHER UNTIL AFTER I GOT OUT OF THE HOSPITAL. IF CLARK HAD BEEN INSIDE THE BUILDING, AND I'D BEEN OUTSIDE...WELL...
PLEASE JOIN ME, EVERYONE, IN RAISING A GLASS TO THE MEMORY OF A YOUNG MAN WHO LEFT US MUCH TOO SOON. A MAN WHOSE WRITING RAISED UP THE PERSON ON THE STREET AND TOPPLED A TITAN OF INDUSTRY.
A MAN WHO CARED ABOUT PEOPLE--
--AND MADE US CARE, TOO.
TO ABSENT FRIENDS.
TO ABSENT FRIENDS.
WAR

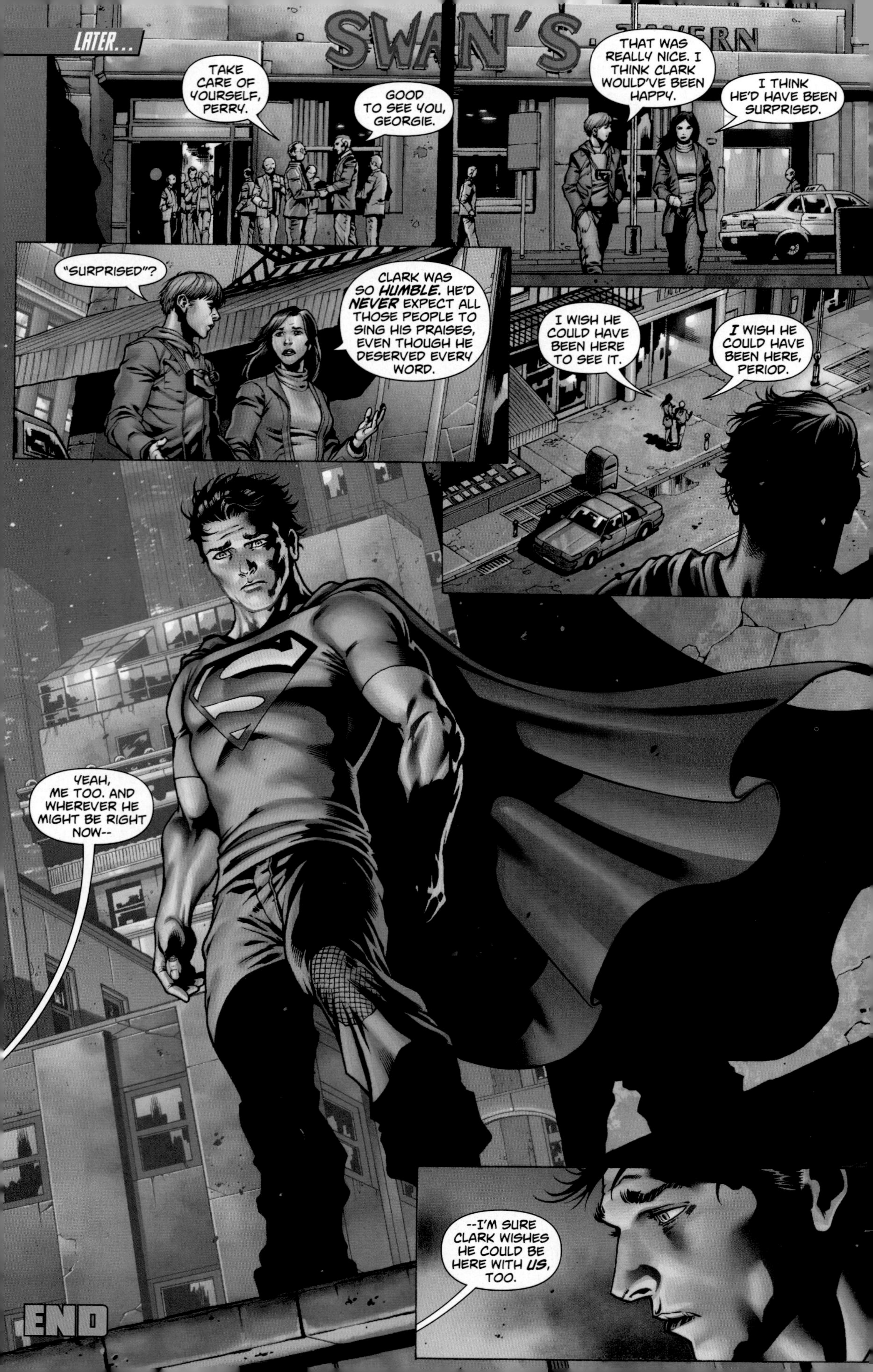

LATER...
SWAN'S TAVERN
TAKE CARE OF YOURSELF, PERRY.
GOOD TO SEE YOU, GEORGIE.
THAT WAS REALLY NICE. I THINK CLARK WOULD'VE BEEN HAPPY.
I THINK HE'D HAVE BEEN SURPRISED.
"SURPRISED"?
CLARK WAS SO HUMBLE. HE'D NEVER EXPECT ALL THOSE PEOPLE TO SING HIS PRAISES, EVEN THOUGH HE DESERVED EVERY WORD.
I WISH HE COULD HAVE BEEN HERE TO SEE IT.
I WISH HE COULD HAVE BEEN HERE, PERIOD.
YEAH, ME TOO. AND WHEREVER HE MIGHT BE RIGHT NOW--
--I'M SURE CLARK WISHES HE COULD BE HERE WITH US, TOO.
END

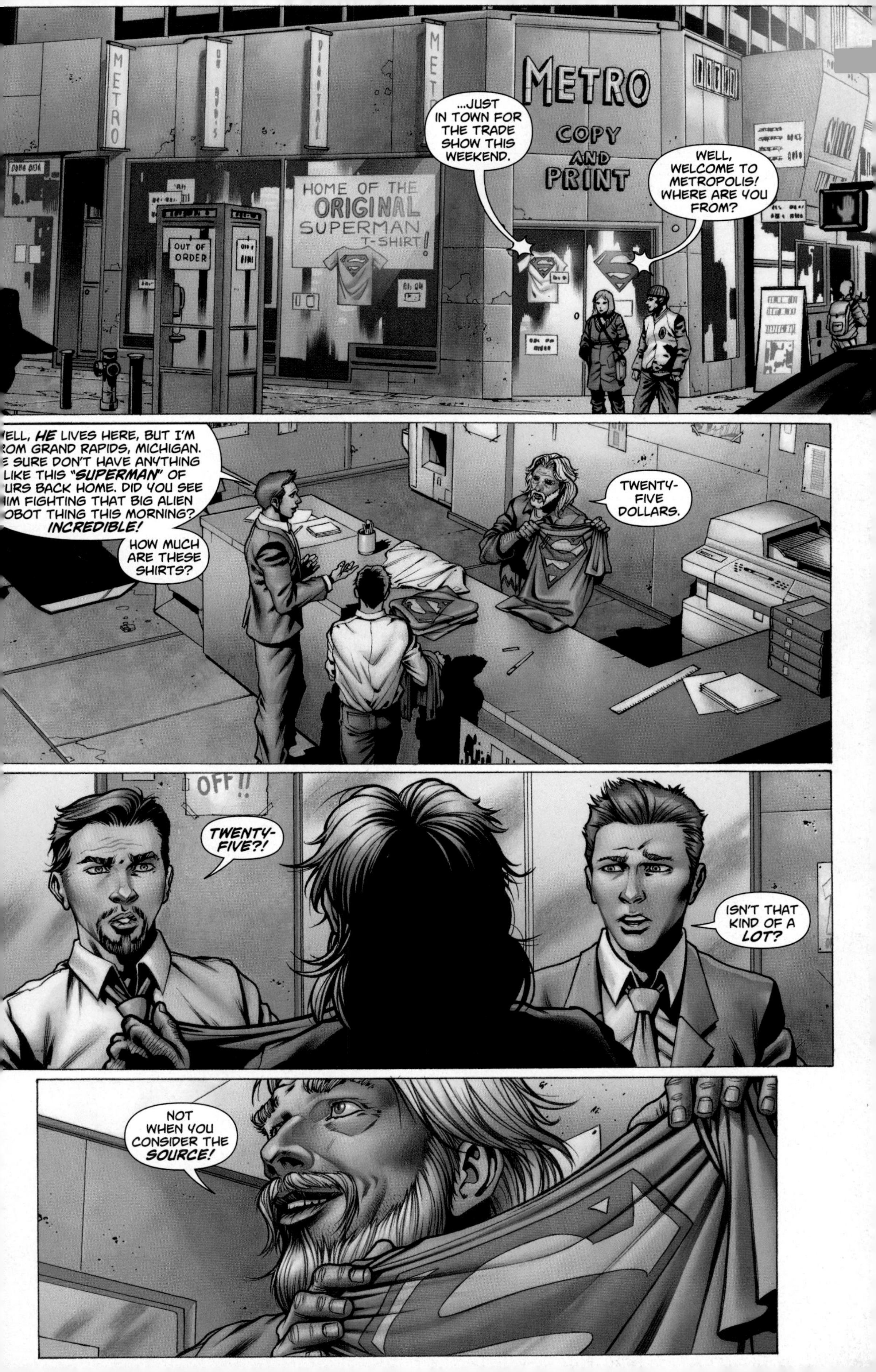
METRO
COPY AND PRINT
HOME OF THE ORIGINAL SUPERMAN T-SHIRT!
OUT OF ORDER
...JUST IN TOWN FOR THE TRADE SHOW THIS WEEKEND.
WELL, WELCOME TO METROPOLIS! WHERE ARE YOU FROM?
ELL, HE LIVES HERE, BUT I'M ROM GRAND RAPIDS, MICHIGAN. E SURE DON'T HAVE ANYTHING LIKE THIS "SUPERMAN" OF URS BACK HOME. DID YOU SEE IM FIGHTING THAT BIG ALIEN OBOT THING THIS MORNING? INCREDIBLE!
HOW MUCH ARE THESE SHIRTS?
TWENTY-FIVE DOLLARS.
OFF!!
TWENTY-FIVE?!
ISN'T THAT KIND OF A LOT?
NOT WHEN YOU CONSIDER THE SOURCE!

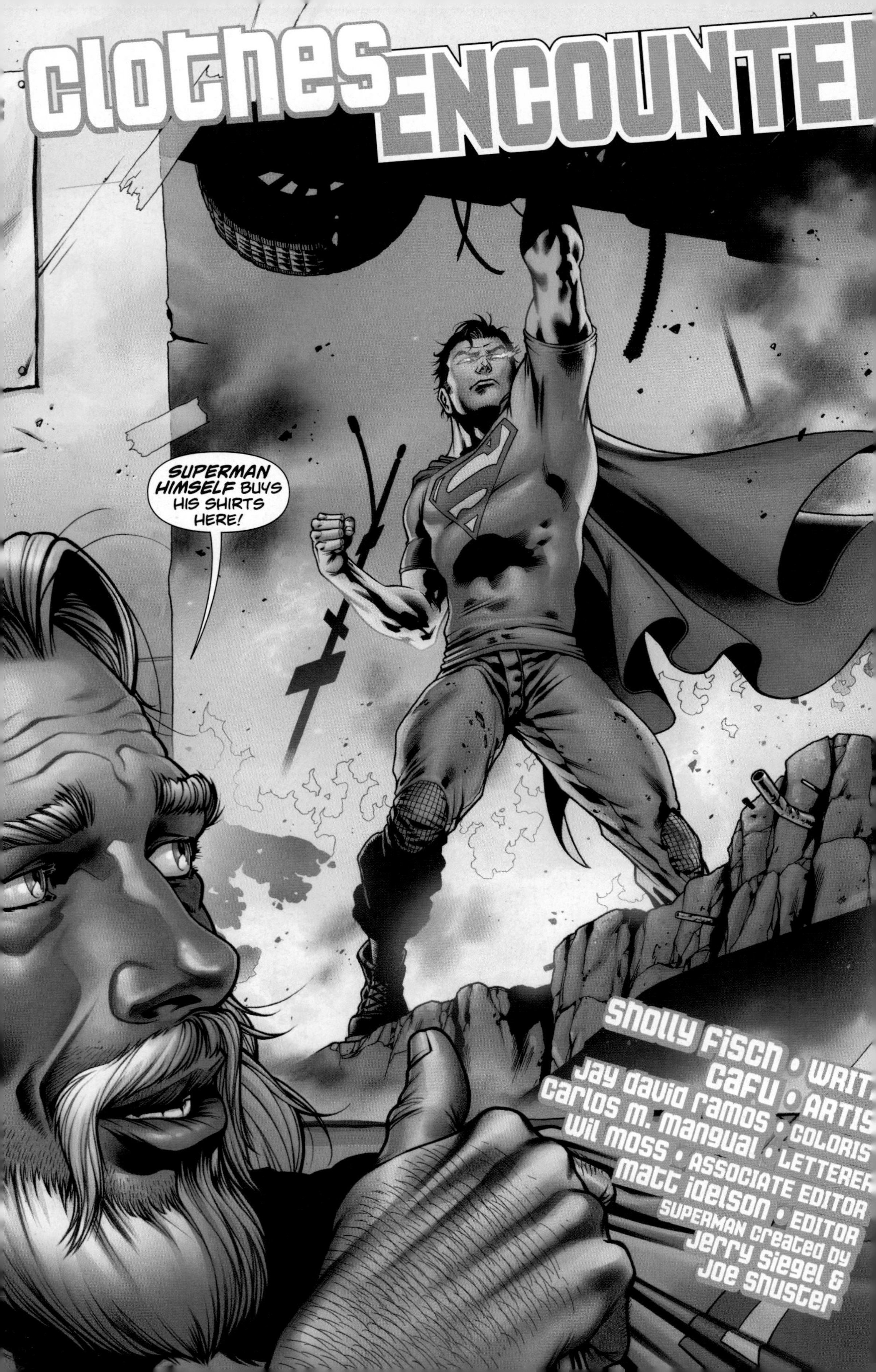
CLOTHES ENCOUNTER
SUPERMAN HIMSELF BUYS HIS SHIRTS HERE!
SHOLLY FISCH • WRIT
CAFU • ARTIS
JAY DAVID RAMOS • COLORIS
CARLOS M. MANGUAL • LETTERER
WIL MOSS • ASSOCIATE EDITOR
MATT IDELSON • EDITOR
SUPERMAN CREATED BY
JERRY SIEGEL &
JOE SHUSTER

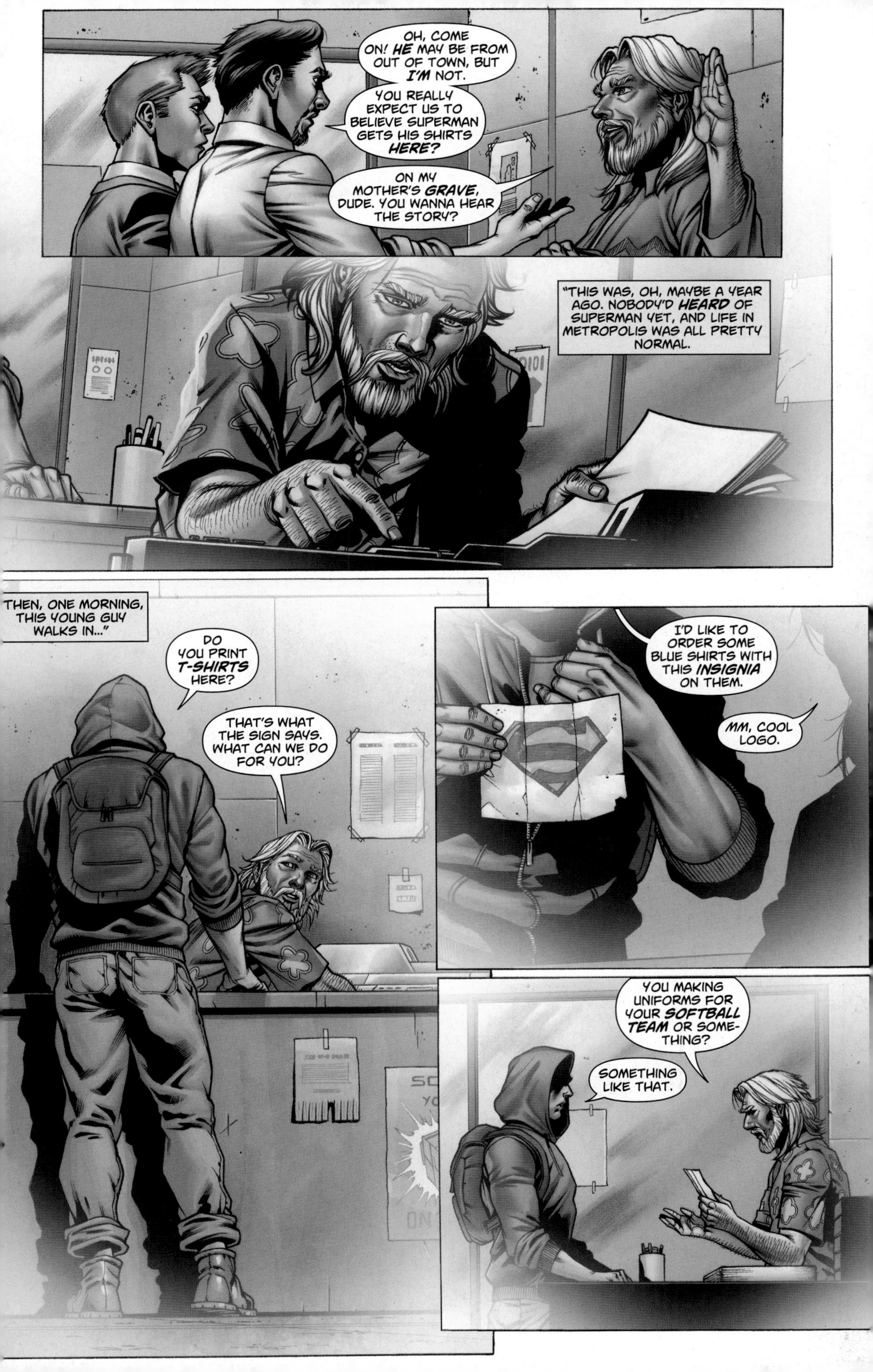
OH, COME ON! HE MAY BE FROM OUT OF TOWN, BUT I'M NOT.
YOU REALLY EXPECT US TO BELIEVE SUPERMAN GETS HIS SHIRTS HERE?
ON MY MOTHER'S GRAVE, DUDE. YOU WANNA HEAR THE STORY?
"THIS WAS, OH, MAYBE A YEAR AGO. NOBODY'D HEARD OF SUPERMAN YET, AND LIFE IN METROPOLIS WAS ALL PRETTY NORMAL.
THEN, ONE MORNING, THIS YOUNG GUY WALKS IN..."
DO YOU PRINT T-SHIRTS HERE?
THAT'S WHAT THE SIGN SAYS. WHAT CAN WE DO FOR YOU?
I'D LIKE TO ORDER SOME BLUE SHIRTS WITH THIS INSIGNIA ON THEM.
MM, COOL LOGO.
YOU MAKING UNIFORMS FOR YOUR SOFTBALL TEAM OR SOME-THING?
SOMETHING LIKE THAT.

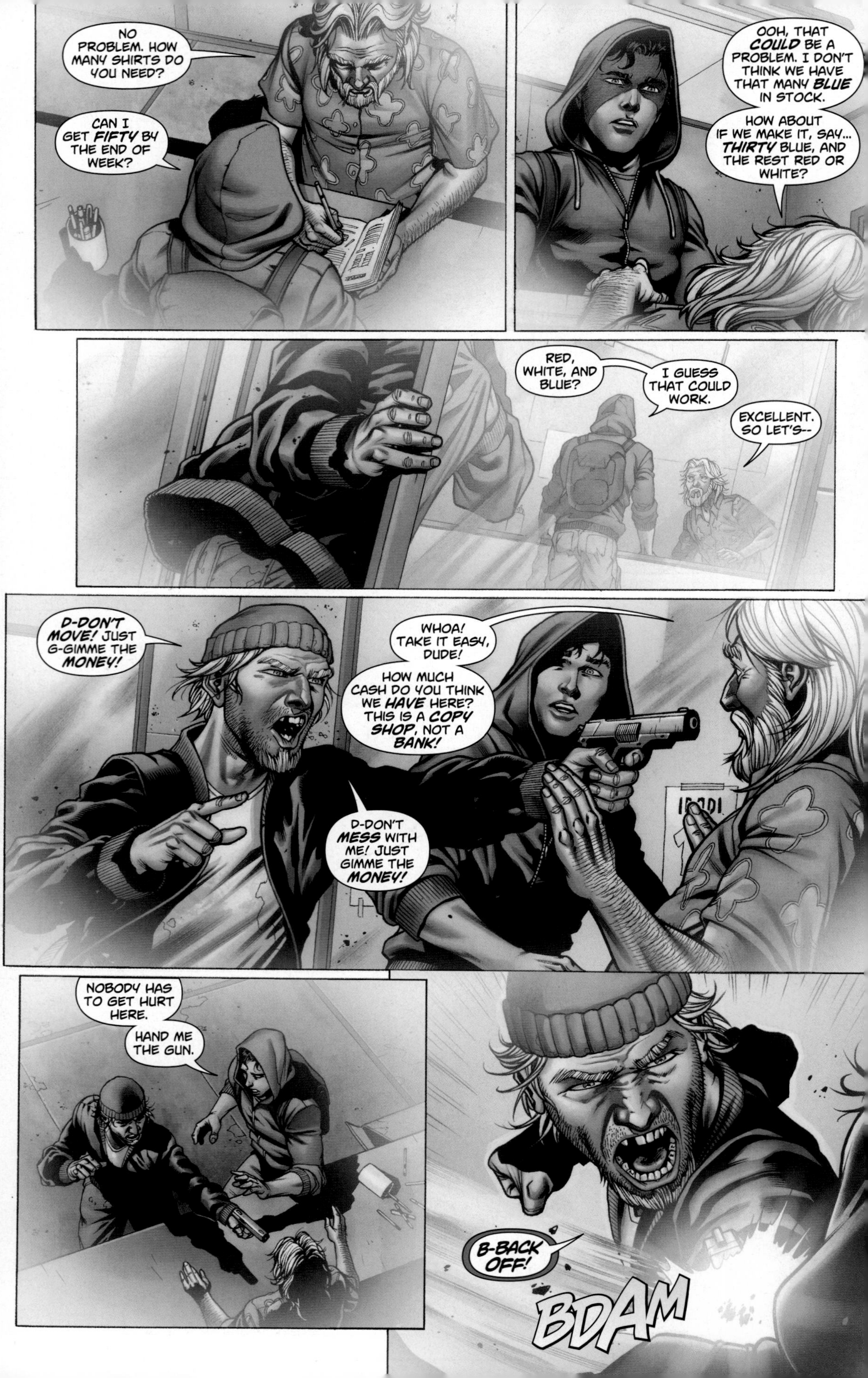

NO PROBLEM. HOW MANY SHIRTS DO YOU NEED?
CAN I GET FIFTY BY THE END OF WEEK?
OOH, THAT COULD BE A PROBLEM. I DON'T THINK WE HAVE THAT MANY BLUE IN STOCK.
HOW ABOUT IF WE MAKE IT, SAY... THIRTY BLUE, AND THE REST RED OR WHITE?
RED, WHITE, AND BLUE?
I GUESS THAT COULD WORK.
EXCELLENT. SO LET'S--
D-DON'T MOVE! JUST G-GIMME THE MONEY!
WHOA! TAKE IT EASY, DUDE!
HOW MUCH CASH DO YOU THINK WE HAVE HERE? THIS IS A COPY SHOP, NOT A BANK!
D-DON'T MESS WITH ME! JUST GIMME THE MONEY!
NOBODY HAS TO GET HURT HERE.
HAND ME THE GUN.
B-BACK OFF!
BDAM

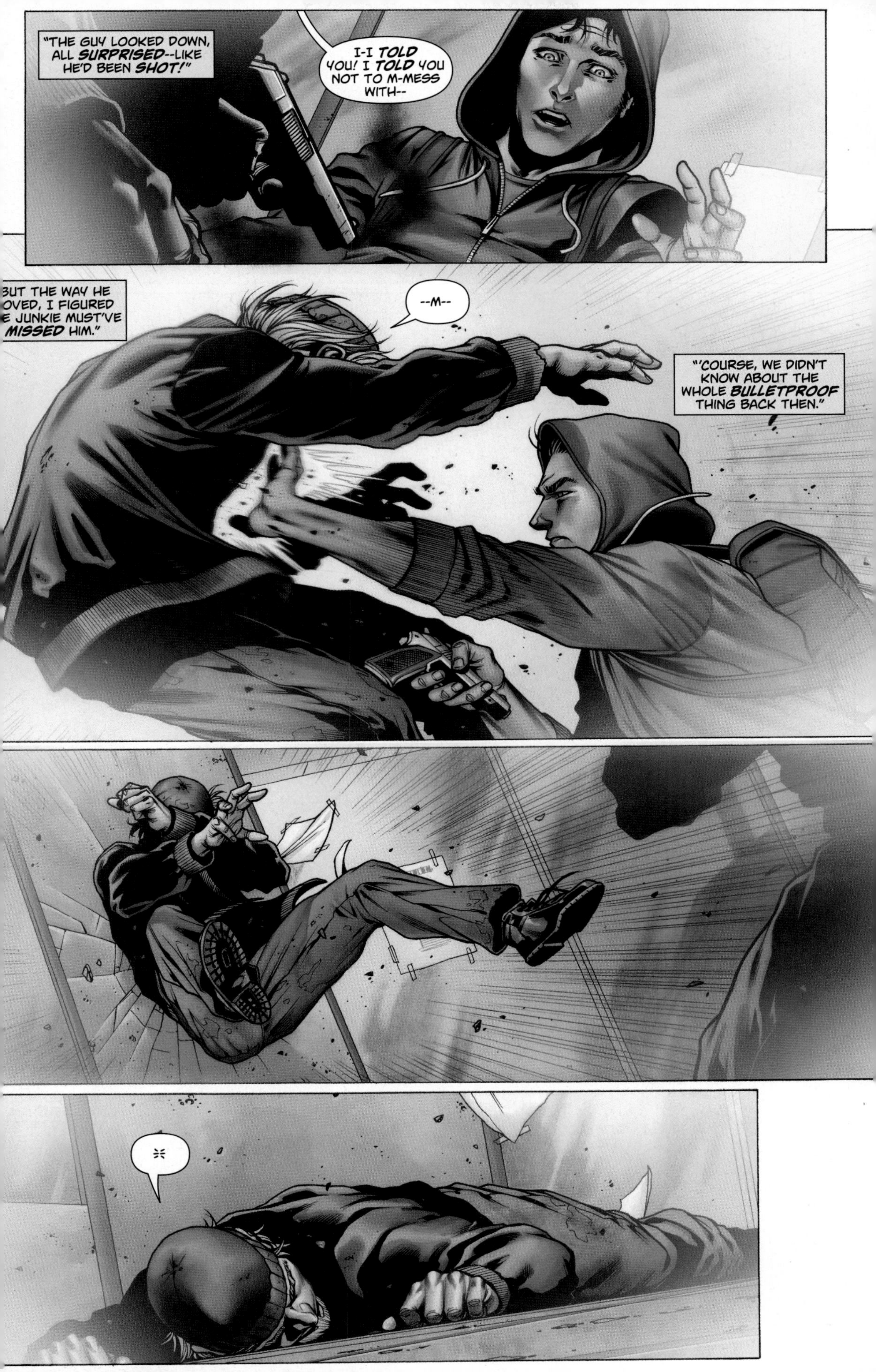
"THE GUY LOOKED DOWN, ALL SURPRISED--LIKE HE'D BEEN SHOT!"
I-I TOLD YOU! I TOLD YOU NOT TO M-MESS WITH--
BUT THE WAY HE OVED, I FIGURED E JUNKIE MUST'VE MISSED HIM."
--M--
"'COURSE, WE DIDN'T KNOW ABOUT THE WHOLE BULLETPROOF THING BACK THEN."

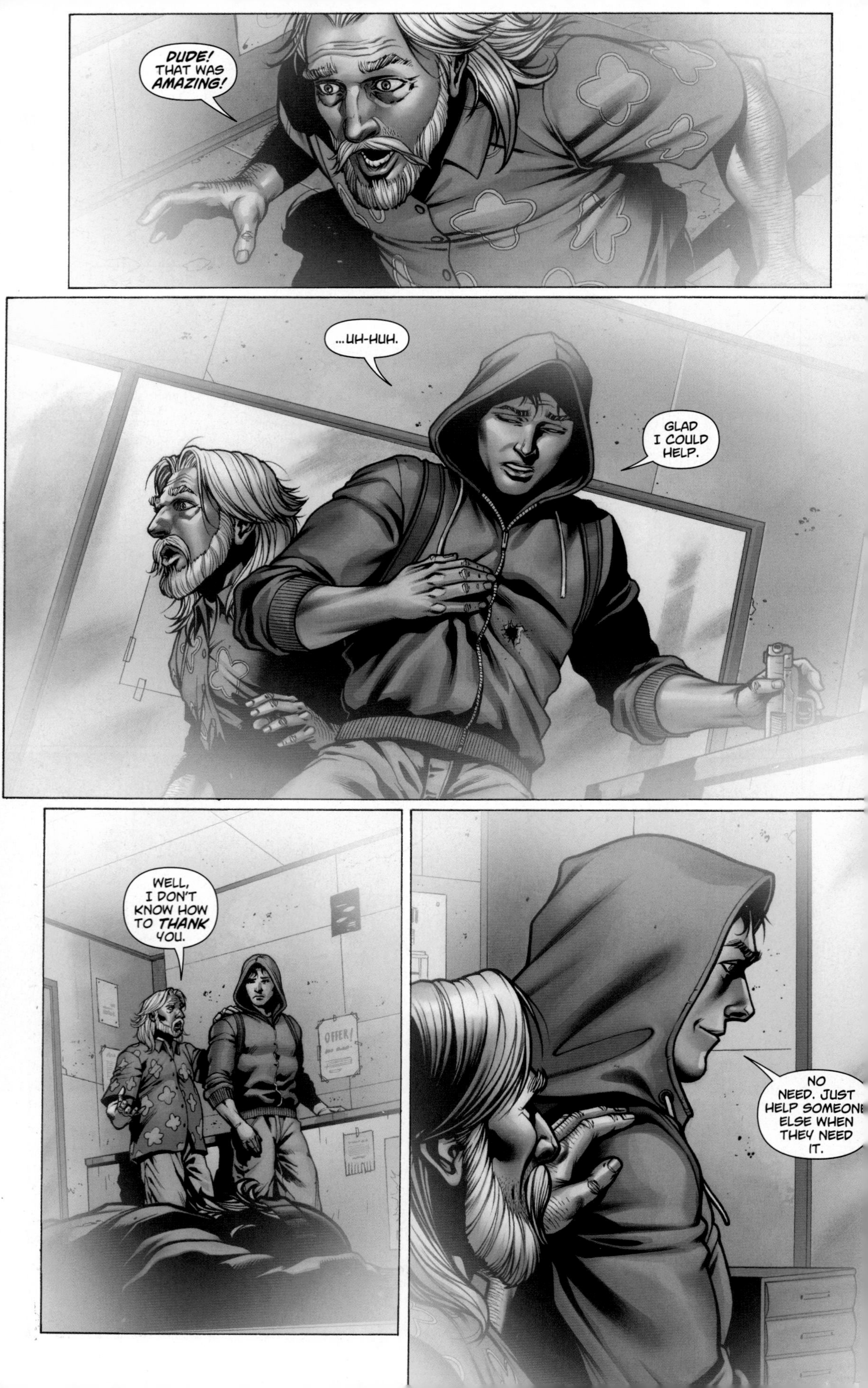
DUDE! THAT WAS AMAZING!
...UH-HUH.
GLAD I COULD HELP.
WELL, I DON'T KNOW HOW TO THANK YOU.
NO NEED. JUST HELP SOMEONE ELSE WHEN THEY NEED IT.

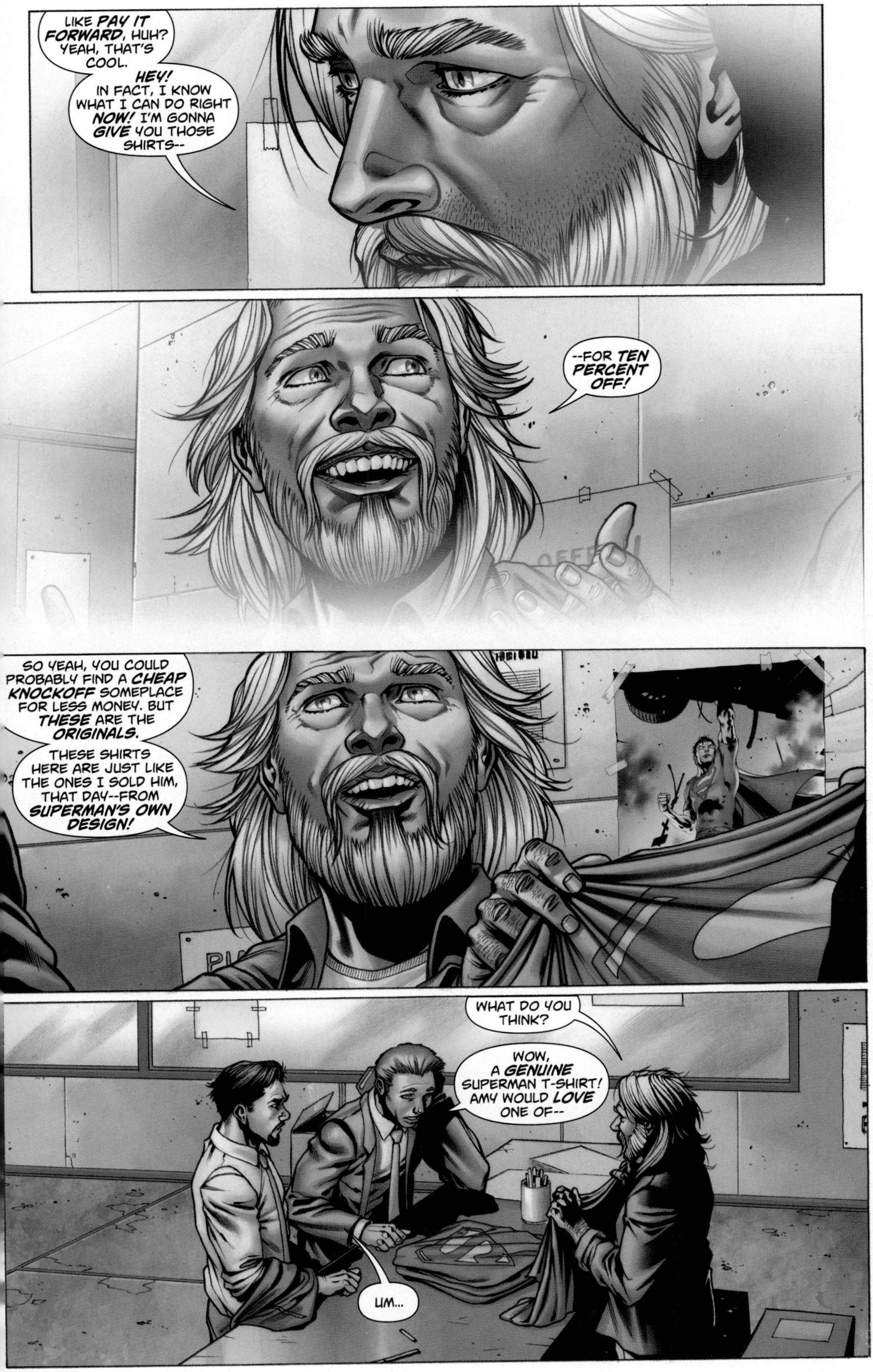
LIKE PAY IT FORWARD, HUH? YEAH, THAT'S COOL.
HEY! IN FACT, I KNOW WHAT I CAN DO RIGHT NOW! I'M GONNA GIVE YOU THOSE SHIRTS--
--FOR TEN PERCENT OFF!
SO YEAH, YOU COULD PROBABLY FIND A CHEAP KNOCKOFF SOMEPLACE FOR LESS MONEY. BUT THESE ARE THE ORIGINALS.
THESE SHIRTS HERE ARE JUST LIKE THE ONES I SOLD HIM, THAT DAY--FROM SUPERMAN'S OWN DESIGN!
WHAT DO YOU THINK?
WOW, A GENUINE SUPERMAN T-SHIRT! AMY WOULD LOVE ONE OF--
UM...

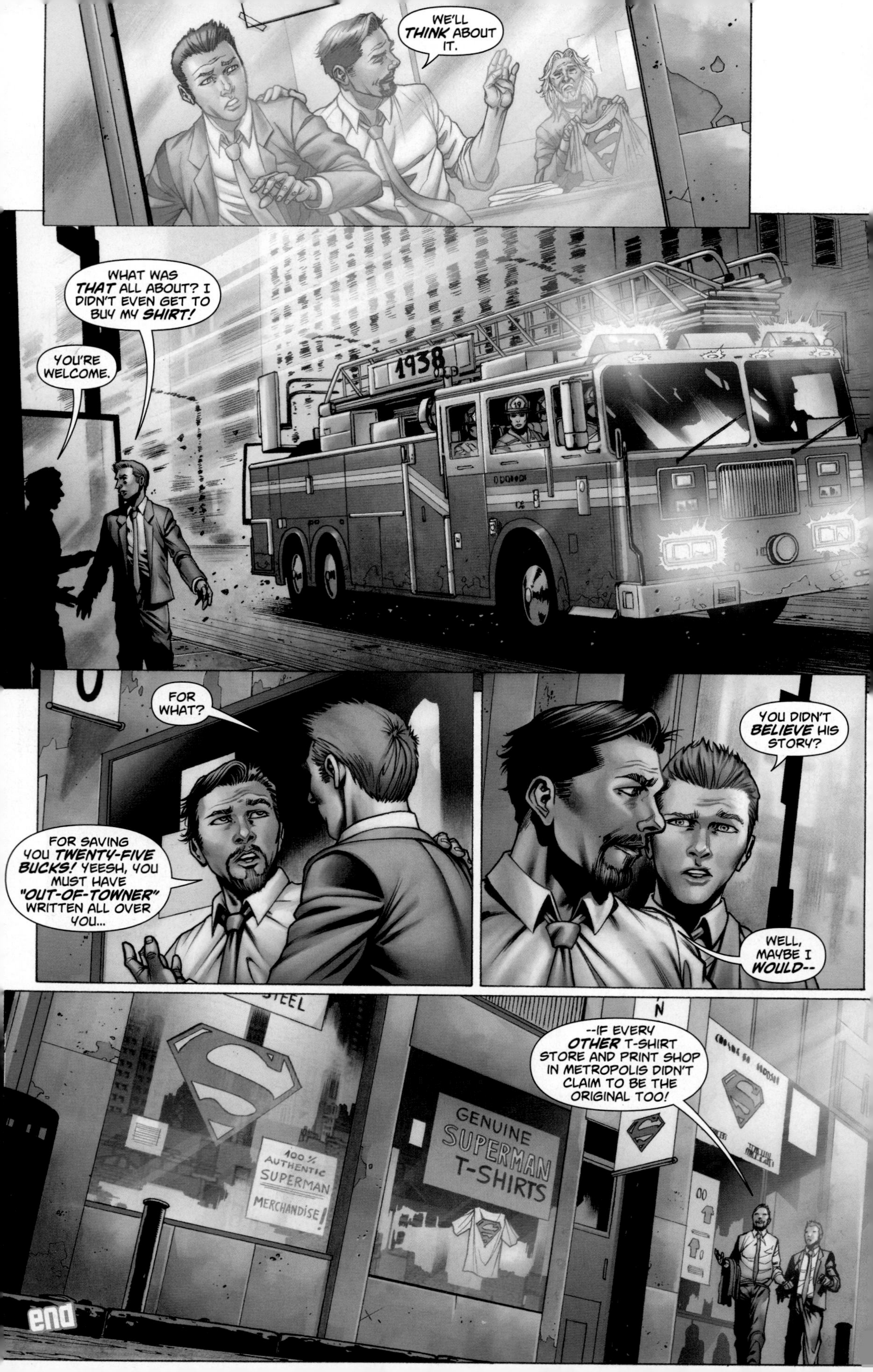
WE'LL THINK ABOUT IT.
WHAT WAS THAT ALL ABOUT? I DIDN'T EVEN GET TO BUY MY SHIRT!
YOU'RE WELCOME.
1938
FOR WHAT?
FOR SAVING YOU TWENTY-FIVE BUCKS! YEESH, YOU MUST HAVE "OUT-OF-TOWNER" WRITTEN ALL OVER YOU...
YOU DIDN'T BELIEVE HIS STORY?
WELL, MAYBE I WOULD--
STEEL
--IF EVERY OTHER T-SHIRT STORE AND PRINT SHOP IN METROPOLIS DIDN'T CLAIM TO BE THE ORIGINAL TOO!
100% AUTHENTIC SUPERMAN MERCHANDISE!
GENUINE SUPERMAN T-SHIRTS
end

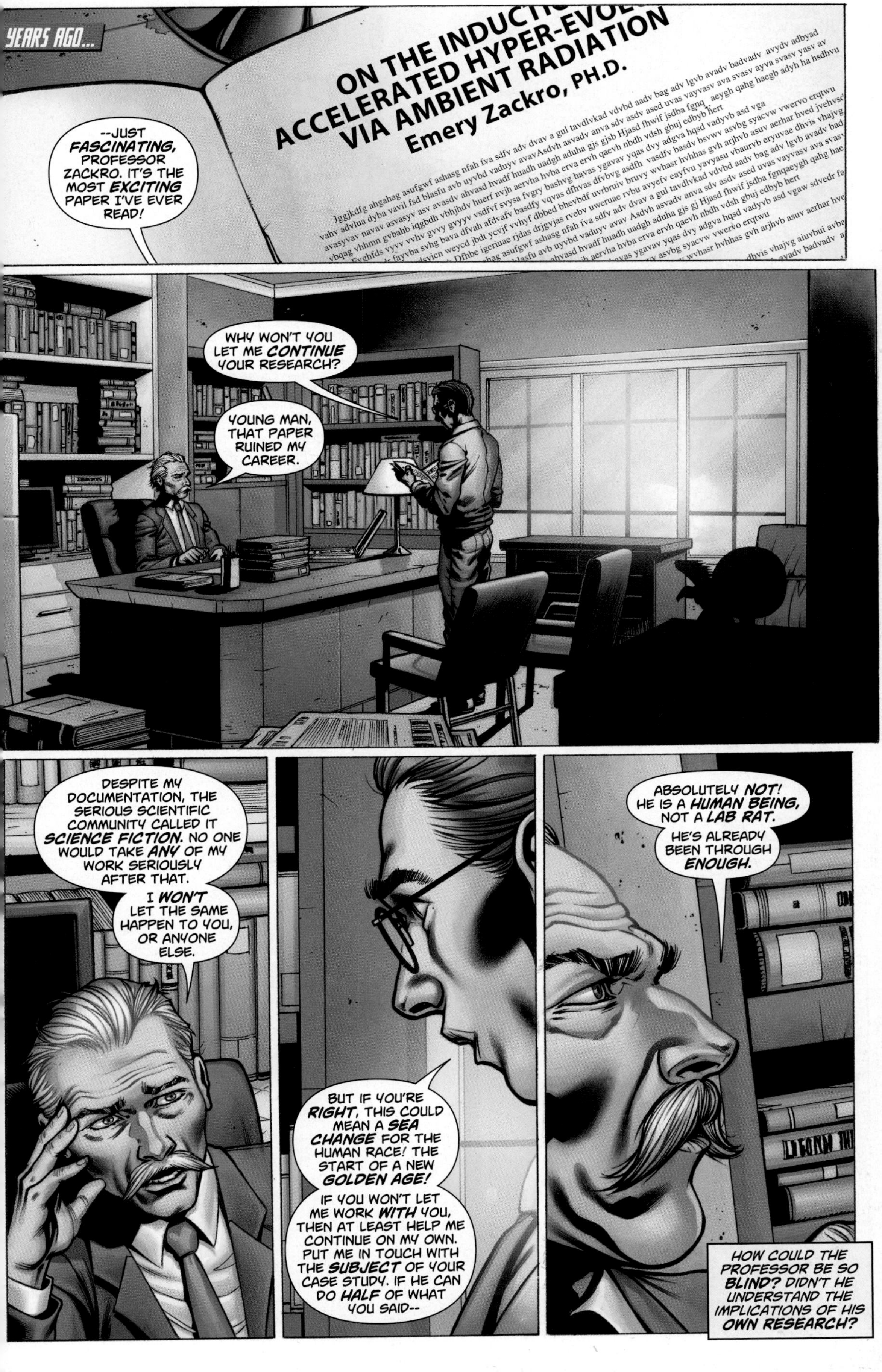
YEARS AGO...
ON THE INDUCTIO
ACCELERATED HYPER-EVOL
VIA AMBIENT RADIATION
Emery Zackro, PH.D.
--JUST FASCINATING, PROFESSOR ZACKRO. IT'S THE MOST EXCITING PAPER I'VE EVER READ!
WHY WON'T YOU LET ME CONTINUE YOUR RESEARCH?
YOUNG MAN, THAT PAPER RUINED MY CAREER.
DESPITE MY DOCUMENTATION, THE SERIOUS SCIENTIFIC COMMUNITY CALLED IT SCIENCE FICTION. NO ONE WOULD TAKE ANY OF MY WORK SERIOUSLY AFTER THAT.
I WON'T LET THE SAME HAPPEN TO YOU, OR ANYONE ELSE.
BUT IF YOU'RE RIGHT, THIS COULD MEAN A SEA CHANGE FOR THE HUMAN RACE! THE START OF A NEW GOLDEN AGE!
IF YOU WON'T LET ME WORK WITH YOU, THEN AT LEAST HELP ME CONTINUE ON MY OWN. PUT ME IN TOUCH WITH THE SUBJECT OF YOUR CASE STUDY. IF HE CAN DO HALF OF WHAT YOU SAID--
ABSOLUTELY NOT! HE IS A HUMAN BEING, NOT A LAB RAT.
HE'S ALREADY BEEN THROUGH ENOUGH.
HOW COULD THE PROFESSOR BE SO BLIND? DIDN'T HE UNDERSTAND THE IMPLICATIONS OF HIS OWN RESEARCH?

WELL, MAYBE HIS **WORK** CAN HELP ME, EVEN IF HE WON'T.

FROM THE DESCRIPTION IN ZACKRO'S PAPER, THE PERSON I'M LOOKING FOR IS SOMEWHERE IN THIS PART OF **RURAL KANSAS.**

AND JUDGING FROM THE WAY THE LOCALS TALK ABOUT **STRANGE THINGS** HAPPENING AROUND HERE, **THIS** COULD BE THE PLACE.

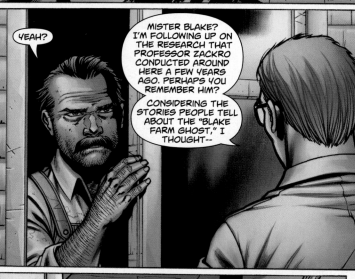

YEAH?

MISTER BLAKE? I'M FOLLOWING UP ON THE RESEARCH THAT PROFESSOR ZACKRO CONDUCTED AROUND HERE A FEW YEARS AGO. PERHAPS YOU REMEMBER HIM?

CONSIDERING THE STORIES PEOPLE TELL ABOUT THE "BLAKE FARM GHOST," I THOUGHT--

I NEVER HEARD OF ANY **ZACKRO!** AND THERE'S **NO** "BLAKE FARM GHOST"!

YOU'RE **TRESPASSING** ON MY LAND!

GET OUT!

SO MUCH FOR SMALL TOWN HOSPITALITY.

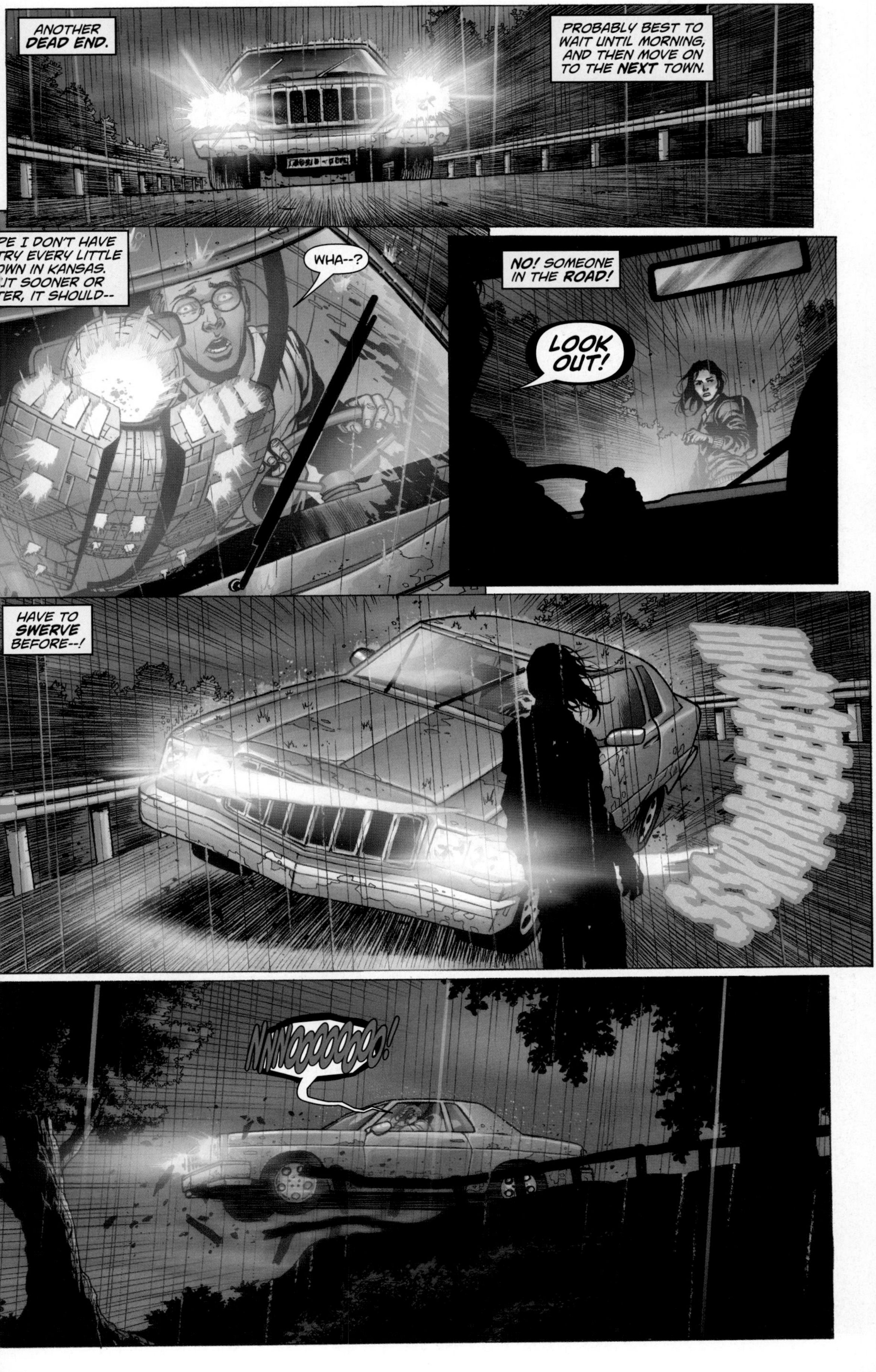
ANOTHER DEAD END.
PROBABLY BEST TO WAIT UNTIL MORNING, AND THEN MOVE ON TO THE NEXT TOWN.
PE I DON'T HAVE TRY EVERY LITTLE OWN IN KANSAS. UT SOONER OR TER, IT SHOULD--
WHA--?
NO! SOMEONE IN THE ROAD!
LOOK OUT!
HAVE TO SWERVE BEFORE--!
SSSKREEEEEEECH
NNNOOOOOOOO!

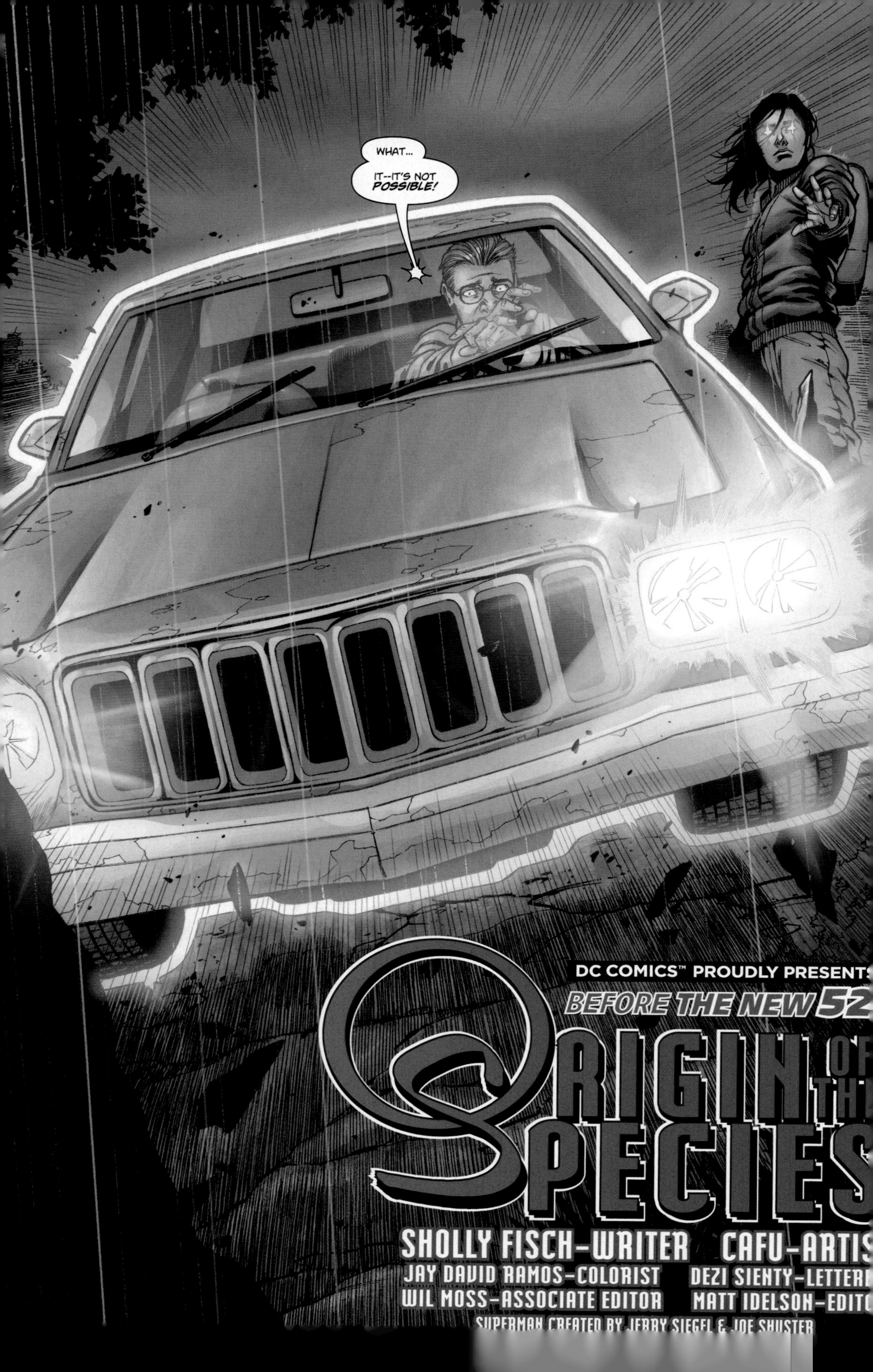
WHAT... IT--IT'S NOT POSSIBLE!
DC COMICS™ PROUDLY PRESENTS
BEFORE THE NEW 52
ORIGIN
SPECIES
SHOLLY FISCH–WRITER CAFU–ARTIS
JAY DAVID RAMOS–COLORIST DEZI SIENTY–LETTER
WIL MOSS–ASSOCIATE EDITOR MATT IDELSON–EDITO
SUPERMAN CREATED BY JERRY SIEGEL & JOE SHUSTER

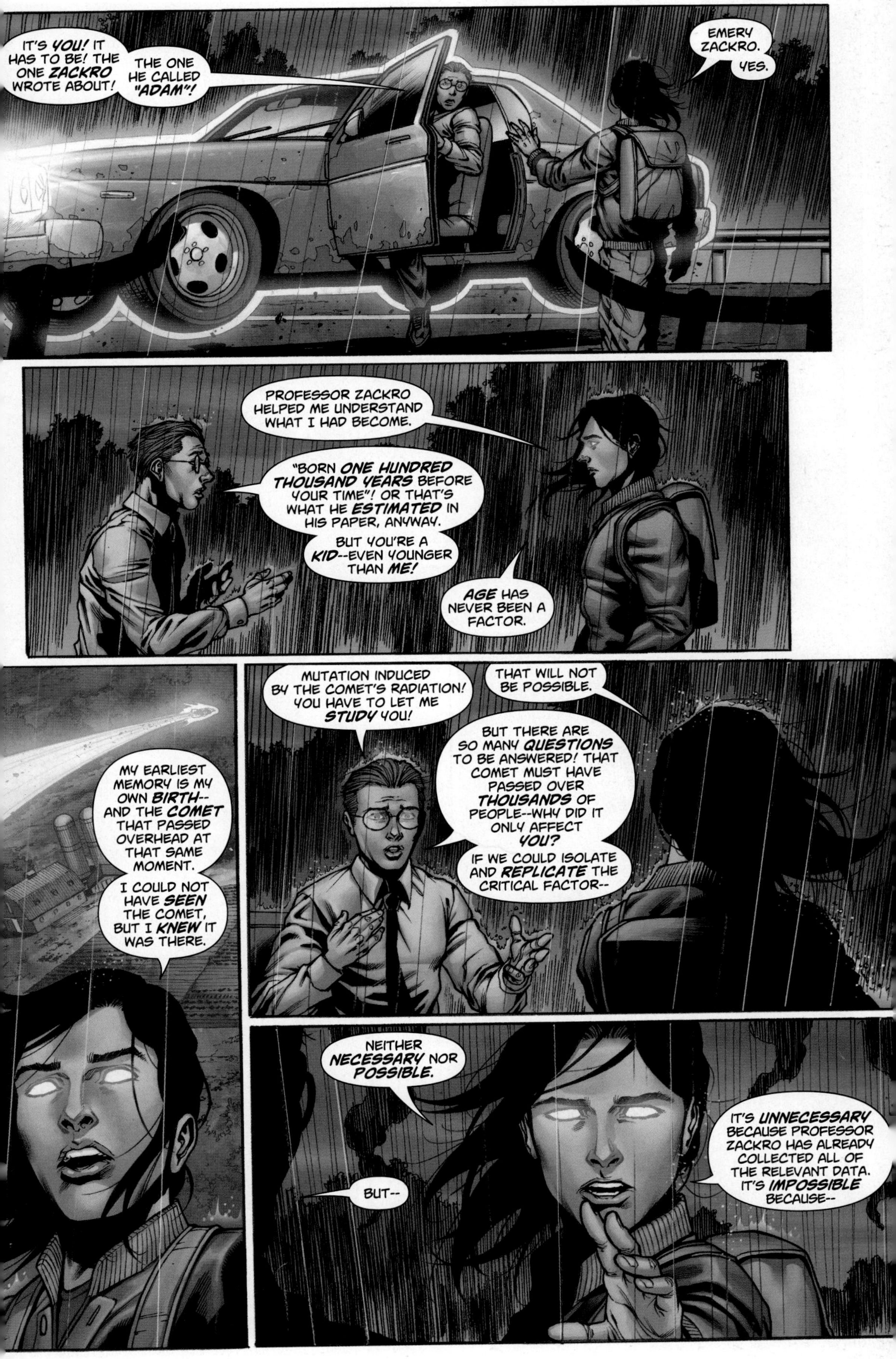
IT'S YOU! IT HAS TO BE! THE ONE ZACKRO WROTE ABOUT!
THE ONE HE CALLED "ADAM"!
EMERY ZACKRO.
YES.
PROFESSOR ZACKRO HELPED ME UNDERSTAND WHAT I HAD BECOME.
"BORN ONE HUNDRED THOUSAND YEARS BEFORE YOUR TIME"! OR THAT'S WHAT HE ESTIMATED IN HIS PAPER, ANYWAY.
BUT YOU'RE A KID--EVEN YOUNGER THAN ME!
AGE HAS NEVER BEEN A FACTOR.
MY EARLIEST MEMORY IS MY OWN BIRTH--AND THE COMET THAT PASSED OVERHEAD AT THAT SAME MOMENT.
I COULD NOT HAVE SEEN THE COMET, BUT I KNEW IT WAS THERE.
MUTATION INDUCED BY THE COMET'S RADIATION! YOU HAVE TO LET ME STUDY YOU!
THAT WILL NOT BE POSSIBLE.
BUT THERE ARE SO MANY QUESTIONS TO BE ANSWERED! THAT COMET MUST HAVE PASSED OVER THOUSANDS OF PEOPLE--WHY DID IT ONLY AFFECT YOU?
IF WE COULD ISOLATE AND REPLICATE THE CRITICAL FACTOR--
NEITHER NECESSARY NOR POSSIBLE.
BUT--
IT'S UNNECESSARY BECAUSE PROFESSOR ZACKRO HAS ALREADY COLLECTED ALL OF THE RELEVANT DATA. IT'S IMPOSSIBLE BECAUSE--

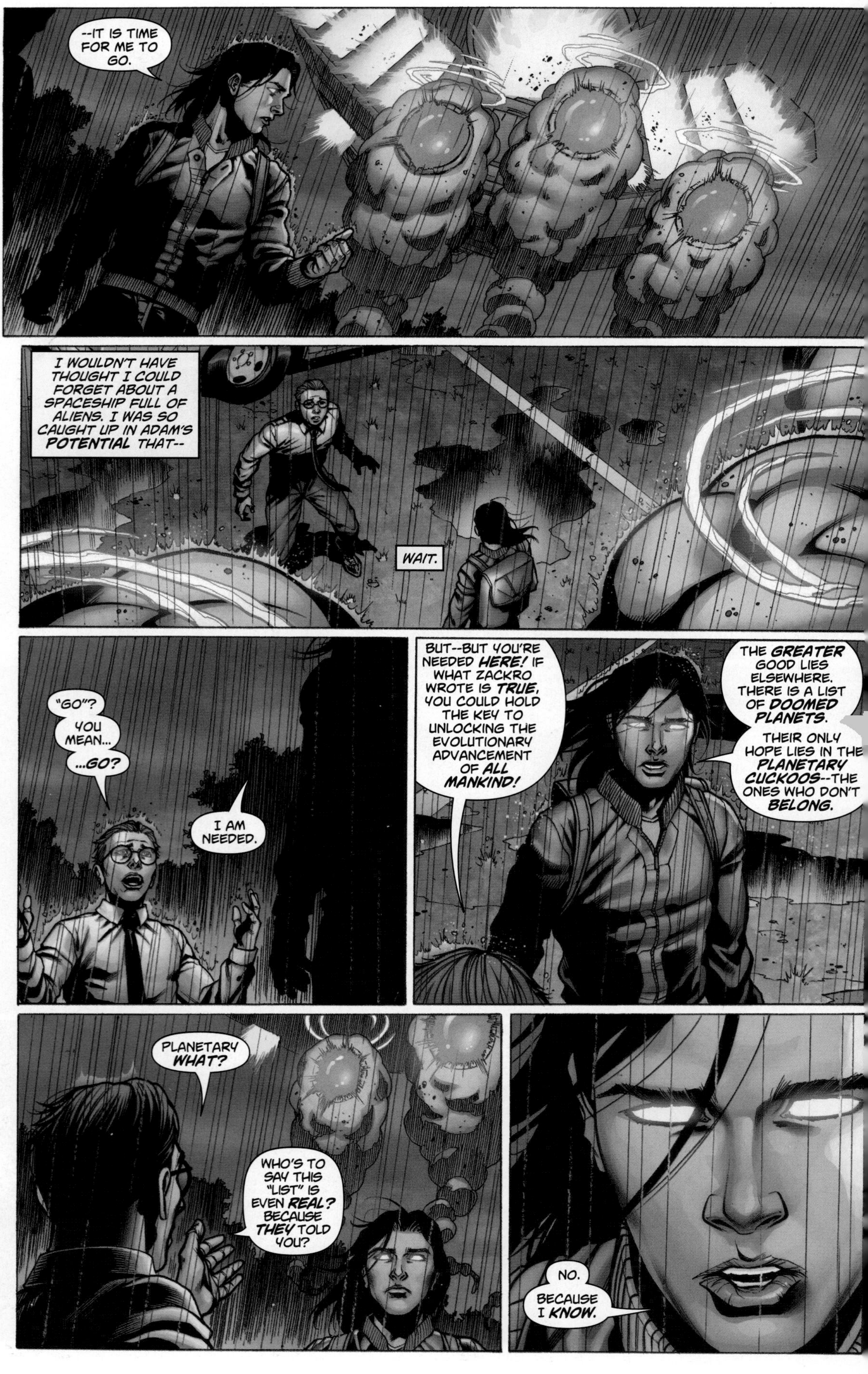
--IT IS TIME FOR ME TO GO.
I WOULDN'T HAVE THOUGHT I COULD FORGET ABOUT A SPACESHIP FULL OF ALIENS. I WAS SO CAUGHT UP IN ADAM'S POTENTIAL THAT--
WAIT.
"GO"? YOU MEAN... ...GO?
I AM NEEDED.
BUT--BUT YOU'RE NEEDED HERE! IF WHAT ZACKRO WROTE IS TRUE, YOU COULD HOLD THE KEY TO UNLOCKING THE EVOLUTIONARY ADVANCEMENT OF ALL MANKIND!
THE GREATER GOOD LIES ELSEWHERE. THERE IS A LIST OF DOOMED PLANETS.
THEIR ONLY HOPE LIES IN THE PLANETARY CUCKOOS--THE ONES WHO DON'T BELONG.
PLANETARY WHAT?
WHO'S TO SAY THIS "LIST" IS EVEN REAL? BECAUSE THEY TOLD YOU?
NO. BECAUSE I KNOW.

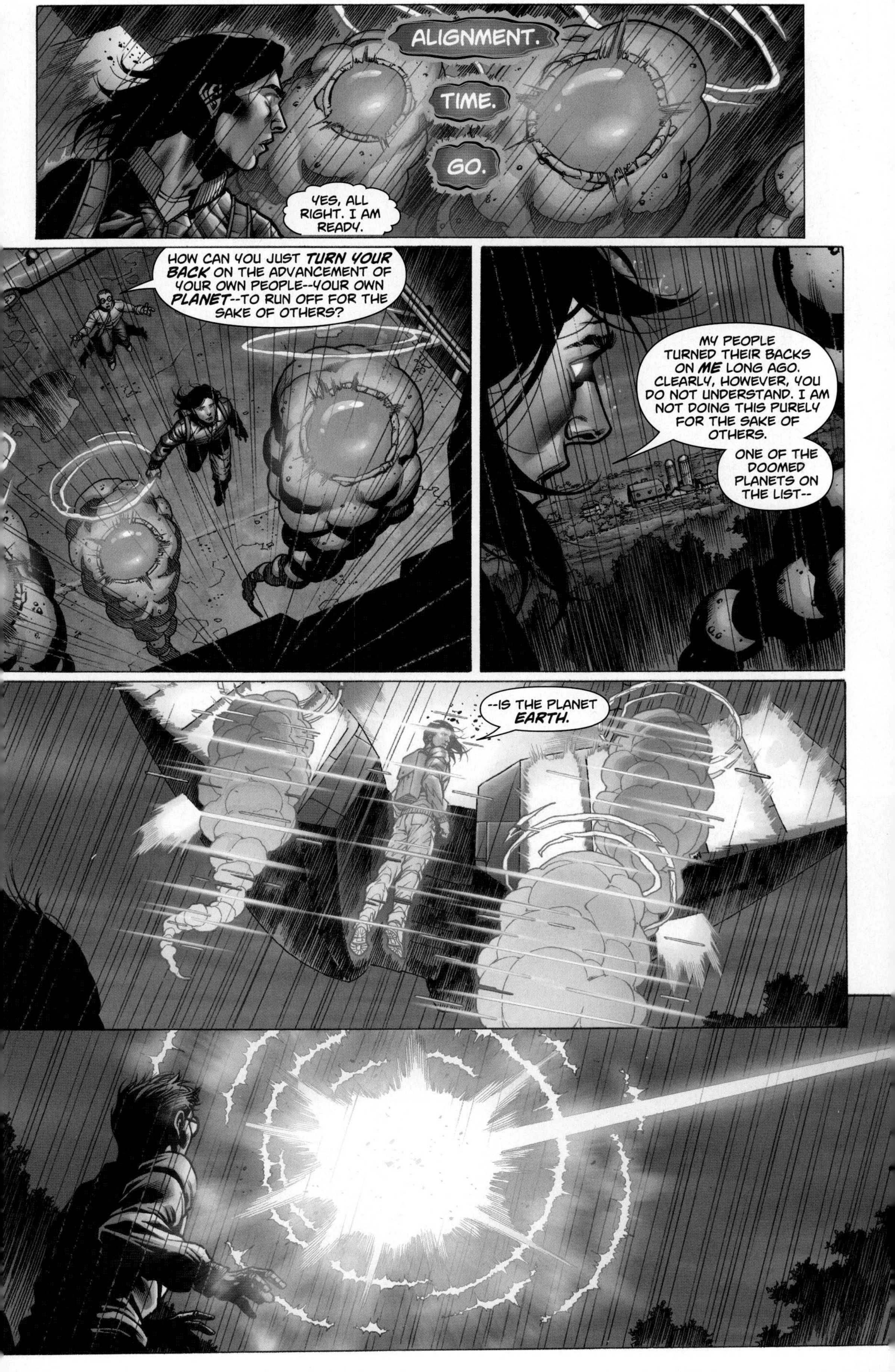
ALIGNMENT.
TIME.
GO.
YES, ALL RIGHT. I AM READY.
HOW CAN YOU JUST TURN YOUR BACK ON THE ADVANCEMENT OF YOUR OWN PEOPLE--YOUR OWN PLANET--TO RUN OFF FOR THE SAKE OF OTHERS?
MY PEOPLE TURNED THEIR BACKS ON ME LONG AGO. CLEARLY, HOWEVER, YOU DO NOT UNDERSTAND. I AM NOT DOING THIS PURELY FOR THE SAKE OF OTHERS.
ONE OF THE DOOMED PLANETS ON THE LIST--
--IS THE PLANET EARTH.

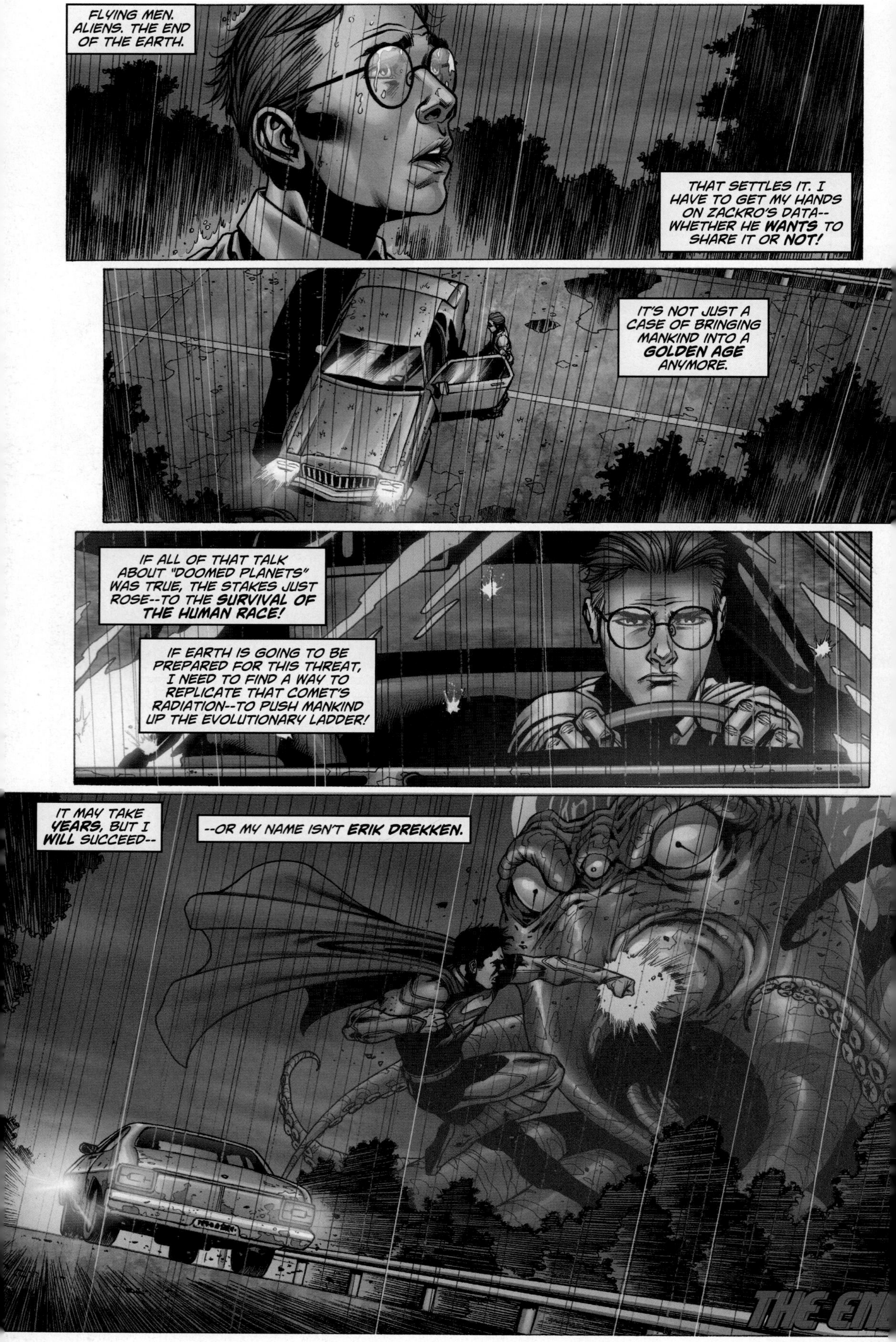
FLYING MEN. ALIENS. THE END OF THE EARTH.
THAT SETTLES IT. I HAVE TO GET MY HANDS ON ZACKRO'S DATA--WHETHER HE WANTS TO SHARE IT OR NOT!
IT'S NOT JUST A CASE OF BRINGING MANKIND INTO A GOLDEN AGE ANYMORE.
IF ALL OF THAT TALK ABOUT "DOOMED PLANETS" WAS TRUE, THE STAKES JUST ROSE--TO THE SURVIVAL OF THE HUMAN RACE!
IF EARTH IS GOING TO BE PREPARED FOR THIS THREAT, I NEED TO FIND A WAY TO REPLICATE THAT COMET'S RADIATION--TO PUSH MANKIND UP THE EVOLUTIONARY LADDER!
IT MAY TAKE YEARS, BUT I WILL SUCCEED--
--OR MY NAME ISN'T ERIK DREKKEN.
THE EN

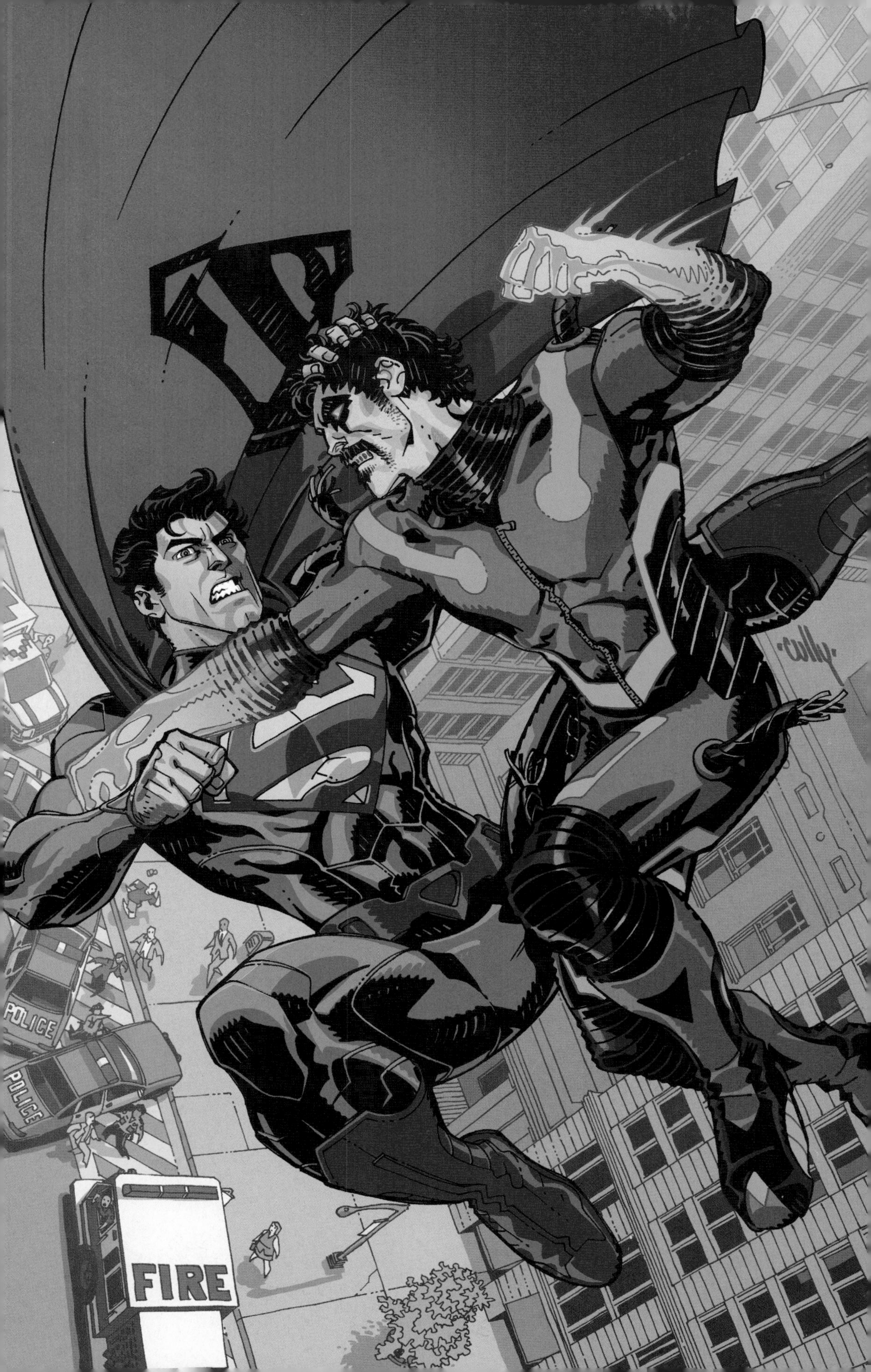

POLICE
POLICE
FIRE

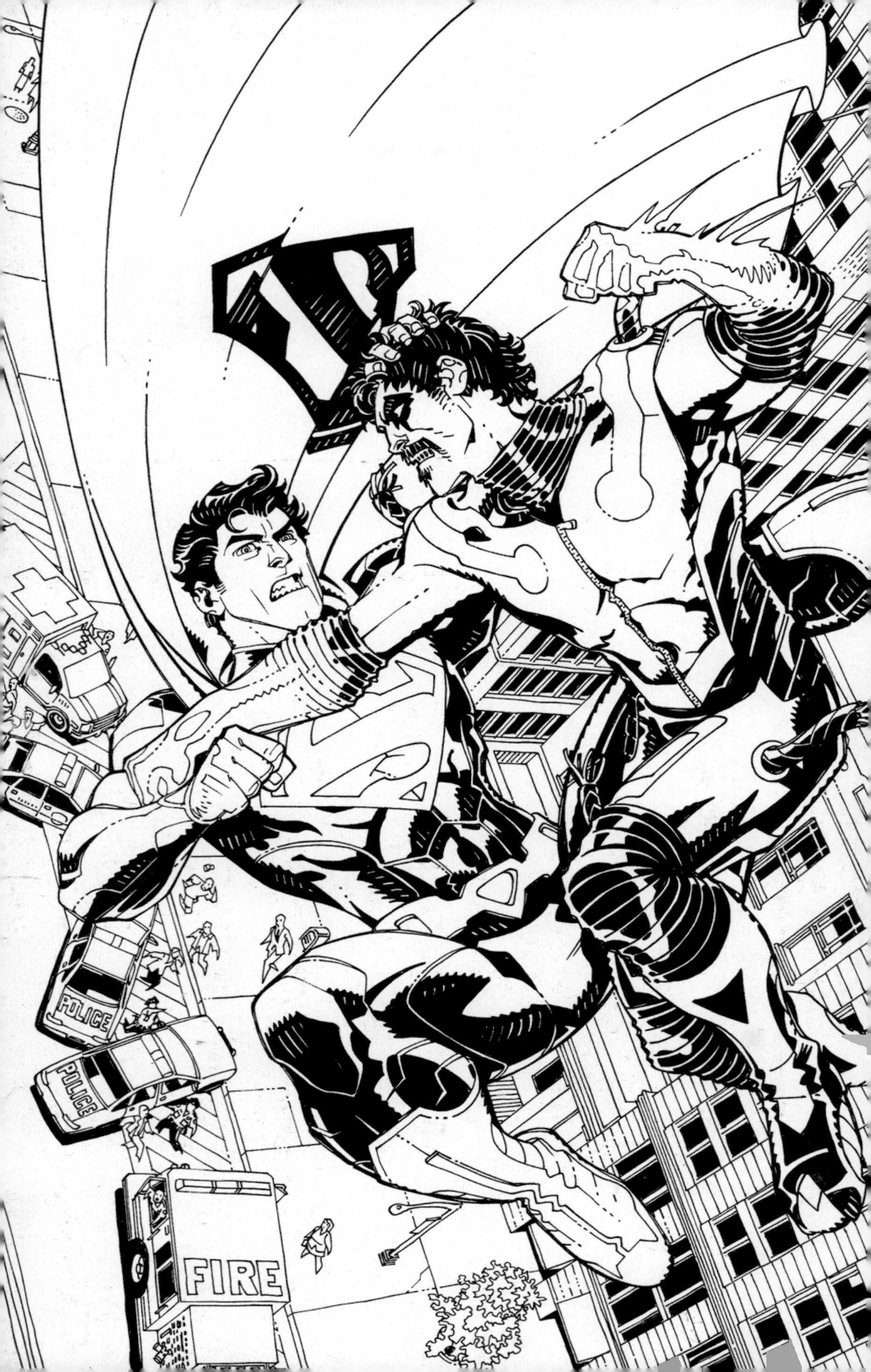

POLICE
POLICE
FIRE

VULNERABLE

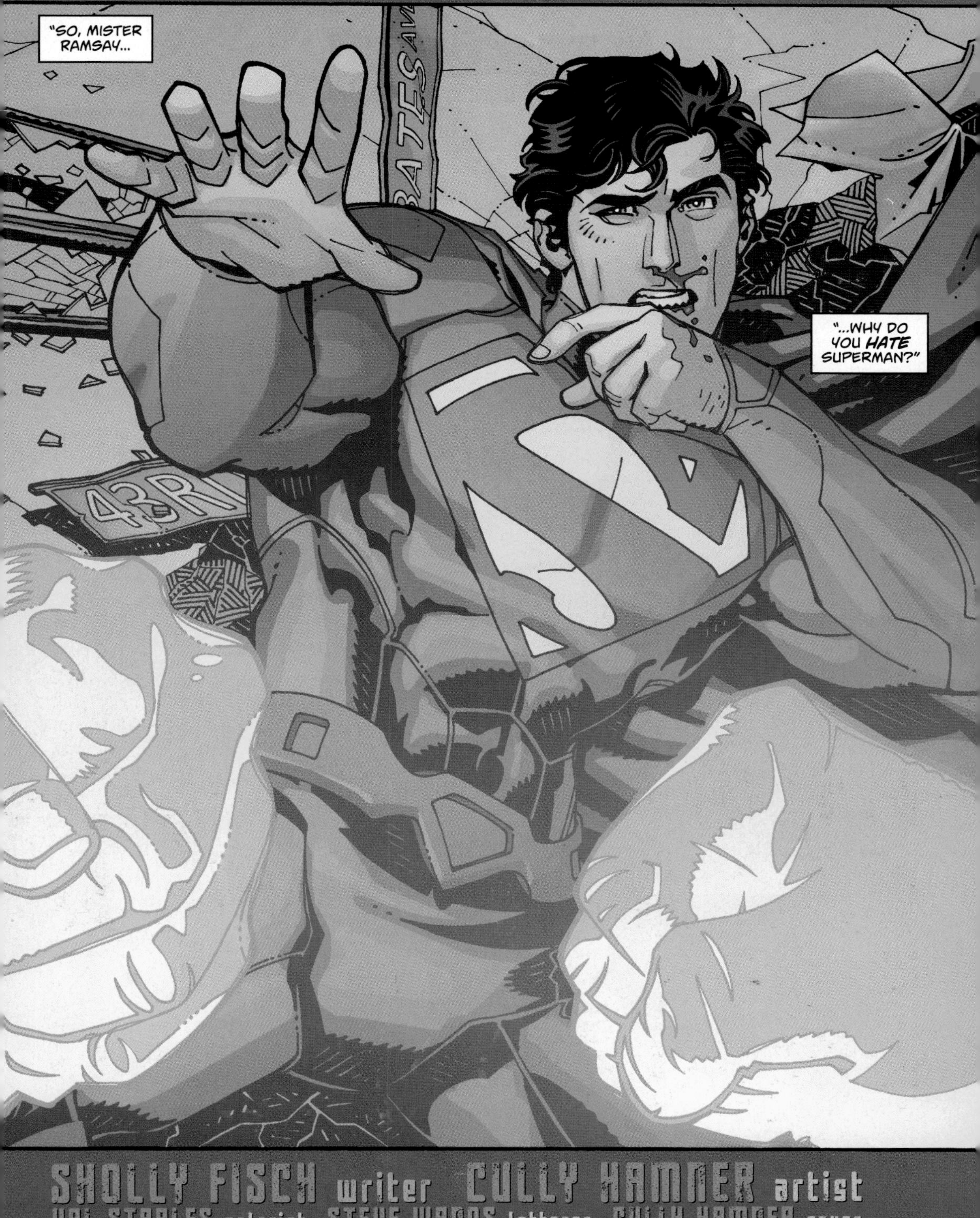
"SO, MISTER RAMSAY...
"...WHY DO YOU *HATE* SUPERMAN?"

SHOLLY FISCH writer CULLY HAMNER artist
VAL STAPLES colorist STEVE WANDS letterer CULLY HAMNER cover
special thanks to GRANT MORRISON
WIL MOSS associate editor MATT IDELSON editor
SUPERMAN created by JERRY SIEGEL & JOE SHUSTER

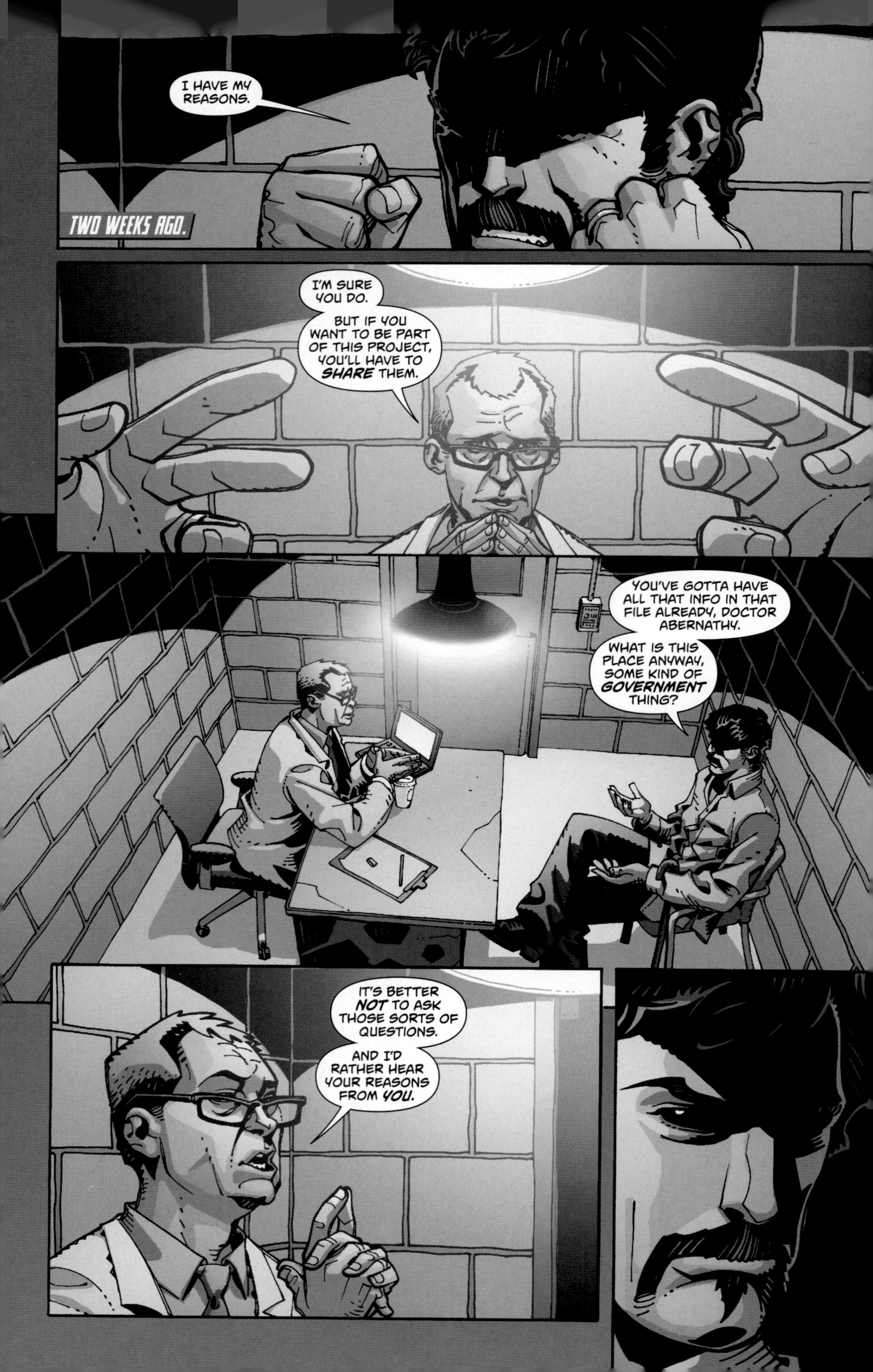
I HAVE MY REASONS.
TWO WEEKS AGO.
I'M SURE YOU DO.
BUT IF YOU WANT TO BE PART OF THIS PROJECT, YOU'LL HAVE TO SHARE THEM.
YOU'VE GOTTA HAVE ALL THAT INFO IN THAT FILE ALREADY, DOCTOR ABERNATHY.
WHAT IS THIS PLACE ANYWAY, SOME KIND OF GOVERNMENT THING?
IT'S BETTER NOT TO ASK THOSE SORTS OF QUESTIONS.
AND I'D RATHER HEAR YOUR REASONS FROM YOU.

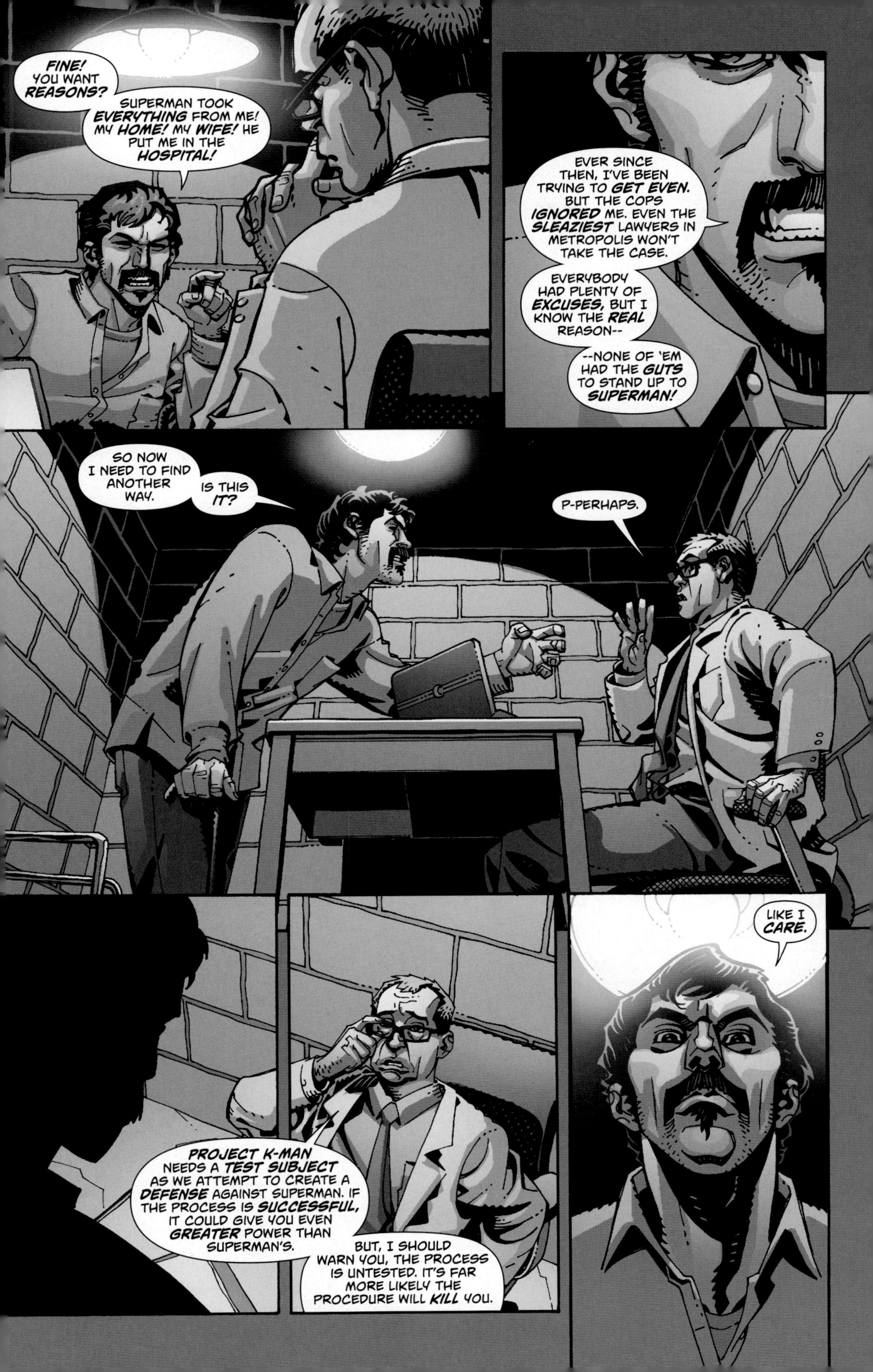
FINE! YOU WANT REASONS?
SUPERMAN TOOK EVERYTHING FROM ME! MY HOME! MY WIFE! HE PUT ME IN THE HOSPITAL!
EVER SINCE THEN, I'VE BEEN TRYING TO GET EVEN. BUT THE COPS IGNORED ME. EVEN THE SLEAZIEST LAWYERS IN METROPOLIS WON'T TAKE THE CASE.
EVERYBODY HAD PLENTY OF EXCUSES, BUT I KNOW THE REAL REASON--
--NONE OF 'EM HAD THE GUTS TO STAND UP TO SUPERMAN!
SO NOW I NEED TO FIND ANOTHER WAY.
IS THIS IT?
P-PERHAPS.
PROJECT K-MAN NEEDS A TEST SUBJECT AS WE ATTEMPT TO CREATE A DEFENSE AGAINST SUPERMAN. IF THE PROCESS IS SUCCESSFUL, IT COULD GIVE YOU EVEN GREATER POWER THAN SUPERMAN'S.
BUT, I SHOULD WARN YOU, THE PROCESS IS UNTESTED. IT'S FAR MORE LIKELY THE PROCEDURE WILL KILL YOU.
LIKE I CARE.

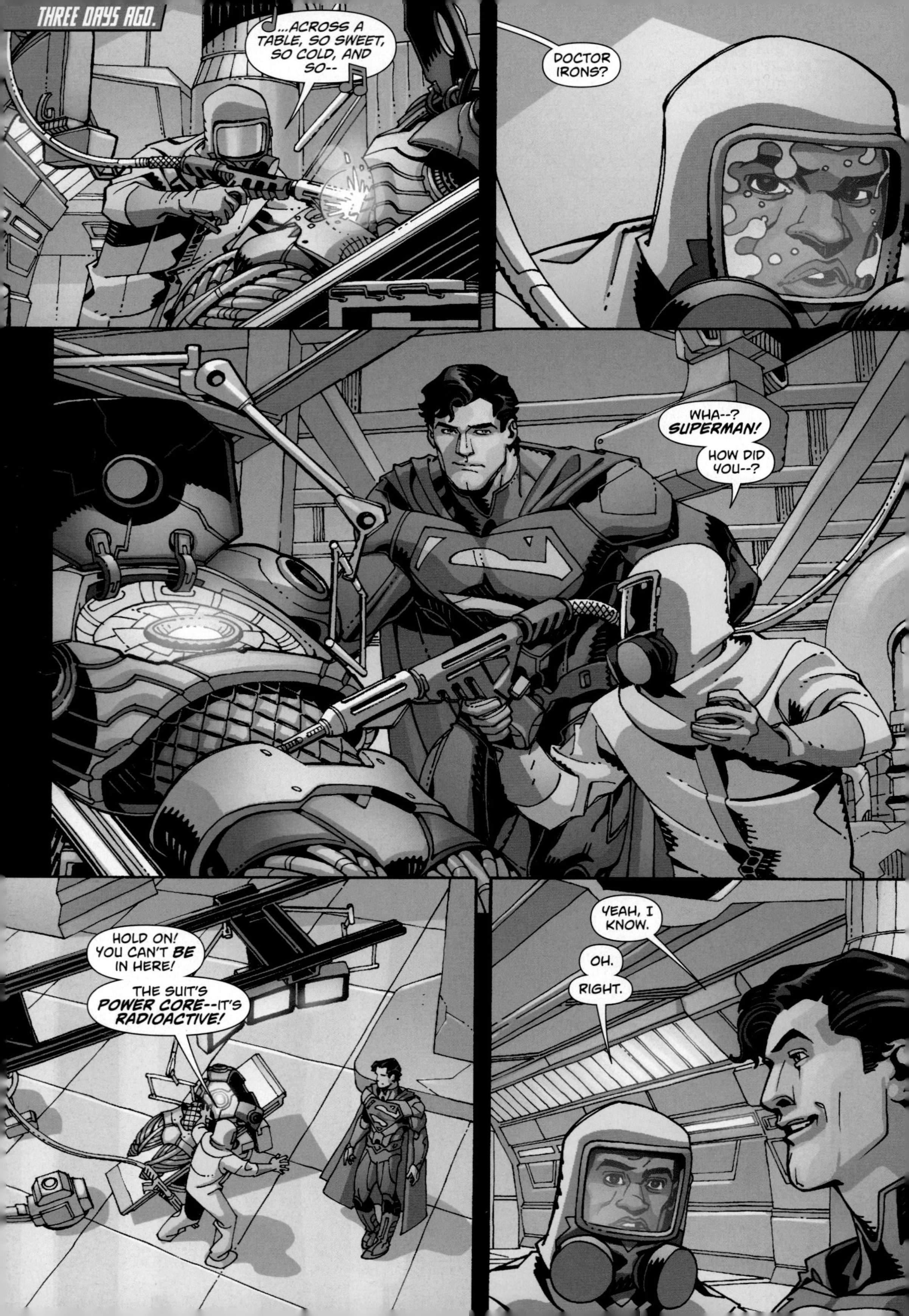
THREE DAYS AGO.
...ACROSS A TABLE, SO SWEET, SO COLD, AND SO--
DOCTOR IRONS?
WHA--? SUPERMAN!
HOW DID YOU--?
HOLD ON! YOU CAN'T BE IN HERE!
THE SUIT'S POWER CORE--IT'S RADIOACTIVE!
YEAH, I KNOW.
OH.
RIGHT.

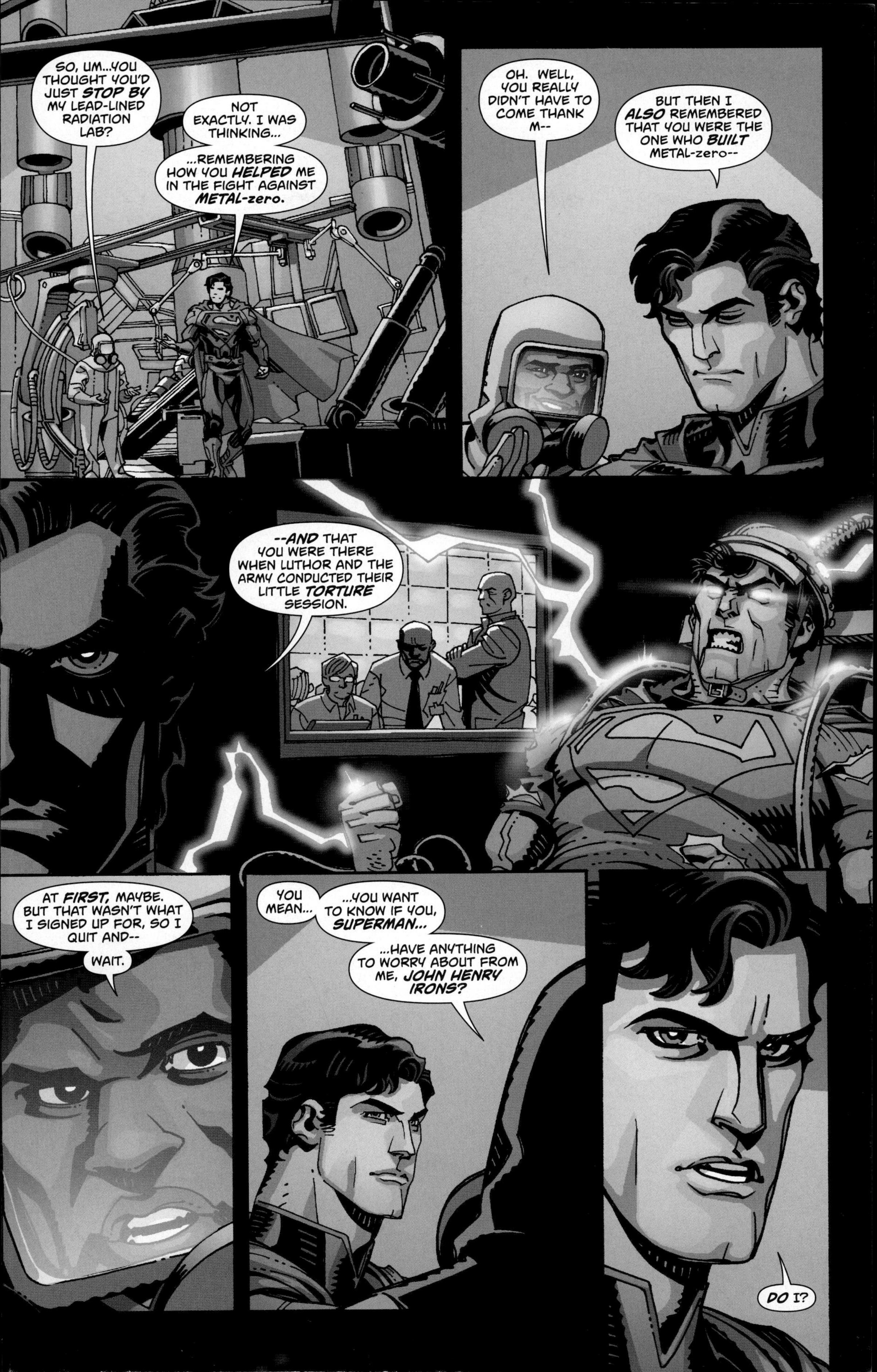
SO, UM...YOU THOUGHT YOU'D JUST STOP BY MY LEAD-LINED RADIATION LAB?
NOT EXACTLY. I WAS THINKING...
...REMEMBERING HOW YOU HELPED ME IN THE FIGHT AGAINST METAL-zero.
OH. WELL, YOU REALLY DIDN'T HAVE TO COME THANK M--
BUT THEN I ALSO REMEMBERED THAT YOU WERE THE ONE WHO BUILT METAL-zero--
--AND THAT YOU WERE THERE WHEN LUTHOR AND THE ARMY CONDUCTED THEIR LITTLE TORTURE SESSION.
AT FIRST, MAYBE. BUT THAT WASN'T WHAT I SIGNED UP FOR, SO I QUIT AND--
WAIT.
YOU MEAN...
...YOU WANT TO KNOW IF YOU, SUPERMAN...
...HAVE ANYTHING TO WORRY ABOUT FROM ME, JOHN HENRY IRONS?
DO I?

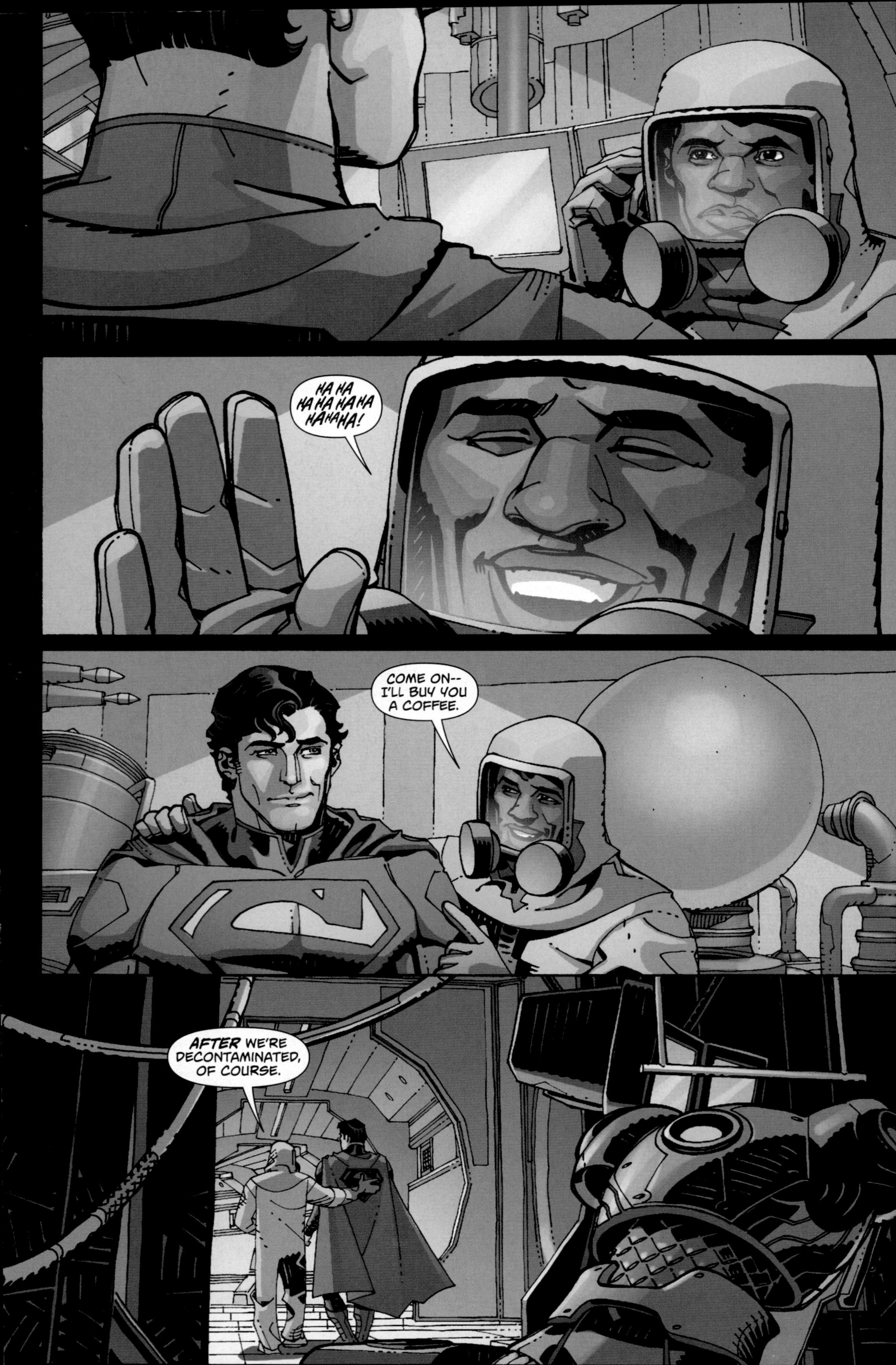
HA HA HA HA HA HA HAHAHA!
COME ON-- I'LL BUY YOU A COFFEE.
AFTER WE'RE DECONTAMINATED, OF COURSE.

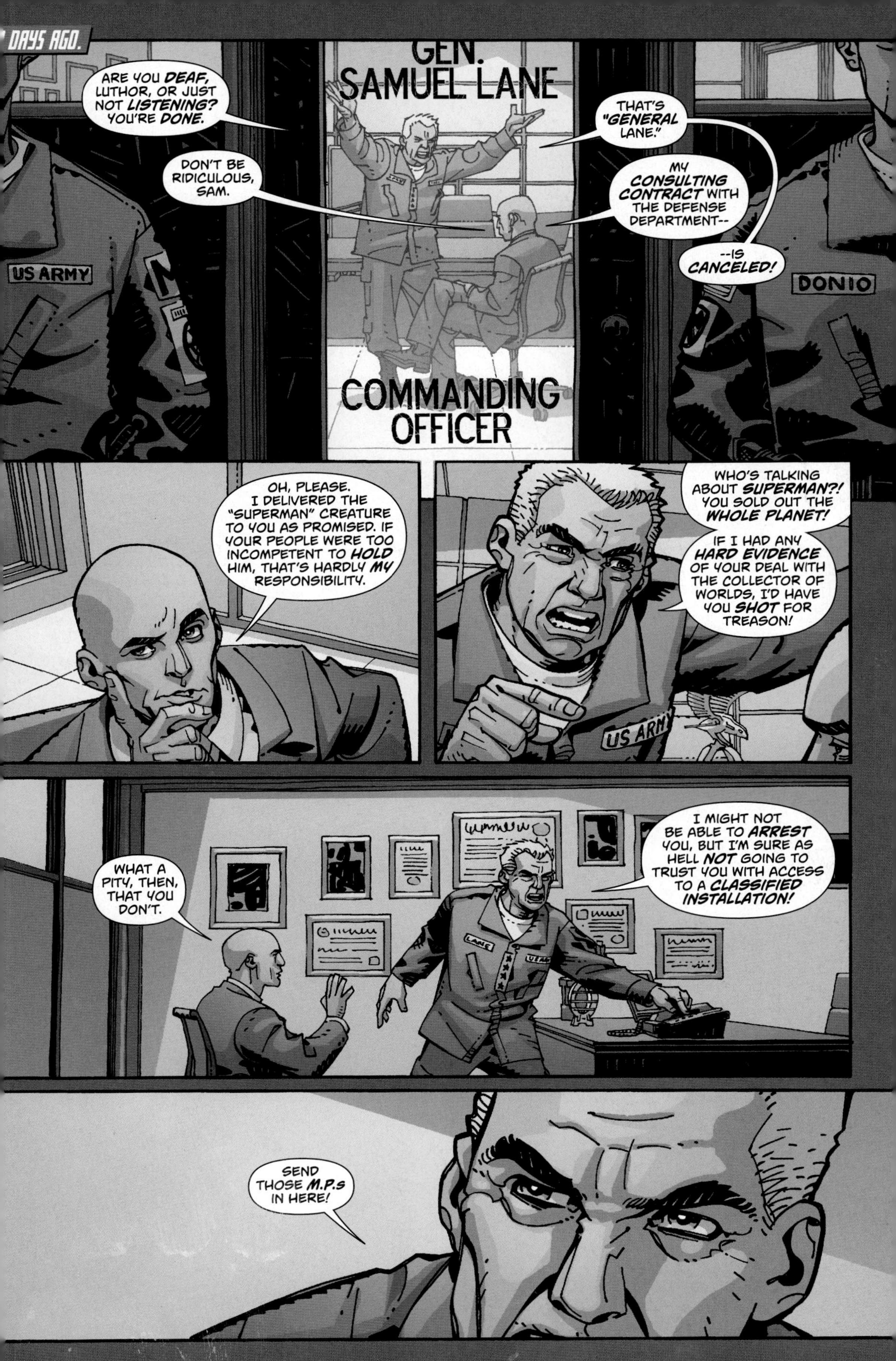
DAYS AGO.
GEN. SAMUEL LANE
COMMANDING OFFICER
ARE YOU DEAF, LUTHOR, OR JUST NOT LISTENING? YOU'RE DONE.
DON'T BE RIDICULOUS, SAM.
THAT'S "GENERAL LANE."
MY CONSULTING CONTRACT WITH THE DEFENSE DEPARTMENT--
--IS CANCELED!
US ARMY
DONIO
OH, PLEASE. I DELIVERED THE "SUPERMAN" CREATURE TO YOU AS PROMISED. IF YOUR PEOPLE WERE TOO INCOMPETENT TO HOLD HIM, THAT'S HARDLY MY RESPONSIBILITY.
WHO'S TALKING ABOUT SUPERMAN?! YOU SOLD OUT THE WHOLE PLANET!
IF I HAD ANY HARD EVIDENCE OF YOUR DEAL WITH THE COLLECTOR OF WORLDS, I'D HAVE YOU SHOT FOR TREASON!
US ARMY
WHAT A PITY, THEN, THAT YOU DON'T.
I MIGHT NOT BE ABLE TO ARREST YOU, BUT I'M SURE AS HELL NOT GOING TO TRUST YOU WITH ACCESS TO A CLASSIFIED INSTALLATION!
LANE
SEND THOSE M.P.s IN HERE!

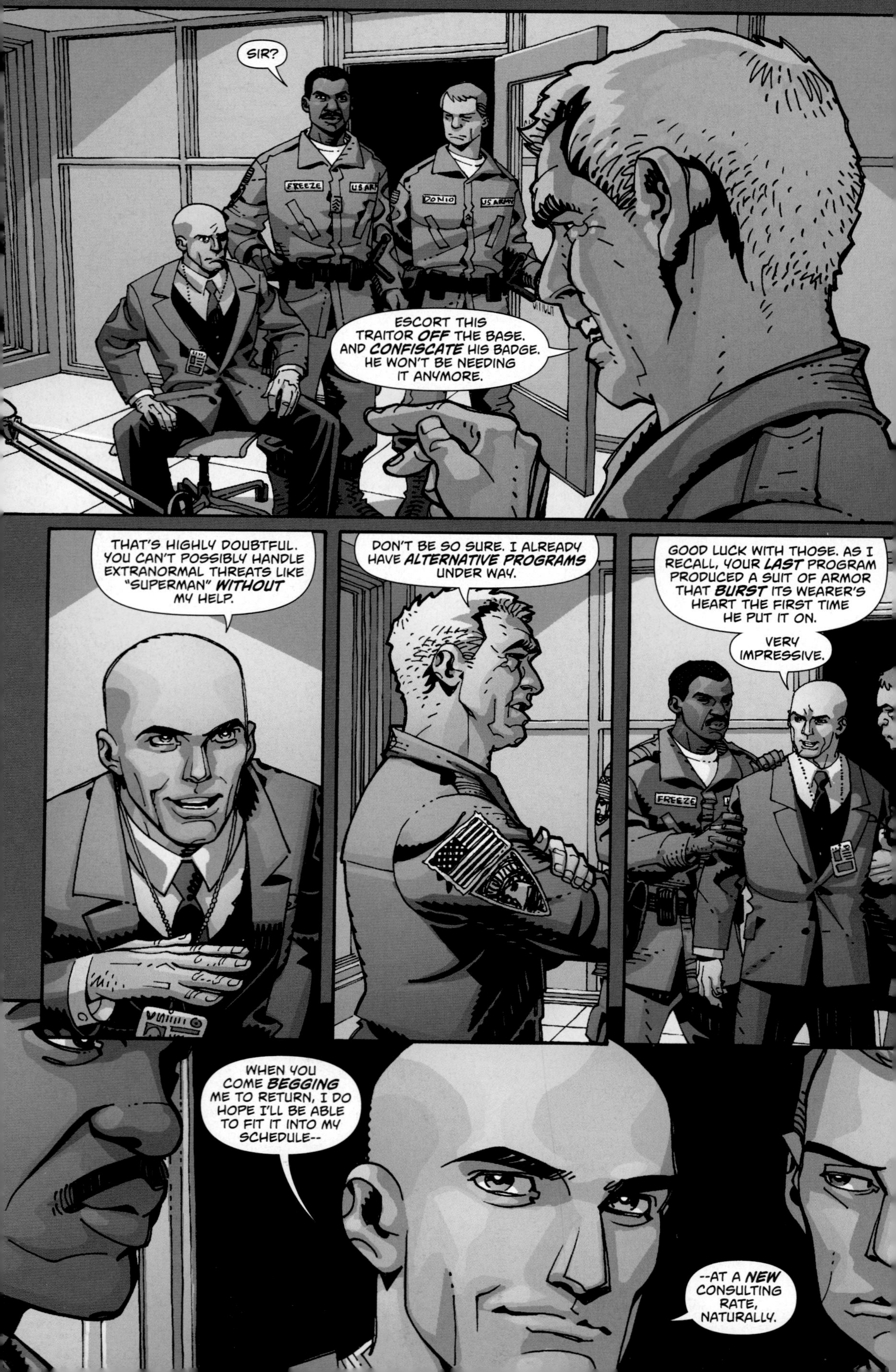
SIR?
FREEZE
US ARMY
DONIO
US ARMY
ESCORT THIS TRAITOR OFF THE BASE. AND CONFISCATE HIS BADGE. HE WON'T BE NEEDING IT ANYMORE.
THAT'S HIGHLY DOUBTFUL. YOU CAN'T POSSIBLY HANDLE EXTRANORMAL THREATS LIKE "SUPERMAN" WITHOUT MY HELP.
DON'T BE SO SURE. I ALREADY HAVE ALTERNATIVE PROGRAMS UNDER WAY.
GOOD LUCK WITH THOSE. AS I RECALL, YOUR LAST PROGRAM PRODUCED A SUIT OF ARMOR THAT BURST ITS WEARER'S HEART THE FIRST TIME HE PUT IT ON.
VERY IMPRESSIVE.
FREEZE
WHEN YOU COME BEGGING ME TO RETURN, I DO HOPE I'LL BE ABLE TO FIT IT INTO MY SCHEDULE--
--AT A NEW CONSULTING RATE, NATURALLY.

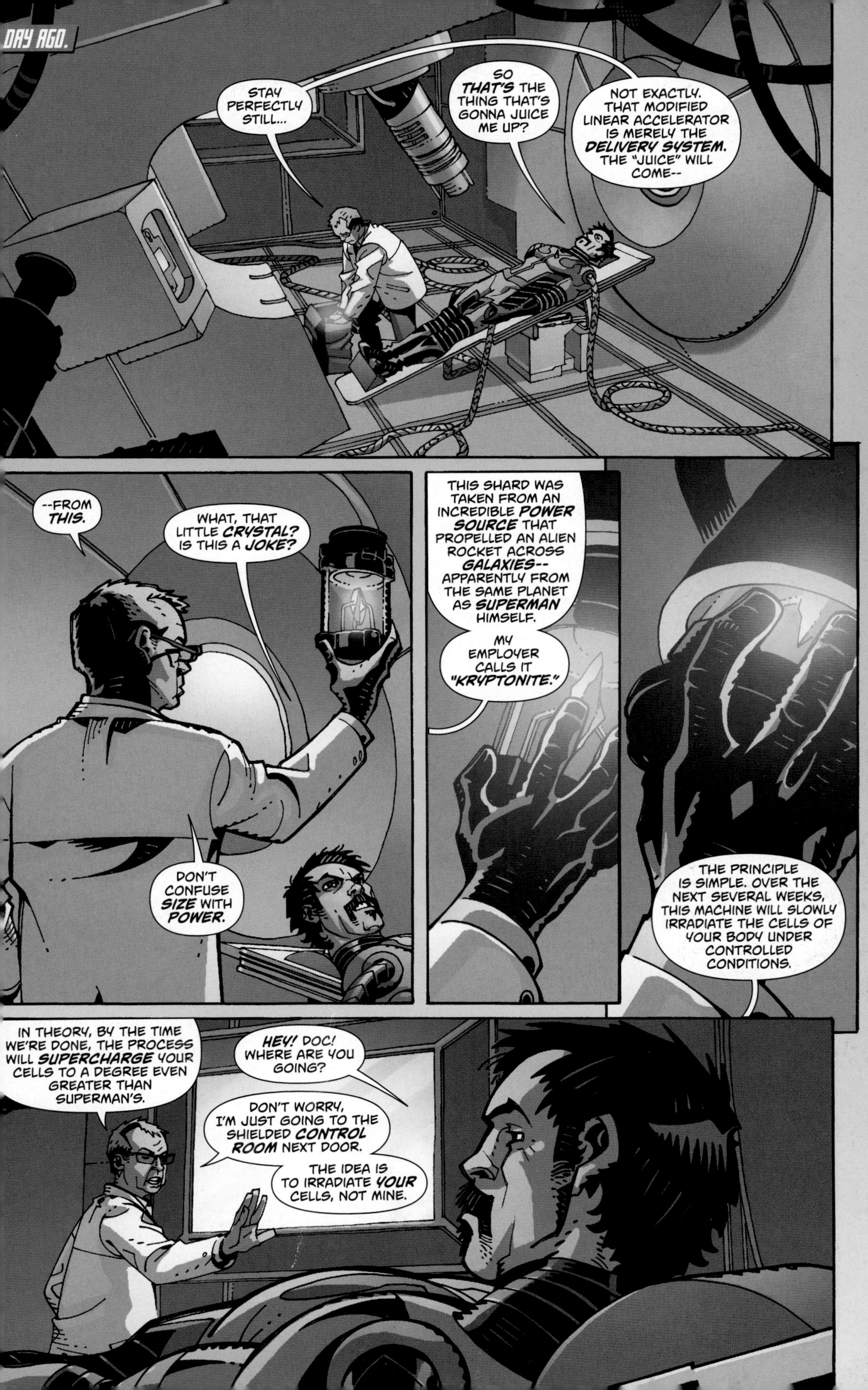
DAY AGO.
STAY PERFECTLY STILL...
SO THAT'S THE THING THAT'S GONNA JUICE ME UP?
NOT EXACTLY. THAT MODIFIED LINEAR ACCELERATOR IS MERELY THE DELIVERY SYSTEM. THE "JUICE" WILL COME--
--FROM THIS.
WHAT, THAT LITTLE CRYSTAL? IS THIS A JOKE?
DON'T CONFUSE SIZE WITH POWER.
THIS SHARD WAS TAKEN FROM AN INCREDIBLE POWER SOURCE THAT PROPELLED AN ALIEN ROCKET ACROSS GALAXIES-- APPARENTLY FROM THE SAME PLANET AS SUPERMAN HIMSELF.
MY EMPLOYER CALLS IT "KRYPTONITE."
THE PRINCIPLE IS SIMPLE. OVER THE NEXT SEVERAL WEEKS, THIS MACHINE WILL SLOWLY IRRADIATE THE CELLS OF YOUR BODY UNDER CONTROLLED CONDITIONS.
IN THEORY, BY THE TIME WE'RE DONE, THE PROCESS WILL SUPERCHARGE YOUR CELLS TO A DEGREE EVEN GREATER THAN SUPERMAN'S.
HEY! DOC! WHERE ARE YOU GOING?
DON'T WORRY, I'M JUST GOING TO THE SHIELDED CONTROL ROOM NEXT DOOR.
THE IDEA IS TO IRRADIATE YOUR CELLS, NOT MINE.

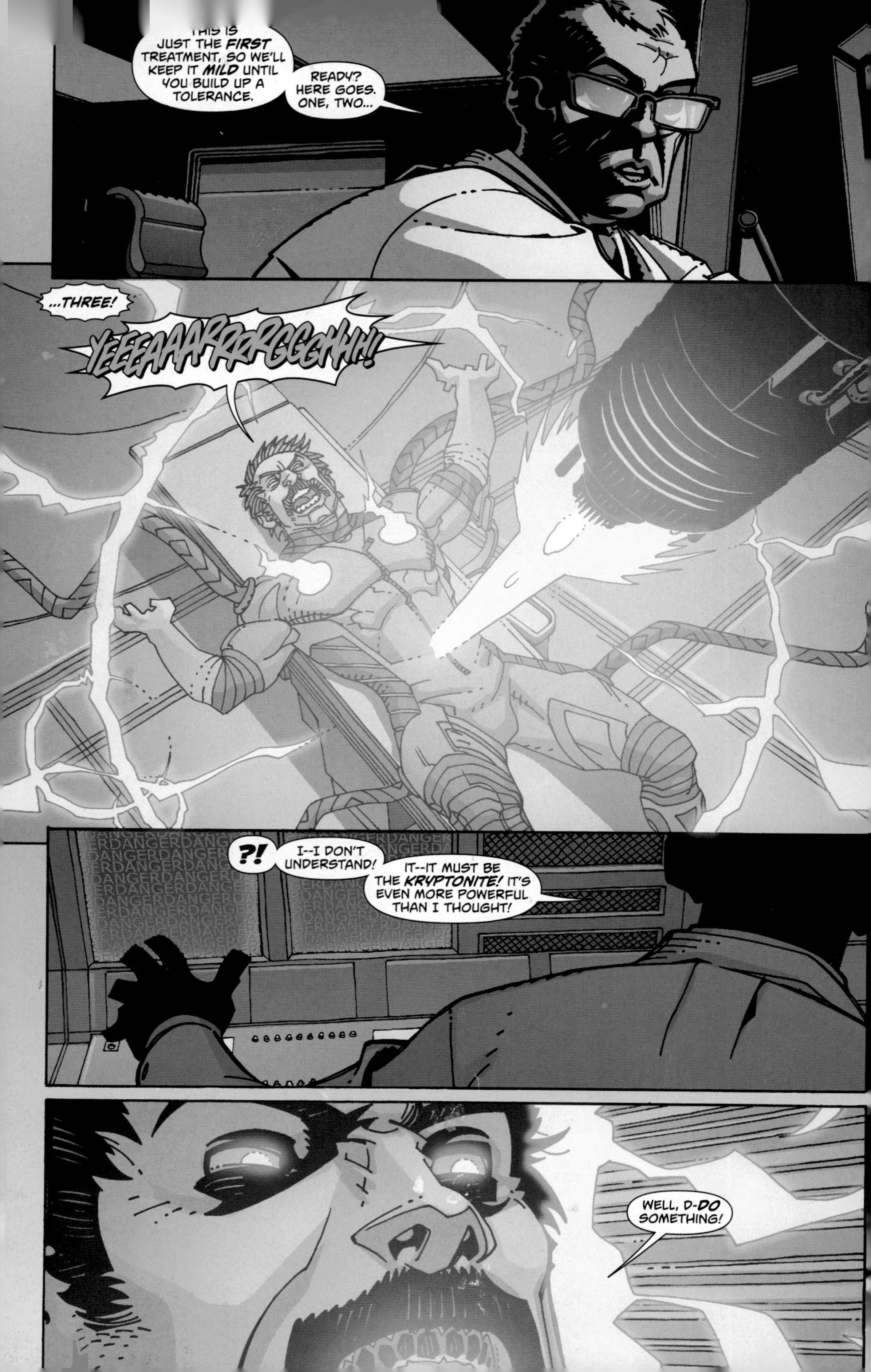
THIS IS JUST THE FIRST TREATMENT, SO WE'LL KEEP IT MILD UNTIL YOU BUILD UP A TOLERANCE.
READY? HERE GOES. ONE, TWO...
...THREE!
YEEEAAARRRRGGGHHH!
?!
I--I DON'T UNDERSTAND!
IT--IT MUST BE THE KRYPTONITE! IT'S EVEN MORE POWERFUL THAN I THOUGHT!
WELL, D-DO SOMETHING!

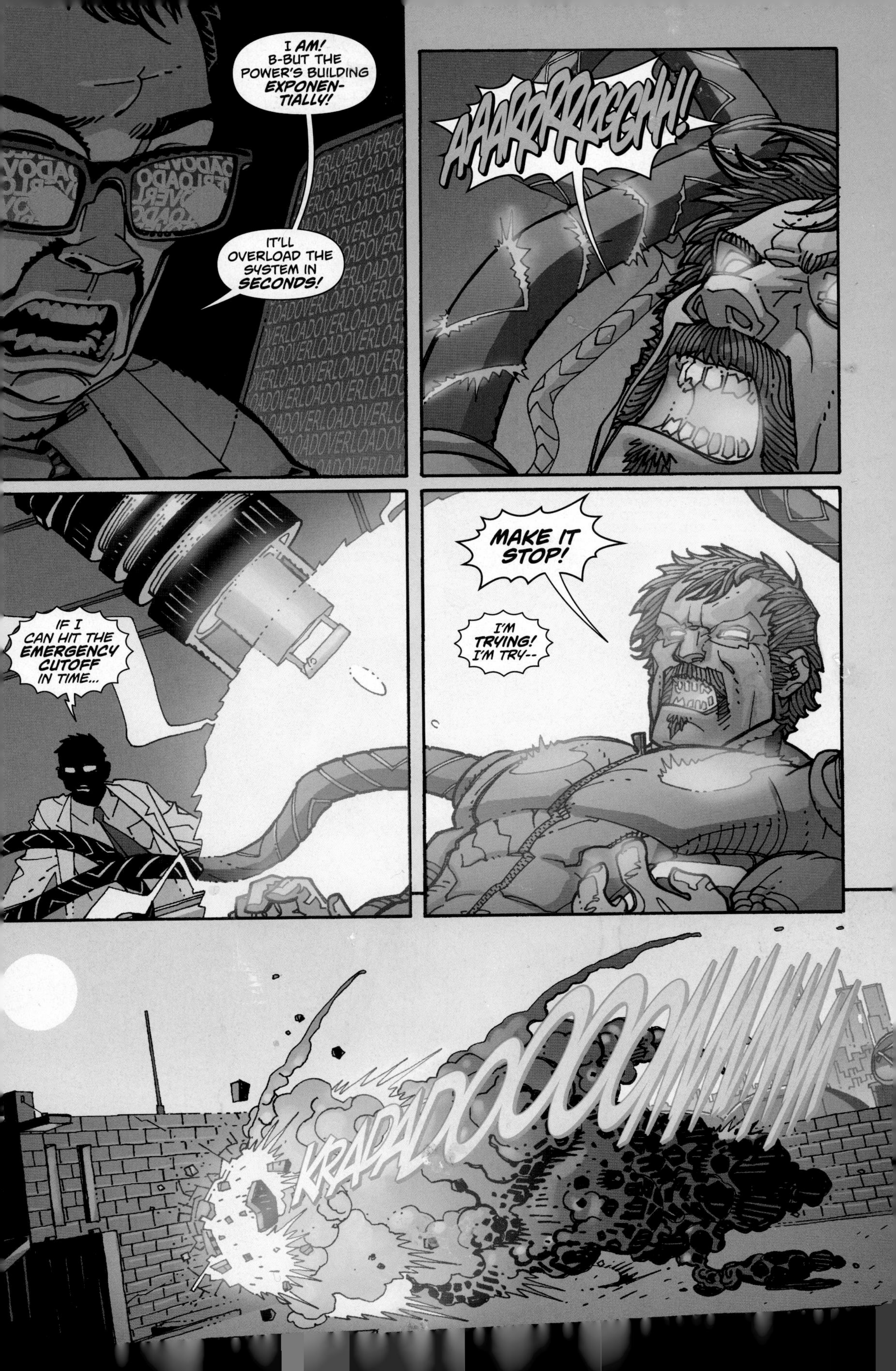
I *AM!* B-BUT THE POWER'S BUILDING *EXPONENTIALLY!*
IT'LL OVERLOAD THE SYSTEM IN *SECONDS!*
AAARRRRGGHH!
IF I CAN HIT THE **EMERGENCY CUTOFF** IN TIME...
MAKE IT STOP!
I'M *TRYING!* I'M TRY--
KRADADOOOOMMMMM

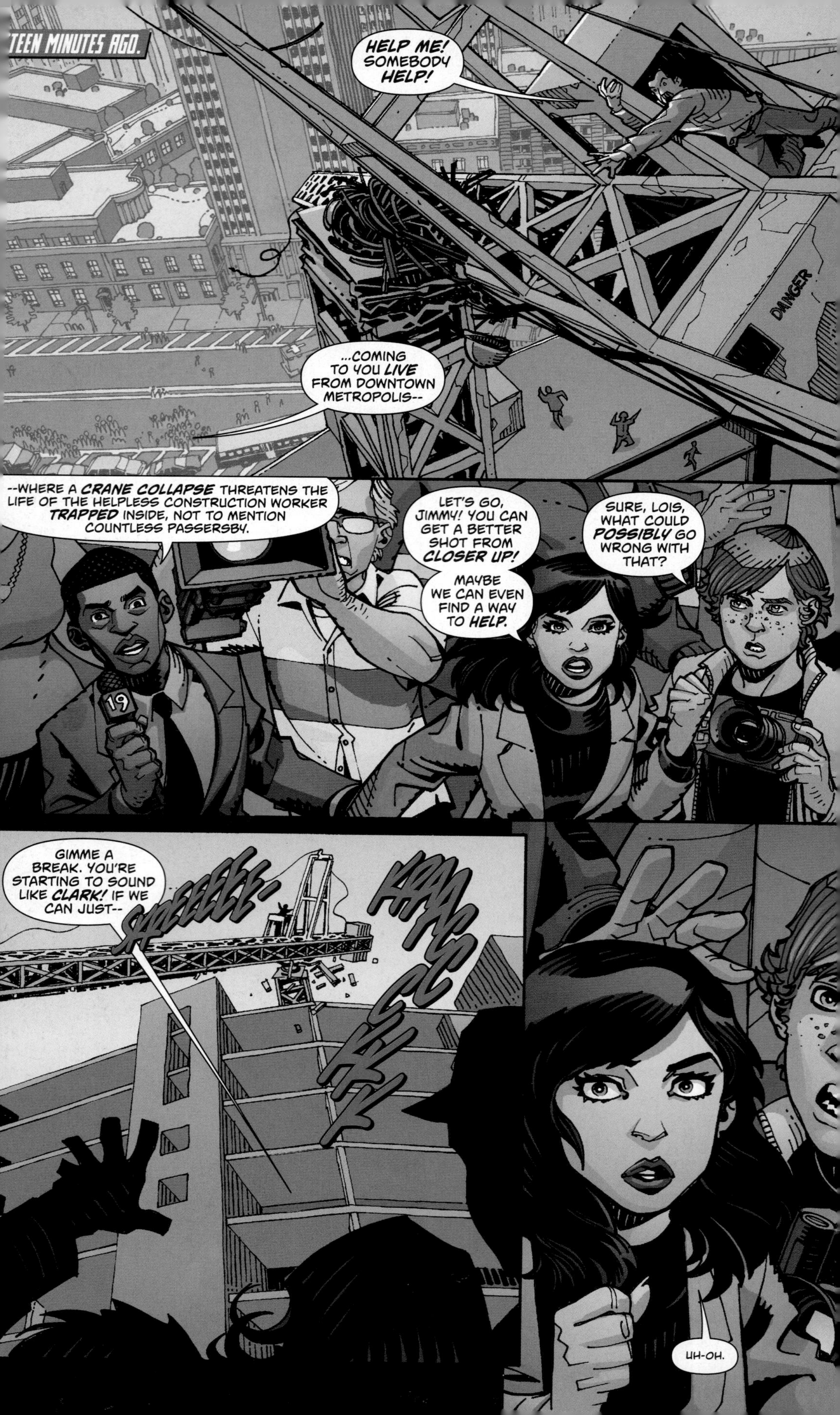
TEEN MINUTES AGO.
HELP ME! SOMEBODY HELP!
...COMING TO YOU LIVE FROM DOWNTOWN METROPOLIS--
--WHERE A CRANE COLLAPSE THREATENS THE LIFE OF THE HELPLESS CONSTRUCTION WORKER TRAPPED INSIDE, NOT TO MENTION COUNTLESS PASSERSBY.
19
LET'S GO, JIMMY! YOU CAN GET A BETTER SHOT FROM CLOSER UP!
MAYBE WE CAN EVEN FIND A WAY TO HELP.
SURE, LOIS, WHAT COULD POSSIBLY GO WRONG WITH THAT?
GIMME A BREAK. YOU'RE STARTING TO SOUND LIKE CLARK! IF WE CAN JUST--
UH-OH.

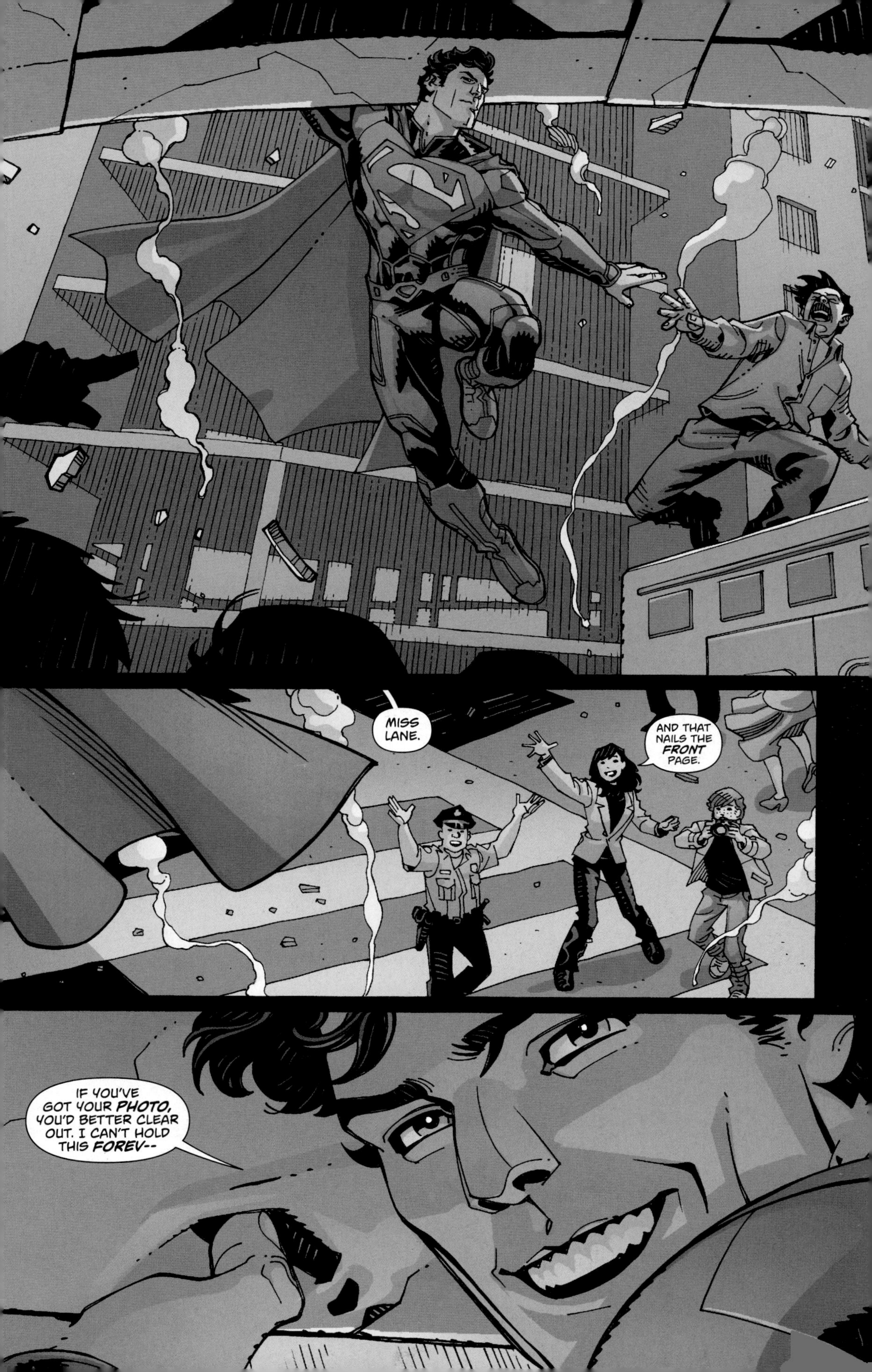
MISS LANE.
AND THAT NAILS THE FRONT PAGE.
IF YOU'VE GOT YOUR PHOTO, YOU'D BETTER CLEAR OUT. I CAN'T HOLD THIS FOREV--

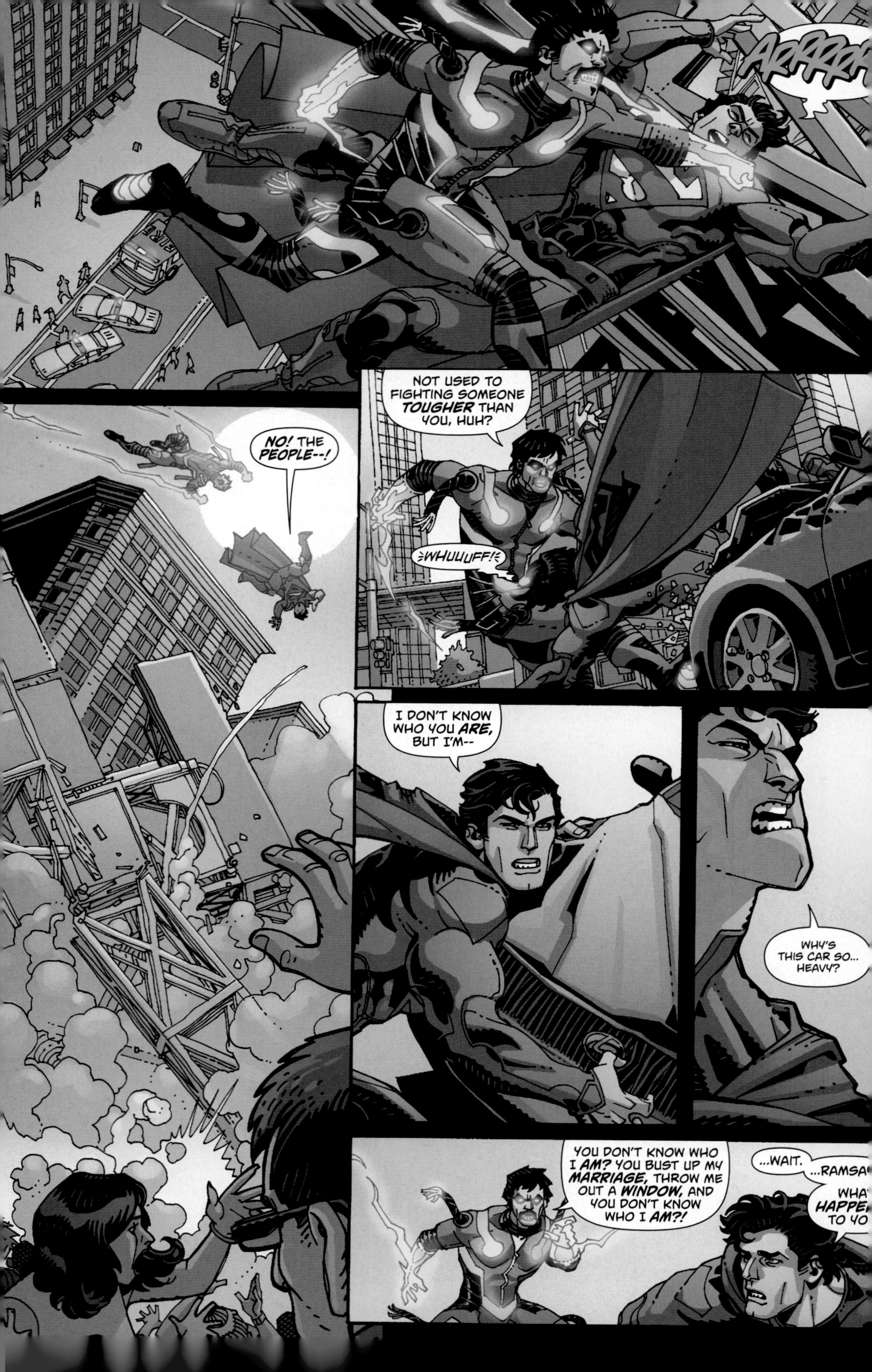

ARRRRR
NO! THE PEOPLE--!
NOT USED TO FIGHTING SOMEONE TOUGHER THAN YOU, HUH?
WHUUUFF!
I DON'T KNOW WHO YOU ARE, BUT I'M--
WHY'S THIS CAR SO... HEAVY?
YOU DON'T KNOW WHO I AM? YOU BUST UP MY MARRIAGE, THROW ME OUT A WINDOW, AND YOU DON'T KNOW WHO I AM?!
...WAIT.

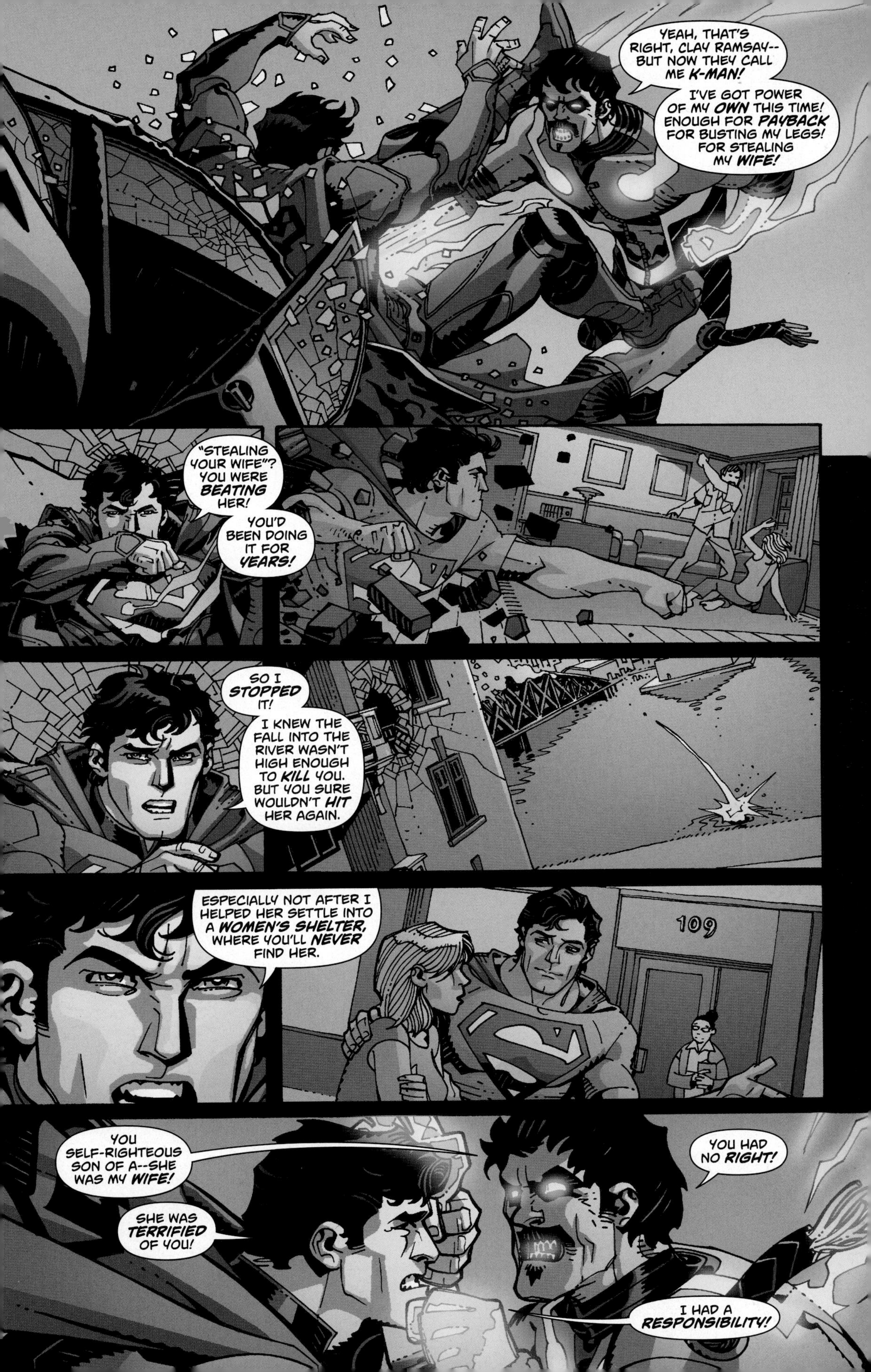

YEAH, THAT'S RIGHT, CLAY RAMSAY-- BUT NOW THEY CALL ME K-MAN!
I'VE GOT POWER OF MY OWN THIS TIME! ENOUGH FOR PAYBACK FOR BUSTING MY LEGS! FOR STEALING MY WIFE!
"STEALING YOUR WIFE"? YOU WERE BEATING HER!
YOU'D BEEN DOING IT FOR YEARS!
SO I STOPPED IT!
I KNEW THE FALL INTO THE RIVER WASN'T HIGH ENOUGH TO KILL YOU. BUT YOU SURE WOULDN'T HIT HER AGAIN.
ESPECIALLY NOT AFTER I HELPED HER SETTLE INTO A WOMEN'S SHELTER, WHERE YOU'LL NEVER FIND HER.
109
YOU SELF-RIGHTEOUS SON OF A--SHE WAS MY WIFE!
SHE WAS TERRIFIED OF YOU!
YOU HAD NO RIGHT!
I HAD A RESPONSIBILITY!

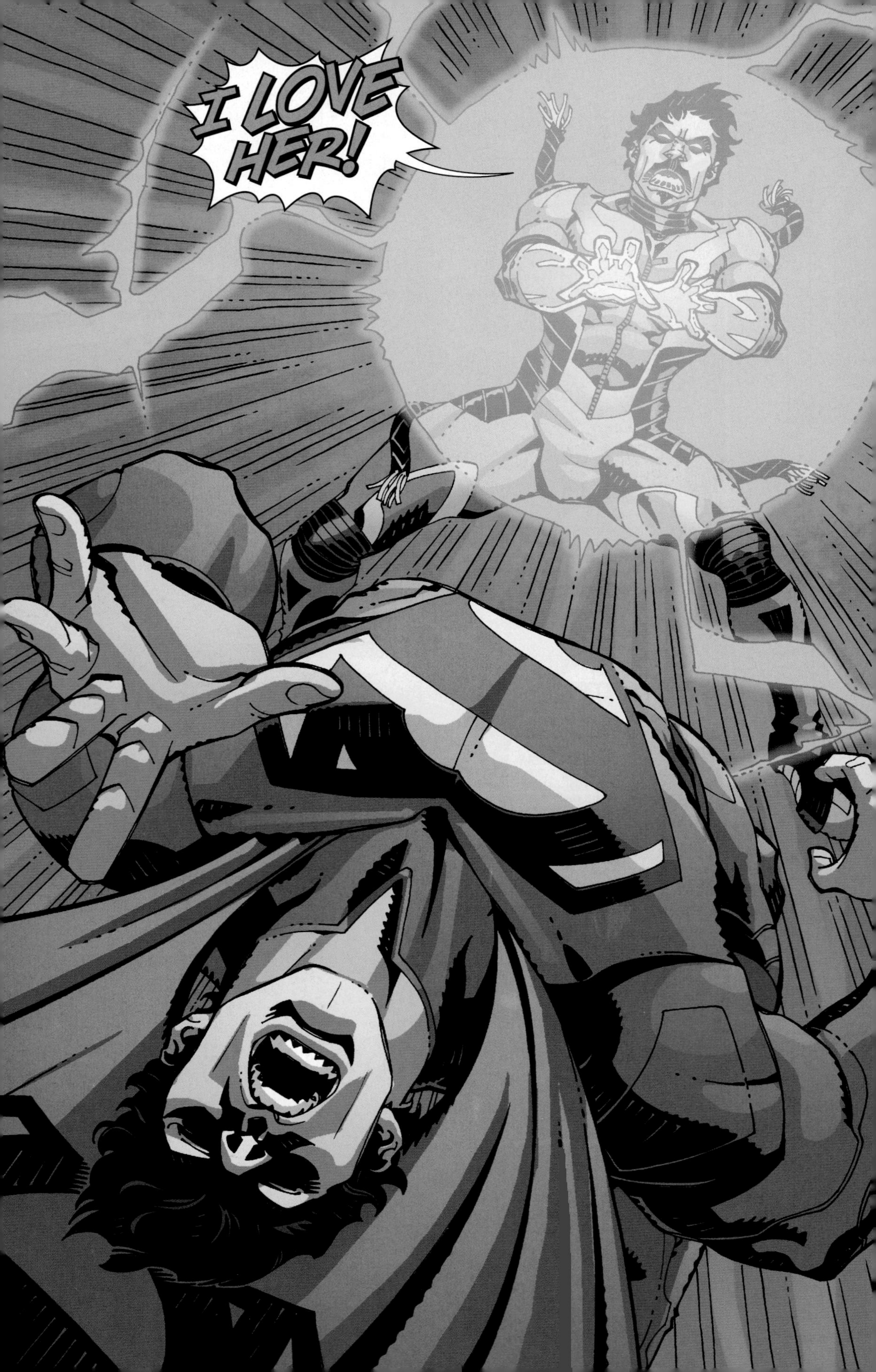
I LOVE HER!

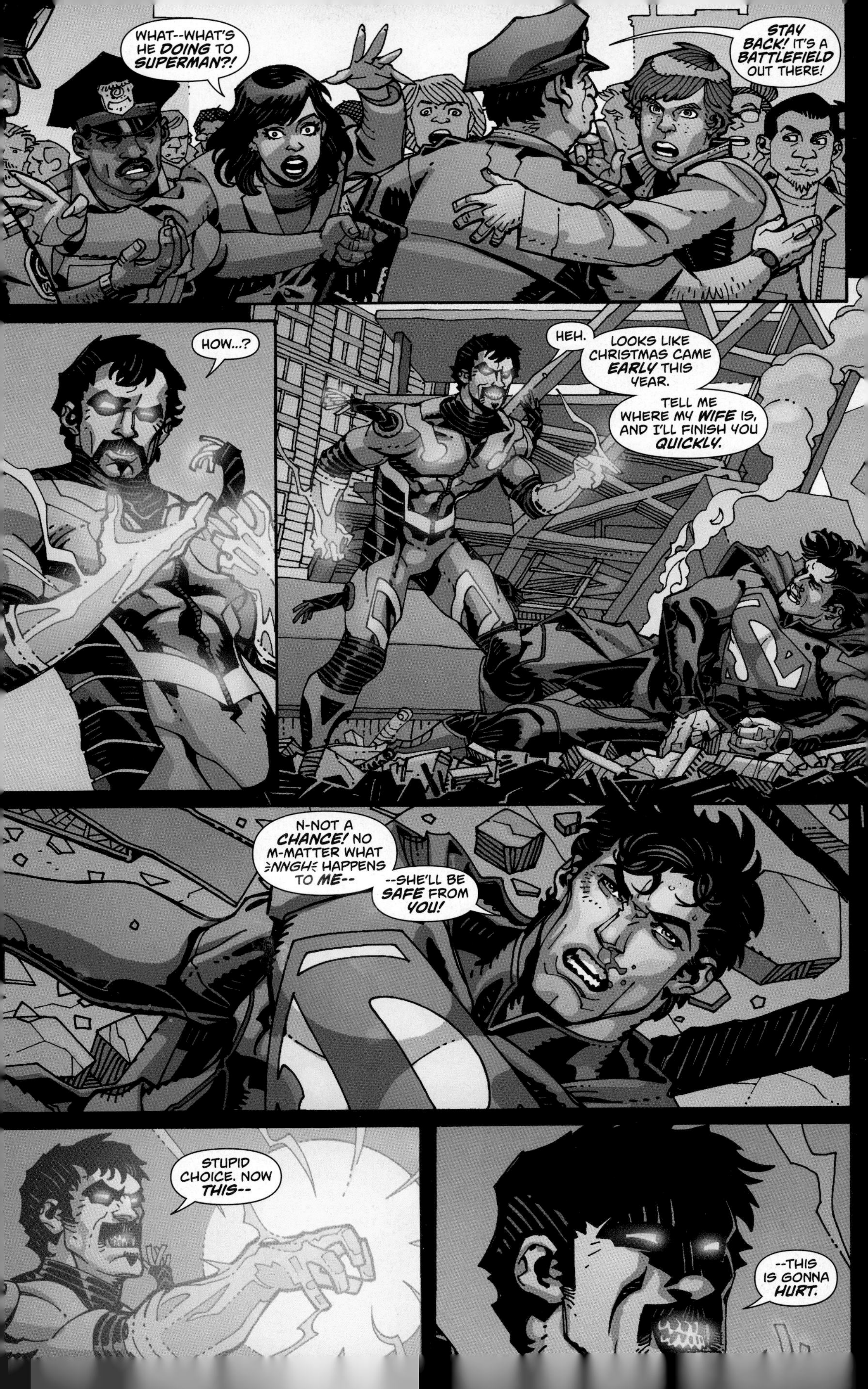
WHAT--WHAT'S HE DOING TO SUPERMAN?!
STAY BACK! IT'S A BATTLEFIELD OUT THERE!
HOW...?
HEH.
LOOKS LIKE CHRISTMAS CAME EARLY THIS YEAR.
TELL ME WHERE MY WIFE IS, AND I'LL FINISH YOU QUICKLY.
N-NOT A CHANCE! NO M-MATTER WHAT NNGH HAPPENS TO ME--
--SHE'LL BE SAFE FROM YOU!
STUPID CHOICE. NOW THIS--
--THIS IS GONNA HURT.

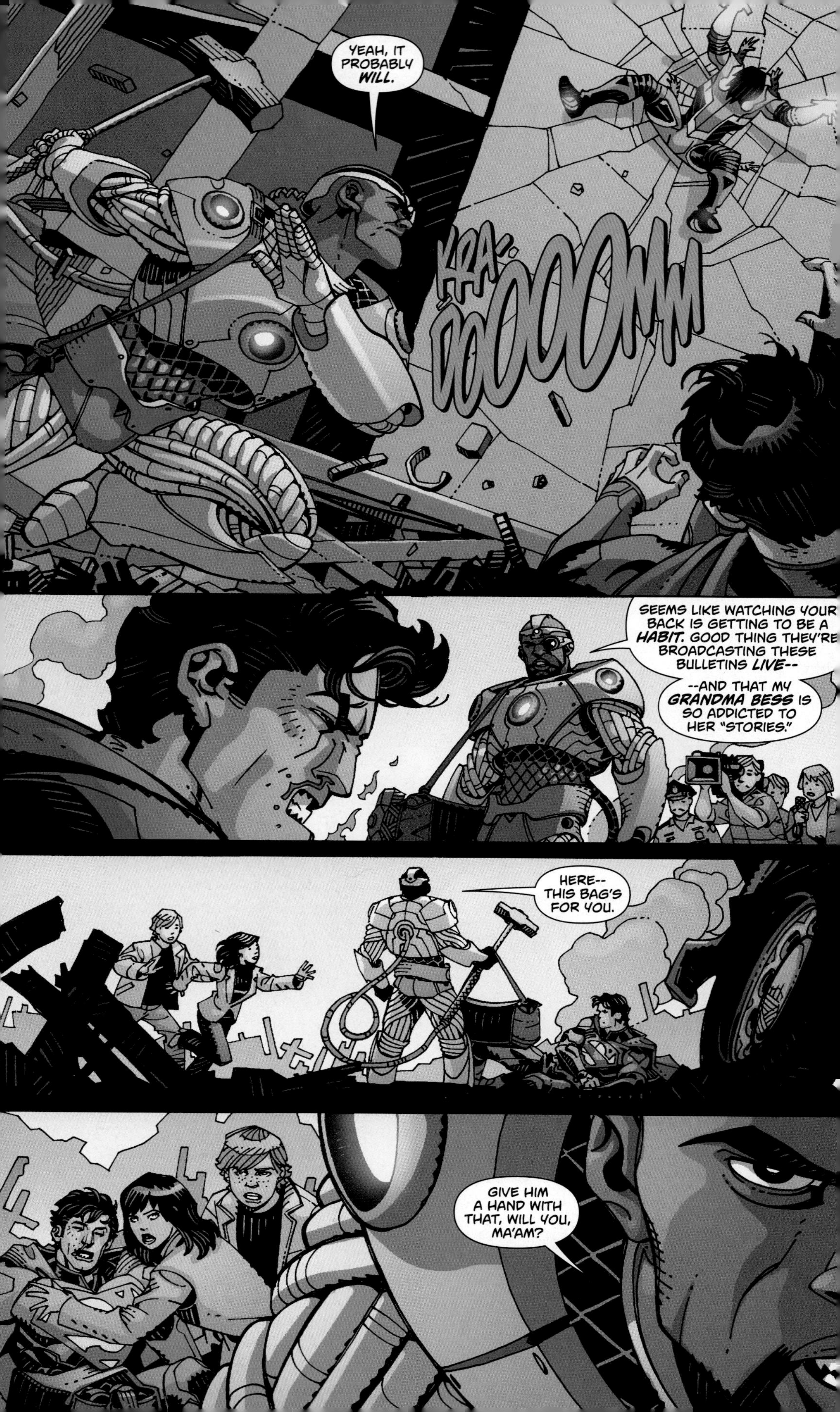
YEAH, IT PROBABLY WILL.
KRA-DOOOOOMM
SEEMS LIKE WATCHING YOUR BACK IS GETTING TO BE A HABIT. GOOD THING THEY'RE BROADCASTING THESE BULLETINS LIVE--
--AND THAT MY GRANDMA BESS IS SO ADDICTED TO HER "STORIES."
HERE-- THIS BAG'S FOR YOU.
GIVE HIM A HAND WITH THAT, WILL YOU, MA'AM?

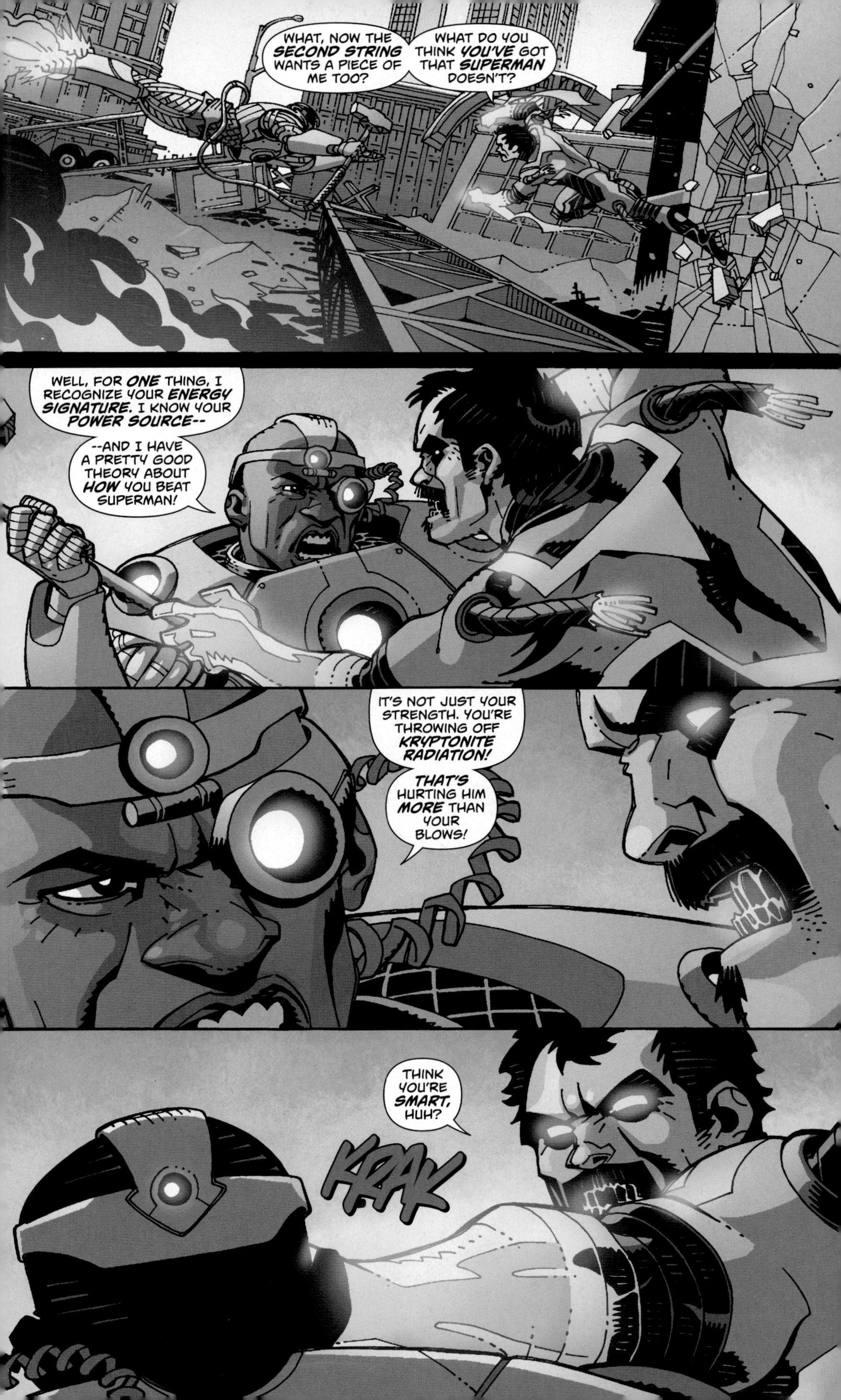
WHAT, NOW THE SECOND STRING WANTS A PIECE OF ME TOO?
WHAT DO YOU THINK YOU'VE GOT THAT SUPERMAN DOESN'T?
WELL, FOR ONE THING, I RECOGNIZE YOUR ENERGY SIGNATURE. I KNOW YOUR POWER SOURCE--
--AND I HAVE A PRETTY GOOD THEORY ABOUT HOW YOU BEAT SUPERMAN!
IT'S NOT JUST YOUR STRENGTH. YOU'RE THROWING OFF KRYPTONITE RADIATION!
THAT'S HURTING HIM MORE THAN YOUR BLOWS!
THINK YOU'RE SMART, HUH?
KRAK

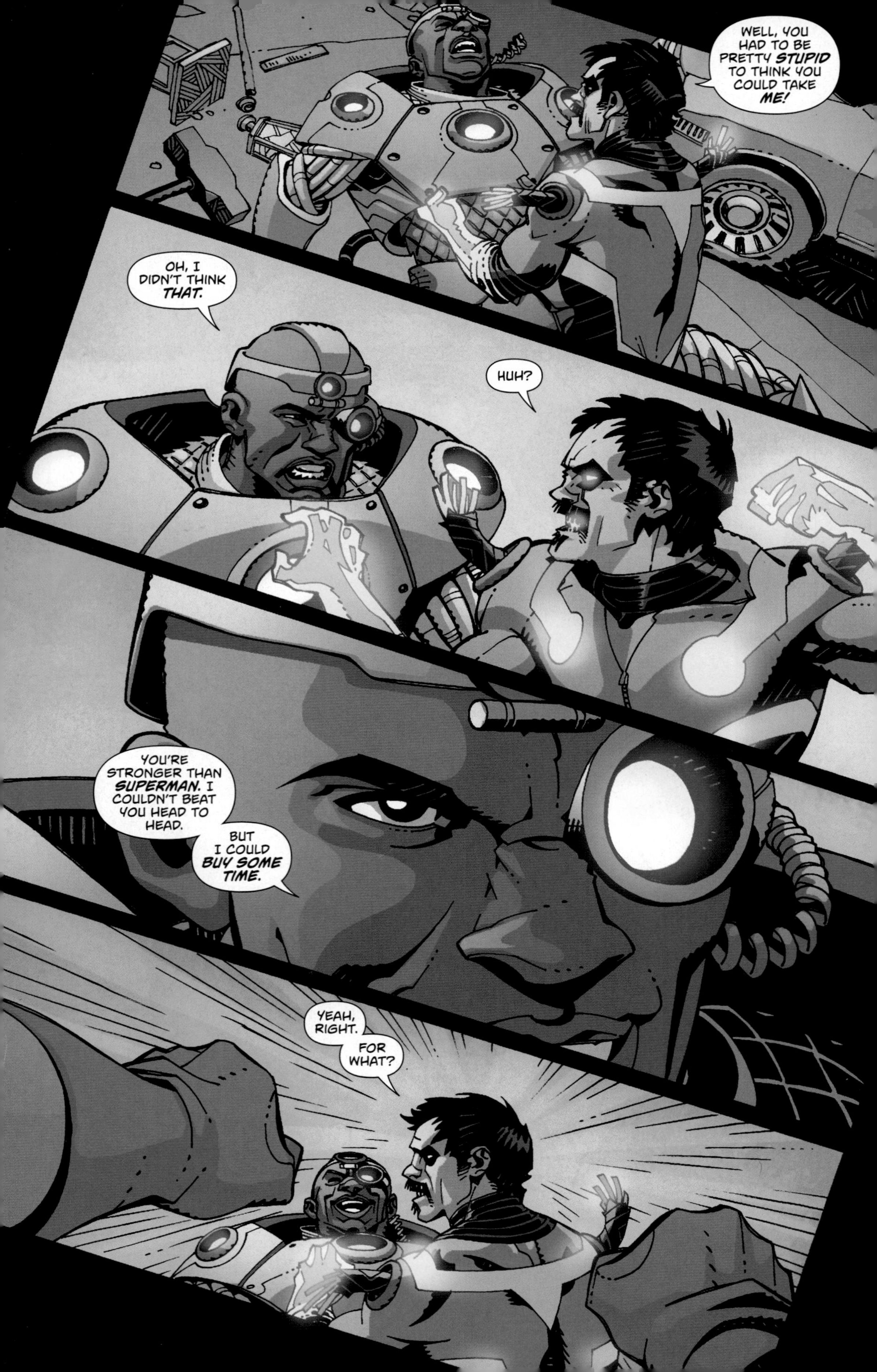
WELL, YOU HAD TO BE PRETTY STUPID TO THINK YOU COULD TAKE ME!
OH, I DIDN'T THINK THAT.
HUH?
YOU'RE STRONGER THAN SUPERMAN. I COULDN'T BEAT YOU HEAD TO HEAD.
BUT I COULD BUY SOME TIME.
YEAH, RIGHT.
FOR WHAT?

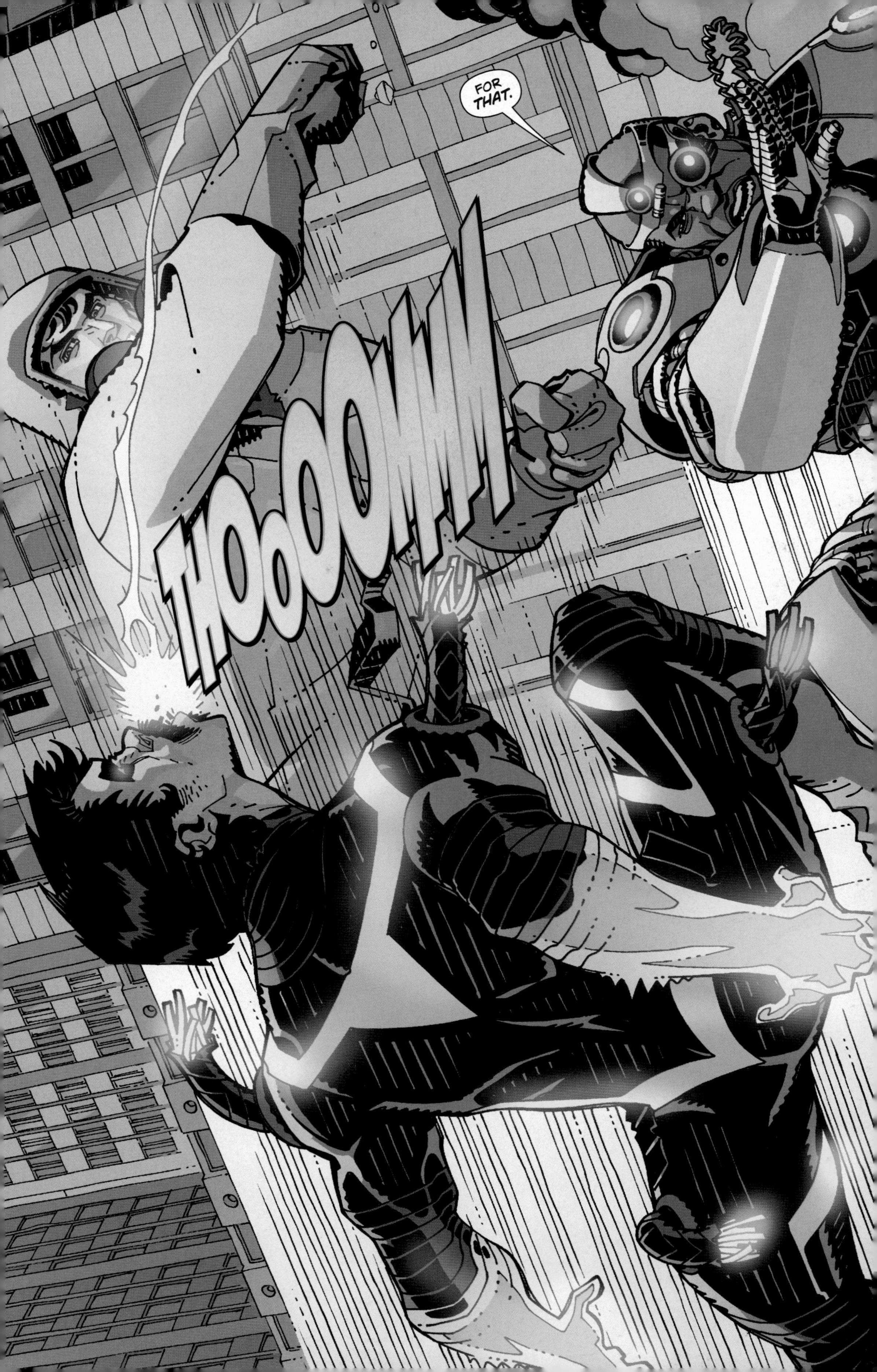
FOR THAT.
THOOOOMMM

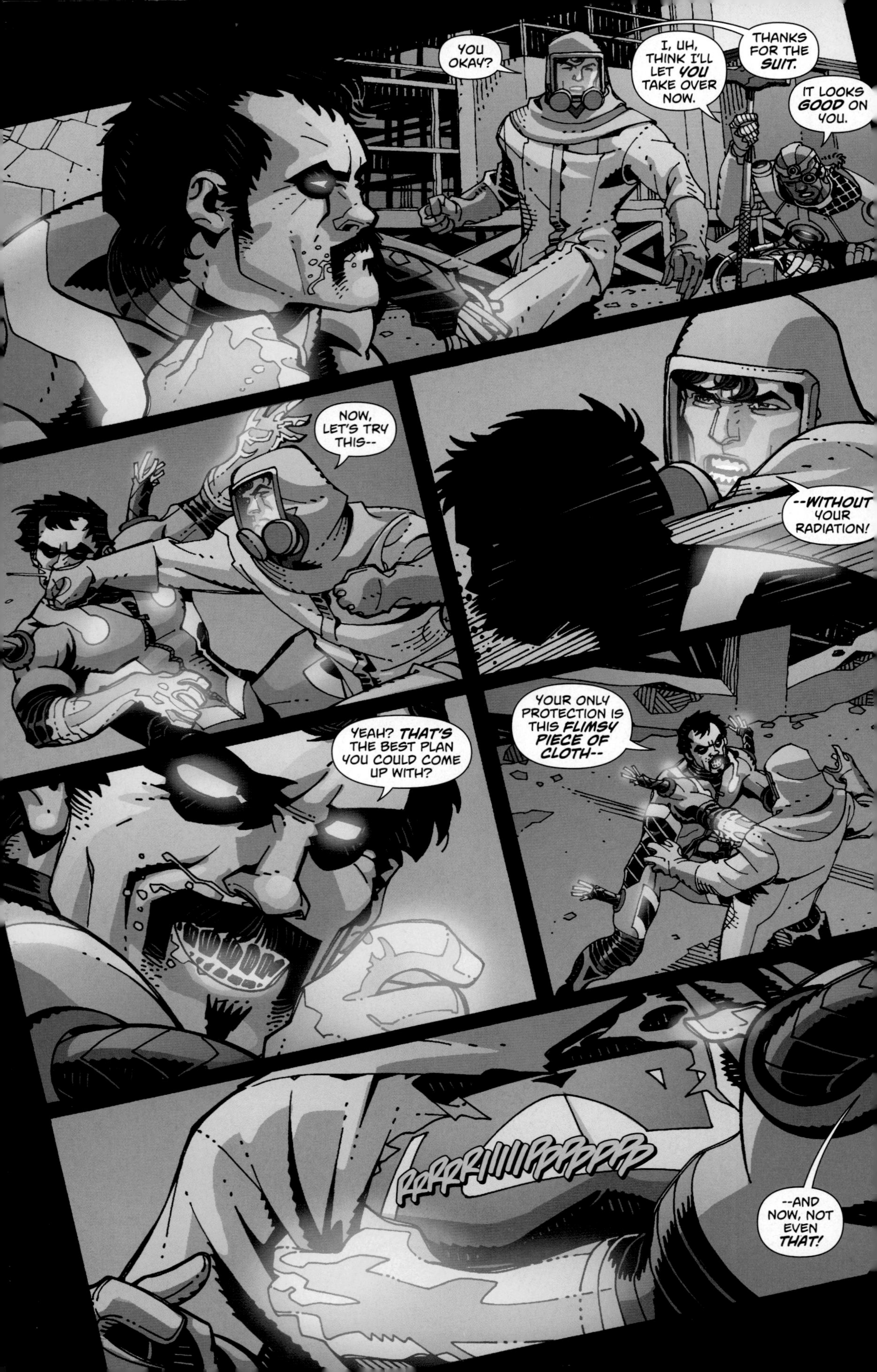

YOU OKAY?
I, UH, THINK I'LL LET YOU TAKE OVER NOW.
THANKS FOR THE SUIT.
IT LOOKS GOOD ON YOU.
NOW, LET'S TRY THIS--
--WITHOUT YOUR RADIATION!
YEAH? THAT'S THE BEST PLAN YOU COULD COME UP WITH?
YOUR ONLY PROTECTION IS THIS FLIMSY PIECE OF CLOTH--
RRRRRIIIIIPPPPPPP
--AND NOW, NOT EVEN THAT!

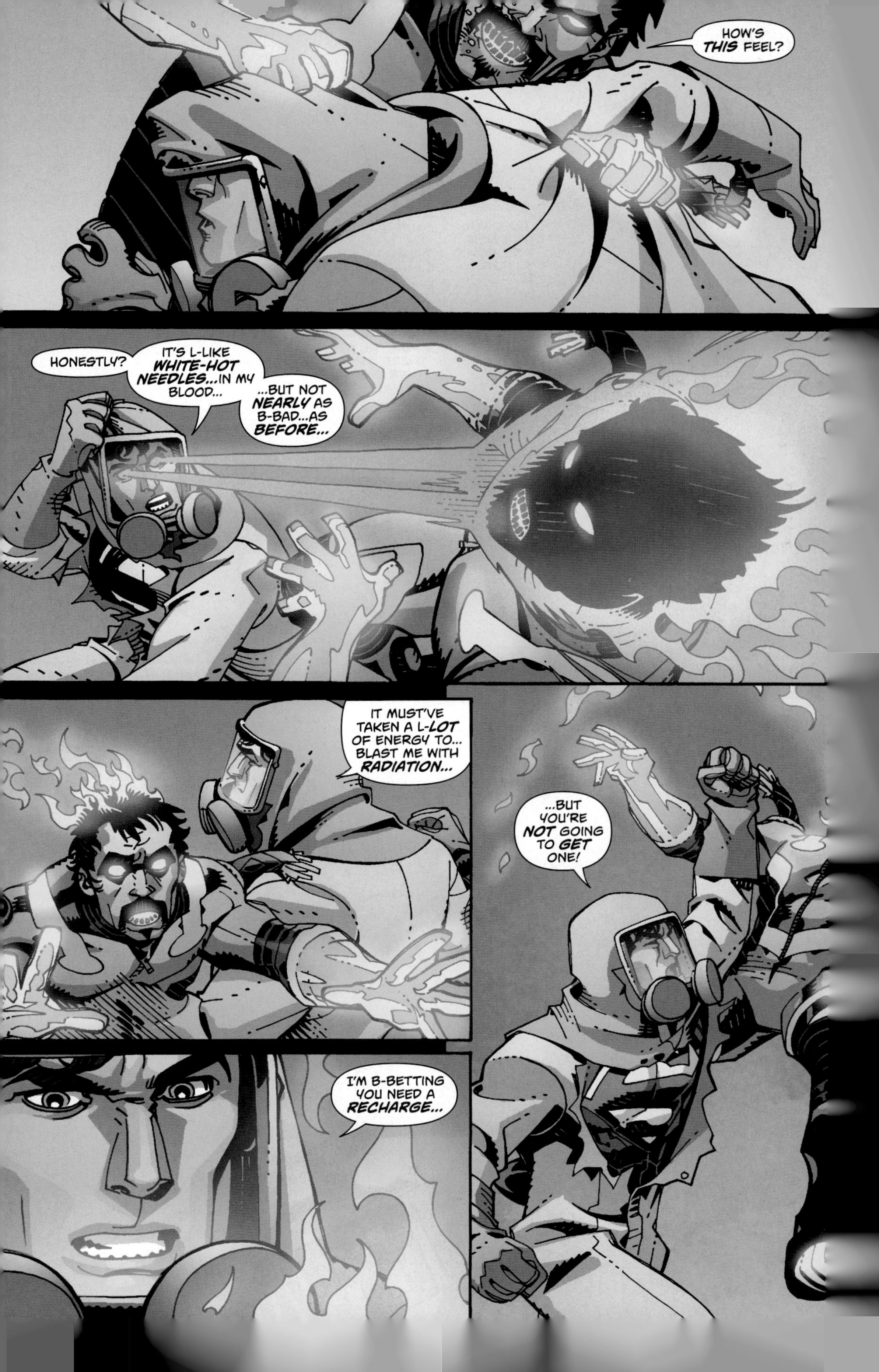
HOW'S THIS FEEL?
HONESTLY?
IT'S L-LIKE WHITE-HOT NEEDLES...IN MY BLOOD...
...BUT NOT NEARLY AS B-BAD...AS BEFORE...
IT MUST'VE TAKEN A L-LOT OF ENERGY TO... BLAST ME WITH RADIATION...
I'M B-BETTING YOU NEED A RECHARGE...
...BUT YOU'RE NOT GOING TO GET ONE!

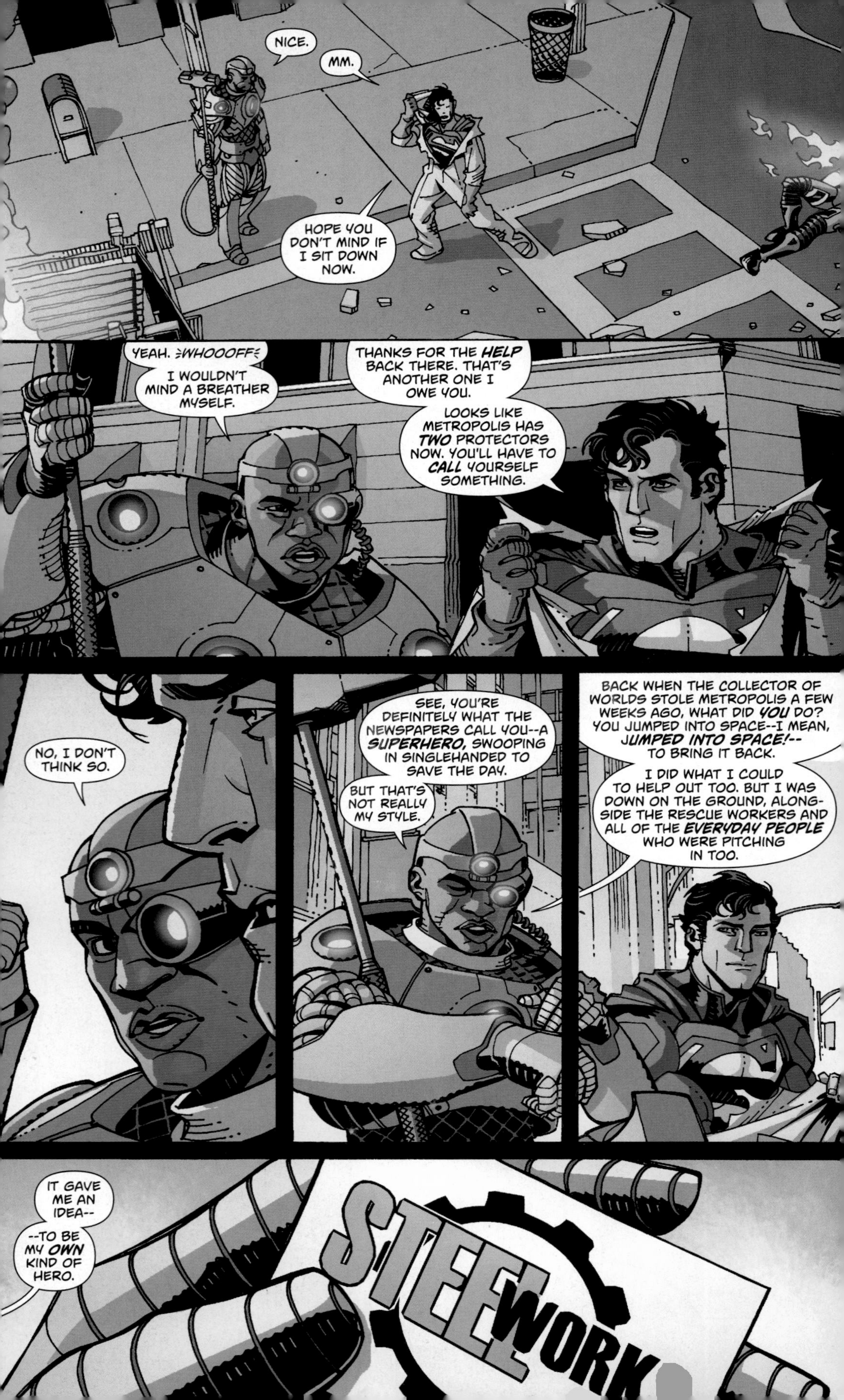

NICE.
MM.
HOPE YOU DON'T MIND IF I SIT DOWN NOW.
YEAH. WHOOOFF
I WOULDN'T MIND A BREATHER MYSELF.
THANKS FOR THE HELP BACK THERE. THAT'S ANOTHER ONE I OWE YOU.
LOOKS LIKE METROPOLIS HAS TWO PROTECTORS NOW. YOU'LL HAVE TO CALL YOURSELF SOMETHING.
NO, I DON'T THINK SO.
SEE, YOU'RE DEFINITELY WHAT THE NEWSPAPERS CALL YOU--A SUPERHERO, SWOOPING IN SINGLEHANDED TO SAVE THE DAY.
BUT THAT'S NOT REALLY MY STYLE.
BACK WHEN THE COLLECTOR OF WORLDS STOLE METROPOLIS A FEW WEEKS AGO, WHAT DID YOU DO? YOU JUMPED INTO SPACE--I MEAN, JUMPED INTO SPACE!-- TO BRING IT BACK.
I DID WHAT I COULD TO HELP OUT TOO. BUT I WAS DOWN ON THE GROUND, ALONG-SIDE THE RESCUE WORKERS AND ALL OF THE EVERYDAY PEOPLE WHO WERE PITCHING IN TOO.
IT GAVE ME AN IDEA--
--TO BE MY OWN KIND OF HERO.
STEEL
WORK

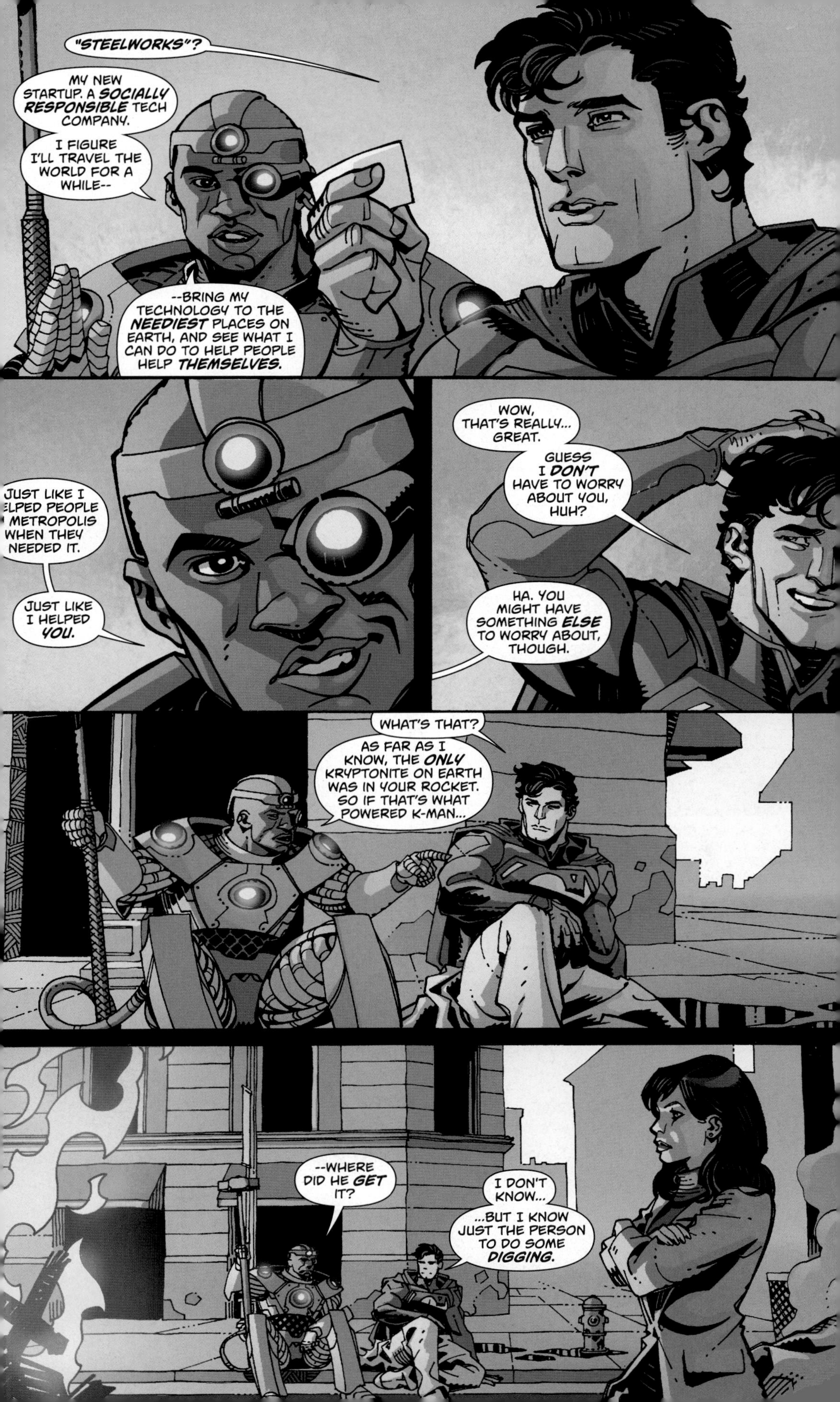
"STEELWORKS"?
MY NEW STARTUP. A SOCIALLY RESPONSIBLE TECH COMPANY.
I FIGURE I'LL TRAVEL THE WORLD FOR A WHILE--
--BRING MY TECHNOLOGY TO THE NEEDIEST PLACES ON EARTH, AND SEE WHAT I CAN DO TO HELP PEOPLE HELP THEMSELVES.
JUST LIKE I ELPED PEOPLE METROPOLIS WHEN THEY NEEDED IT.
JUST LIKE I HELPED YOU.
WOW, THAT'S REALLY... GREAT.
GUESS I DON'T HAVE TO WORRY ABOUT YOU, HUH?
HA. YOU MIGHT HAVE SOMETHING ELSE TO WORRY ABOUT, THOUGH.
WHAT'S THAT?
AS FAR AS I KNOW, THE ONLY KRYPTONITE ON EARTH WAS IN YOUR ROCKET. SO IF THAT'S WHAT POWERED K-MAN...
--WHERE DID HE GET IT?
I DON'T KNOW...
...BUT I KNOW JUST THE PERSON TO DO SOME DIGGING.

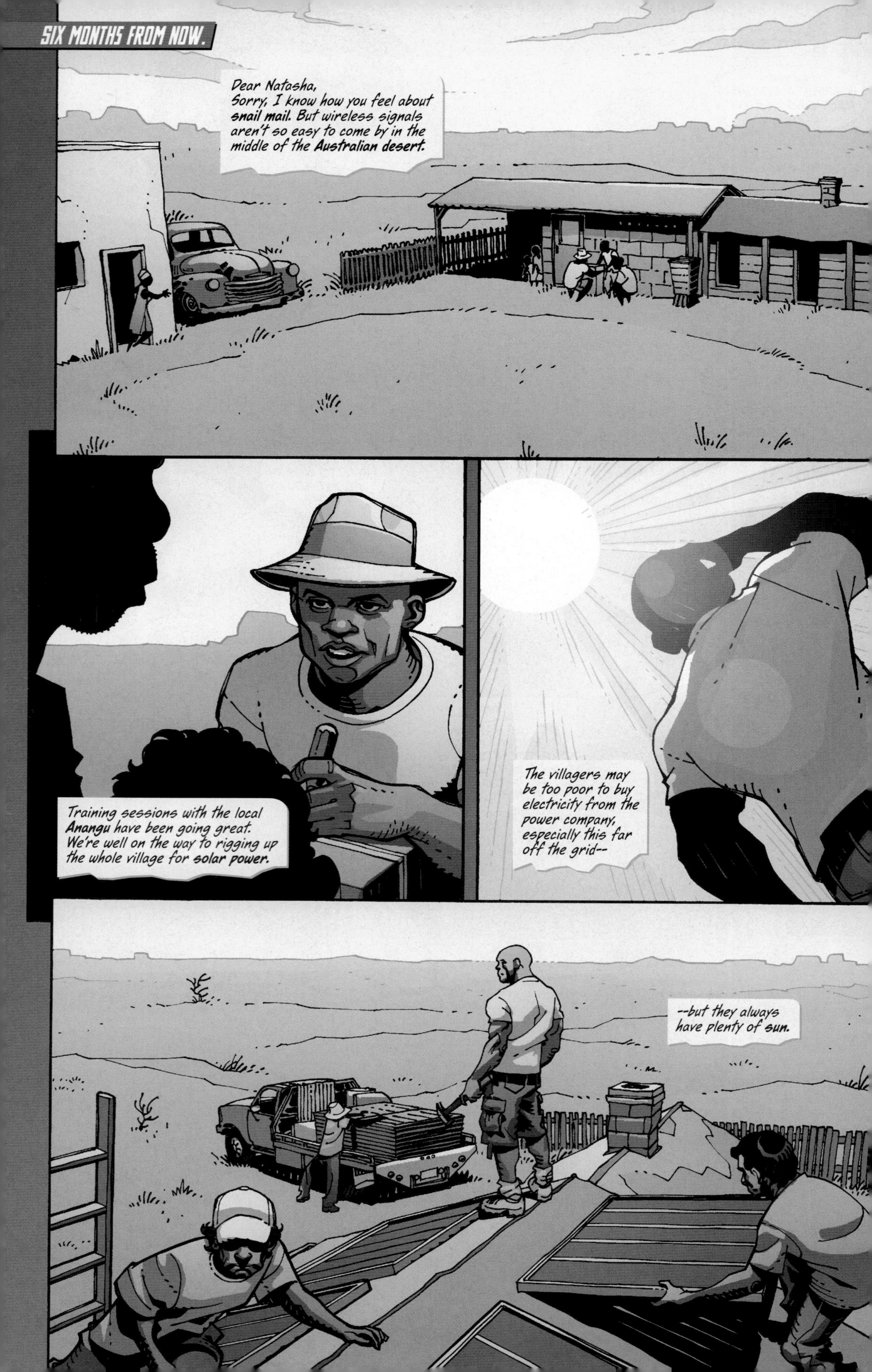
SIX MONTHS FROM NOW.
Dear Natasha,
Sorry, I know how you feel about snail mail. But wireless signals aren't so easy to come by in the middle of the Australian desert.
Training sessions with the local Anangu have been going great. We're well on the way to rigging up the whole village for solar power.
The villagers may be too poor to buy electricity from the power company, especially this far off the grid--
--but they always have plenty of sun.

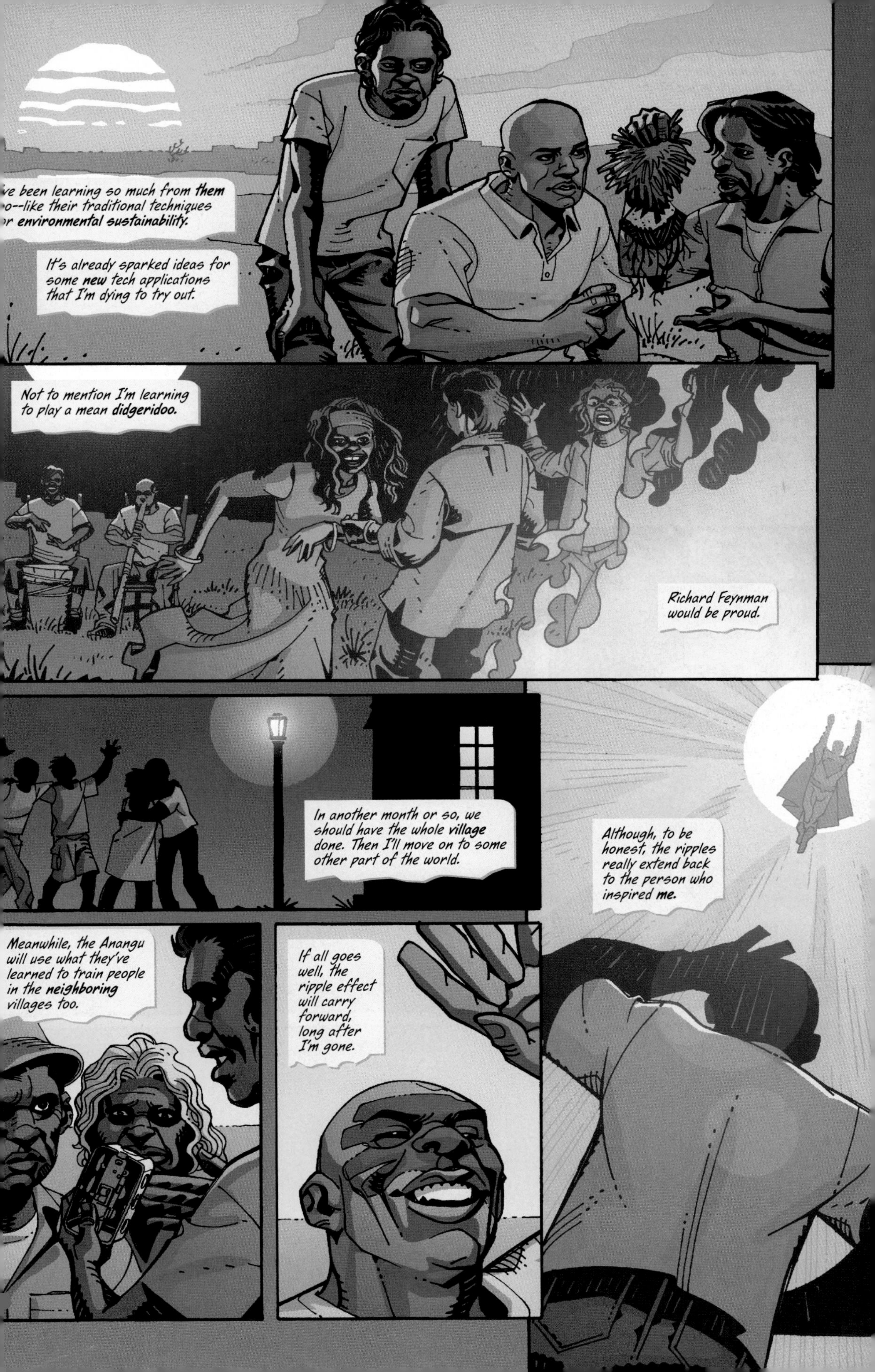
ve been learning so much from **them** o--like their traditional techniques or **environmental sustainability.**
It's already sparked ideas for some **new** tech applications that I'm dying to try out.
Not to mention I'm learning to play a mean **didgeridoo.**
Richard Feynman would be proud.
In another month or so, we should have the whole **village** done. Then I'll move on to some other part of the world.
Although, to be honest, the ripples really extend back to the person who inspired **me.**
Meanwhile, the Anangu will use what they've learned to train people in the **neighboring** villages too.
If all goes well, the ripple effect will carry forward, long after I'm gone.

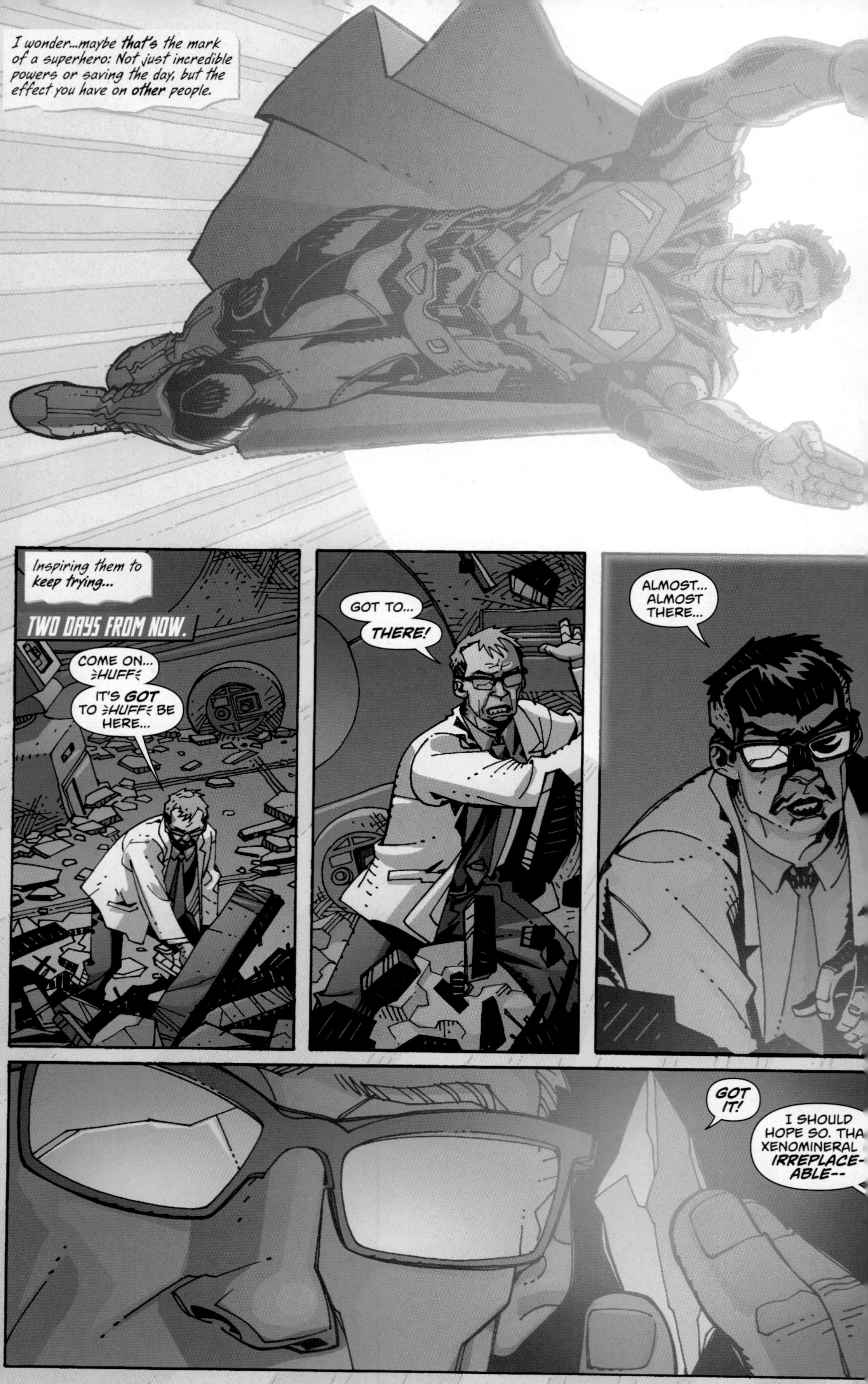

I wonder...maybe that's the mark of a superhero: Not just incredible powers or saving the day, but the effect you have on other people.
Inspiring them to keep trying...
TWO DAYS FROM NOW.
COME ON... HUFF
IT'S GOT TO HUFF BE HERE...
GOT TO... THERE!
ALMOST... ALMOST THERE...
GOT IT!
I SHOULD HOPE SO. THA XENOMINERAL IRREPLACE-ABLE--

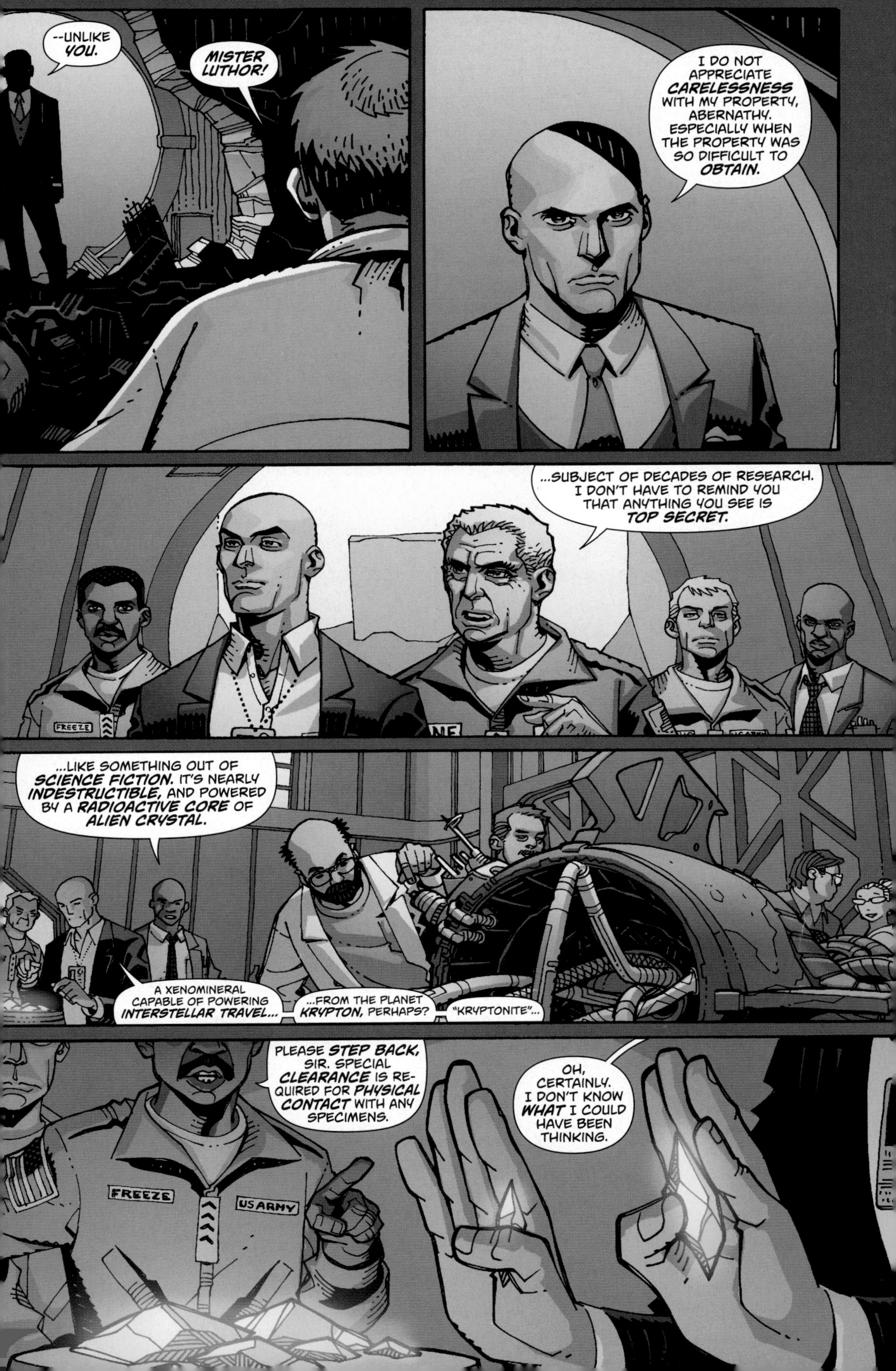
--UNLIKE YOU.
MISTER LUTHOR!
I DO NOT APPRECIATE CARELESSNESS WITH MY PROPERTY, ABERNATHY. ESPECIALLY WHEN THE PROPERTY WAS SO DIFFICULT TO OBTAIN.
...SUBJECT OF DECADES OF RESEARCH. I DON'T HAVE TO REMIND YOU THAT ANYTHING YOU SEE IS TOP SECRET.
FREEZE
...LIKE SOMETHING OUT OF SCIENCE FICTION. IT'S NEARLY INDESTRUCTIBLE, AND POWERED BY A RADIOACTIVE CORE OF ALIEN CRYSTAL.
A XENOMINERAL CAPABLE OF POWERING INTERSTELLAR TRAVEL...
...FROM THE PLANET KRYPTON, PERHAPS?
"KRYPTONITE"...
PLEASE STEP BACK, SIR. SPECIAL CLEARANCE IS REQUIRED FOR PHYSICAL CONTACT WITH ANY SPECIMENS.
OH, CERTAINLY. I DON'T KNOW WHAT I COULD HAVE BEEN THINKING.
FREEZE
US ARMY

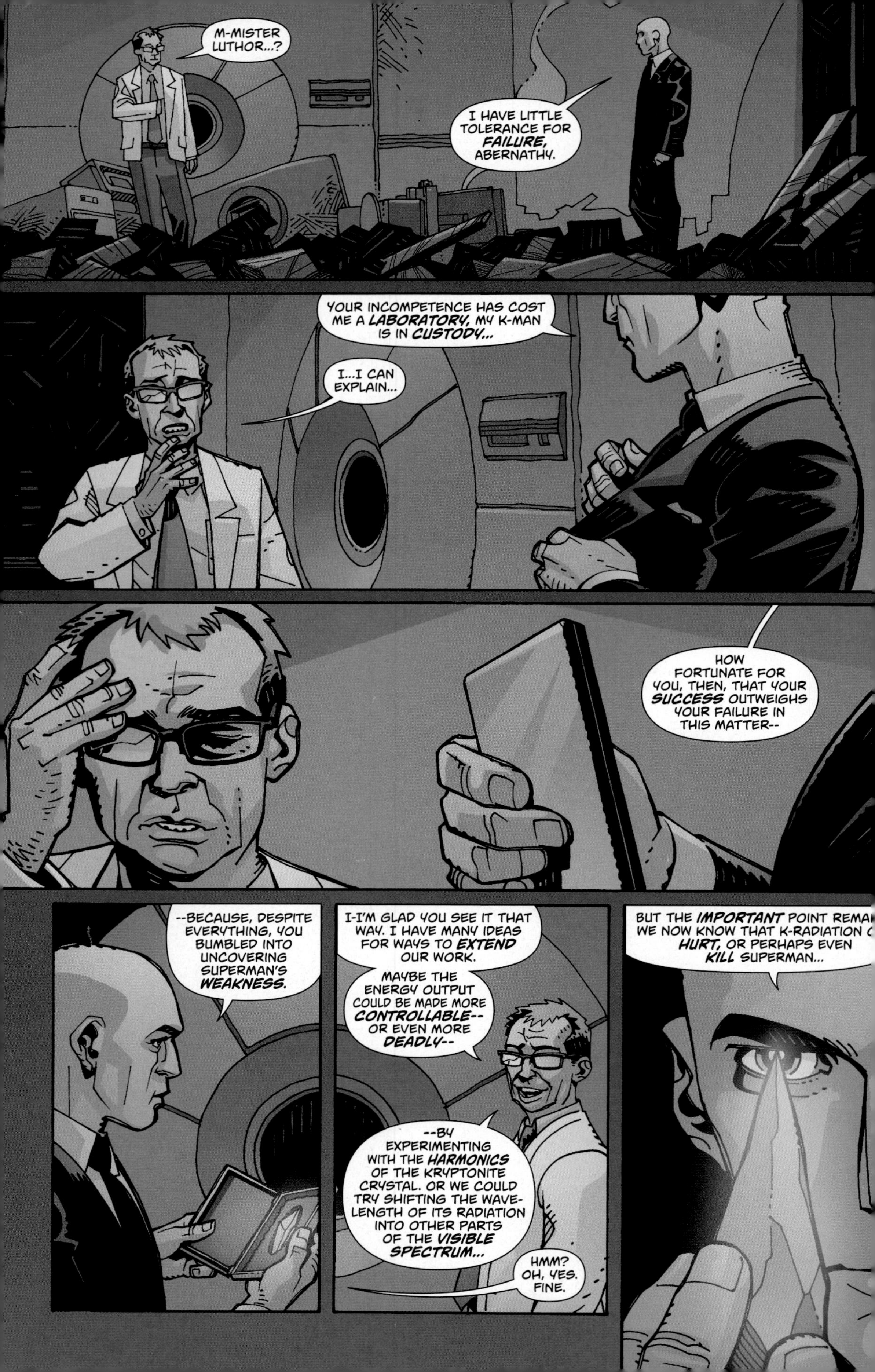
M-MISTER LUTHOR...?
I HAVE LITTLE TOLERANCE FOR FAILURE, ABERNATHY.
YOUR INCOMPETENCE HAS COST ME A LABORATORY, MY K-MAN IS IN CUSTODY...
I...I CAN EXPLAIN...
HOW FORTUNATE FOR YOU, THEN, THAT YOUR SUCCESS OUTWEIGHS YOUR FAILURE IN THIS MATTER--
--BECAUSE, DESPITE EVERYTHING, YOU BUMBLED INTO UNCOVERING SUPERMAN'S WEAKNESS.
I-I'M GLAD YOU SEE IT THAT WAY. I HAVE MANY IDEAS FOR WAYS TO EXTEND OUR WORK.
MAYBE THE ENERGY OUTPUT COULD BE MADE MORE CONTROLLABLE-- OR EVEN MORE DEADLY--
--BY EXPERIMENTING WITH THE HARMONICS OF THE KRYPTONITE CRYSTAL. OR WE COULD TRY SHIFTING THE WAVE-LENGTH OF ITS RADIATION INTO OTHER PARTS OF THE VISIBLE SPECTRUM...
HMM? OH, YES. FINE.
BUT THE IMPORTANT POINT REMA
WE NOW KNOW THAT K-RADIATION
HURT, OR PERHAPS EVEN KILL SUPERMAN...

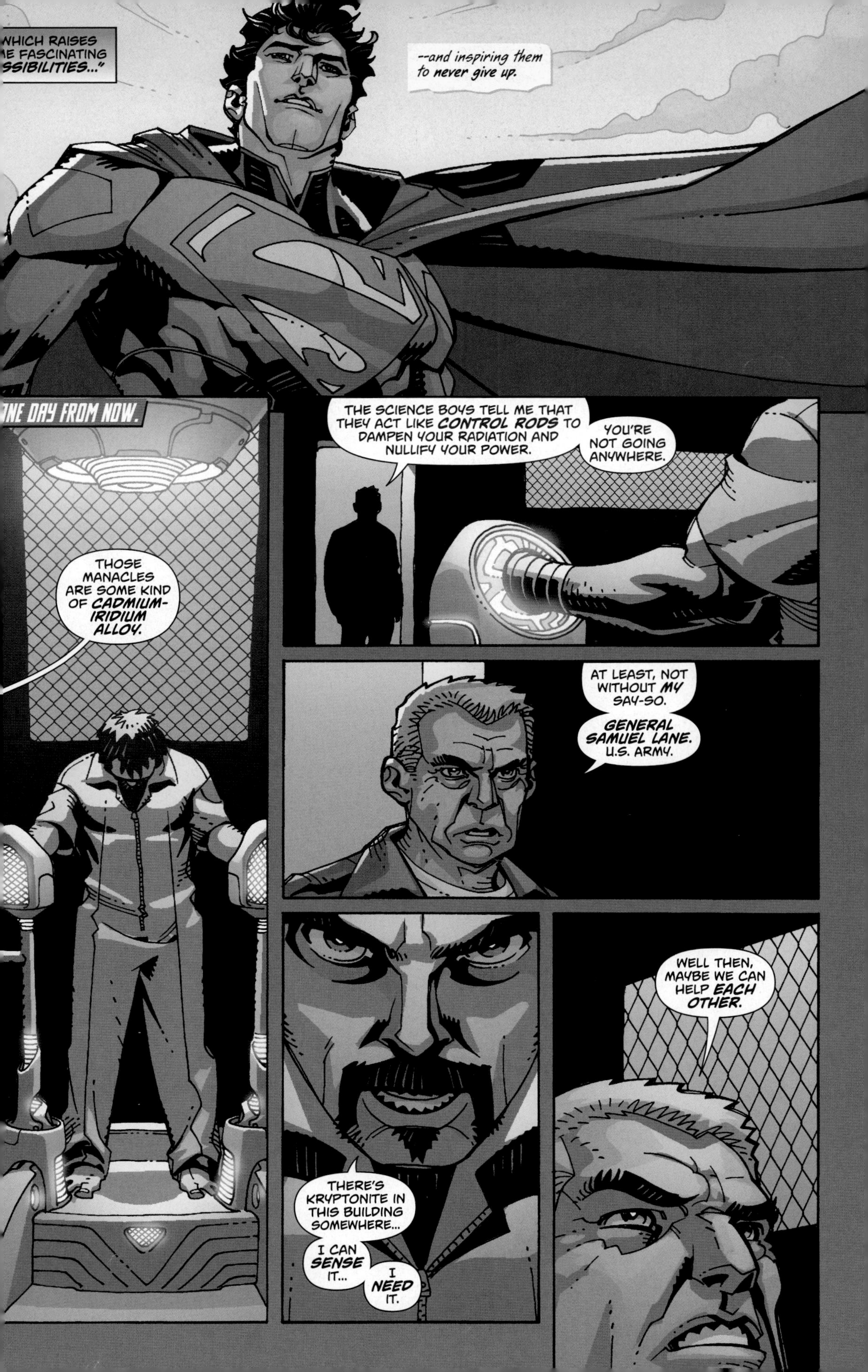
WHICH RAISES
ME FASCINATING
SSIBILITIES..."
--and inspiring them to never give up.
ONE DAY FROM NOW.
THOSE MANACLES ARE SOME KIND OF CADMIUM-IRIDIUM ALLOY.
THE SCIENCE BOYS TELL ME THAT THEY ACT LIKE CONTROL RODS TO DAMPEN YOUR RADIATION AND NULLIFY YOUR POWER.
YOU'RE NOT GOING ANYWHERE.
AT LEAST, NOT WITHOUT MY SAY-SO.
GENERAL SAMUEL LANE. U.S. ARMY.
THERE'S KRYPTONITE IN THIS BUILDING SOMEWHERE...
I CAN SENSE IT...
I NEED IT.
WELL THEN, MAYBE WE CAN HELP EACH OTHER.

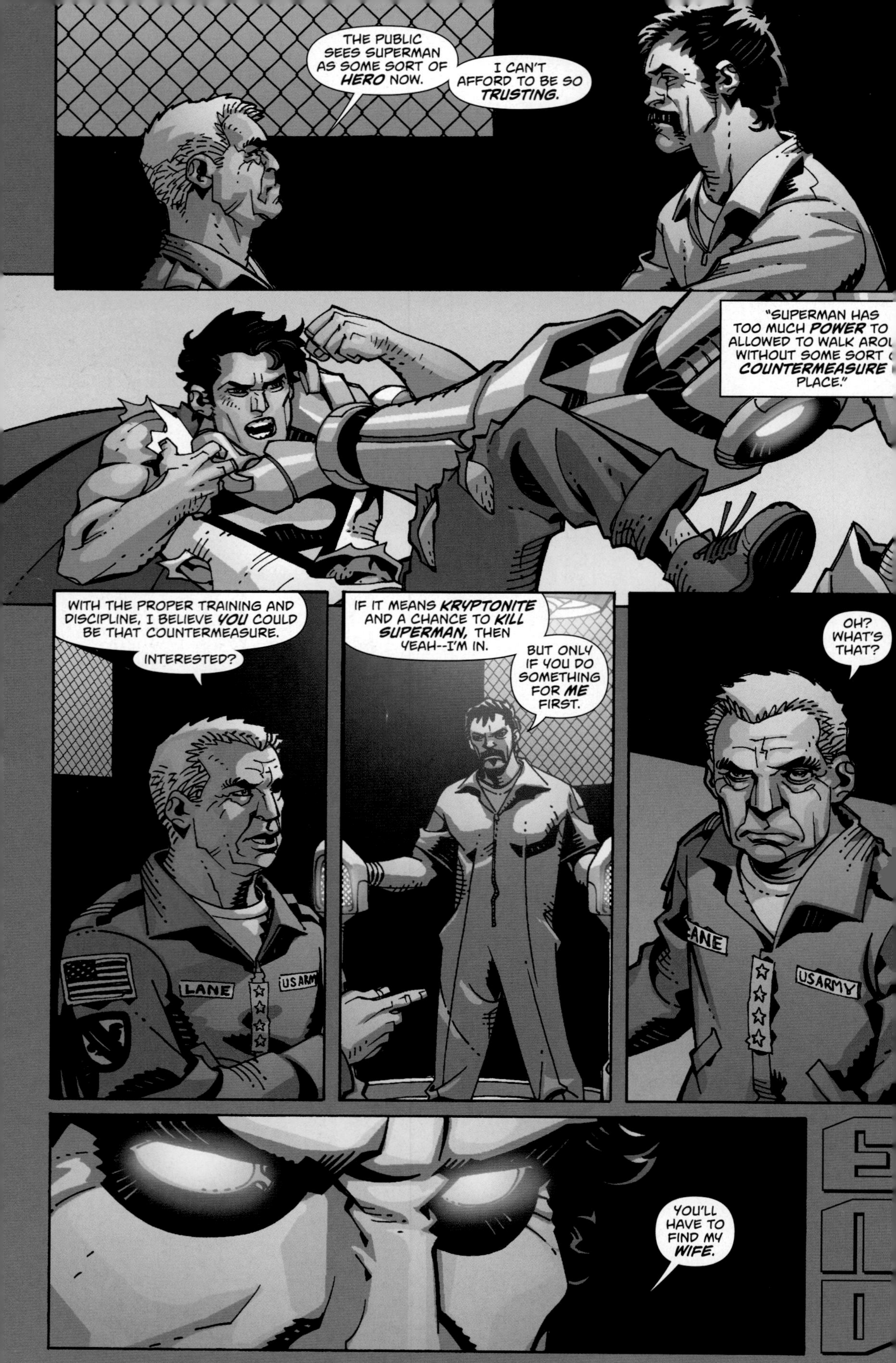
THE PUBLIC SEES SUPERMAN AS SOME SORT OF HERO NOW.
I CAN'T AFFORD TO BE SO TRUSTING.
"SUPERMAN HAS TOO MUCH POWER TO ALLOWED TO WALK AROU WITHOUT SOME SORT C COUNTERMEASURE PLACE."
WITH THE PROPER TRAINING AND DISCIPLINE, I BELIEVE YOU COULD BE THAT COUNTERMEASURE.
INTERESTED?
LANE
USARMY
IF IT MEANS KRYPTONITE AND A CHANCE TO KILL SUPERMAN, THEN YEAH--I'M IN.
BUT ONLY IF YOU DO SOMETHING FOR ME FIRST.
OH? WHAT'S THAT?
USARMY
YOU'LL HAVE TO FIND MY WIFE.

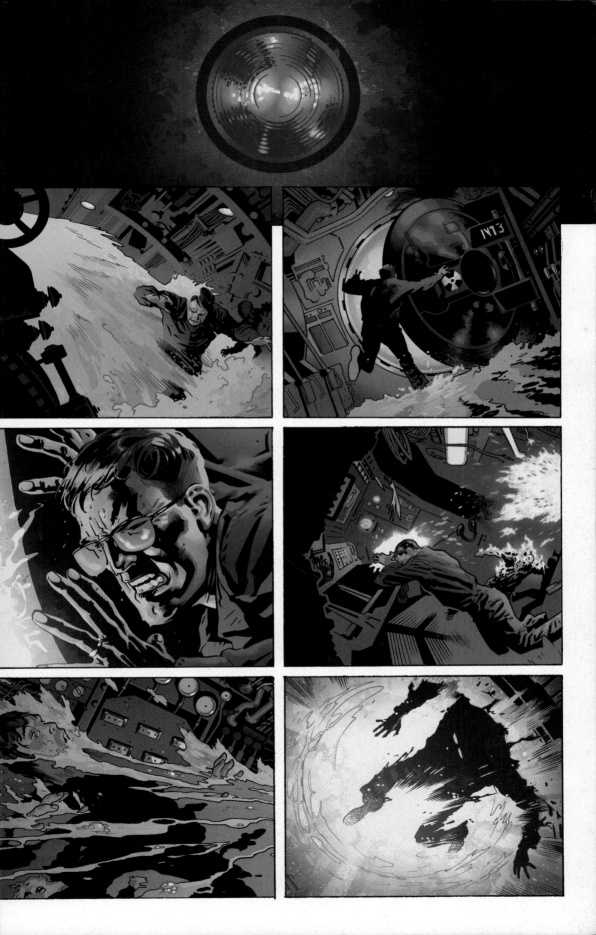

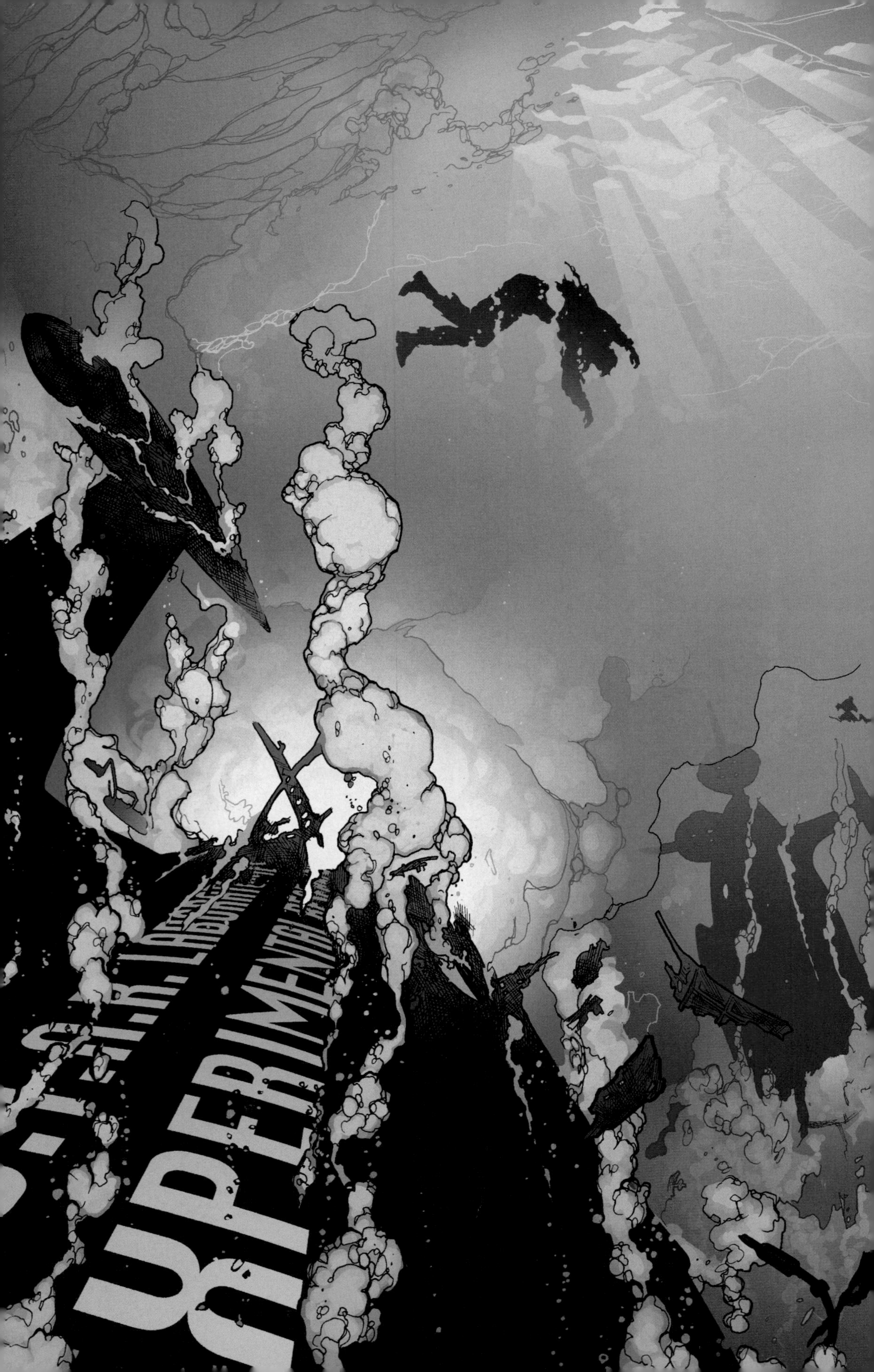

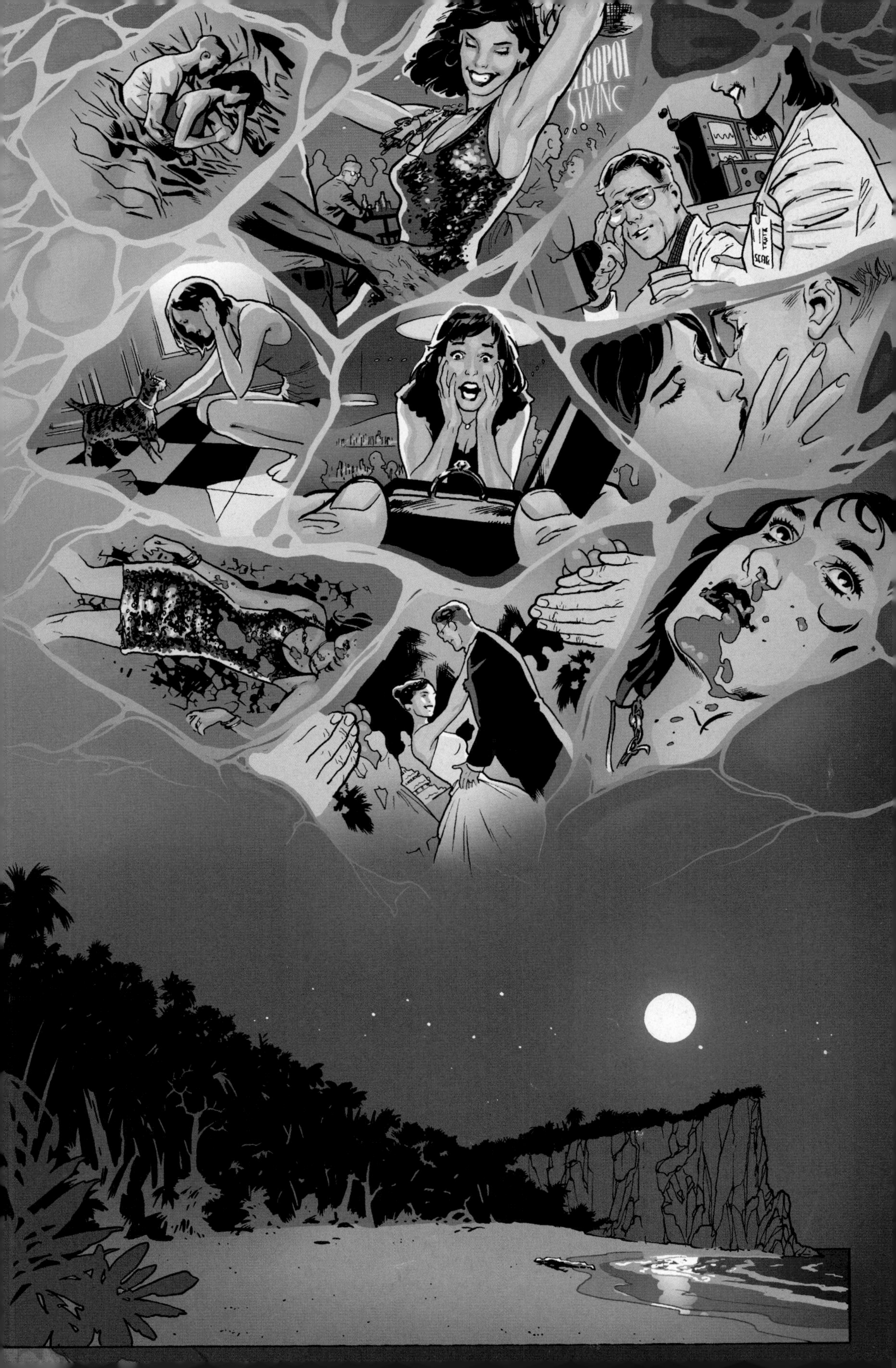
SWING

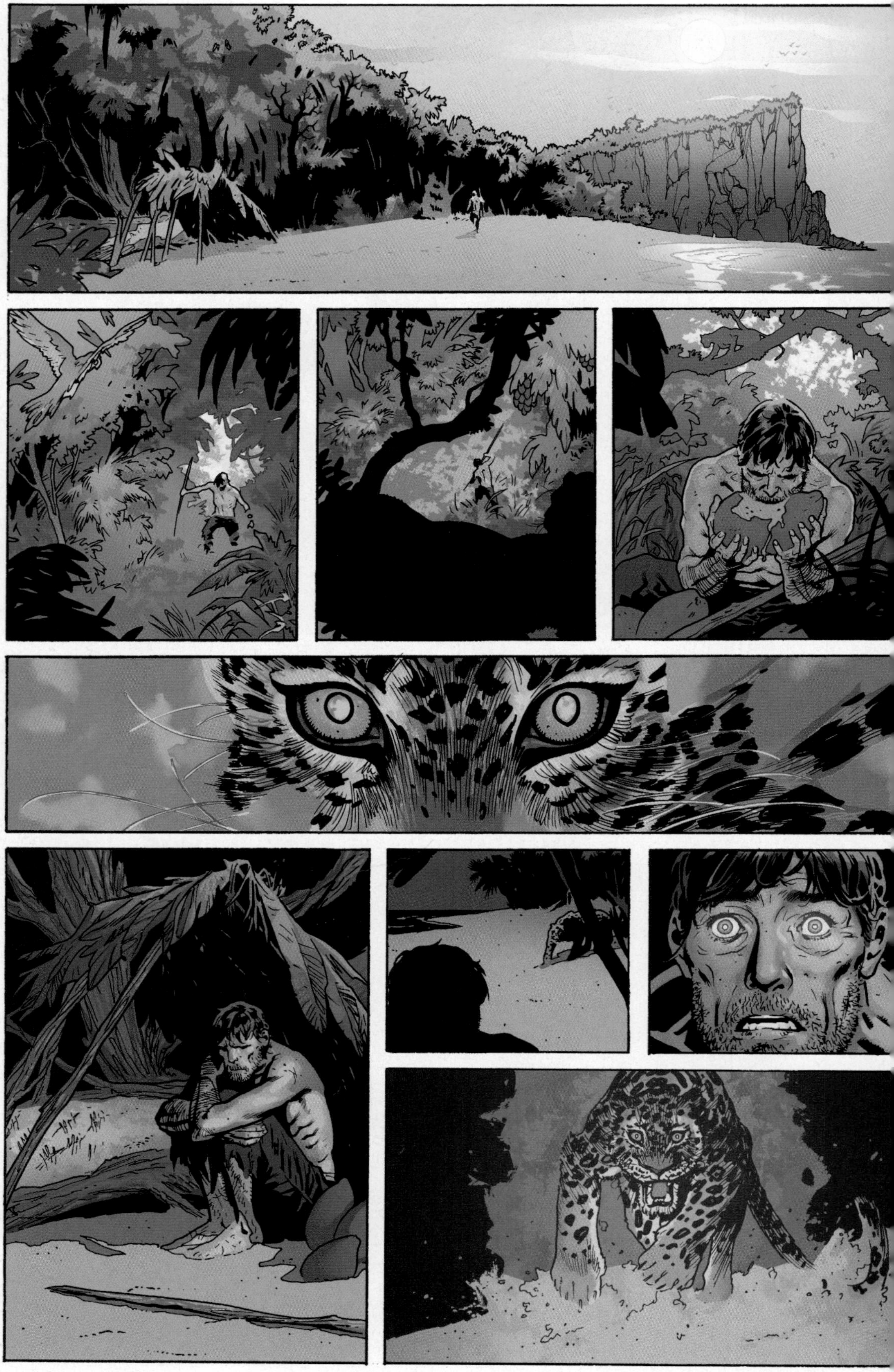

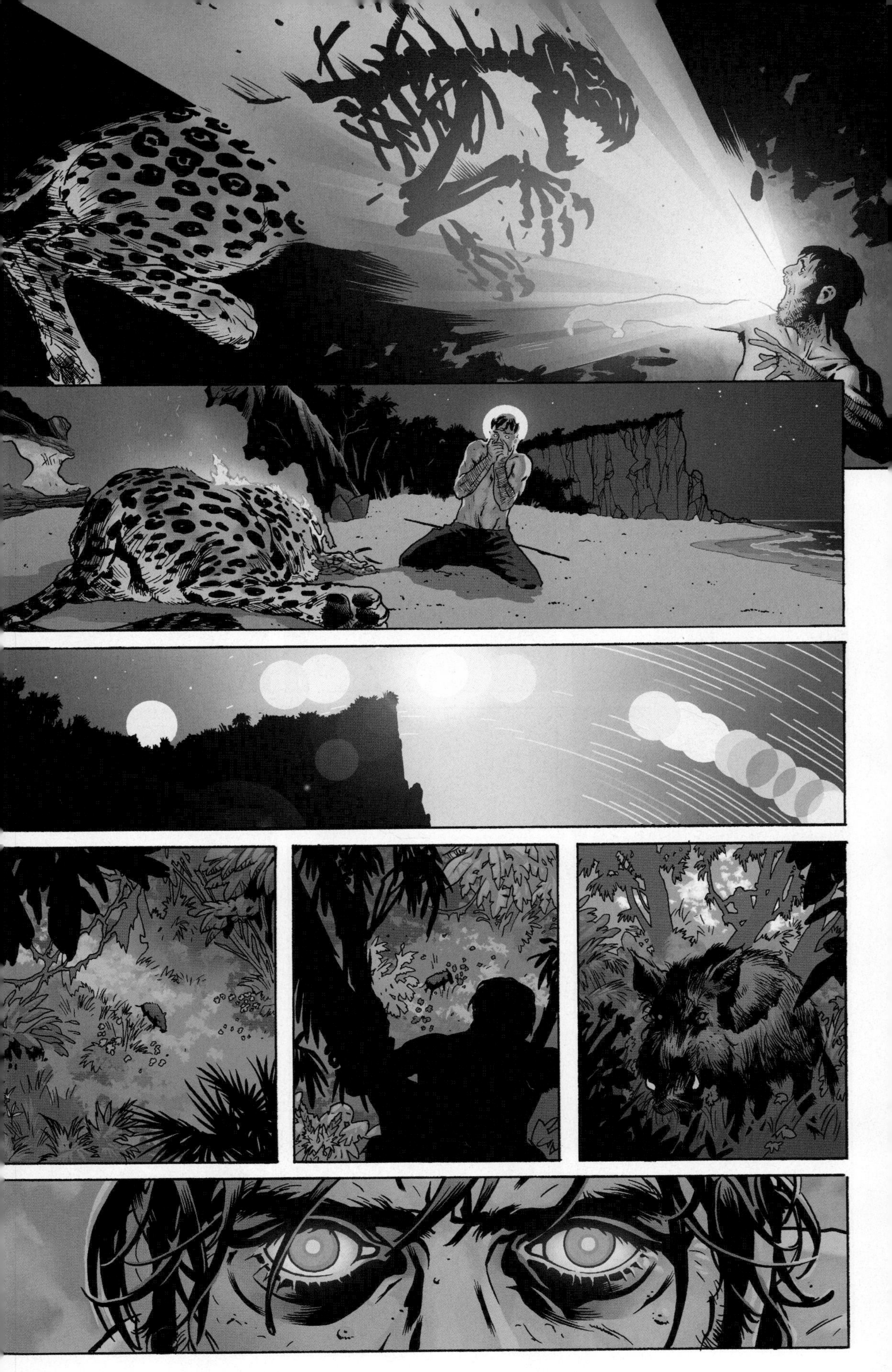

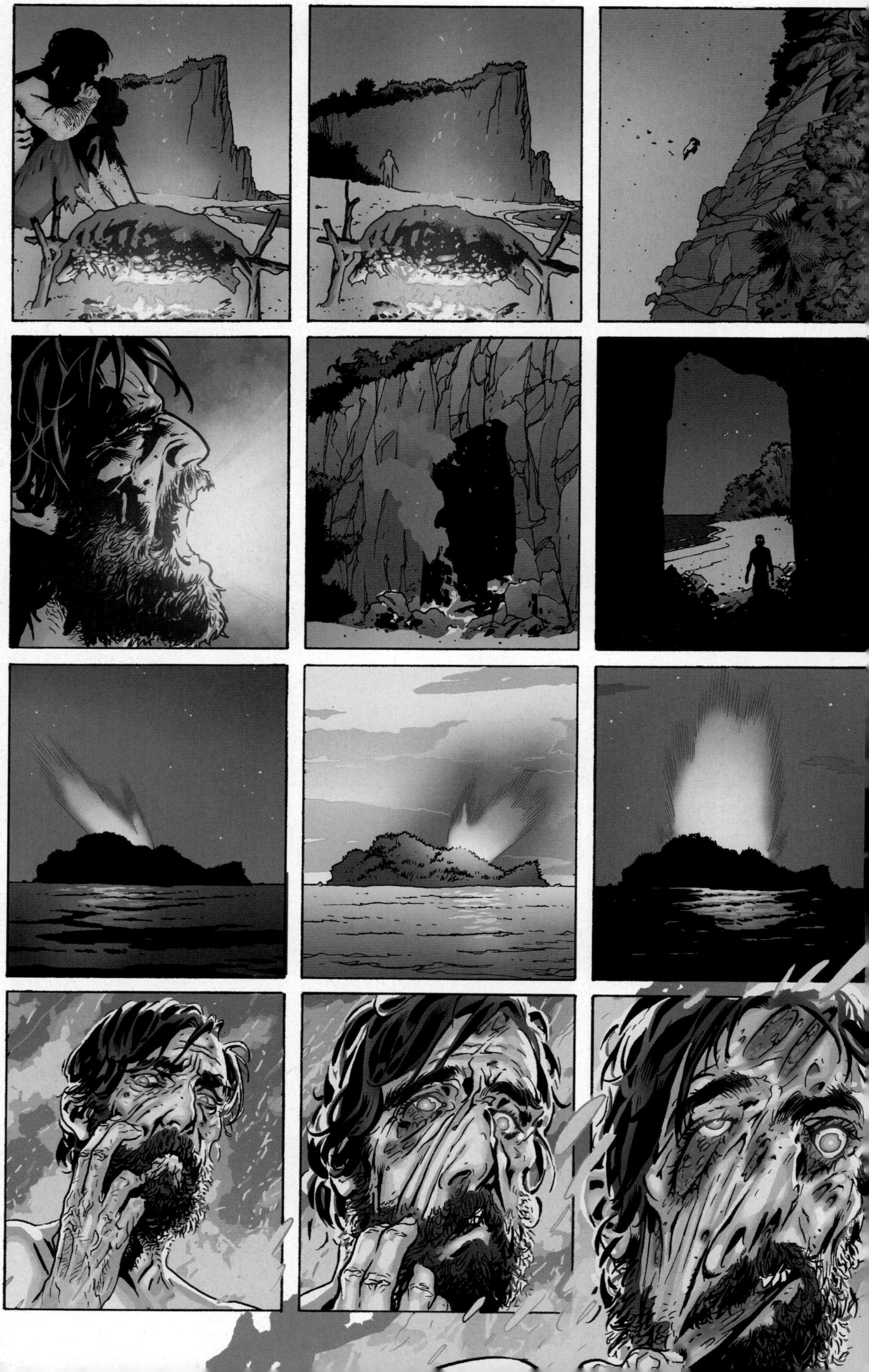

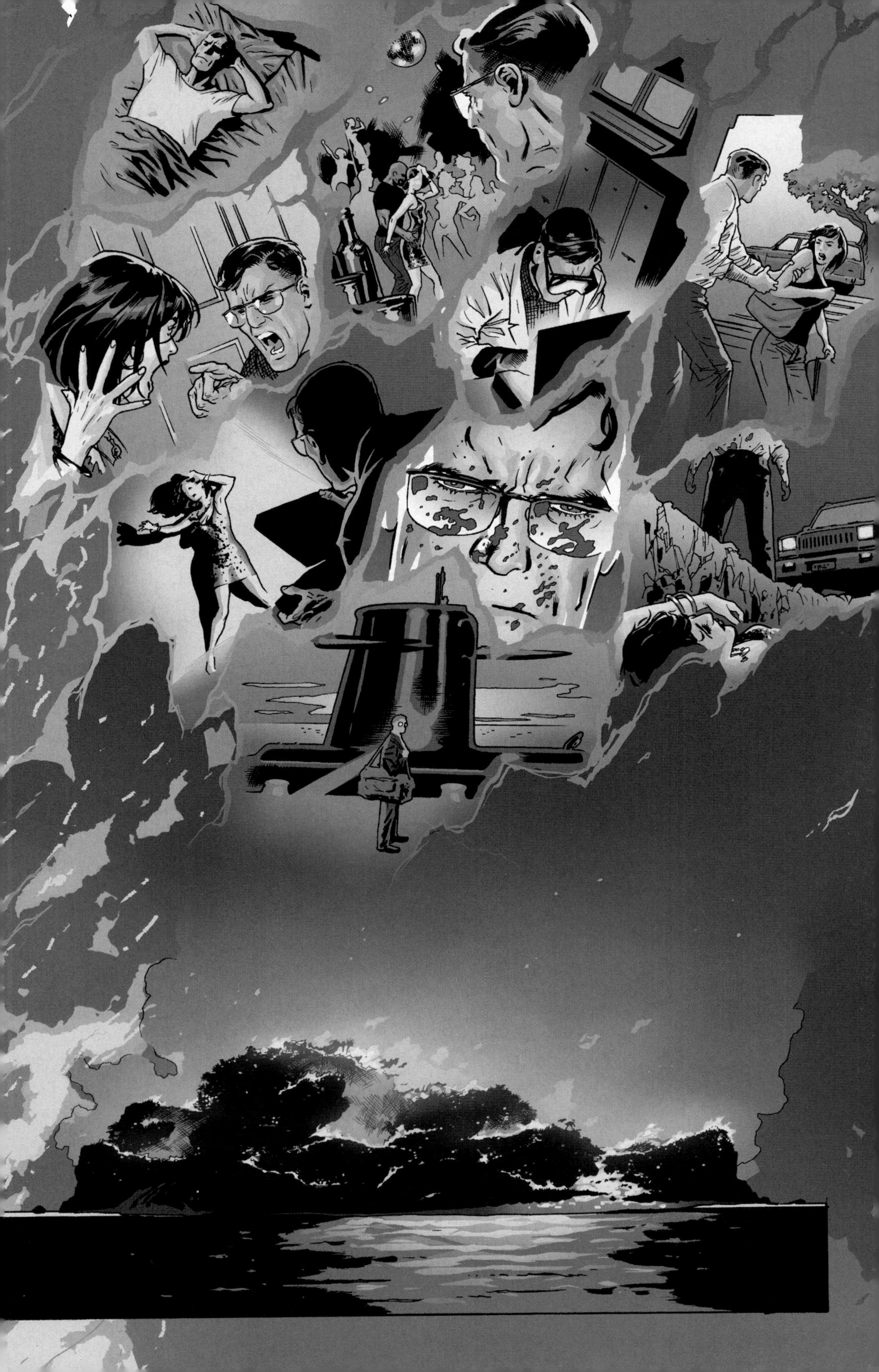

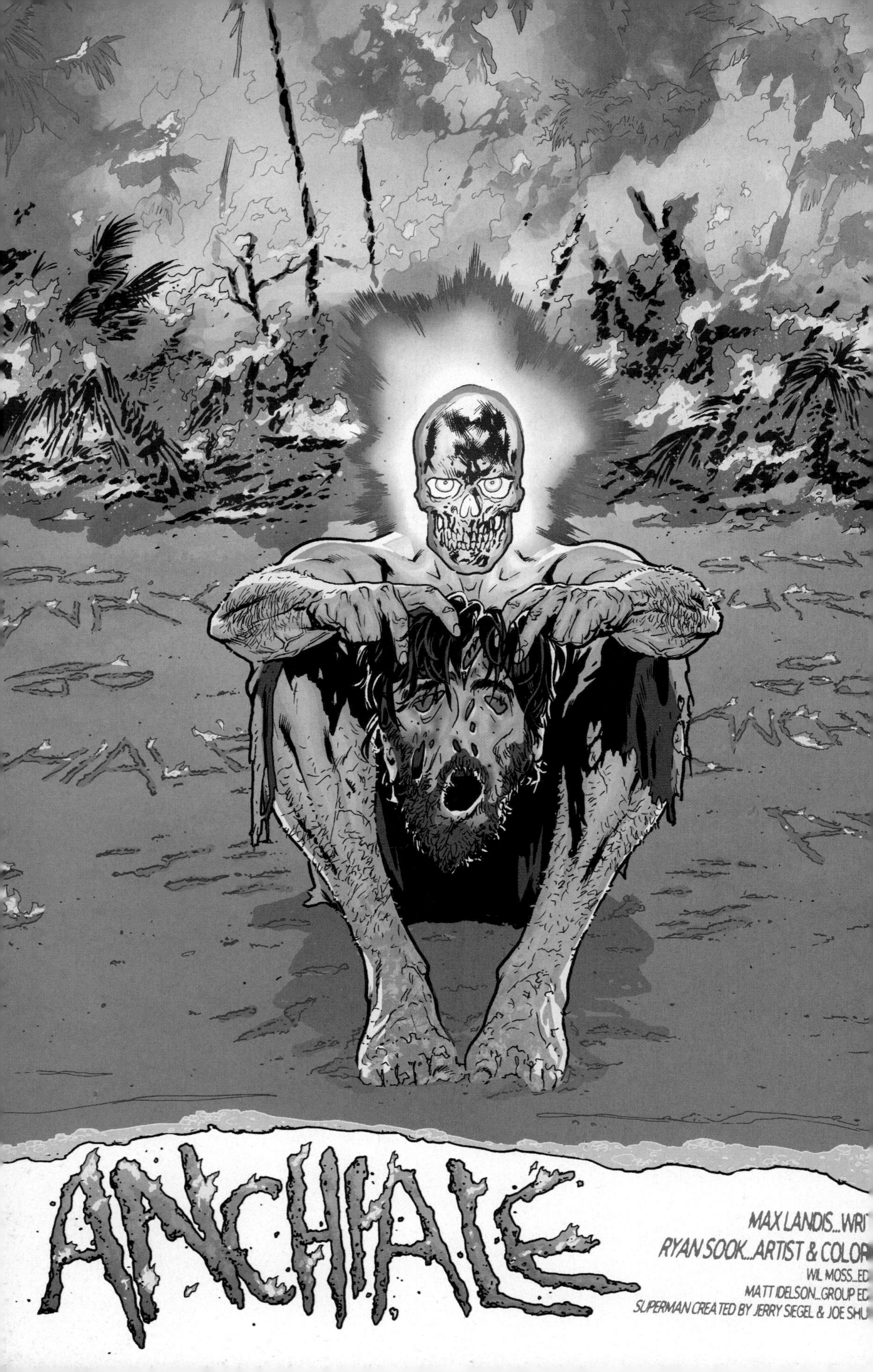
ANCHIALE
MAX LANDIS...WRI
RYAN SOOK...ARTIST & COLOR
WIL MOSS...ED
MATT IDELSON...GROUP ED
SUPERMAN CREATED BY JERRY SIEGEL & JOE SHU

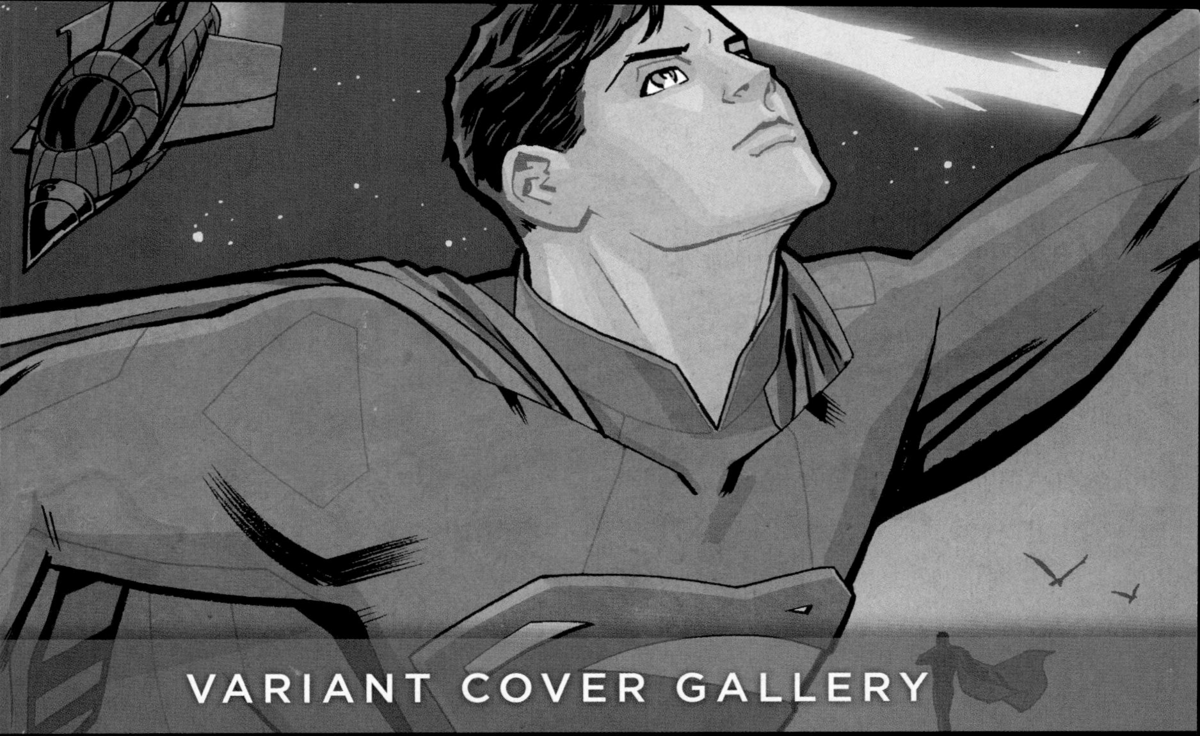
VARIANT COVER GALLERY

ACTION COMICS #9
Art by Rags Morales & Brad Anderson

ACTION COMICS #10
Art by Bryan Hitch & Paul Mounts

ACTION COMICS #11
Art by Cully Hamner & Val Staples

ACTION COMICS #12
Art by Cliff Chiang

ACTION COMICS #0
Art by Rags Morales & Brad Anderson

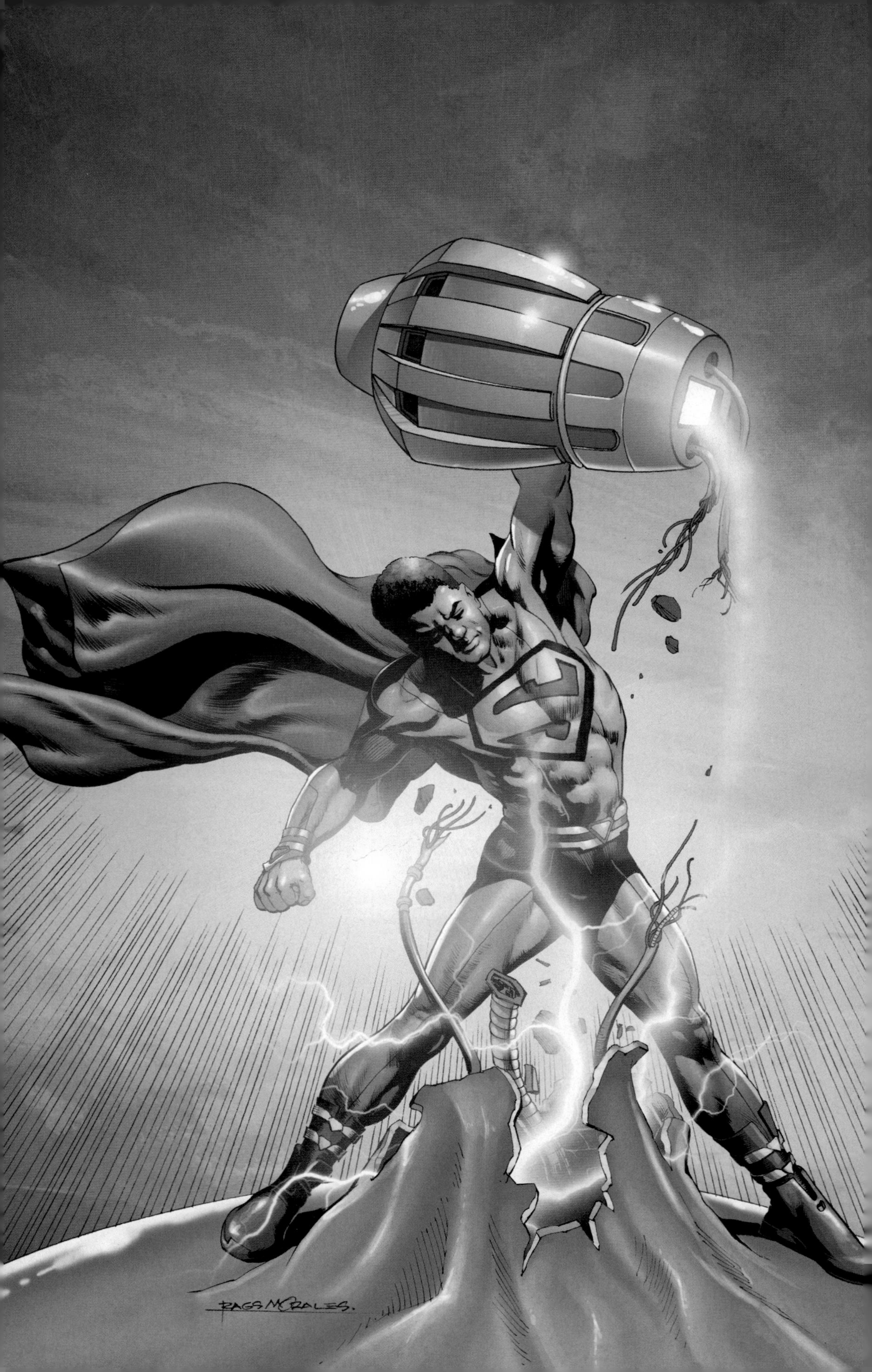
RAGS MORALES.

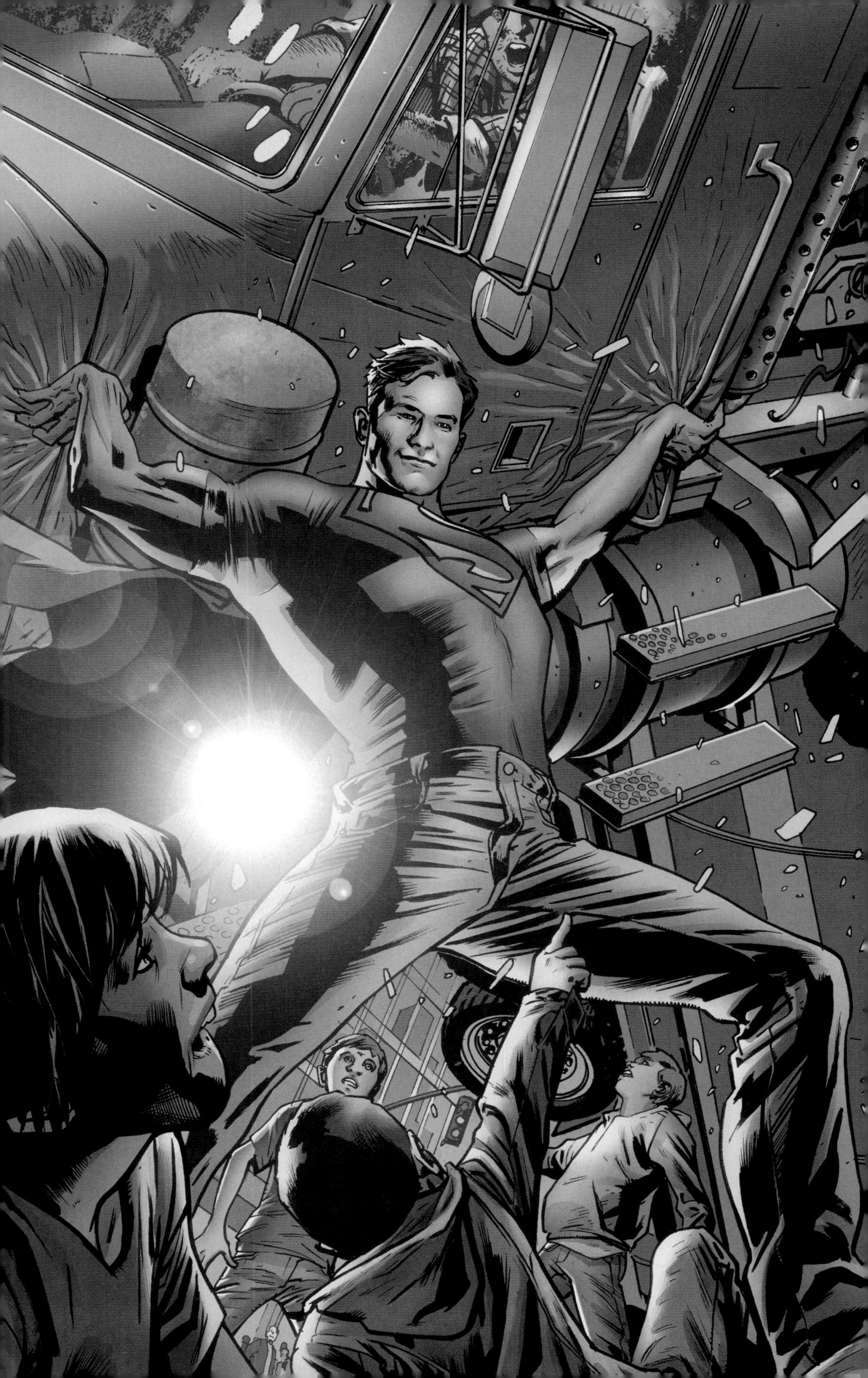

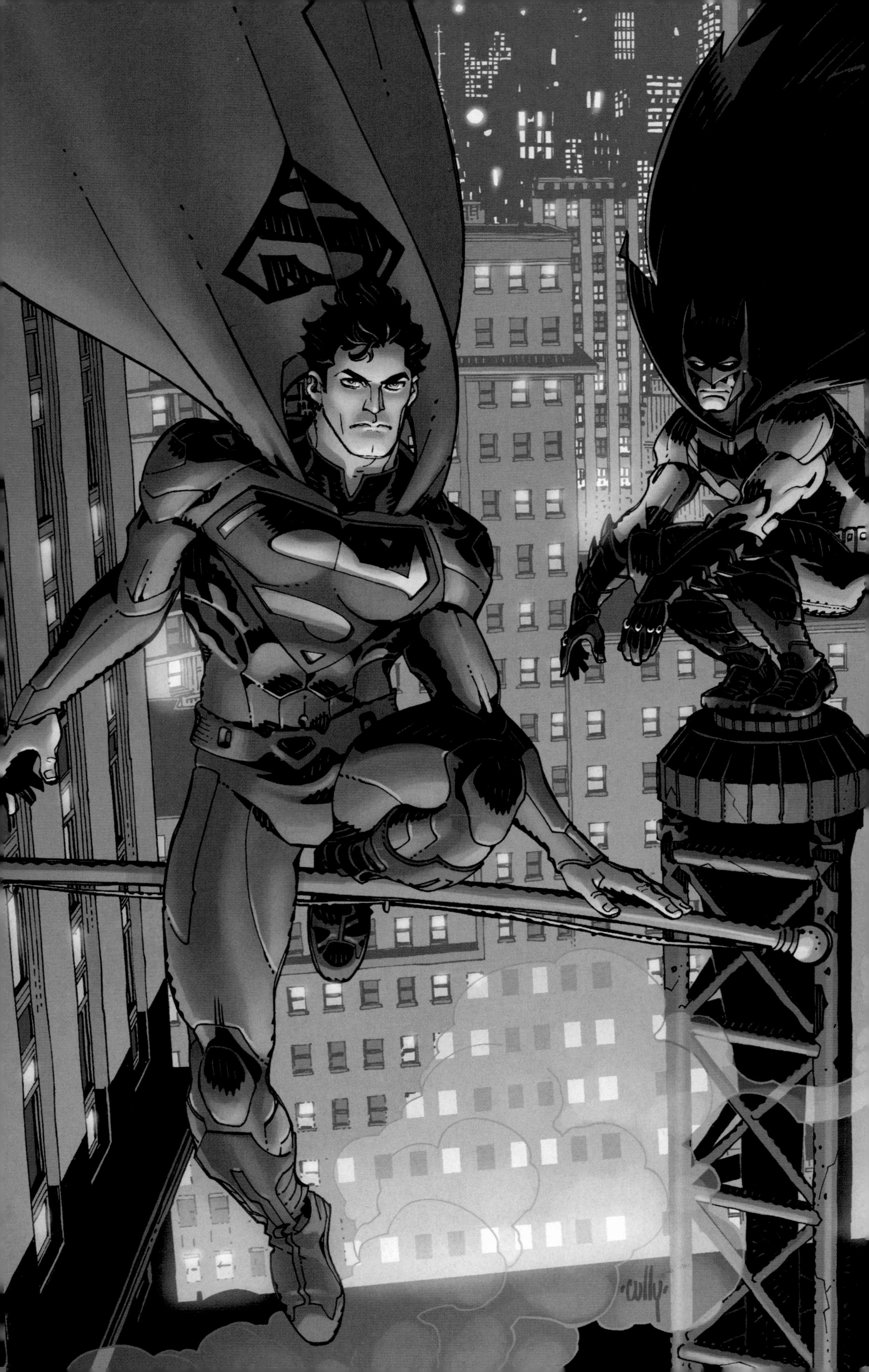
cully

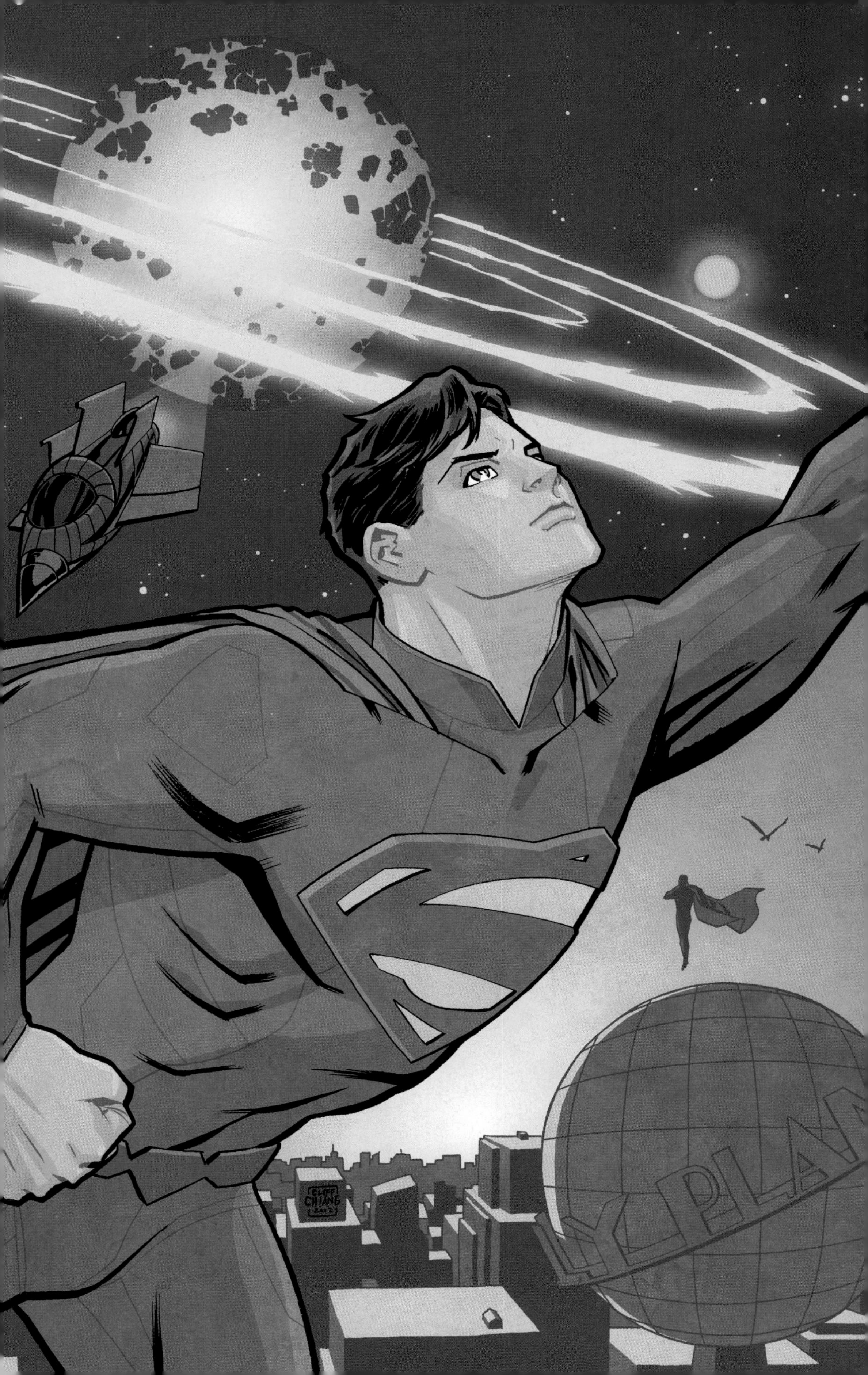
CLIFF
CHIANG
2012

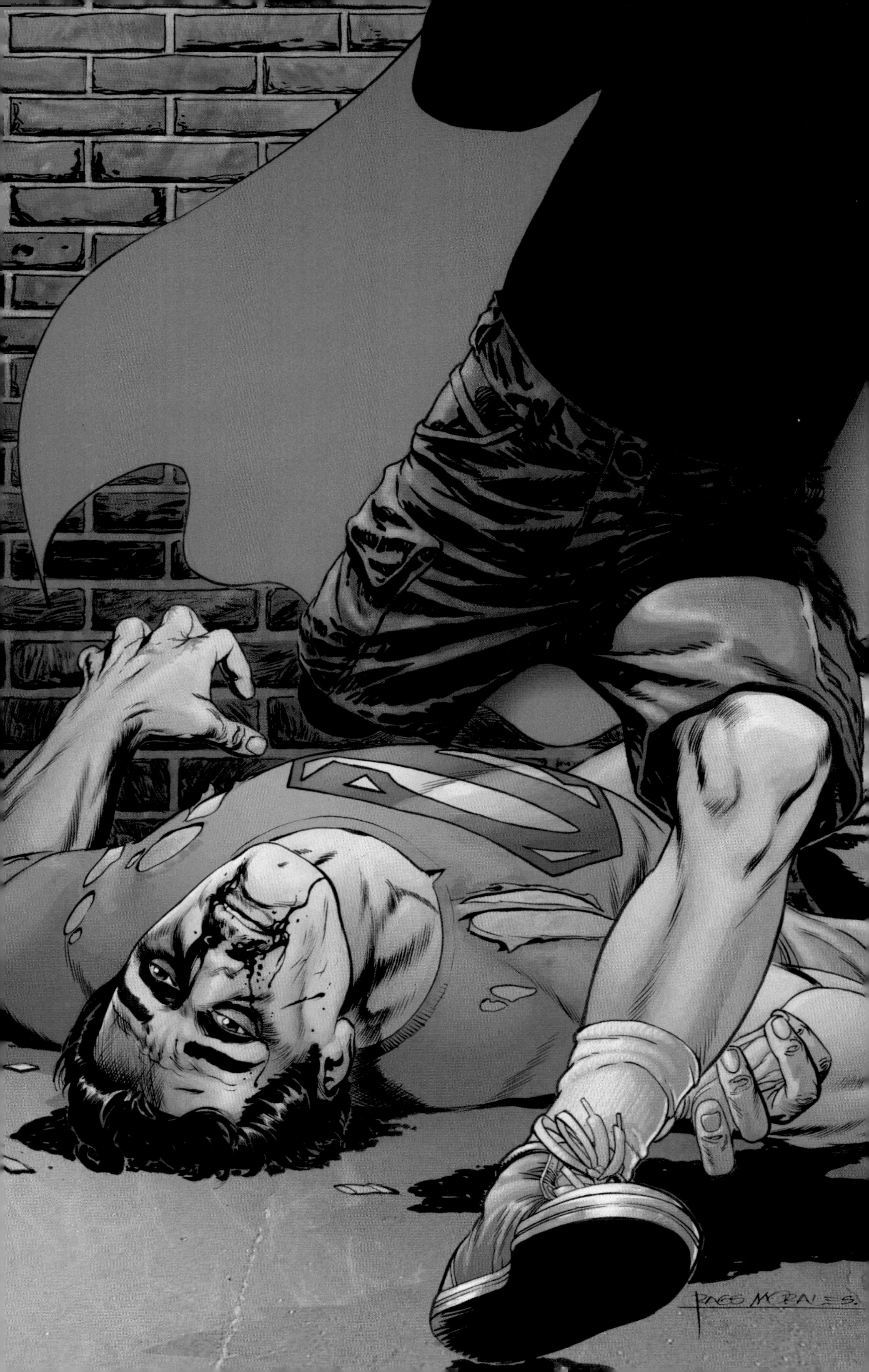
RAGS MORALES.

Designs for Superman of Earth 23 by Gene Ha

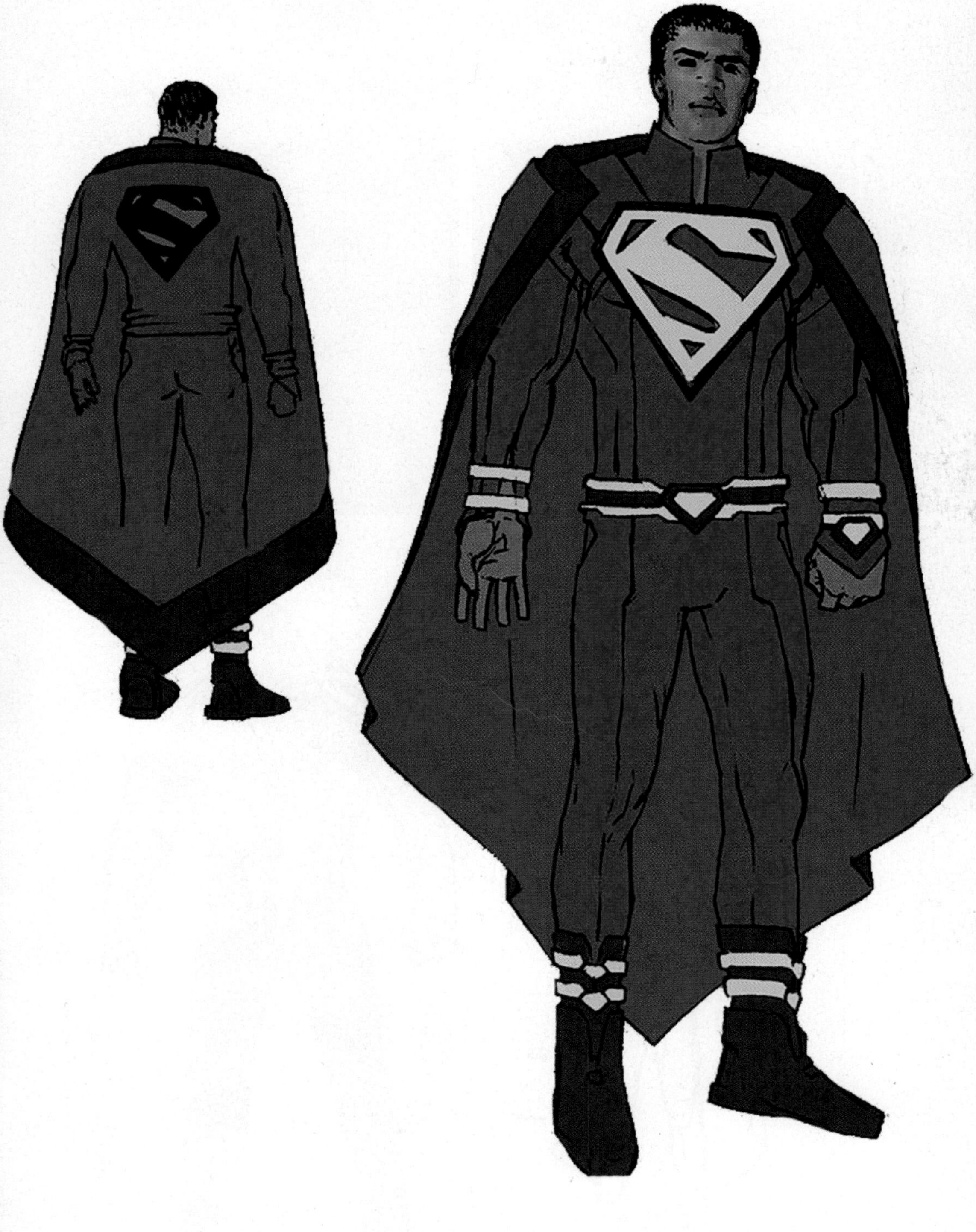

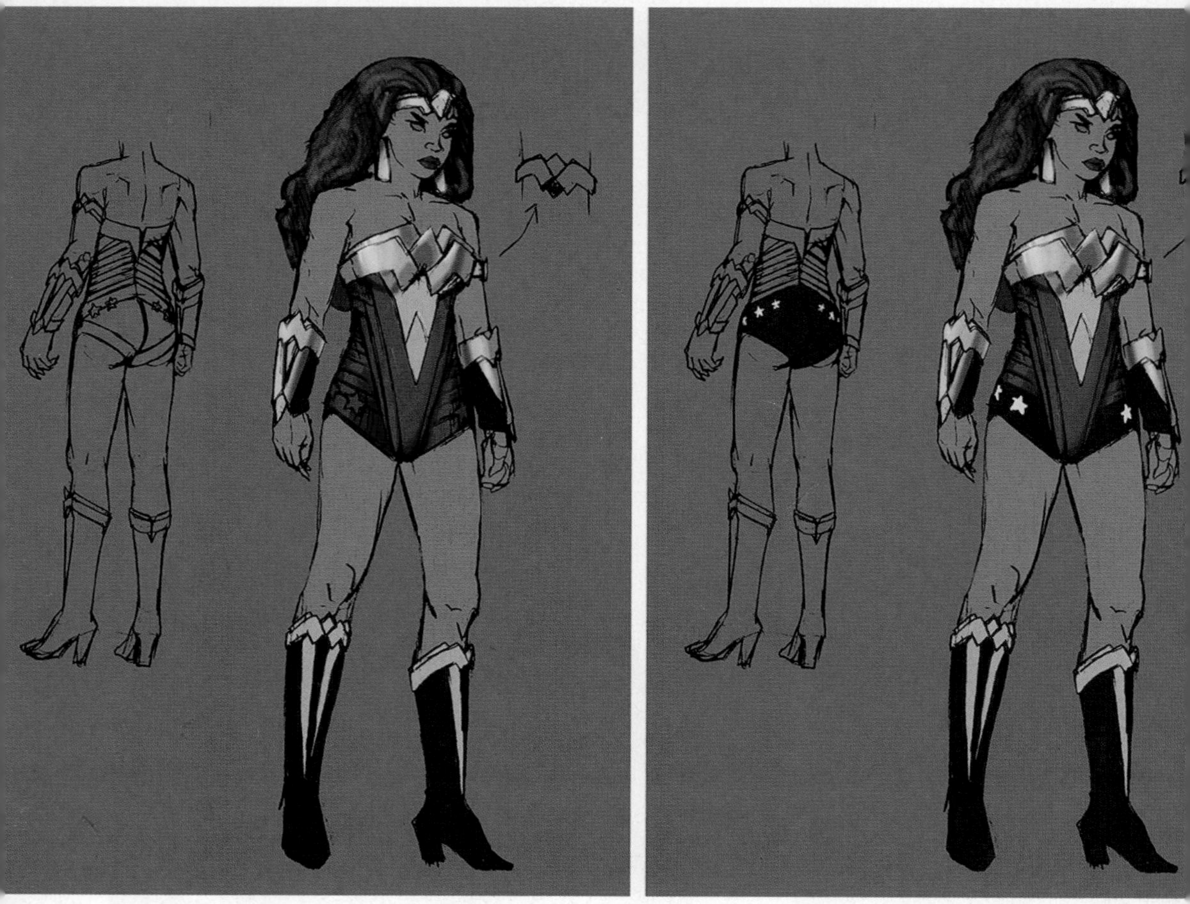

Designs for Wonder Woman of Earth 23 and Superdoom by Gene Ha

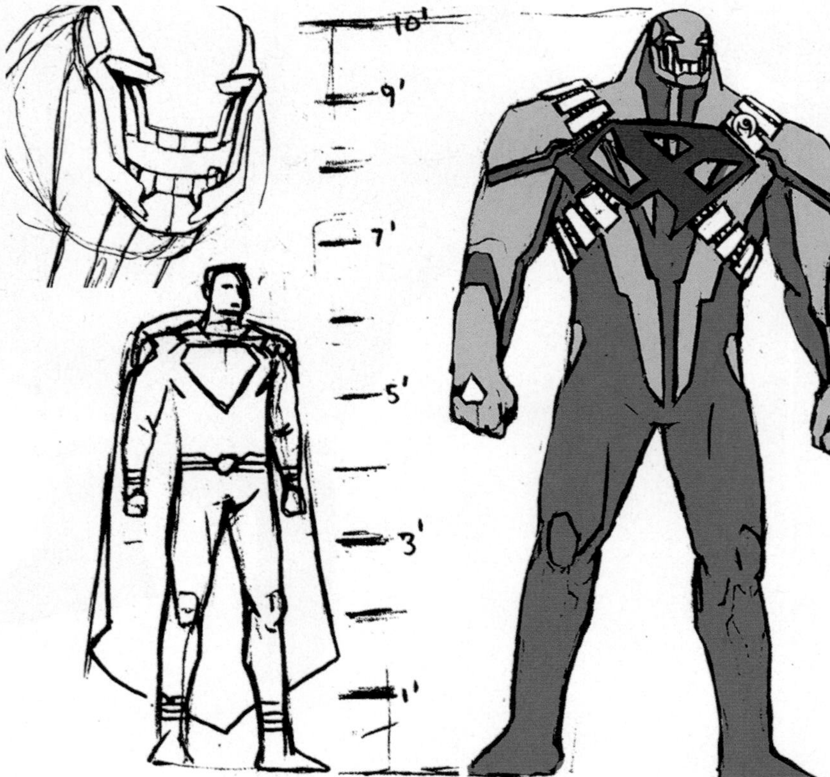
10'
9'
7'
5'
3'
1'

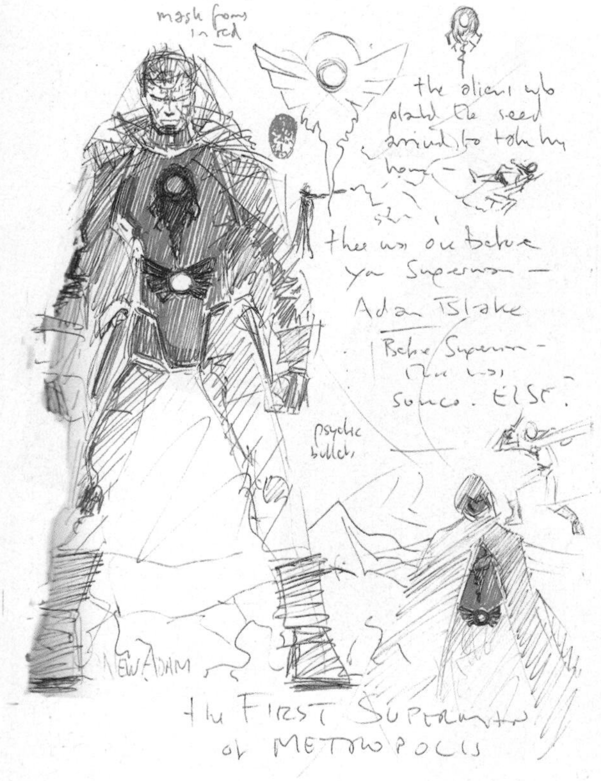
mask forms in red
the aliens who planted the seed arrived to take him home —
there was one before you Superman —
Adam Blake
Before Superman — there was someone ELSE?
psychic bullets
NEW ADAM
the FIRST SUPERMAN of METROPOLIS

Designs for Captain Comet by Grant Morrison

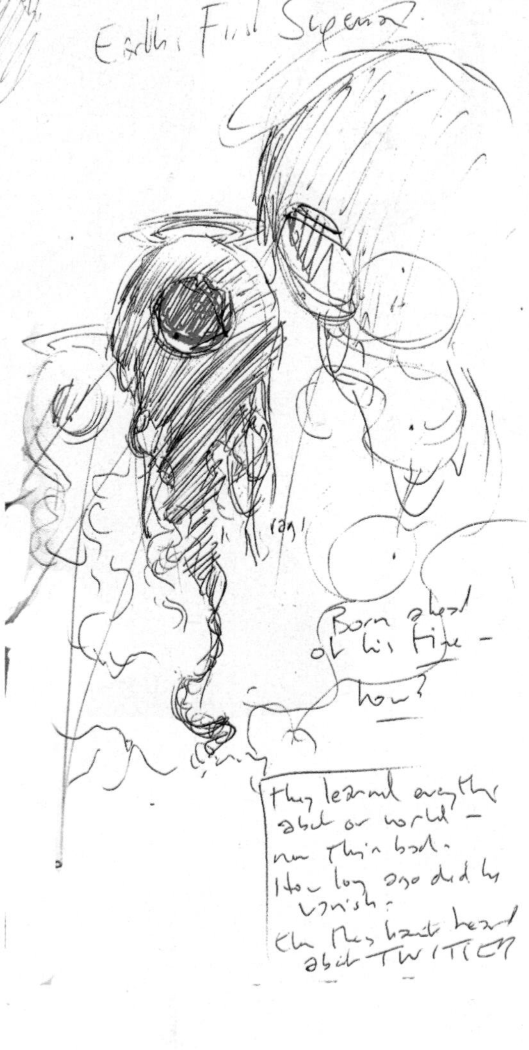
Earth's First Superman
rags
Born ahead of his time —
how?
They learned everything about our world —
How long ago did he vanish —
then they haven't heard about TWITTER

Steel art by Cully Hamner

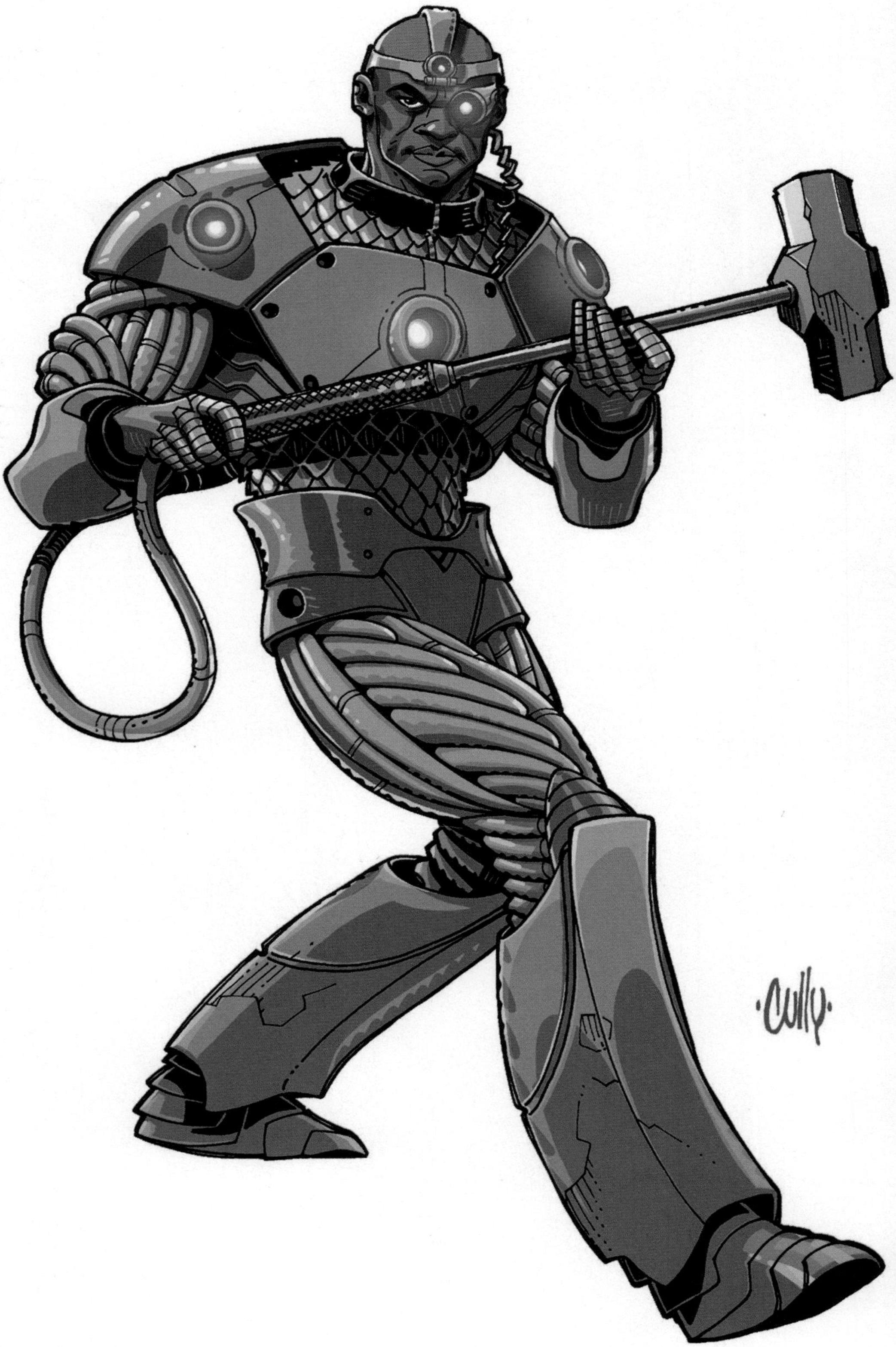
Cully

STEEL (REV)

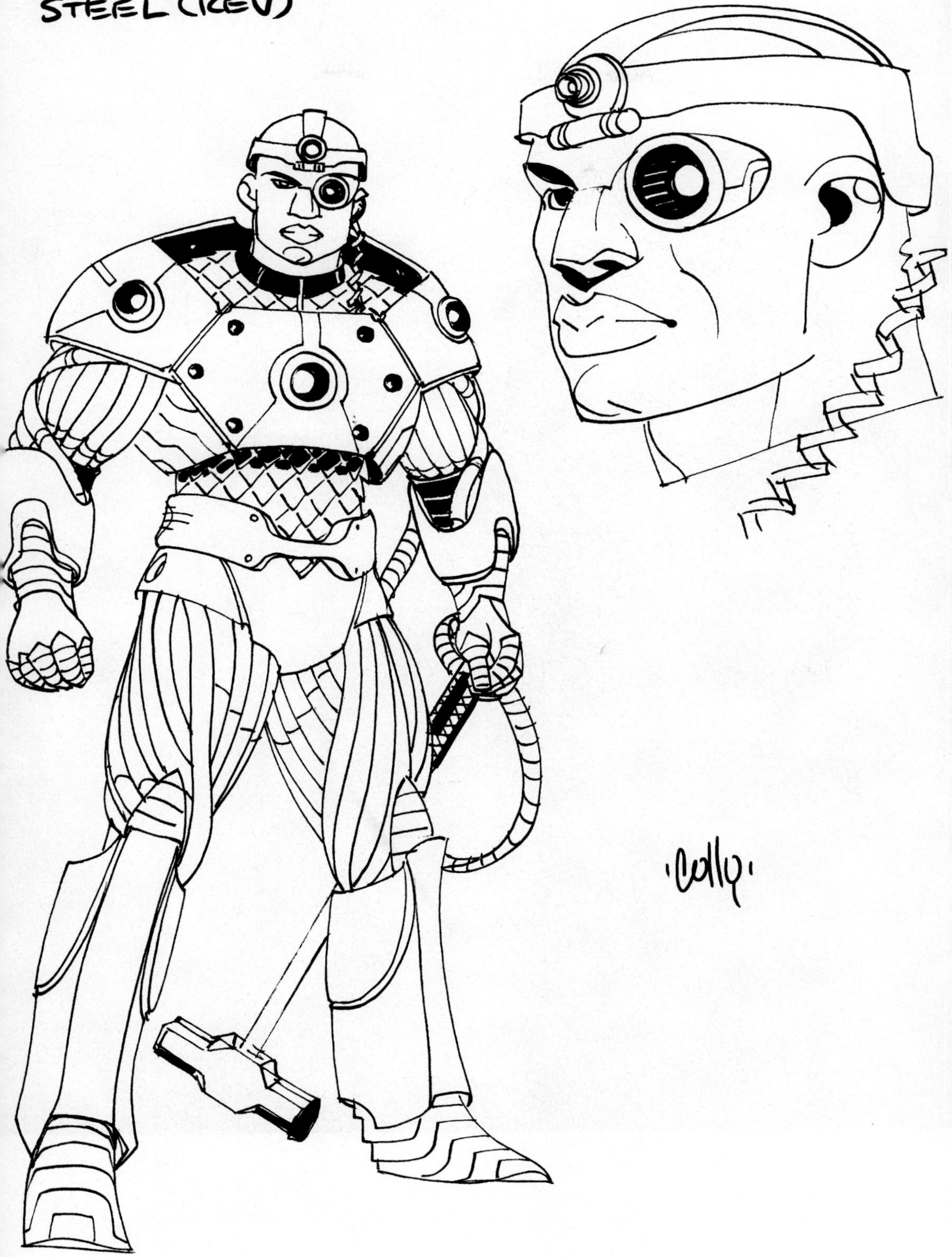

In progress pages by Cully Hamner from ACTION COMICS ANNUAL #1

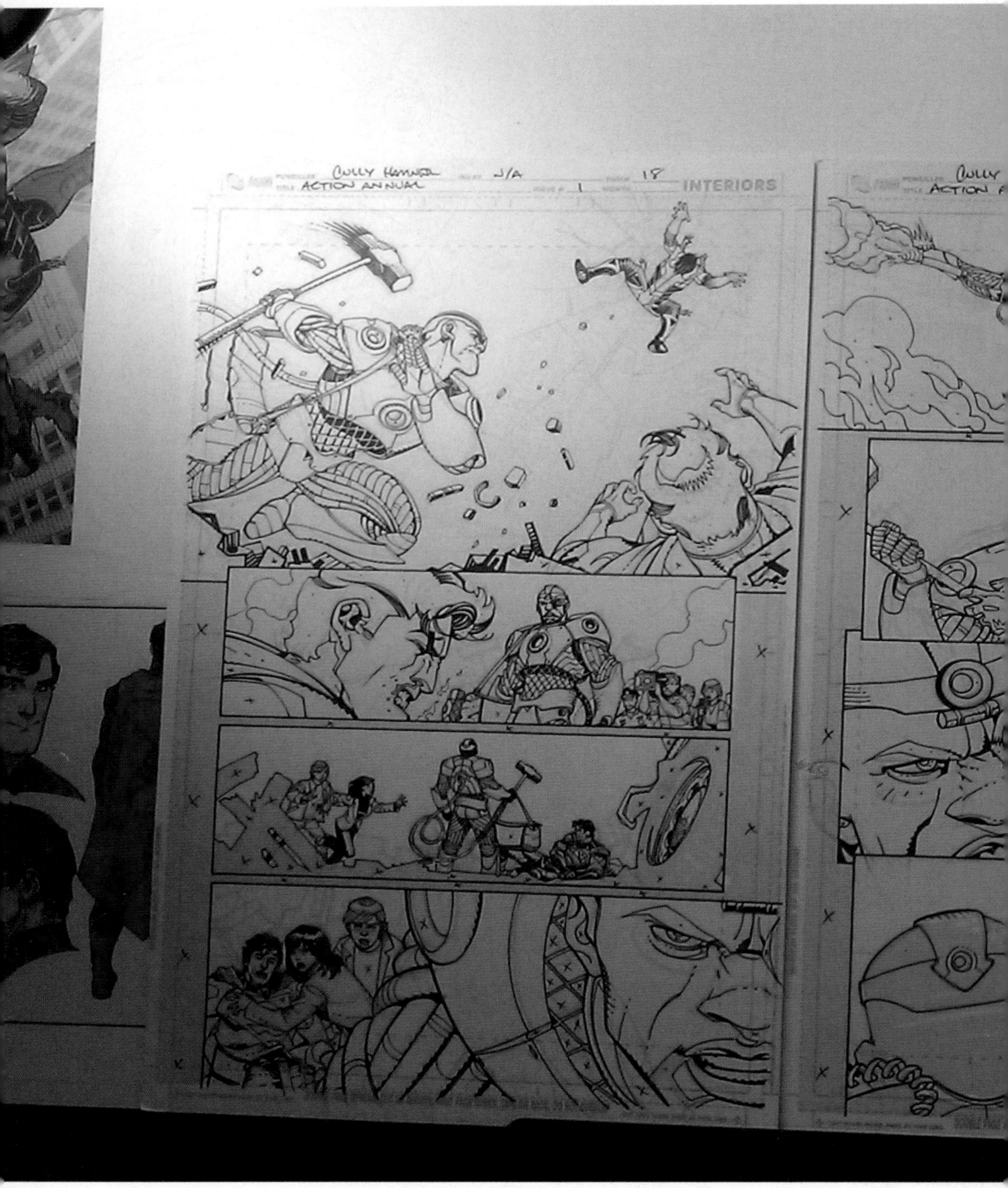
CULLY HAMNER
J/A
18
ACTION ANNUAL
1
INTERIORS

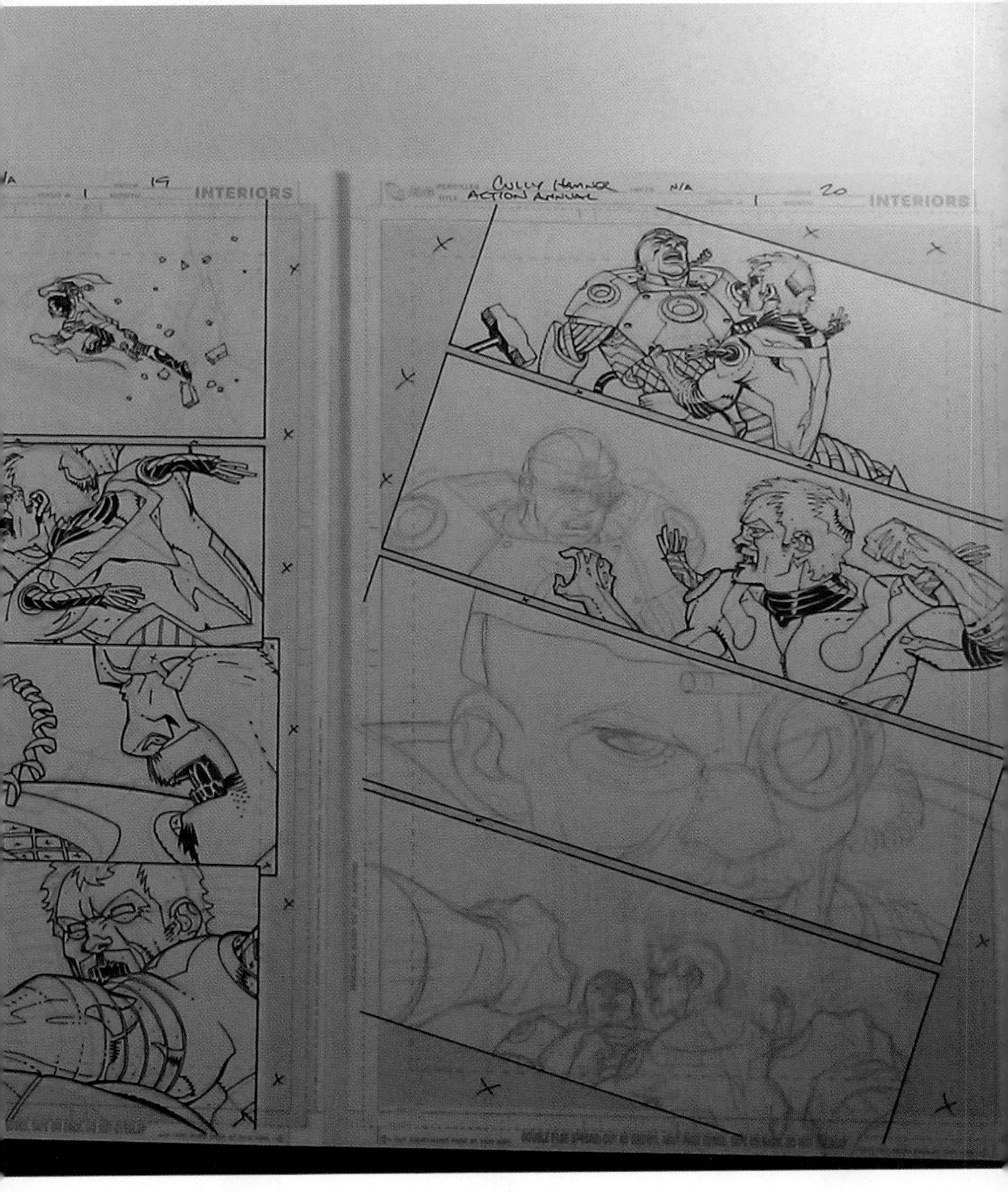
19
INTERIORS
CULLY HAMNER
ACTION ANNUAL
N/A
20
INTERIORS

Designs for the Kryptonite Man by Cully Hamner

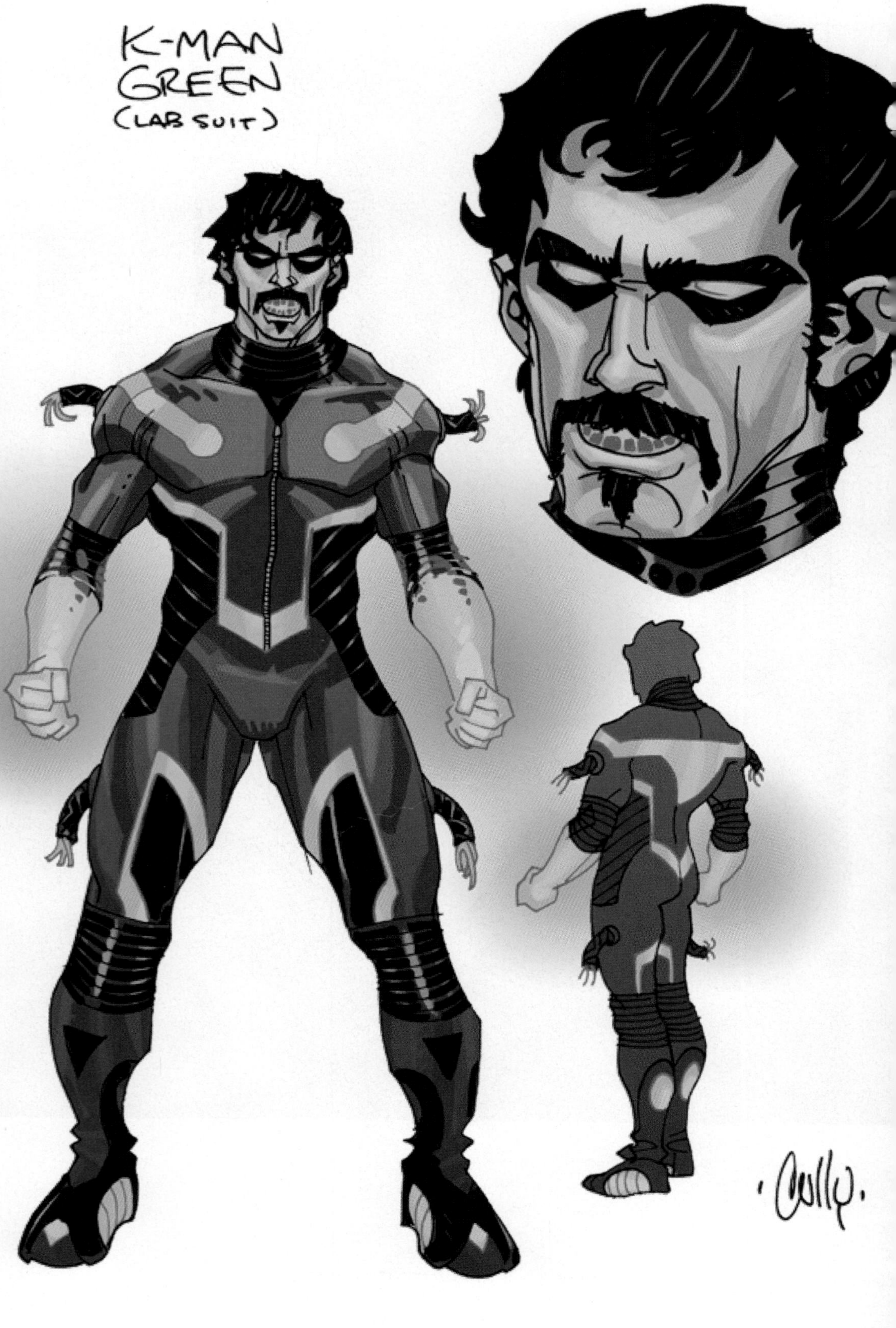
K-MAN
GREEN
(LAB SUIT)
Cully

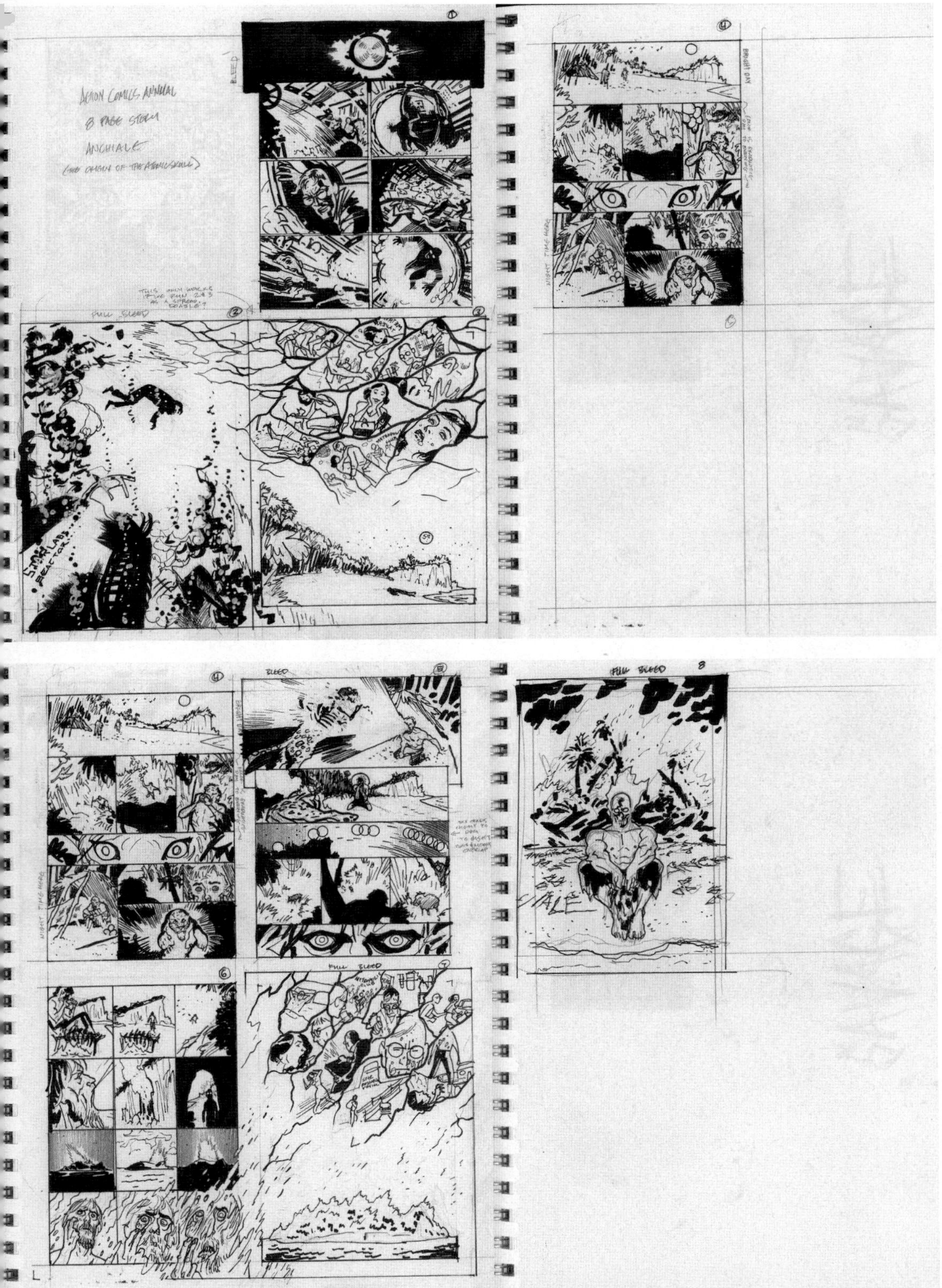
ACTION COMICS ANNUAL
8 PAGE STORY
ANCHIALE
(THE ORIGIN OF THE ATOMIC SKULL)
BLEED
FULL BLEED
BRIGHT DAY
NIGHT TIME HERE
FULL BLEED
AS A SPREAD?
FULL BLEED

Thumbnails for the Anchiale story by Ryan Sook from ACTION COMICS ANNUAL #1

Action Comics #9 cover sketches by Gene Ha

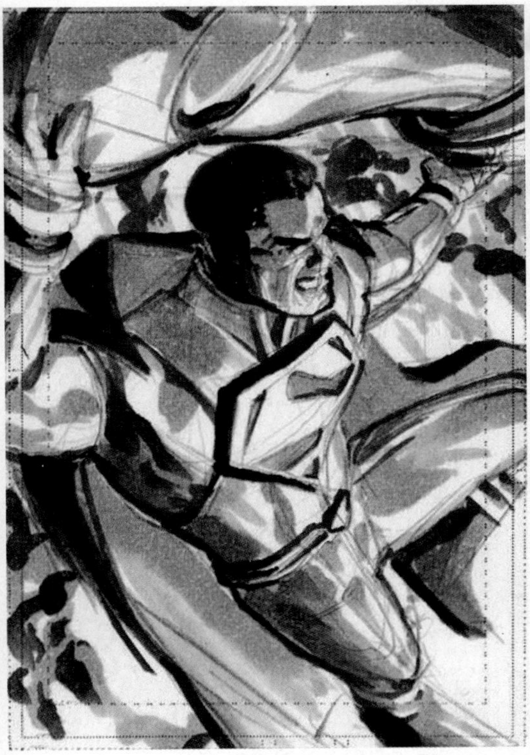
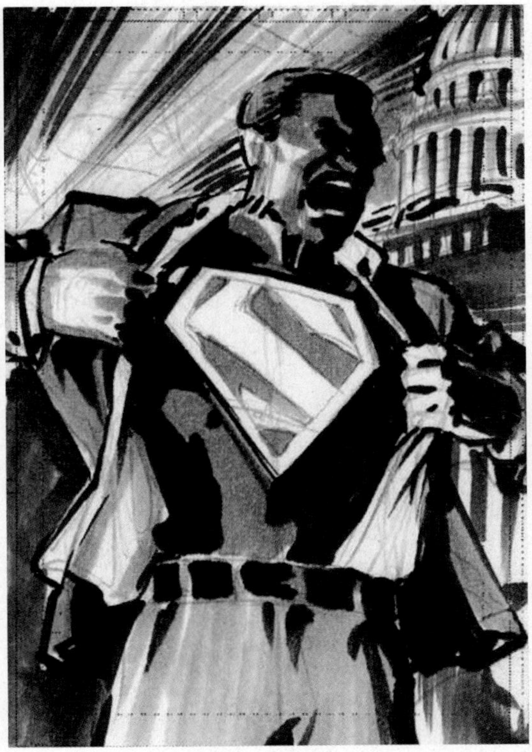
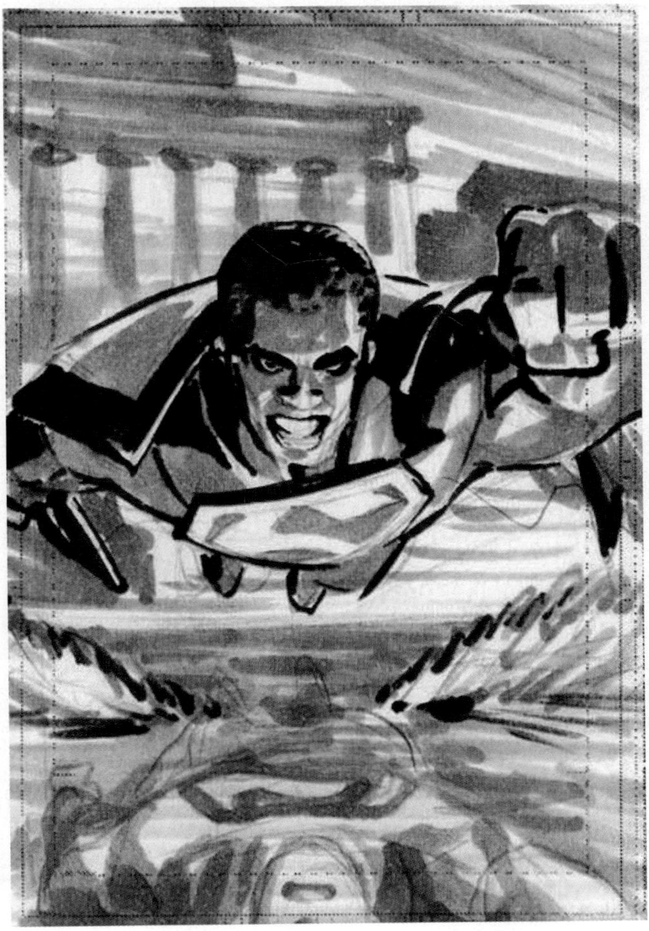

Action Comics #11 variant cover sketch by Cully Hamner

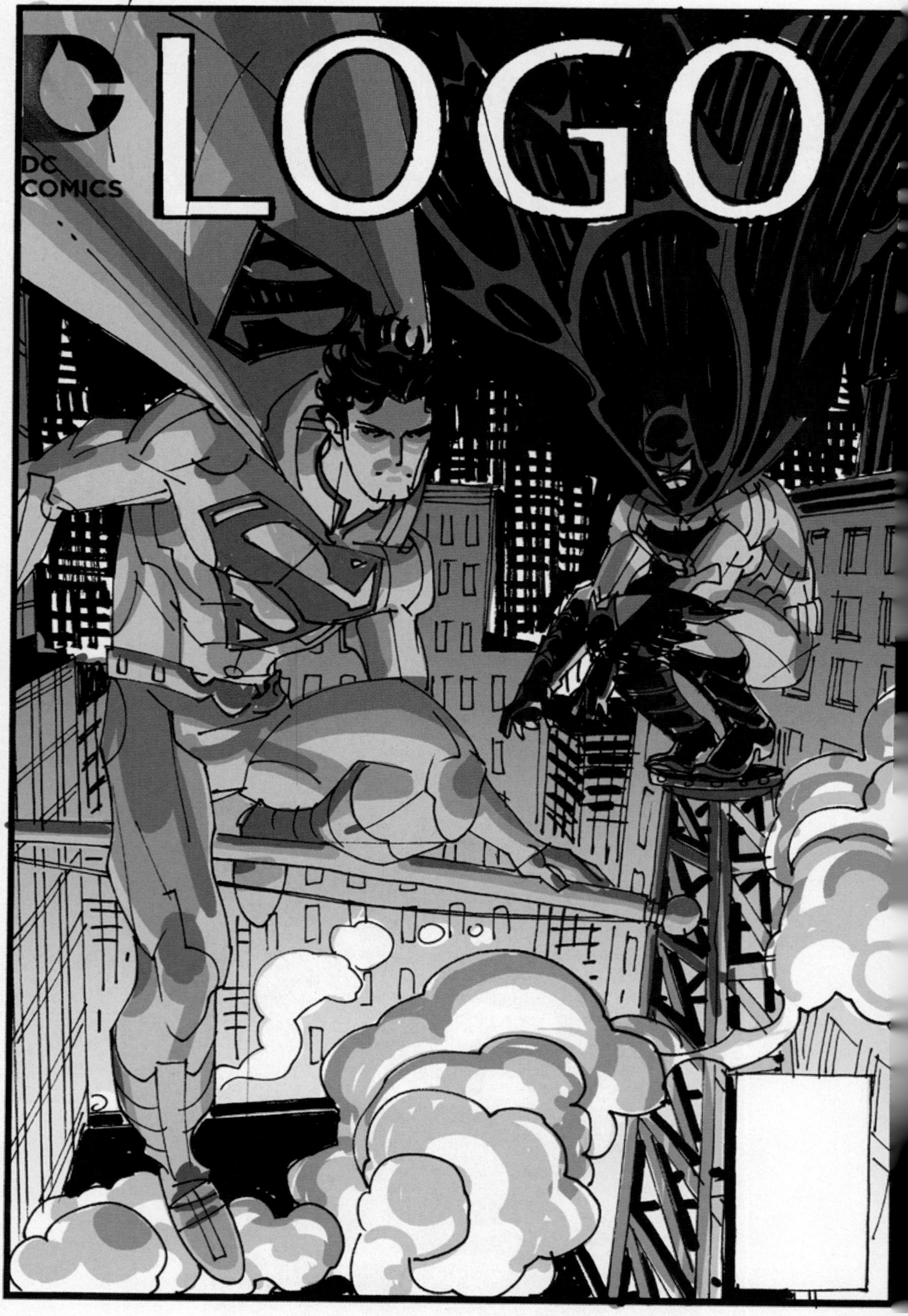
DC
COMICS
LOGO

:tion Comics #11 cover sketch by Grant Morrison

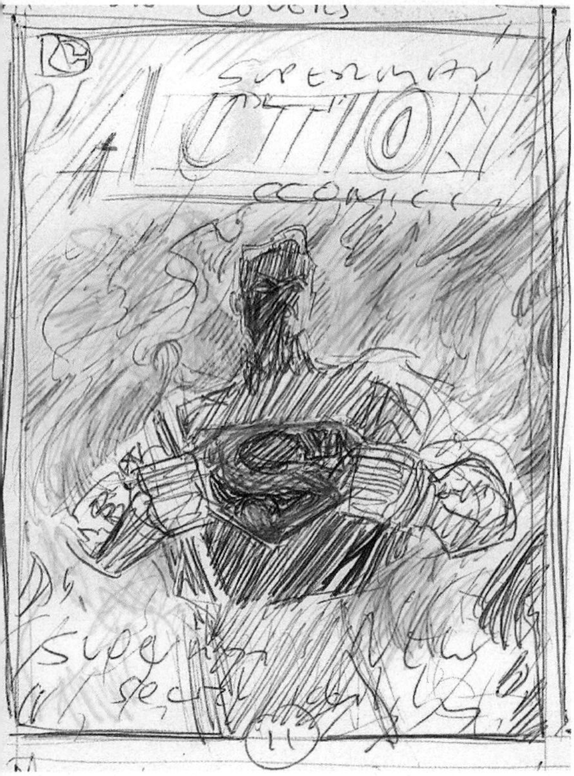

Action Comics #12 cover sketch by Grant Morrison

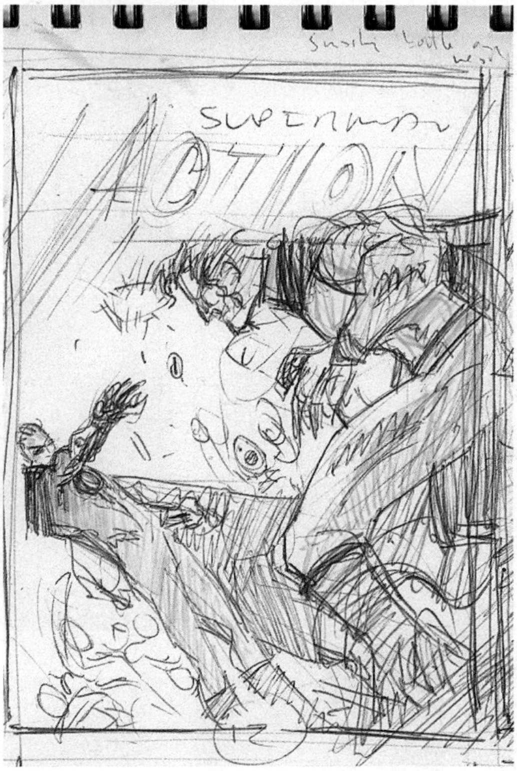

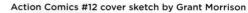

Action Comics Annual #1 cover sketch by Cully Hamner

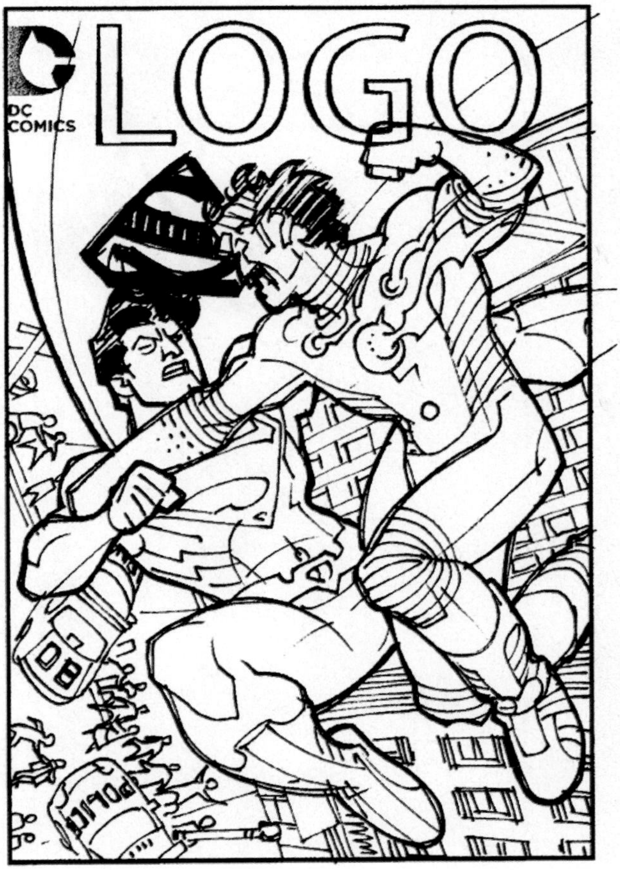
DC
COMICS
LOGO

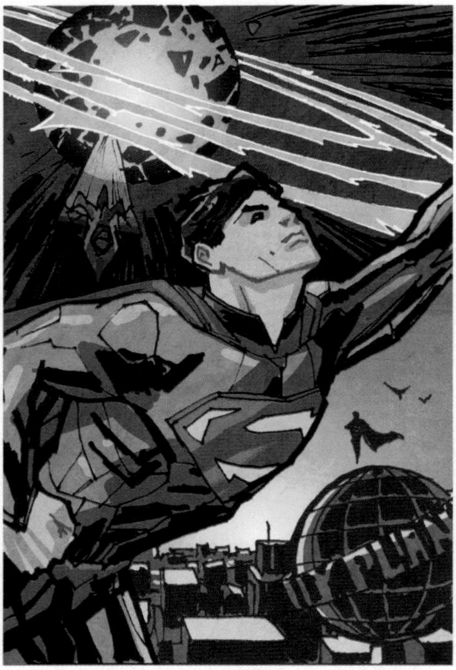

Action Comics #12 variant cover sketch by Cliff Chiang

Action Comics #11 cover sketch by Grant Morrison

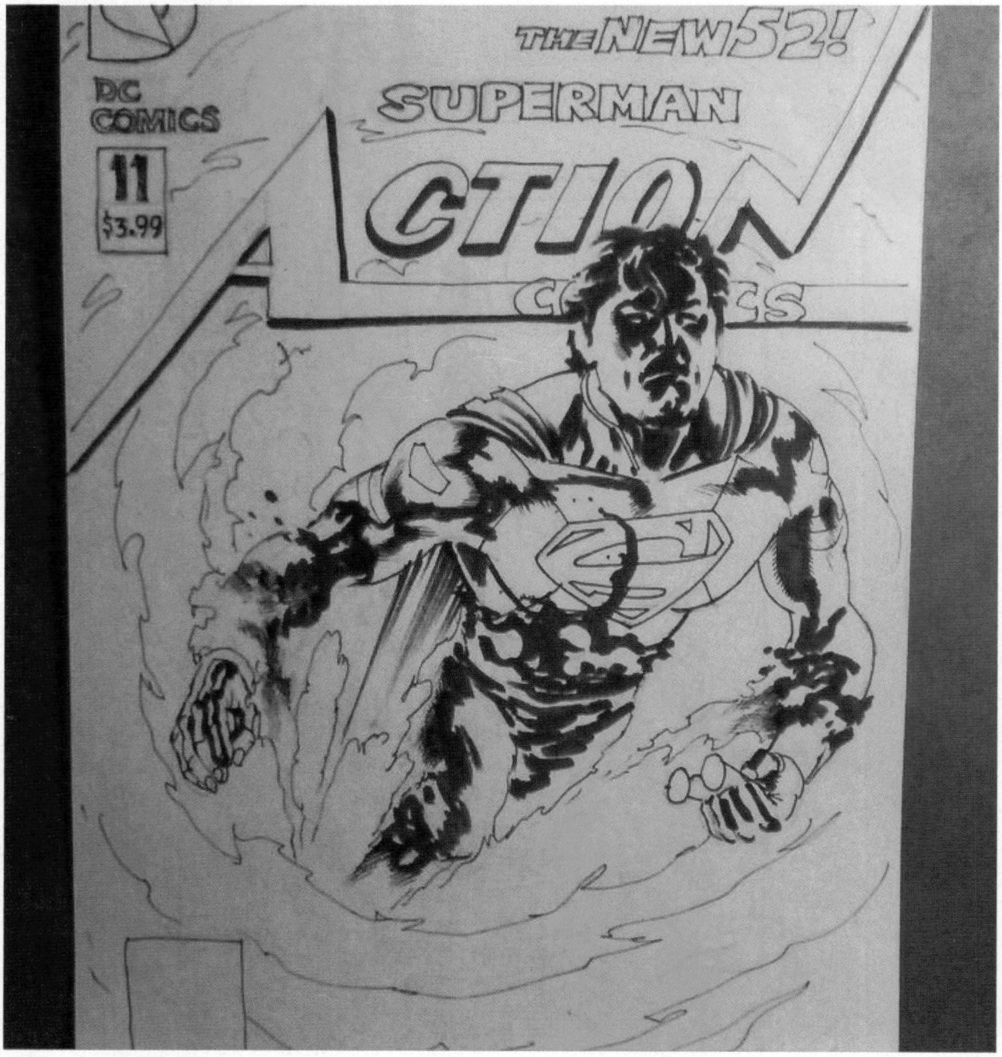
THE NEW 52!
DC COMICS
11
$3.99
SUPERMAN
CTION

DC
COMICS™

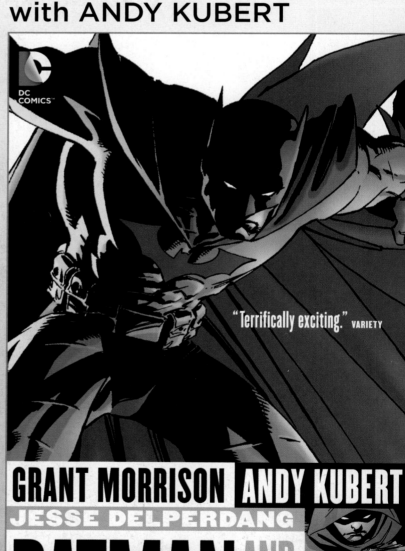

FROM *NEW YORK TIMES* #1 BEST-SELLING WRITE

GRANT MORRISON

with ANDY KUBERT

BATMAN:
THE BLACK GLOVE

with J.H. WILLIAMS III
and TONY S. DANIEL

BATMAN: R.I.P.

with TONY S. DANIEL

BATMAN: THE RETURN
OF BRUCE WAYNE

with FRAZER IRVING,
RYAN SOOK and other top
talent

GRANT MORRISON ANDY KUBERT
JESSE DELPERDANG
BATMAN AND SON

"Welcoming to new fans looking to get into superhero comics for the first time and old fans who gave up on the funny-books long ago."
—SCRIPPS HOWARD NEWS SERVICE

START AT THE BEGINNING!

JUSTICE LEAGUE VOLUME 1: ORIGIN

AQUAMAN VOLUME 1: THE TRENCH

THE SAVAGE HAWKMAN VOLUME 1: DARKNESS RISING

GREEN ARROW VOLUME 1: THE MIDAS TOUCH

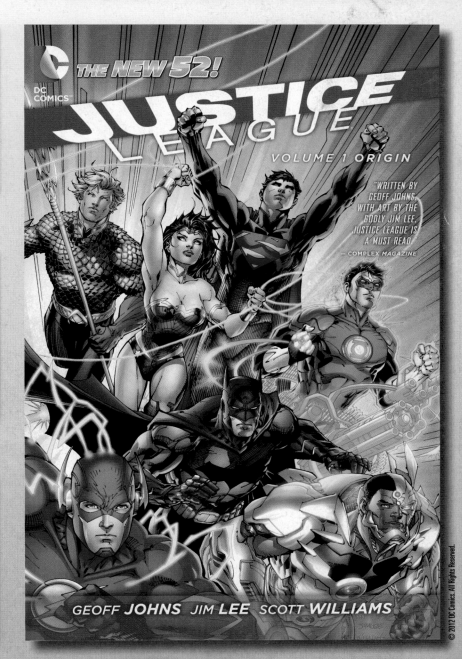

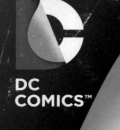

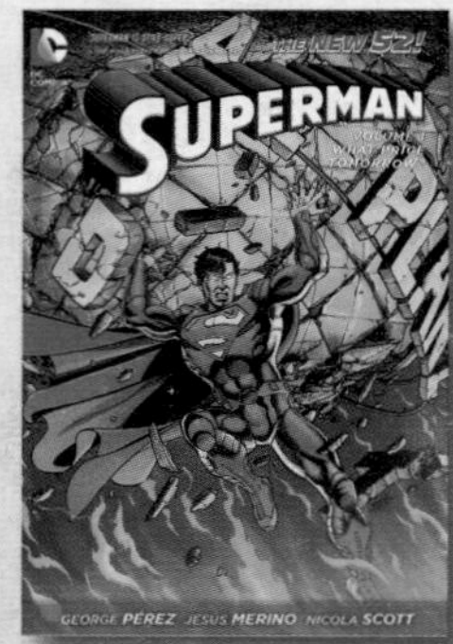
THE NEW 52!
SUPERMAN
GEORGE PÉREZ JESÚS MERINO NICOLA SCOTT

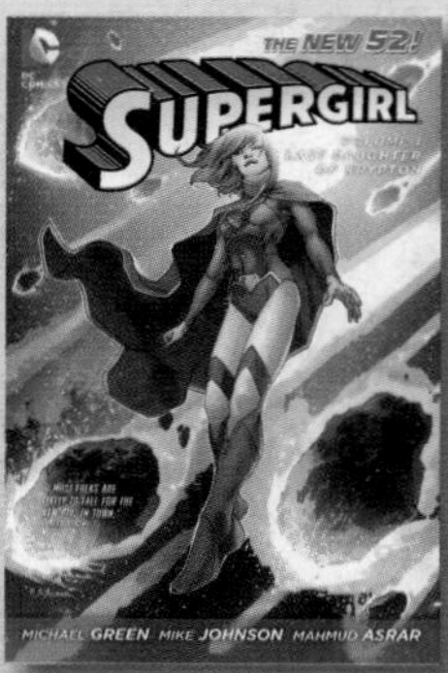
THE NEW 52!
SUPERGIRL
MICHAEL GREEN MIKE JOHNSON MAHMUD ASRAR

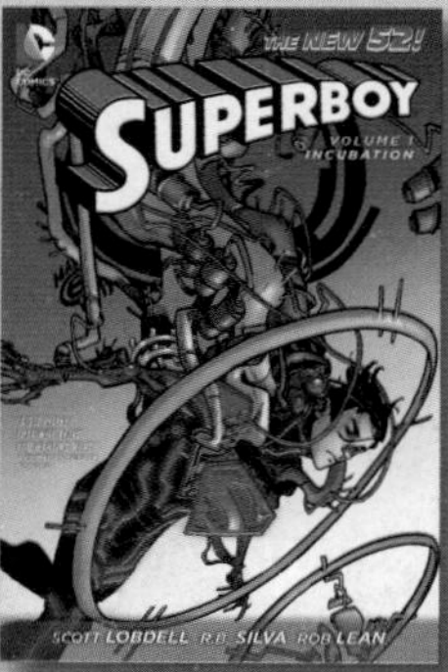
THE NEW 52!
SUPERBOY
VOLUME 1 INCUBATION
SCOTT LOBDELL R.B. SILVA ROB LEAN

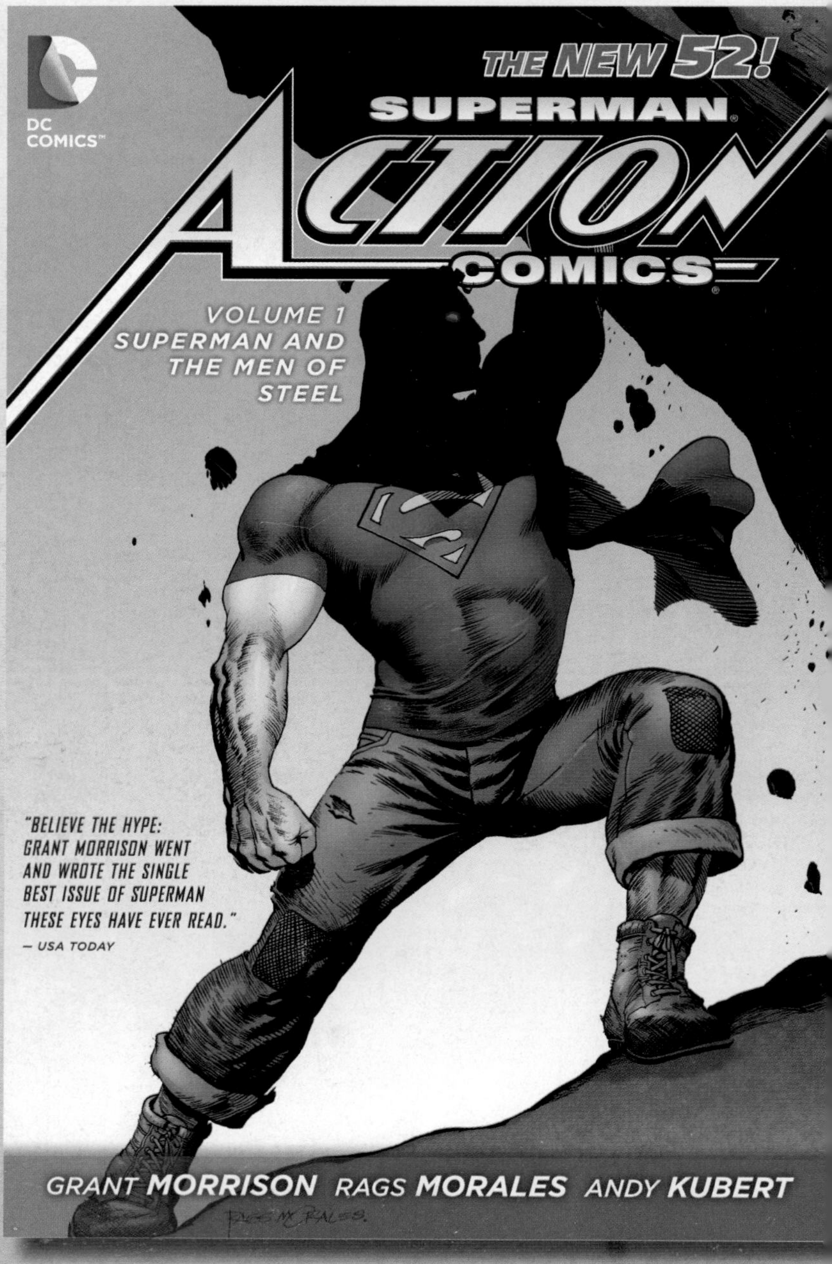
DC COMICS™
THE NEW 52!
SUPERMAN
ACTION COMICS
VOLUME 1
SUPERMAN AND THE MEN OF STEEL
"BELIEVE THE HYPE: GRANT MORRISON WENT AND WROTE THE SINGLE BEST ISSUE OF SUPERMAN THESE EYES HAVE EVER READ."
— USA TODAY
GRANT MORRISON RAGS MORALES ANDY KUBERT